The Language of Politics

Series Editor

Ofer Feldman, Doshisha University, Kyoto, Japan

Editorial Board

Christ'l De Landtsheer, University of Antwerp, Antwerp, Belgium

Catalina Fuentes-Rodríguez, University of Seville, Sevilla, Spain

Augusto Gnisci, University of Campania "Luigi Vanvitelli", Caserta, Italy

Michael Hameleers, University of Amsterdam, Amsterdam, The Netherlands

Ken Kinoshita, Faculty of Socio-Environmental Studies, Fukuoka Institute of Technology, Fukuoka, Japan

Michael Alan Krasner, City University of New York, New York, USA

Sam Lehman-Wilzig, Bar-Ilan University, Ramat Gan, Israel

Hongna Miao, Nanjing University, Nanjing, China

Katarzyna Molek-Kozakowska, University of Opole, Opole, Poland

Gene Segarra Navera, National University of Singapore, Singapore, Singapore

Debbita Ai Lin Tan, Universiti Sains Malaysia, Penang, Malaysia

Annemarie Walter, University of Nottingham, Nottingham, UK

Ruth Wodak, Lancaster University, Lancaster, UK

Sonja Zmerli, Sciences Po Grenoble, St. Martin d'Hères, France

The Language of Politics series is an interdisciplinary, critical, and analytical forum for the publication of cutting-edge research regarding the way language is used by political officials. It focuses mainly on empirically-based research aiming to analyze and discuss the role, function, and effects of the vocabulary used by politicians and other officials in Western and non-Western societies. Such language can be broadcast live in venues such as parliamentary debates and deliberations, election campaign assemblies, political party conventions, press conferences, media interviews, and even non-broadcast (but later reported) speeches in front of support groups or during international negotiations – in traditional as well as social media (e.g., Facebook, Twitter). It can include polite, respectful, and deferential public speaking, or conversely, impolite verbal discourse, debasing and derisive comments, and the use of crude, vulgar, or abusive terms – including curses and obscenities – through irony, sarcasm, cynicism, ridicule, and mockery, to demean, degrade, humiliate, and insult individuals, the political opposition, or groups in society.

The series is located at the intersection of several social science disciplines including communication, linguistics, discourse studies, political sociology, political science, and political psychology. It aims to bring together multiple political and social theories and concepts; qualitative, quantitative, or mixed methodological approaches; and in-depth, empirical, communication- and language-oriented analyses. By addressing critical issues such as the use of words, terms, and expressions in parliamentary debate and political negotiations, and their effect from novel perspectives, it can expose the weaknesses of existing discourse analysis concepts and arguments, or reassess the topic in other ways through the introduction of different ideas, the integration of perspectives from disparate sub-fields or even disciplines. By challenging existing paradigms, authored books in the series will enrich current debates surrounding several complex, discourse relationships: between politicians' and citizens; between decision-makers and their colleagues; and in general, the way language shapes political culture in an increasingly globalized world. All proposals and books in this series are peer-reviewed by international experts in the aforementioned fields.

Ofer Feldman
Editor

Political Humor Worldwide

The Cultural Context of Political Comedy, Satire, and Parody

 Springer

Editor
Ofer Feldman
Faculty of Policy Studies
Doshisha University
Kyoto, Japan

ISSN 2731-7617 ISSN 2731-7625 (electronic)
The Language of Politics
ISBN 978-981-99-8489-3 ISBN 978-981-99-8490-9 (eBook)
https://doi.org/10.1007/978-981-99-8490-9

© The Editor(s) (if applicable) and The Author(s), under exclusive license to Springer Nature Singapore Pte Ltd. 2024

This work is subject to copyright. All rights are solely and exclusively licensed by the Publisher, whether the whole or part of the material is concerned, specifically the rights of translation, reprinting, reuse of illustrations, recitation, broadcasting, reproduction on microfilms or in any other physical way, and transmission or information storage and retrieval, electronic adaptation, computer software, or by similar or dissimilar methodology now known or hereafter developed.

The use of general descriptive names, registered names, trademarks, service marks, etc. in this publication does not imply, even in the absence of a specific statement, that such names are exempt from the relevant protective laws and regulations and therefore free for general use.

The publisher, the authors, and the editors are safe to assume that the advice and information in this book are believed to be true and accurate at the date of publication. Neither the publisher nor the authors or the editors give a warranty, expressed or implied, with respect to the material contained herein or for any errors or omissions that may have been made. The publisher remains neutral with regard to jurisdictional claims in published maps and institutional affiliations.

This Springer imprint is published by the registered company Springer Nature Singapore Pte Ltd.
The registered company address is: 152 Beach Road, #21-01/04 Gateway East, Singapore 189721, Singapore

Paper in this product is recyclable.

To the Hatanis—
Akifumi, Asaya, and Usa

Who have just started to write their own hopefully joyful stories

Preface

Exactly 30 years ago, in 1993, I was invited to join a panel on comparative political humor organized during the annual meeting of the International Society of Political Psychology. The feedback to the presentations in that panel was overwhelming. Through this feedback I learned about the vast interest in humor and its role in politics, especially in a comparative context with non-Western societies such as Japan, characterized (at least at that time) with scarcity of empirical knowledge on related issues, and regarding the place of humor within political culture. Motivated by this feedback, I initiated several studies and published a series of journal papers and book chapters on political humor in Japan, focusing specifically on the language of politicians and the media, also detailing political cartoons and *senryû* (short poetry) verses in the national dailies (e.g., Feldman 2004). Since then, the idea of having an international collaboration on political humor was always in my thoughts.

Further impetus for such a collaboration arose during the late 1990s and at the beginning of this century. These years were typified by increasing appearances of politicians and aspiring politicians on televised talk shows in a variety of countries including Japan, but most notably in the U.S., especially in such late-night shows as hosted by David Letterman and Jay Leno, and political satire programs on the cable network including *The Daily Show, The Colbert Report,* and *Saturday Night Live.* Clearly, over the last 20 years these programs have drawn wide popular, journalistic, and scholarly attention to the content and effects of such nontraditional modes of political information on the audience. The rich and varied results on such matters from researchers in areas as communication, political science, and psychology, identified and detailed the manifold aspects of humor in politics, its function and effect on the political attitudes and engagement of media users and voters, portraying humor as an alternative and important means of political communication.

From the start, I felt there was more than only such talk shows to focus on in a study of humor in politics. Humor, with all the expressions it embraces, including satire, irony, comedy, parody, jokes, and cartoons, was also found in the Social Networking Service (SNS)—Facebook, YouTube, Instagram, Twitter, and TikTok— in deliberative bodies, in art, and in popular culture. Considering these aspects two years ago, I exchanged views with my friend and colleague Sam Lehman-Wilzig on initiating a project on political humor and jokes around the world. Eventually, we decided to withdraw from this idea as I assumed that some chapters about specific countries (that do not encourage humor on politics) wouldn't be longer than one page. Things changed, though, after the publication of my recent two edited books *Political Debasement: Incivility, Contempt, and Humiliation in Parliamentary and Public Discourse*, and *Debasing Political Rhetoric: Dissing Opponents, Journalists, and Minorities in Populist Leadership Communication* (both published in 2023). While editing these books, I noted that there was enough material overlapping with humor (in a "bad" sense), and thus I went back to the original plan on organizing a publication project on political humor worldwide.

This is the result that yielded two books, both examining the diversity of dimensions related to the nature and use of humorous expressions in the public sphere in selected countries around the globe. Whereas the present volume focuses on humor in deliberative bodies, ethno-national humor in religion, art, and in popular culture, the ensuing volume entitled *Communicating Political Humor in the Media: How Culture Influences Satire and Irony* generally centers, as the title suggests, on humor in the media, including political cartoons and comics, and the language of television programs hosts, SNS users, public opinion leaders, and voters in different countries. Together, both books detail verbal and nonverbal dimensions of humor in politics. Both address the discourse of public figures, reporters, political cartoonists, *manga* artist, comedians, performers, and artists including painters and musicians, subject-matter experts, and the general public. Both books call attention to the idea that humor in politics, satire, comedy, or jokes about political issues and personnel is deeply contextual, related to socio-cultural elements embedded in a given society, and thus may be interpreted differently by individuals. Humoristic aspects that are accepted and appreciated by members of one society as amusing and resulting in laughter could be regarded as rude and unpleasant to members of another society. At the heart of this project is thus the notion that culture is a powerful element that affects and determines the content, nature, and characteristics of humor about political issues and personnel, and the reaction to these in the public domain.

In the ensuing chapters, contributors from diverse fields of research and disciplinary backgrounds, specializing in communication, rhetoric, discourse analysis, social and political psychology, political science, history, and philosophy, bring multinational, multidisciplinary diversity, and a range of theoretical/conceptual approaches and research methods, to examine and determine how culture is relevant (or affects) political humor in a given country, society, or an ethnic group.

As the editor I wish to thank those involved in this project. First, thanks to each of the contributors, whose competent, patient, and collaborative activity made possible the completion of this volume and the following volume. Sonja Zmerli was always in the background to listen and encourage, and Daphna Birenbaum-Carmeli offered valuable feedback and helpful advice. I am also grateful to Michael Krasner who provided useful and practical comments on earlier version of submitted chapters and for his constructive criticism on many of the issues considered in this book. My deepest gratitude to Sam Lehman-Wilzig, who shared the stress throughout the current project, and for carrying out the linguistic and copy-editing task.

All the contributors are deeply indebted to him for his suggestions and advice that improved the quality of our publication. Finally, thanks are due to Juno Kawakami, our editor at Springer, who has given us constant encouragement and support throughout the whole process. Needless to mention, as in my previous projects, none of the above-mentioned individuals bear any responsibility for any mistake or flaws in this book—except perhaps my three grandchildren Akifumi (4 years old), Asaya (2 years old), and Usa (250 days) to whom this book is dedicated.

Kyoto, Japan   Ofer Feldman

References

Feldman, O. (2004). *Talking politics in Japan today*. Sussex Academic Press.
Feldman, O. (Ed.). (2023a). *Political debasement: Incivility, contempt, and humiliation in parliamentary and public discourse*. Springer.
Feldman, O. (Ed.). (2023b). *Debasing political rhetoric: Dissing opponents, journalists, and minorities in populist leadership communication*. Springer.
Feldman, O. (Ed.). (2024). *Communicating political humor in the media: How culture influences satire and irony*. Springer.

Contents

1 **Humor and Politics: A Conceptual Introduction** 1
   Ofer Feldman

Part I Humor in Legislative Bodies

2 **Founding Contradictions, Contemporary Expressions: Political Humor in American Culture** 31
   Michael Phillips-Anderson

3 **Humorous Genres and Modes in Greek Political Discourse** 49
   Marianthi Georgalidou

4 **British Phlegm and Individualism in Humorous Political Advertising** 67
   Kostoula Margariti, Leonidas Hatzithomas, and Christina Boutsouki

5 **"*Kapwa*" and Filipinos' Fixation with Presidential Jokes** 85
   Rogelio Alicor L. Panao and Ronald A. Pernia

6 **Holocaust Humor in Israel as a Political Tool of the Left-Wing** 101
   Liat Steir-Livny

Part II Ethno-National Humor in Religion, Art, and Popular Culture

7 **Cultural Wars in Polish Political Humor** 117
   Dorota Brzozowska and Władysław Chłopicki

8 **Jewish Humor as a Survival Tool and a Bridge to Social Justice** 139
   Linda Weiser Friedman and Hershey H. Friedman

9 **Humor and Cynical Political Parody in Italian Movies and Newspaper Cartoons** 159
   Benedetta Baldi

10	**The Power of Funny: Indigenous High Art as Quiescence and Rebellion** .... Liz Sills and Pamela G. Monaghan-Geernaert	175
11	**The Cultural Background of Political Humor "Sung" by the Spanish People** .... María del Mar Rivas-Carmona and María del Carmen García-Manga	193

Part III Framing and Analyzing Political Humor

12	**Political Humor in American Culture: From Affability to Aggression** .... Michael Alan Krasner	217
13	**Political Humor: Theoretical Questions, Methodological Suggestions** .... Sam Lehman-Wilzig	239

Index 249

Contributors

Benedetta Baldi Department of Humanities and Philosophy, University of Florence, Florence, Italy

Christina Boutsouki School of Economics, Aristotle University of Thessaloniki, Thessaloniki, Greece

Dorota Brzozowska Institute of Linguistics, University of Opole, Opole, Poland

Władysław Chłopicki Institute of English Studies, Jagiellonian University, Kraków, Poland

Ofer Feldman Faculty of Policy Studies, Doshisha University, Kyoto, Japan

Hershey H. Friedman Koppelman School of Business, Brooklyn College, City University of New York, New York City, USA

Linda Weiser Friedman Faculty in Business and Jewish Studies, Baruch College, City University of New York, New York City, USA

María del Carmen García-Manga Faculty of Philosophy and Letters, University of Córdoba, Córdoba, Spain

Marianthi Georgalidou Department of Mediterranean Studies, University of the Aegean, Rhodes, Greece

Leonidas Hatzithomas Department of Business Administration, University of Macedonia, Thessaloniki, Greece

Michael Alan Krasner Taft Institute for Government and Civic Education, Queens College, City University of New York, New York City, NY, USA

Sam Lehman-Wilzig Department of Communications, Peres Academic College, Rehovot, Israel

Kostoula Margariti Department of Business Administration, University of Macedonia, Thessaloniki, Greece

Pamela G. Monaghan-Geernaert Department of History and Social Sciences, Northern State University, Aberdeen, SD, USA

Rogelio Alicor L. Panao Department of Political Science, College of Social Sciences and Philosophy, University of the Philippines Diliman, Quezon City, Philippines

Ronald A. Pernia Political Science Program, College of Social Sciences, University of the Philippines Cebu, Cebu, Philippines

Michael Phillips-Anderson Department of Communication, Monmouth University, West Long Branch, NJ, USA

María del Mar Rivas-Carmona Faculty of Philosophy and Letters, University of Córdoba, Córdoba, Spain

Liz Sills Department of English, Communication, and Global Languages, Northern State University, Aberdeen, SD, USA

Liat Steir-Livny Sapir Academic College, Sderot, Israel;
Open University of Israel, Ra'anana, Israel

Chapter 1
Humor and Politics: A Conceptual Introduction

Ofer Feldman

Abstract This introductory chapter details the goals of the book, defines the scope of political humor and the rhetorical tools through which this humor is circulated verbally, also presenting a brief theoretical approach guiding the subsequent chapters. This is followed by three sections addressing key aspects in the study and analysis of political humor, considered among the different contributions: First, that humoristic expressions related to politics can be employed for good and bad purposes, illustrated by a discussion of the role played by stereotypes and prejudice in creating ethno-national humor; second, that members of the public, the political elite, and the media employ humorous expressions in politics while using different means for different goals; third, humor about political matters is a highly contextual and subjective phenomenon that can be perceived differently by individuals, with different cultures shaping the content, nature, and characteristics of such humor. The chapter suggests that knowledge of political humor contributes to a better understanding of political rhetoric, information processing and organization, attitude formation and change, persuasion, and political engagement.

1.1 Introduction

Political humor is a form of humorous expression communicated via any medium that addresses aspects of, or directed at, the power structure, including the political system and process, political institutions, political leaders, and issues in the public sphere. This expression is found in verbal messages including jokes, puns, parody, comedy, satire, and metaphors, and in non-oratorical discourse and visual representations such as caricatures, cartoons, pictures, *manga* (comic or satiric strips), or graffiti.

Humorous expressions can be articulated and convey by politicians, journalists, political pundits, and in particular members of the public. Arguably, political legitimacy implies deference for the government, its institutions, and representatives. This is the fundamental principle underlying all types of political systems. Humor

O. Feldman (✉)
Faculty of Policy Studies, Doshisha University, Kyoto, Japan
e-mail: ofeldman@mail.doshisha.ac.jp

© The Author(s), under exclusive license to Springer Nature Singapore Pte Ltd. 2024
O. Feldman (ed.), *Political Humor Worldwide*, The Language of Politics,
https://doi.org/10.1007/978-981-99-8490-9_1

that is directed at the power structure is created and circulated by citizens on the assumption that this may satisfy a need for disrespect of political authority and a relief from the trivial stress and frustrations people feel toward political institutions or policies.[1] In this sense, such humor may be seen as weapons of political criticism and contempt, as methods of individuals coping with disliked policies, politicians, and circumstances, and an instrument to get even with oppressors.

Four rhetorical tools are at the center of this book project on political humor: Parody, comedy, satire, and jokes. Parody is a humorous imitation of style. It draws on the audience's earlier knowledge of an event, concept, or people, by exaggerating (or being ironic regarding) its most recognized aspects (Gray et al., 2009).

A comedy show (and program) expresses criticism by emphasizing the positive as well as the negative universal aspects of human behavior and attitudes, and as such can readily be perceived and understood in different countries without losing their relevance. Its main objective is to make people laugh, thus not always satirical in nature (Young, 2016).

In comparison, satire is a form of social criticism that aims to draw attention to certain persons, events, organization, or a social practice or norms, considered unjust—expecting a swift change in these phenomena. It focuses on situations specific to a given society and time. Political satire, by such means as incongruity, ridicule, and irony, draws attention to the negative facets in the political system e.g., officeholders' dishonesty and deceitfulness, or questioning the inadequacies and flaws in the political or social order, thereby aiming to change or reform society. To understand political satire, the audience must have knowledge about the social and political background of the discussed society. By its focus on the detrimental aspects of politics, indicating what could or should be done to better the citizens' wellbeing, its targets (e.g., political leaders, government officials) often perceive it as a threat to their authority and rule. In totalitarian countries, for example, satire directed against the ruling powers is prohibited, and satirists could experience severe consequences. In such circumstances, humorous attacks on a regime take place in the underground (Baumgartner, 2021).

Finally, jokes are (like graffiti) a distinct genre of humor, communicated orally (or written on walls). Jokes and graffiti are typically short stories, brief sentences, or figments of imagination—ideational constructs within a setting that is possible in some sense. There must be at least three elements in a situation when a joke is told: a storyteller (or initiator), a victim (target), and a listener (audience) (cf. Dwyer, 1991). A good joke, like a good proverb, has three characteristics: few words, a fine use of metaphor, and perspicacity. Some jokes are apparently not "good" in this sense, since they require lengthy explanations, or in the words of Sigmund Freud (1905/1960, p. 109), a joke loses its effect of laughter

> as soon as someone is required to make an expenditure on intellectual work in connection with it. The allusions made in a joke must be obvious and the omissions easy to fill; an awakening of conscious intellectual interest usually makes the effect of the joke impossible.

---

[1] I thank Tom Bryder for this observation.

As with satire, without having any idea regarding a particular context, one would not be able to understand what is politically funny in jokes (and graffiti). Moreover, some jokes cannot be translated since the puns are based on linguistic idiosyncrasy. The most tormenting aspect of translation is that what is idiomatic in one language is often idiotic in another.

Political humor draws upon two significant concepts. First, the common experiences and stereotypes around which identities and perceptions toward the self and the other are formed. Political jokes, for example, rely on unconscious fear, expectations, frustrations, and release of various energies (Freud, 1905/1960), rarely on cognition, reasoning, and logic. As such, they satisfy needs which are more psychological and symbolic than political, more in the domain of amusement than in realizing public goals. In this respect, it is a discourse of persuasion and opinion, attitude formation and change, almost always against the political elite, oppressors, and the "other." Based on this premise, the rhetoric of political humor is ultimately political.

Second, political humor relies on the semantics and pragmatics of political language, contextual information, the culture, norms, values, and beliefs of a given society or an ethnic group, and the political culture of a given country (Bergson, 2008, p. 11). Humor in general, and humor about political issues and personnel in particular, can thus be seen as a highly contextual and subjective phenomenon that could be interpreted differently by individuals. As a complex social interaction, it might incorporate feelings of amusement, can be funny for some people and evoke laughter, but could also result in unexpected or unpleasant outcomes, including nervousness and embarrassment, by offending and upsetting others (Kim & Plester, 2019).

The idea that context affects political humor is central to this book, with a special focus on the cultural circumstances. Chapters assess how the force of humor reverberates in culturally specific contexts, detailing the extent that culture shapes the content, nature, and characteristics of humor in selected countries and social groups. The message that evolves from this work is about the distinctive power of humor: studying political humor leads to a better understanding of political rhetoric, information processing, attitude formation and change, persuasion, and political engagement.

In this introductory chapter, following a brief theoretical consideration, I detail three selected aspects at the heart of political humor that are relevant to the ensuing chapters: Sect. 1.3 first discusses the notion that political humor can be employed for both good and bad purposes, followed by discussion of the role played by stereotypes in affecting ethno-national humor. Section 1.4 details each of the three main groups—the public, politicians, and the mass media—that employ humorous expressions in politics, detailing the means they use and their goals in doing so. Section 1.5 discusses the cultural context in which humor evolves and is employed. Finally, the chapter details the structure of the book and briefly describes each of the contributions.

1.2 Theoretical Considerations

Research in different fields of knowledge including psychology, sociology, anthropology, linguistic, philosophy, literature, history, theology, medicine, and health care have shown in recent years a growing interest in diverse aspects of the study of humor, examining its role and functions in ancient and contemporary societies. Some of these works, notably in the fields of psychology, sociology, and linguistics, have attracted considerable attention and developed theories to explain humor's role in society, its impact on the audience, and especially the circumstances that enable humor to be adequate, interesting, and amusing.

In their attempt to explore the question of what conditions predict laughter and amusement, Warren and his associates (2021) noted more than 20 different psychological theories that attempt to identify a set of psychological conditions, or characteristics, that elicit laughter, and the perception that something is funny. These are split into three categories that explain humor appreciation: superiority, incongruity, and relief/release. Contemporary humor scholars seem to agree that while distinct, these three predominant theories of humor are not exclusive to each other; they are often linked and share the same concepts (e.g., Lintott, 2016; Martin, 1998; Morreall, 1987; Smuts, 2006). The three theories and their relevance to political humor are detailed below.

1.2.1 Superiority Theory

Superiority theory is the most ancient theory. It suggests that the purpose of humor is to demonstrate one's superiority, dominance, hostility, derision, or power over others or some objects, and also over the persons' own former position or a former version of themselves (Lintott, 2016; Smuts, 2006). Aggressive, cruel, non-empathetic, and mocking humor that belittles the stupidity or weaknesses of a targeted victim or group is a clear way to display one group's "superiority" over others. Generally, superiority theory works well in the realm of political humor, as laughs can easily be gained at the expense of another individual or groups in society. It is reflected in racist and sexist attitudes that intend to derogate or humiliate members of minorities such as ethnic groups, women, LGBTQ, and physically handicapped persons (see Feldman, 2023a, 2023b), and in humor demeaning members of certain populations. Through such humor the initiator aims to enhance their own or their groups' self-esteem.

Here are two jokes that fall under this category: first, the imprudence and lack of intelligence of Russians; second, a joke to show the comparative "intelligence" of Poles. Both illustrate aspects discussed later in the section on ethno-national humor:

> A Russian researcher conducted a study. He took a fly, tore off one of its leg and told it "Fly, jump." The fly jumped. So the researcher wrote in the notebook, "A fly with five legs can jump." He then tore off the fly's other leg and told it "Jump" and as soon as the fly jumped the researcher added in the notebook, "A fly with four legs can jump." He then tore off the fly's other leg and told it "Jump" and right after the fly jumped he wrote in his notebook that

"A fly with three legs can jump." And so on, until the fly had only one leg. The researcher then tore off the fly's last leg and told it "Jump!" The fly did not move. He tried again and repeatedly ordered "Jump!" but the fly didn't move at all. The researcher then recorded in the notebook: "A fly without legs does not hear."

Three men were all applying for the same job as a detective. One was Polish, one was Jewish, and one was Italian. Rather than ask the standard questions during the interview, the chief decided to ask each applicant just one question and base his decision upon that answer. When the Jewish man arrived for his interview, the chief asked, "Who killed Jesus Christ?" The Jewish man answered without hesitation "The Romans killed him." The chief thanked him and he left. When the Italian man arrived for his interview the chief asked the same question, to which the Italian replied "Jesus was killed by the Jews." Again, the chief thanked the man who then left. When the Polish man arrived for his interview, he was asked the exact same question. The Polish thought for a long time, before saying, "Could I have some time to think about it?" The chief said, "OK, but get back to me tomorrow with your answer." When the Polish man arrived home, his wife asked "How did the interview go?" He replied, "Great, I got the job—and I'm already investigating a murder!"

1.2.2 Incongruity Theory

A second major theory focuses on the cognitive or intellectual aspects of humor. It is based upon the premise that humor results from a contrast between what is logically expected and what actually takes place or what is said. In other words, it is based on the mismatch between two or more normally unrelated ideas or events that are brought together in an unanticipated, inappropriate, or surprising manner. The laughter comes upon the discovery of the incongruity and the realization that the statement was a joke (Shultz, 1976, pp. 12–13). Consider the following examples:

At the funeral of the richest man in town, a stranger saw a woman crying very loudly. The stranger asked, "Are you a relative of the deceased?"
The woman: "No."
The stranger: "Then why are you crying?"
The women: "That's why!"

A man told his friend: "I've been married for 34 years, and I'm still in love with the same woman. If my wife ever finds out, I'll be in big trouble!

Feinstein returned home from a business trip to discover that his wife had cheated on him. Furiously he roared:"Who was it? That bastard Wolf?"
Feinstein: "Was it Green, that creep?"
Wife: "No, it wasn't Wolf."
Wife: "No, it wasn't him."
Feinstein: "I know—it must have been that idiot Sherman."
Wife: "No, it wasn't Sherman, either."
Feinstein got inflamed and cried: "What's a matter? None of my friends is good enough for you?"

1.2.3 Relief/Release Theory

Third, the relief/release theory relates less to what makes something funny and more to the purpose of laughter and its physiological effects, the release of tension—asserting that humor and the resulting laughter are necessary to discharge energy and stress (Smuts, 2006). Here, humor appears as a socially acceptable vehicle to relieve tension about sensitive issues, such as violence and racism, that individuals might find difficult or uncomfortable to discuss. In his version of relief theory, Freud (1905/1960, pp. 797–803) suggested that laughter is related to the release of various energies, such as hostility, aggression, sexual impulses, and distressing emotions, and that repressed feelings can escape through humor. Laughter can thus be used as a substitute for violent behavior and helps people avoid conflict. Relief/release theory may best explain the importance of humor in healing. It can also explain why people laugh at an inappropriate moment, such as at a funeral, or why teenagers enjoy sexual humor. In contrast to the aforementioned theories, the relief/release theory is not of much use in the study of political humor because while it describes the process of laughter, it does not contribute to the discussion of purposeful humor provided by incongruity and superiority theories.

Taken together, the three theories are an essential framework for presenting the volume of classical approaches. They are, however, incomplete and by themselves not adequate to fully describe the phenomenon. As such, scholars proposed comprehensive theories that encompass all aspects of humor development within a framework that makes sense of contemporary matters.

1.2.4 Comprehensive Theories

One example of a comprehensive theory is *John* Morreal's (1983) theory that combines the traditional approaches of superiority, incongruity, and release, emphasizing that all laughter results from a pleasant psychological shift (that can also elicit a physiological response) of the individual, in response to the humorous stimulus. Another one is Avner Ziv's model for understanding humor (Ziv, 1984), that emphasizes five functions rather than psychological change: aggressive, sexual, social, humor as a defense mechanism, and intellectual. I now detail them in order.

1.2.4.1 The Aggressive Function

The aggressive function of humor involves victimization of individuals (e.g., doctor humor, judge humor, psychiatrist humor), groups (e.g., folklore, ethnic humor), or institutions (e.g., political humor), through ridicule or disparagement, and creates a sense of superiority in the teller. This humor is believed to have already existed in prehistoric times, and is used to monitor and limit the expression of aggression; that is, the enjoyment of this type of humor leads to eliminating the severity of aggressive emotions. Here are a few examples of this type of humor:

> Male Patient: "Dr., I fell in love with a horse."
> Psychiatrist: "Male or female?"
> Male Patient: "Of course a female. Do you think I'm psychotic?"
>
> Doctor: "Your cough this morning is much better."
> Patient: "It's because I trained all night."
>
> Polish border guard at the airport: "Nationality?"
> German tourist: "German."
> Border guard: "Occupation?"
> German tourist: "Nein, nein, only vacation."

1.2.4.2 The Sexual Function

The sexual function of humor deals with the socially acceptable ways to express and reduce sexual tension (i.e., what society considers taboo). Sexual humor can indicate enjoyment, anxiety, or disappointment in sex, allowing people to tackle such taboos in a pleasurable manner. An example in this regard:

> One man was standing at a train station and overheard a farewell conversation between two men. One said: "I enjoyed staying at your place Bill! Everything was great, the food, the pool, and even your wife, I enjoyed sleeping with her." After the host left, the astonished man turned to the guest and asked him: "Did I hear correctly? Did you tell the host that you enjoyed sleeping with his wife?" "Well," replied the guest, "the truth is that I didn't enjoy it that much, but Bill is a good friend of mine and I didn't want to tell him the truth and insult him."

1.2.4.3 The Social Function

The social function of humor is characterized by two aspects. First, relationships within a group—the social system within which one can find personal acquaintants and interaction between and among group members. Second, society as a whole or of social phenomena. Humor's role is to reform aspects of these, including strengthening group relations, opening up interpersonal relations, accepting others into one's group, cultivating social intimacy, and reinforcing group cohesiveness. Conversely, humor can be used to exclude members from the group (Ziv, 1984, p. 3). Humor in this regard can be a way of improving society, working as a social corrective by acting as a safety valve for the release of tensions and frustration. Satire, for example, conveys a social message, expressing social problems, struggles, and aspirations. Its purpose is to educate through the guise of humor.

Israel is an example in this regard. Israeli humor and satire are much like Israelis themselves—direct, defiant, and exaggerated. Israel's equivalent of *Saturday Night Live*—*Eretz Nehederet* (A Wonderful Country)—is a prime-time television satirical sketch comedy show that premiered in 2003, known for its parodies of famous political and cultural leaders and for providing a satirical twist to the weekly news. It forces Israelis to take a good look in the mirror, to laugh, but also to think about a variety of social and political issues (Steinberg, 2022).

Satire has been part of Israeli society for a long time. At the end of 1950s, the Theater Club Quartet sang a song entitled "How the bug got up," written by Haim Hefer, whose many songs are considered Israeli classics. The hymn described a bug, who was born in mouse fur, but strove to move forward in life and was able to outwit the laws of nature on his way to the top. It left the mouse and moved to the dog. The life of a dog did not satisfy him, and he aspired to rise higher and higher. He then went from the puppy to the donkey and from the donkey to the horse. And so it rose, rose, rose until he reached the government. The song wondered: "How did the bug succeed in his promotional campaign?" The answer is in the repeating chorus: "Always say yes," then you will be able to climb. This resulted from bewilderment that a small and wretched man has reached a position of influence and power, and even though the song didn't include the name of a person, the whole country knew that it referred to Shimon Peres, who later served as Israel prime minister (1984–1986; 1995–1996), and the president of the country (2007–2014).

1.2.4.4 The Defensive Function

Humor as a defense mechanism is a means of providing us with a way to deal with our anxieties. Two characteristic forms of humor as a defense mechanism are detailed, both helping to protect an individual's self-image and emotional balance. First, humor acts as a form of self-inoculation against what scares us in a form of "gallows humor" or "black humor" (i.e., sick humor, cynical humor), the type of humor that makes light of a subject often considered taboo, serious, or too painful to discuss; for example, death, crime, discrimination, terrorism, genocide including the Holocaust (e.g., Patt, 2020, see also Chapter 6, and Chapter 8). It is instrumental in actively helping us to handle threats and horror instead of yielding to it, and can be described as the humor of survival (Ziv, 1984, p. 58). Here are few examples of "black humor:"

> Question: What is good about Alzheimer's?
> Answer: Every day you meet new people.

> One Frenchman bought his wife a grave plot as a birthday present. A year later, he didn't buy her anything.
> Wife: "Why didn't you buy me a present for my birthday?"
> Husband: "Because you still haven't used the gift I bought you last year."

> Rabbi Altmann and his secretary were sitting in a coffeehouse in Berlin in 1935. "Herr Altmann," said his secretary, "I notice you're reading Der Stürmer! I can't understand why. A Nazi libel sheet! Are you some kind of masochist, or, God forbid, a self-hating Jew?"
> "On the contrary," Frau Epstein. "When I used to read the Jewish papers, all I learned about were pogroms, riots in Palestine, and assimilation in America. But now that I read Der Stürmer, I see so much more: That the Jews control all the banks, that we dominate in the arts, and that we're on the verge of taking over the entire world. You know—it makes me feel a whole lot better!"

The second characteristic form of humor as a defense mechanism is self-disparagement or self-deprecating humor i.e., the ability to laugh at oneself or their group, considered the "highest" form of humor by some (Ziv, 1984, p. 3). By revealing the joke-teller's weakness, self-disparaging humor aims at discharging any hostility towards them by impeding aggressive motives, gaining sympathy from others who identify with the humorist's shortcomings, and at the same time enabling them to actively grapple with their fear and weaknesses. Freud (1905/1960, p. 111) noted that self-deprecating jokes by Jews point to positive attributes of the Jewish people at the same time even as they poked fun at perceived negatives. In the analysis of the psychology of Jewish humor, Freud saw it as an acceptable mode of expressing hostility and as one-upmanship, as if to say: "We know our faults and can mock them much better than you ever could." Freud (1905/1960, pp. 111–112) writes:

> The jokes made about Jews by foreigners are for the most part brutal comic stories in which a joke is made unnecessary by the fact that Jews are regarded by foreigners as comic figures. The Jewish jokes which originate from Jews admit this too; but they know their real faults as well as the connection between them and their good qualities, and the share which the subject has in the person found fault with creates the subjective determinant (usually so hard to arrive at) of the joke-work. Incidentally, I do not know whether there are many other instances of a people making fun to such a degree of its own character.

Here are examples:

> Two beggars are sitting side by side on the street in Rome. One has a cross in front of him, the other a Star of David. Many people go by, but only put money into the hat of the beggar sitting behind the cross. A priest comes by, stops and watches throngs of people giving money to the beggar sitting behind the cross, but none give to the beggar sitting behind the Star of David. Finally, the priest goes over to the beggar behind the Star of David and says: "Don't you understand? This is a Catholic country. People aren't going to give you money if you sit there with a Star of David in front of you, especially if you're sitting beside a beggar who has a cross. In fact, they would probably give to him triple the amount just out of spite to you."
> The beggar behind the Star of David listened to the priest, turned to the other beggar with the cross and said: "Aaron, look who's trying to teach us marketing."

> A teacher asked her kindergarten children: "Who is the most important person in history; whoever gets it right gets 5 dollars." One of the kids yells, "Abe Lincoln." The teacher smiles and shakes her head "No!" Another kid yells, "George Washington." Again, the teacher shakes her head. The class becomes quiet as they all begin to think before one of the children goes, "Jesus!" The teacher responds, "That's right! But wait, aren't you Jewish?" To which the child replies: "Well, the correct answer is Moses, but business is business."

1.2.4.5 The Intellectual Function

Fifth and finally, the intellectual function. Based on word play and absurdities, intellectual humor provides temporary release from strict rules and rational thought, an escape to the absurd. When a funny story is presented, the person delivering it must assume that the receiver has some background knowledge. The listener or viewer then makes the intellectual connection of the funny story with the background information, that leads to understanding the message, providing enjoyment and satisfaction. The intellectual function of humor involves comprehension and problem solving, that Ziv (1984, pp. 70–80) suggests is a two-dimensional concept involving the appreciation and production of humor. In his view, understanding is a part of the thought process, and the enjoyment of humor calls for an intellectual activity like the kind required in problem solving. The need for intellectual activity is even more pronounced where creating humor is involved. Here are related examples:

> I ordered a chicken and an egg from Amazon. I'll let you know.

> My friend refuses to leave Sweden.
> She said Sweden is actually nice and deserves sympathy.
> I think she's developed Stockholm Syndrome.

> An Australian bought a new boomerang.
> But he couldn't get rid of the old one.

> What is President Donald Trump's favorite nation?
> Discrimination

Perhaps also included in this category is the Japanese *dajare* (literally, "wordplay"), a linguistic device, similar in spirit to a pun, that relies on similarities in the pronunciation of words to create a simple jokes. These homophones (and Japanese has plenty of these), have a different "spelling." Most of the time the pun relies on the phrase being spoken (different from writing when different kanji, i.e., logographic Chinese characters, will be used for the same sounds). Thus, while speaking, one can use context or explain later, but when writing something down, kanji specifies the meaning apart from the pronunciation. *Dajare* are also associated with *oyaji gyagu* (literally "old man gag" or "old man joke"), the Japanese equivalent of the dad ("old man") jokes in English (see Toshiko, 2022).

1.3 Self and Other: The Fabric of Ethno-National Humor

Inferring from the above theories on general humor, political humor can be employed for both positive and malevolent purposes. Humor creates positive behavior (laughter) through a shared experience between the person providing the mirth and the person enjoying the benefits of the humor (the laughing person). In this regard, humor can serve as a means of an alternative form of communication between individuals, a manifestation of cheerful optimism. It facilitates communication across social differences and hierarchies, helps in gaining acceptance more quickly and easily, serves as a bonding, solidarity tool that ties people together, and creating a friendly atmosphere in a given social group. Humor is used in a positive manner through which it creates a sense of belonging in the workplace, a tool for healing, enhancing self-esteem, helping in relieving stress, to maintain social justice, and enhance teamwork in the workplace (e.g., Friedman & Friedman, 2019; Hey, 2000; Warren et al., 2021).

Conversely, it may serve as mocking discreditation and thus function as a tool for ridiculing, criticizing, demeaning, degrading, humiliating, belittling, and manipulating other people. Some humor is built on bad taste, using metaphors that reveal prejudice purposefully insulting and harmful. Such "humor" can be seen as attempts to handle feelings of anxiety by depreciating "the other" (the victim) on the presupposition that that they engage in socially undesirable acts such as being untidy, or simply being silly or stupid. This may stem from the need to reinforce one's own self-esteem often at the expense of other people and relationships with them in order to enhance one's superiority and domination (Feldman, 2023a, 2023b). Many such jokes require empathy to be understood. In a large number of cases, comparisons between good and evil, heaven and hell, and winners and losers, are involved, and rhetorical devices are usually employed, as discussed in the following section.

1.3.1 Contrasts in Humor

In considering the interaction between speakers and their audiences, Atkinson (1984, cited in Bull & Feldman, 2011) noted that two of the most useful rhetorical devices to elicit reactions from listeners (mostly applause but also laughter, see Feldman & Bull, 2012) are a "list of three items" and "contrast." In the case of the former, once the listeners recognize that a list of three items is under way, it is possible to anticipate the completion point and hence the end of the speaker's utterance (before reacting, e.g., with a laugh). In the case of the latter, contrasts can be used to do a number of things, including boasting about one's own side, attacking the opposition, or doing both things at the same time. To be effective, the second part of the contrast should closely resemble the first in the details of its construction and duration, so that the audience can the more easily anticipate the point of completion (and then react with laughter). According to this model, the contrast is by far the most frequently used device for obtaining the intended audience reaction, and the skilled use of both contrasts and three-part lists is characteristic of "charismatic" speakers. The most classic humoristic expression in this regard is a story that includes three persons in a comparative manner, such as the following examples:

> Three men are stuck on an island. One day, as they were walking along the beach, they discover a magic lamp. They rub and rub, and sure enough, out pops a genie.
> The genie says: "Since I can only grant three wishes, you may each have one."
> The first says: "I've been stuck here for years. I miss my family, my wife, and my kids. I just want to go home." Poof, he's gone!
> The second says: "I've been stuck here for years as well. I miss my family, and my life. I wish I could go home too." Poof, he's gone!
> The third man starts crying uncontrollably. The genie asks: "My dear, what's the matter?"
> The man whimpers: "I wish my friends were still here."
>
> A powerful Emperor advertised for a new Chief Samurai. Only three applied for the job: a Japanese, a Chinese, and a Jewish Samurai. "Demonstrate your skills!" commanded the Emperor. So the Japanese samurai stepped forward, opened a tiny box, and released a fly. He drew his samurai sword and "swish," the fly fell to the floor, neatly divided in two!
> "What a feat!" said the Emperor. "Number Two Samurai, show me what you can do."
> The Chinese samurai smiled confidently, stepped forward and opened a tiny box, releasing a fly. He drew his samurai sword and "swish," the fly fell to the floor, neatly quartered!

"That is skill!" nodded the Emperor. "How are you going to top that, Number Three Samurai?"

The Jewish samurai stepped forward, opened a tiny box, release one fly, drew his samurai sword, and "swoooooosh," flourished his sword so mightily that a gust of wind blew through the room. But the fly was still buzzing around!

In disappointment, the Emperor said, "What kind of skill is that? The fly isn't even dead."

"Dead, schmed," replied the Jewish Samurai. "Dead is easy. What takes REAL skill is circumcision."

1.3.2 Comparing Ethnic Groups

In humor related to politics, "contrast" is most "effective" in creating laughter when social groups that share cultural practices, including language, religion, customs, and common behavior patterns, are compared to other groups. Ethnic groups or nationalities that engender a sense of belonging and ethnic and national identity (see Geertz, 1963) are examples in this regard.

Humor concerning ethnicity is prevalent mostly because of the use of the term "ethnocentrism," that is, applying one's ethnicity or culture as a frame of reference to judge people from other ethnicities according to racial, customary, behavioral, and other cultural traits. Members of a certain group tend to see themselves as the focus, take pride in their relative "superiority" and glorify themselves compared to the "inferiority" of the "other." Employing humor with the intention of denigrating the "other" (e.g., for being part of a minority group) raises the group's self-image, fosters its self-esteem and feelings of superiority. Much of this ethnocentrism is based on a stereotypical image that is attached to the "other," how any particular group of people behave or what they look like, justifying hostility towards them. Stereotypes constitute a shared set of assumptions crucial to, and necessary for, ethnic humor (Apte, 1985, pp. 113–114).

Ethnic humor gives direct or indirect expression to the socio-cultural characteristics of the group, encourages a strong ethnic identity and a positive self-image of the members of the group. It is often used to hurt or degrade other groups. In Israel, for example, it can be toward such groups as Arabs and Sephardim or Sephardic Jews, descendants of Jews from Spain, Portugal, North Africa and the Middle East (see below, Sect. 1.5); in the U.S. toward Afro-Americans, and other minorities. Or it can be also directed at religious practices such as the following two jokes regarding Jews:

> An old rabbi decided that he wanted to try pork, forbidden in the Torah. But because he's the rabbi, he can't risk being seen by anyone in his congregation. So he decided to take a vacation. He buys his tickets, flies to Brazil, finds an expensive restaurant and orders the roast pork. As he's waiting, however, a couple from his congregation walk into the same restaurant. They instantly recognize him, walk up to him, and just as they're saying hello, the Rabbi's pork is brought out: A giant pig on massive platter with a big red apple in its mouth. As it's placed in front of him, to the shock of the couple, the Rabbi exclaims: "My goodness...so this is how they serve apples here!"

A woman on a train walked up to a man across the table and asked:"Excuse me, but are you Jewish?"
"No," replied the man.
A few minutes later the woman returned again: "Excuse me, are you sure you're not Jewish?"
"I'm sure," said the man.
But the woman was not convinced, and a few minutes later she approached him a third time.
"Are you absolutely sure you're not Jewish?" she asked.
"All right, all right," the man said. "You win. I'm Jewish."
"That's funny," said the woman." You don't look Jewish."

1.3.3 Comparing National Characters

Stereotypes, images, along with prejudice, enter politics also through humor, particularly jokes, regarding countries and nations. Like ethnic groups, countries are quite different as each has its own values, accepted behavior, and customs (Feldman, 2021). Much of this has to do with the concept of national character, defined as the traits apparent in the consciousness and behavioral tendencies shared by the majority of the population (e.g., Feldman, 1997). Here is how cultural stereotypes found their way as classic jokes to illustrate differences in national character:

One Brit, without difficulty, makes a queue.
Two Jews, without trouble, make three political parties.
Three Japanese easily make four trading companies.

When a fly falls into a cup of coffee:
The Italian throws the cup, breaks it, and walks away in a fit of rage.
The German carefully washes the cup, sterilizes it, and makes a new cup of coffee.
The Frenchman takes out the fly, and drinks the coffee.
The Chinese eats the fly and throws away the coffee.
The Russian drinks the coffee with the fly, since it was extra with no charge.
The Israeli sells the coffee to the Frenchman, sells the fly to the Chinese, sells the cup to the Italian, drinks a cup of tea, and uses the extra money to invent a device that prevents flies from falling into coffee.
The Palestinian blames the Israeli for the fly falling into his coffee, protests the act of aggression to the UN, takes a loan from the European Union to buy a new cup of coffee, uses the money to purchase explosives and then blows up the coffee house where the Italian, the Frenchman, the Chinese, the German, and the Russian are all trying to explain to the Israeli that he should give away his cup of tea to the Palestinian so there will be peace in the Middle East.

The United Nations decided to conduct a world-wide survey. So they sent a letter to the representatives of each country with the following question: "Would you please give your honest opinion about solutions to the food shortage in the rest of the world?" The survey was a huge failure:
None of the European countries knew the meaning of "scarcity."
The African nations did not know what "food" meant.
In Eastern Europe they didn't know what "honest" meant.
In Western Europe they didn't know what "shortage" meant.
In China they didn't know what "opinion" meant.
In the Middle East they didn't know what "solution" meant.
In South America they didn't know what "please" meant.
The North Americans didn't know what "the rest of the world" meant.

1.4 Creating and Exploiting Political Humor

Three groups that employ humorous expressions in politics can be distinguished. Each does it through different means to realized different goals: The public, politicians, and the mass media. Here I examine each of these groups, concluding with actual acts of such humor.

1.4.1 The Public

The general public use humoristic expressions as a means of trying to express power and resisting the power structure and social injustice. As "the powerless," citizens overtly try to make fun of the political system, institutions, and political oppressors. Humoristic expressions are a reaction of citizens to the stress they feel in everyday life, where there is a gap between the self and society i.e., the two codes of reference and behavior that exist between the public and the private. The way citizens want to spend their lives and the way they are regulated, restricted, and disciplined by rulers turns out to be a perfect subject for humor.

Freud (1905/1960) observed that jokes, for example, especially serve the purpose of aggressiveness toward, or defense against, the people in high positions, for the reasons mentioned above. He noted (1905/1960, p. 103): "By making our enemy small, inferior, despicable or comic, we achieve in a roundabout way the enjoyment of overcoming him." "Enemy" in this regard are also politicians. Humor is thus used by those who have no political power as a means of political criticism and contempt, as a method of an individual's coping with disliked policies, politicians, and circumstances, and as an instrument to get even with oppressors.

To the extent that a regime cannot explicitly forbid political humor but can silence it by laws against harming national morale and the like, political humor can go underground, especially in authoritarian, dictatorial, and undemocratic governments, appearing in the form of graffiti and other anonymous, unidentifiable, and secret publications. Once political laughter becomes a way of coping in everyday life, providing a form of political protest to challenge the power and the social injustice, and a hope for restoration of self-respect and human dignity, the storytellers and audience make it a habit to insert joking comments whenever there is a perceived need for it. Consider the ensuing two, short, put-down humorous comments on the government, followed by a joke on the politicians, that spread during the 2008 U.S. presidential campaign:

> The problem with political jokes is they get elected
> (anonymous. Attributed to Henry Cate, VII).

> What's the difference between the government and the Mafia?
> One of them is organized.

> John McCain, Mitt Romney, and Sarah Palin were all caught in Iraq and sentenced to death by firing squad. John McCain was told to stand in front of the wall. Just before the firing

squad was given the order to shoot, he yelled, "Earthquake!" The squad took cover and McCain escaped over the wall. Mitt Romney took his turn and as the squad took aim, he yelled, "Tornado!" The squad panicked and Romney jumped over the wall. Then it was Sarah Palin's turn. As the firing squad pointed their rifles at her, she considered how her colleagues had escaped and yelled, "Fire!".

Political humor by citizens can include humoristic comments, assumptions, and jokes on the nature of politics and decision-making processes, social issues, and the working style, attitudes, and characteristics of political leaders. Consider for example the issue of morals, ethics, and integrity in politics. Niccolò Machiavelli (1469–1527) talked about morals as distant from politics. In the present era, within democratic and not so democratic societies, citizens wonder how far away can morality be in the world of politics, regarding what politicians do. For some citizens, the paradox of politics is that during election campaigns politicians appeal to the electorate by saying "Trust me, I am a politician." From a cynical perspective, one is not supposed to trust politicians, because according to the general view, trust and honesty are traits politicians do not often have. To illustrate:

A man visiting Washington, D.C. had to make a brief stop at the Capitol. As he parked his car he saw a man standing nearby. "I have to leave my car here for a few minutes," the visitor said. "If you're going to be here, would you mind watching it for me?" "Don't you realize I'm a United States Senator?" the bystander asked. The driver responded, "No, I didn't, but it's okay, I'll trust you anyway."

Some voters with a skeptical view will say that "The only time politicians tell the truth is when they call each other liars." Or: "Politicians lie, even when they're telling the truth." It seems that some politicians couldn't agree more regarding this attitude attributed to them. Nikita Khrushchev, the prominent Soviet politician who served as First Secretary of the Communist Party of the Soviet Union (1953–1964), observed that "Politicians are the same all over. They promise to build a bridge even where there is no river." During the time he served as Finance Minister of Israel, Levi Eshkol (who later became prime minister) uttered his famous expression: "Yes, I promised, but did I promise to keep my promise?" (Leshem, 2020). It's not surprising, then, to hear a voter asking: "How many presidents does it take to change a light bulb?" The answer, "None. They only promise change." With such doubting of politicians' morals, others say that there is no feature that politicians use more than a weak memory (of theirs and their electorate). Politicians, especially at the time of election, rely on the short memory of the electorate vis-à-vis promises they made in the previous elections.

The sarcastic view regarding the morality and (lack of) integrity of decision-makers isn't found only in Western (or former Eastern) societies. In Japan, former justice minister Hatano Akira seriously claimed that "To seek such virtues as honesty or cleanliness in [Japanese] politicians is like asking for fish at a vegetable shop" (Feldman, 2004, p. 190). And in Israel, Prime Minister Menachem Begin (1977–1983) entertained his audience by saying that when people saw on a tombstone in the cemetery the remembrance message "Here lies an honest politician," they asked if it was a custom to put two people in the same grave.

At the same time, humorous expressions can be created and circulated by the public (including publicists, authors and writers, scholars, political pundits, and journalists) not only against members of the political elite but also towards groups within society, including put-down jokes of lawyers, doctors, businessmen and the like, especially jokes told by members of one ethnic, religious, professional group aiming to ridicule and belittle members of another group; as noted above, especially prejudiced or rival groups. Thus, Blacks will tell jokes about White supremacists; women will tell jokes about male chauvinists; and Jews will tell jokes about anti-Semites (see Friedman & Friedman, 2019).

1.4.2 The Politicians

For their part, politicians are well aware of humor's power. When used wisely, humor carries a considerable benefit for office holders and political candidates. This includes politicians' casual utterances during parliamentarian deliberations, spontaneous comments during a political party meeting or election campaign, and statements in media interviews (see Chaps. 3 and 4). In all these capacities, Michael Krasner (Chap. 12) observed how humor affects politicians' interaction with the electorate and the public along two dimensions. First, humor enables politicians to control the immediate social situation by, for example, focusing attention on themselves, putting them in the superior position of knowing something the rest of the listeners don't know, re-establishing deference, creating temporary unity in the audience, relieving tension, defusing stressful situations, and controlling the immediate threatening situation. President John F. Kennedy, as one example, used jokes to dismiss as unimportant the accusations against him, reestablishing himself among the media and the public as a worthy leader. Second, humor enables politicians to decisively influence the audience's perception of the potentially damaging issue that is at stake—in fact, redefining the situation to the politicians's advantage. Using witty remarks enables the leader to influence the choice of schema by which journalists and the wider public perceive the situation.

In Japan (Feldman, 2021, pp. 6–7), politicians are remote and inaccessible, and humor lets them relate to the voters. Many savvy and novice politicians and political candidates blend their speeches in front of supporters and crowds in the streets with humoristic episodes and funny comments. When addressing followers in their constituencies or when appealing to voters during election campaigns, rather than limiting themselves to the dry facts of current political affairs, they "spice up" their lectures with witty antecedents and remarks, sometimes even satirical statements. They often share with their audience amusing observations regarding other political groups and politicians, aiming to entertain the listeners at hand and by that to attract attention, strengthen familiarity, and elicit enthusiastic reactions (in terms of applause, laughter, or encouraging shouts) from the attendees, that enable them to eventually mobilize voters. On the negative side, at times (sometime too often), their humor offends key electoral groups, insulting minority groups, and draws fire from leaders of opposition parties, citizens' groups, or the media; some of them have been forced to either publicly explain their humoristic comments, retract their remarks and apologize, or submit their resignation.

In the Philippines, too (Feldman, 2021, pp. 6–7), President Rodrigo Duterte, in his presidential discourse, as his predecessors, entertained his audience with jokes i.e., a particular type of jokes, about his female cabinet members and Filipina as tourist attractions, seemingly acceptable and even appreciated by Filipinos, as Duterte has consistently enjoyed high ratings of support (more on this recent Philippines President's humor is detailed in Chap. 5).

American presidents, in particular, starting from George Washington and Abraham Lincoln through John Kennedy, Ronald Reagan, and Barack Obama, used humor while campaigning and while in office (see Chap. 2). Probably because they knew that even a mediocre joke or a witty remark has very strong effects on the audience, many of them went as far as hiring joke writers to improve their speeches (Gardner, 1994, pp. 18, 21; Katz, 2003).

Consider, for example, President Reagan who was known as *"The Great Communicator"* and the "Master of the Joke" (Harris, 2009). One of Reagan's most effective uses of humor occurred during his 1984 debate with Walter Mondale. After being asked a question about his age (he was already at that time the oldest president in history), Reagan responded, "I will not make age an issue of this campaign. I am not going to exploit for political purposes my opponent's youth and inexperience." The effect of this remark was remarkable (see Chap. 12). Reagan also demonstrated his humor even when his life was at risk. On March 30, 1981, he was shot, and as he was placed on the operating table at the hospital, bleeding, with a bullet in his lung, he looked up and said to his doctors, "I hope you're all Republicans."

In the same manner as Reagan made his age less of an issue by appearing clearly comfortable with it and joking about it, President Barack Obama too used humor to appear at ease with his own background. On one occasion he joked that his middle name was given to him "by someone who didn't think I'd ever run for president," and later added that his middle name was actually "Steve." In another occasion, Obama joked about his celebrity status, saying he was surprised people would ask who he truly was replying that "The answer is right there on my Facebook page" (cited in Harris, 2009, p. 27). Many politicians and aspiring politicians recognize the fact that appearances on late night satire and comedy television shows provides positive exposure, a better image, and possibly some votes (Compton, 2008, p. 45; 2018). Probably based on this notion and the idea that he would be able to access youngsters as well as the politically active, Obama secured his appearance on *The Daily Show* the same evening that his paid infomercial aired on major commercial broadcast television networks (Harris, 2009).

Because many office holders know humor can shape their image, they often utilize humor to relate to their profession, their groups, and their colleagues. Referring jokingly to his profession, President Reagan noted once that "It has been said that politics is the second oldest profession. I have learned that it bears a striking resemblance to the first" (Humoropedia, n.d.). In Israel, Simha Erlich, who served as Minister of Finance (1977–1979) under Prime Minister Begin, referred to his colleagues in the Liberal Party, Gideon Pat, Abraham Sharir, and Yitzhak Modai, as "the first is Pat, the second is antipat[hy], and the third psychopath! And the French general Charles de Gaulle, who led the Free French Forces against the Nazi Germany in WWII and founded the Fifth Republic, serving as the President of France, revealed that "I have come to the conclusion that politics is too serious a matter to be left to the politicians."

1.4.3 The Mass Media

Another group is the mass media—through which journalists, columnists, political pundits and critics, and subject matter experts (and also general public who use the media for opinion columns and pages, letters to the editors)—create and spread humor. The print media, newspapers and magazines, provide the public with comic columns, comic strips, editorial cartoons, and *manga*. The internet includes such sites as Facebook, YouTube, Instagram, Twitter, and TikTok that have turned into battlegrounds for humoristic messages, cartoons, and jokes by politicians among themselves and by the general public (see Feldman, 2024).

Broadcast media too, including movies and in particular television, provides the public with humor in the form of comedy shows, standup performances, joke tellers, humorous advertisements, and witty comments (see Chap. 9). Most notably are satire televised programs in the U.S., including late-night talk shows such as *The Daily Show, The Colbert Report,* and *Saturday Night Live,* where presidents and presidential candidates, their characteristics and habits, are the focus of the majority of jokes told, overwhelmingly negative in tone, and relatively little humor concerns itself with policy or process (Baumgartner et al., 2014; Niven et al., 2003).

Survey and experimental research revealed that such political satire or comedy are very powerful forces, indicating that exposure to political humor in these channels matters. First, such programs serve as a major source of news for viewers, especially for youngsters. Humor in these programs plays a key role helping viewers to make sense of the political world, affecting the way they interpret the political process. By covering politics in an entertaining way, humor affects their knowledge of events and activities, their political attitudes and involvement, including increasing their attention to politics and spurring discussion about politics with friends, family, and coworkers, and influencing their support for certain candidates. As this fact is known to politicians, they try to appear on these programs to their advantage, as mentioned above. Such programs can motivate politically inattentive viewers to seek out additional political information, increase attention to political stories, as well as issue-specific news items, and increase the salience of certain issues or constructs in the minds of the audience (e.g., Compton, 2008, 2018; Feldman, 2013; Goldman, 2013; Gray et al., 2009; Hoffman & Young, 2011; Jones, 2010; Mankoff, 2012; Ross & Rivers, 2017). Notably, political parody and satire affect citizens' political attitudes and behavior not only in the U.S. but also in a variety of Western and non-Western societies (e.g., Baym & Jones, 2013; Chen et al., 2017).

1.4.4 Live Performances

Last, there are live show performances such as satire, comedy, and parody theater, and festivals and carnivals such as Spain's Cádiz Carnival, where groups compose and perform humorous and satirical lyrics that portray current social and political issues concerning the country. Such humorous lyrics spread quickly and widely through the internet and social networks, criticizing political powers from the local to the national levels (see Chap. 11). Likewise, artistic work in posters, photograph, film, pictures, and popular culture also serve as vehicles of humor in Europe and the U.S. (e.g., Chaps. 7 and 10).

1.5 The Cultural Dimension

As alternative forms of communication between individuals, as noted above, humor doesn't develop in a vacuum. It evolves as part of the interaction between individuals and their surroundings. Humor is, therefore, influenced by specific circumstances, culture, language, religion, history, and social values and norms. People from different cultural backgrounds, Western and non-Western—Asian and Middle Eastern—societies, individualistic and collectivist cultures, perceive, interpret, use, and are affected by humor in different ways (e.g., Chen & Martin, 2007; Chen et al., 2013; Kazarian & Martin, 2004; Martin & Ford, 2018; Saroglou & Scariot, 2002; Taher et al., 2008; Yue & Hui, 2015; See also Chap. 9) There are cultures and political cultures where humor plays an important role in social life, where humor on its diverse forms is accepted, and conversely, cultures where humor is not encouraged in everyday life.

Consider, for example, two countries that I am familiar with, Israel and Japan. Both are culturally homogeneous societies in which a majority of the population share a large number of cultural similarities (ethnicity, race, religion, language, values, beliefs, customs, and practices), but also smaller minority groups that differ from the dominant culture. Yet apart from this, Japanese and Israeli societies are almost mirror images in terms of their approach to humor regarding the usage and acceptability of political parody, satire, and jokes.

In Israel, humor has its roots in Jewish humor, originating from the Jewish history of suffering rejection, misery, and despair. The fact that Jews tended to laugh and joke (also about themselves) in difficult times is probably their most conspicuous connection with humor (Friedman & Friedman, 2019; see also Chap. 8). Contemporary Israeli humor, however, is distinct from the "old" Jewish humor, reflecting a shift from self-disparagement humor to aggressive humor, focusing on political and current affairs, including references to the Holocaust (Kotler-Fux, 2018; Steir-Livny, 2016; Ziv, 1988).

Since its establishment, political humor was always present in Israel. Jokes about political leaders, most notably prime ministers and ministers, even about presidents, were an integral part of the Israeli culture. The most famous ones were the collection of jokes published in 1966 and 1967 about Prime Minister Levi Eshkol in tiny booklets entitled *"Kol Bedichot Eshkol"* (All Eshkol's Jokes), which included jokes that for the most part made the prime minister into a laughingstock (All Eshkol's Jokes, n.d.).

One of the jokes asked: "Why should Eshkol retire?" And the reply was, "There are 71 reasons for this, and soon he will turn 72." Another example:

> A man who was passing by the Prime Minister's Office slipped and fell. At that exact moment Eshkol emerged from the building. As soon as he saw what happened, he rushed to the man and helped him to stand up. The man was grateful and asked Eshkol if he is able to reward him with something. "Right now I don't need anything," Eshkol replied. "'But in two years, at the time of elections, I would ask you to vote for me." "Sorry Mr. Eshkol," the man replied. "Surely you didn't notice: I fell on my rear and not on my head."

Another collection of jokes was about David Levy who served in different ministerial positions including Minister of Foreign Affairs (1990–1992; 1996–1998; 1999–2000) (Salamon, 2007). Levy jokes were quite popular in the 1980s only because of the perceived gap between the Ashkenazi "intelligent" group and Levy as a stereotype of "the savages," the "inferior" Moroccans i.e., North African immigrants. He was depicted as a simple person, uneducated, who couldn't speak foreign languages. One joke referred to his alleged poor English:

> David Levy attended a party at the White House. At a certain moment he was seen on the roof of the House. When asked what he was doing there he replied that he was looking for the whiskey as he heard the "whiskey is on the House."

Another set of jokes depicted Levy as not a very clever, knowledgeable person. For example:

> When David Levi died, he reached the gates of heaven, knocked on the door and the angels inside asked him who he was. "I am David Levy, I have done good for the Jewish people, I deserve to enter," he replied. The angels thought for a moment and said, "OK, but how will you prove to us you are David Levy. When Mozart came he wrote us a new piece, we saw it, were impressed and believed he was Mozart. When Picasso came, he drew us an amazing painting, proved to us who he was, and entered.
> But how will you prove you are David Levy?" To this David Levy replied: "Don't worry, I'll prove it to you, but first tell me who are Mozart and Picasso?" Hearing this, the angels opened the gates and said to him: "It's okay, you can come in."

Another notable politician that was often the main target for mocking jokes was Pinchas Sapir who served in Eshkol's cabinet as the Minister of Finance (1963–1968). He was presented as a beggar, detached, ugly, and as incompetent, unable to deal with the economic crisis Israel experienced. One joke referred to one of his trips to the U.S., trying to garner financial support for Israel. As he was leaving his hotel in New York, he handed a coin from his pocket to a *beggar.* "Where are you from?" asks the beggar. "I don't know you from around here." "I am the Israeli Minister of Finance" answered Sapir. "If so, don't give me anything," said the beggar. "I don't take money from friends of my profession."

Here is another joke about Sapir:

The post office decided to issue a special stamp with Sapir's portrait. The proud finance minister walked into a post office and asked the clerk how well his stamp was being sold. "Not good," sighed the officer. "Why?" asked Sapir in anger. "The stamp doesn't stick," explained the postman. "Give me one stamp," said Sapir. He took a stamp, spat on its back and stuck it on a piece of paper. "What are you talking nonsense?" he said, "After all, the stamp sticks perfectly!" "Yes," sighed the officer, "'the trouble is that people spit on the other side."

In comparison, in Japan one finds significantly fewer expressions of political humor than in many Western societies. Jokes about leading politicians, the prime minister, Cabinet members, or government officials are rare. Jokes about the emperor are unthinkable. One seldom sees politically-oriented messages in public places such as walls or fences around public institutions, the street, or in public toilets. Political satire is extremely rare and ridiculing public officials on the media is unwelcome (see Feldman, 2000). For example, on January 3, 2015, the Japanese public broadcaster, NHK, refused to allow a popular comedy duo Bakusho Mondai to joke about politicians on its New Year's television show entitled *"Hatsuwarai Tozai Yose 2015"* (New Year's laughter—East–West Comedy Theater 2015) featured dozens of comedians and traditional comic storytellers from all over Japan. While Bakusho Mondai were choreographing their stand-up comedy performance, NHK staff reviewed the duo's material for the show and were told the broadcaster wouldn't allow any jokes about politicians, shutting down their performance (RBBToday, 2015).

Rather than making fanciful jokes about their governing institutions and individuals, Japanese laugh at anecdotes and purportedly true episodes related to politicians. During election campaigns, for example, candidates often share with the audience incidents and encounters they have experienced, sometimes from their childhood e.g., about losing the list of items mother asked them to bring from the grocery shop, up to the current campaign, mentioning, for example, their meeting with the oldest woman in the community who talked with an accent they didn't understand. Another example is an anecdote related to Prime Minister Yoshida Shigeru (1946–1947, 1948–1954) who once replied to the question what he ate, with,"I ate a human being." This episode became a famous joke in Japan because his choice of words—*hito wo kutta* (literally, "I ate a human being")—sounds arrogant. Few Japanese would speak that way, and it is funny to hear a person in a leading position talking like this. Like many other anecdotes, this story loses a great deal in translation.

Another politician whose remarks made Japanese laugh, was Sakurauchi Yoshio, who served as Foreign Minister for one year from November 1981. It was humor that he was aiming for when he surprised Washington officials during a March 1982 visit to the U.S. by often introducing himself by saying "I am the Japanese Yul Brynner," while pointing to his bald head. In a similar vein, the Japanese humoristically talked about the "Buchi-phone"—a mutation of "push phone," Japanese for a push-button telephone—used by Prime Minister Obuchi Keizô in late 1999. Obuchi reportedly rang up people who did not expect to hear from him, and opened the conversation by saying something like, "Hello, this is Obuchi Keizô, I mean the prime minister." Almost no one believed it was really him, but Obuchi went ahead and chatted about social issues.

Perhaps the only exception in this genre was a joke regarding the lack of English skills of Mori Yoshiro, an unpopular prime minister who had already become an object of derision for having made several untoward verbal gaffes during his short time in office (2000–2001), coming under fire from different citizen groups and voters (see Feldman, 2004). He was ridiculed about confusing the English words "how" and "who" while greeting U.S. President Bill Clinton (Nakamura, 2000). Before the July 2000 Group-of-Eight Summit in Okinawa, Prime Minister Mori was coached in a bit of English. Upon meeting President Clinton, he was supposed to say: "How are you?" The response was supposed to be: "I'm fine, thank you. And you?" Mori was to answer: "Me too." When they actually met, Mori made a small slip-up and asked: "Who are you?" Clinton replied, "I'm Hillary's husband." To which Mori replied, "Me too."[2]

As I am detailing here the difference in humor between the Israel and Japan, I note that the only common humor issue between the two countries is in regard to the inability of selected leaders to make fast decisions. In Israel, Prime Minister Eshkol was considered to be hesitant, stubborn, a man of compromises, eternally undecided, that there were two famous related jokes on him:

> Why does Eshkol never bathe?
> Because every time he enters the bath he sees two taps, for the hot water and the cold water, and he can't decide which one to open.

> A waiter approaches Eshkol and asked:
> "Do you want tea or coffee, sir?"
> Eshkol hesitated, hesitated, and after a long hour decides:
> "Give me half tea and half coffee" (Galili, 2017).

Eshkol's counterpart (in this regard) in Japan, Prime Minister Kaifu Toshiki (1989–1991) was characterized in his attempt to win concessions and even to change policies in response to aggressive U.S. moves related to trade, earning him personal praise from President George Bush. Political observers in Japan complained that Kaifu would not do anything without first consulting with President Bush. They jokingly started calling the telephone in Kaifu's residence a "Bush-phone" instead of a "push-phone" (compare "Buchi-phone" above).

The cultural dimension constitutes the core of the following chapters. Culture is regarded as a central element of communications i.e., culture guides and affects communication and language (Feldman, 2021, p. 1ff.) As such, culture influences, in the context of this project, the use of humoristic expressions in parliament bodies, in political party conferences, and in public halls where voters and supporters are gathered. Satire and parody is also voiced in the mass media, and during live performances in carnivals, festivals, and other popular shows. Language, and in this regard, humoristic language about political issues and personnel, is seen as a way to describe human experience—awareness of, and reaction to, their socio-political surroundings,

---

[2] The same joke had appeared in the U.S. press several months earlier, at that time attributed to Kim Young-sam, who served as President of South Korea for five years beginning in 1993. The same apocryphal tale has also been told about any number of non-English speaking politicians from various countries. It was nonetheless reported by some mainstream media outlets.

1 Humor and Politics: A Conceptual Introduction   23

as well as their frustrations and hopes, fears, and desires regarding the political system and its leaders. All this does not exist apart from culture.

Furthermore, this book and the following one (Feldman, 2024) call attention to the idea that humor in politics, and about political subjects, is profoundly contextual. It is related to socio-cultural elements rooted in a given society, and thus may be interpreted differently by different people. Humoristic expressions that are appreciated and valued by members of one society as amusing, might be regarded as rude and unpleasant to members of another society. At the center of this project is thus the idea that culture is a powerful factor that determines the content, nature, and characteristics of humor about political issues and personnel, and the reaction to these in the public domain.

Focusing on different countries and groups, the chapters examine the extent to which cultural factors are related to (reflect, shape, determine) the nature and characteristics of political humor expressed in the groups under examination.

1.6 Overview of the Volume

Overall, three intellectual goals motivated the writing of this book and the following one (Feldman, 2024). The first to clarify the relationship between culture (broadly defined, involving norms of behavior, values, attitudes, beliefs, etc. in all walks of life) and political humor (including satire, parody, comedy, and jokes). For that matter, each of the contributions focuses on one country, one society, or an ethnic group, and examines how cultural factors (that are related to, affected, and shaped by social and family structure, social relationships, shared historical experiences of individuals and groups, religion, economic systems, majority/minority relations, individualism/collectivism, and national character) affect the content, type, and style of the humorous expressions used in the analyzed group. Chapters thus also reveal the relationship between culture and the uses of humor in the "good sense" (i.e., as funny and amusing), and the "bad" one (i.e., reflected in rudeness, meanness, irony, sarcasm, etc.).

The second goal is to probe the source of this humor: Who utilizes humoristic expressions and for what reason? Chapters detail public officials, including politicians, political candidates, government officials, and others who use humor during speeches delivered in parliaments, parliamentary debates, election campaigns, in front of supporters and voters, during media interviews, and in the social media. Other chapters focus on professionals, including comedians, artists (painters, musicians, etc.), and the general public. Members of the different groups are examined as their humoristic expressions target fellow politicians, the political system, citizens, minorities, foreigners, religion, and the "self."

Last, the third goal is to discuss the social, political, psychological effects or potential effects of political humor in a given polity. Here chapters discuss aspects related to the influence of politicians on public attitudes towards political participation, perception of the "other," ethnic group, and the "self."

To this end, the remainder of the book is organized in three parts revealing some "cross-sectional" material (and even "cross-book" data with the following book, Feldman, 2024) e.g., where individual chapters deal with the media and not only with parliamentary speeches.

The first part of the volume, *Humor in Legislative Bodies* gives particular consideration to the effect of culture in the discourse of political leaders. Chapter 2 assesses the interplay between humor and culture in a time of political polarization and division in the U.S. The chapter notes that humor that exploits the gap between the ideal and the real is found often in diverse texts of American humor, including in the discourse of political leaders, most notably in that of President Donald Trump. Chapter 3 investigates aspects of political humor in the context of Greek cultural trends, discussing humorous political satire texts, as well as texts from parliamentary speeches and media talk that interact with the humorous mode in various ways. Chapter 4 looks at the U.K. and British phlegm, a somewhat dismissive and frequently ironic comedic understatement, showcasing the ability of the humorist to maintain a composed demeanor in challenging situations. The chapter details this phenomenon by focusing on the individualistic cultural orientation of the British people, discussing various examples of humorous political speeches and electoral campaigns by a select number of recent prime ministers, that have emerged in response to historical events. Chapter 5 probes the extent to which humor in the Philippines helps a public figure and when. Examining data about presidents from 1987 to the present, the chapter indicates that Filipinos rarely find jokes offensive as long as they are told by someone who conforms to their popular expectation of what a leader should be: he or she are sincere, caring, giving, pro-people, and anti-elitist. This is rooted in a national character that puts a premium on leadership based on the idea of *"kapwa,"* a Filipino term widely understood as not simply establishing a relationship but a connection with the collective. Chapter 6 details Israeli Holocaust humor, satire, and parody and how it has been a part of the left-wing struggle against the right-wing, the latter governing Israel for most of the past 46 years. The analysis discloses the extent to which speeches and declarations by right-wingers who used the Holocaust to characterize threats to the country, inspired left-wing scholars and intellectuals to produce Holocaust humor, satire, and parodies that reprimanded these attitudes and beliefs as false and manipulative.

Part II of the book focuses on the *Ethno-National Humor in Religion, Art, and Popular Culture*. Chapter 7 explores the degree to which Polish culture is reflected in different genres of political humor. The discussion focuses on the sources of political humor, including religion, class system, literary tradition, art, film, and popular culture in general, along with socio-political polarization between conservative and liberal forces in the polity. Chapter 8 pays special attention to social justice humor as political in nature, detailing how Jewish humor can exemplify their political and cultural oppression. Social justice humor can be a tool for educating bigots, for promoting the self-esteem of the oppressed, or for simply getting even. Chapter 9 looks at historical events that affected Italian movies, revealing that a more crude and cynical satire of politics, typically in the form of social criticism, appeared as more effective in denouncing problems in the post-war period's society. Social satire has been able to interpret the widespread mistrust towards politicians, reflecting the long impasse of civil and social rights in Italian democracy and the growing cultural changes in society over the last 40 years. Chapter 10 elaborates on the effects of Native humor, analyzing the rhetoric of Apsáalooke artist Wendy Red Star's work, exploring the rhetorical tropes within the image and the implications of the choice to express the message in a high art format, lending itself to an extra-cultural audience to jarring and subversive effect. Chapter 11 examines the relationship between culture, politics, and humor in one of Spain's most popular celebrations, the Cádiz Carnival. It looks in particular at the discourse written by the ordinary people to be sung, and on groups that compose and rehearse humorous, satirical, and even biting lyrics that portray current events, competing for weeks in an official contest broadcast live on television.

The last part, *Framing and Analyzing Political Humor* is devoted to consideration of framing and analyzing political humor. Chapter 12 presents an original concept of the author to analyze the power of political leaders' humor and to indicate how changes in American leaders' humor reflect and reinforce changes in American political culture, especially the change from legitimacy (when leaders used gentle humor to gain acceptance within that system), to illegitimacy (when they use crude, aggressive humor to debase establishment rivals), and the rise of an extreme right-wing movement that has captured one of the two major American political parties. The concluding chapter, Chapter 13, presents several theoretical issues related to the study of political humor, and provides a few methodological suggestions for future research on this topic.

Overall, we hope this project will provide a broader source of information and perspective to encourage others to follow up with additional thoughts, discussion, and related research on political humor around the globe.

References

All Eshkol's Jokes. (n.d.). Wikipedia. https://he.wikipedia.org/wiki/%D7%9B%D7%9C_%D7%91%D7%93%D7%99%D7%97%D7%95%D7%AA_%D7%90%D7%A9%D7%9B%D7%95%D7%9C (in Hebrew).

Apte, M. L. (1985). *Humor and laughter: An anthropological approach*. Cornell University Press.

Baumgartner, J. C., Lichter, S. R., & Morris, J. (2014). *Politics is a joke! How TV comedians are remaking political life*. Westview.

Baumgartner, J. C. (2021). Political humor. In T. Ford & M. Strick (Eds.), *The social psychology of humor* (pp. 20–38). Routledge. https://doi.org/10.4324/9781003042440.

Baym, G., & Jones, J. P. (Eds.). (2013). *News parody and political satire across the globe*. Routledge. https://www.routledge.com/News-Parody-and-Political-Satire-Across-the-Globe/Baym-Jones/p/book/9781138109377.

Bergson, H. ([1911]2008). *Laughter: An essay on the meaning of the comic* [trans. C. Brereton & F. Rothwell]. Macmillan. https://www.templeofearth.com/books/laughter.pdf.

Bull, P., & Feldman, O. (2011). Invitations to affiliative audience responses in Japanese political speeches. *Journal of Language and Social Psychology, 30*(2), 158–176. https://doi.org/10.1177/0261927X10397151

Chen, G., and Martin, R. A. (2007). A comparison of humor styles, coping humor, and mental health between Chinese and Canadian university students. *Humor, 20*, 215–234. doi:https://doi.org/10.1515/HUMOR.2007.011.

Chen, G. H., Watkins, D., & Martin, R. A. (2013). Sense of humor in China: The role of individualism, collectivism, and facework. *Psychologia, 56*, 57–70. https://doi.org/10.2117/psysoc.2013.57

Chen, H-T., Gan, C., & Sun, P. (2017). How does political satire influence political participation? Examining the role of counter- and proattitudinal exposure, anger, and personal issue importance. *International Journal of Communication, 11*, 3011–3029. https://ijoc.org/index.php/ijoc/article/view/6158/2098.

Compton, J. (2008). More than laughing? Survey of political humor effects research. In J. C. Baumgartner & J. S. Morris (Eds.), *Laughing matters: Humor and American politics in the media age* (pp. 39–63). Routledge.

Compton, J. (2018). Inoculating against/with political humor. In J. Baumgartner & A. B. Becker (Eds.), *Political humor in a changing media landscape: A new generation of research* (pp. 95–114). Lexington Books.

Dwyer, T. (1991). Humour, power and change in organizations. *Human Relations, 44*(1), 1–19.

Feldman, L. (2013). Cloudy with a chance of heat balls: The portrayal of global warming on The Daily Show and The Colbert Report. *International Journal of Communication, 7*, 430–451. https://ijoc.org/index.php/ijoc/article/view/1940.

Feldman, O. (1997). Culture, society, and the individual: Cross-cultural political psychology in Japan. *Political Psychology, 18*(2), 327–353. https://doi.org/10.1111/0162-895X.00060.

Feldman, O. (2000). Non-oratorical discourse and political humor in Japan: Editorial cartoons, satire and attitudes toward authority. In C. De Landtsheer & O. Feldman (Eds.), *Beyond public speech and symbols: Explorations in the rhetoric of politicians and the media* (pp. 165–191). Praeger.

Feldman, O. (2004). *Talking politics in Japan today*. Sussex Academic Press.

Feldman, O. (2021). Introduction: Assessing cultural influences on political leaders' discourse. In O. Feldman (Ed.), *When politicians talk: The cultural dynamics of public speaking* (pp. 1–14). Springer. https://doi.org/10.1007/978-981-16-3579-3_1.

Feldman, O. (Ed.). (2023a). *Political debasement: Incivility, contempt, and humiliation in parliamentary and public discourse*. Springer.

Feldman, O. (Ed.). (2023b). *Debasing political rhetoric: Dissing opponents, journalists, and minorities in populist leadership communication*. Springer.

Feldman, O. (Ed.). (2024). *Communicating political humor in the media: How culture influences satire and irony*. Springer.

Feldman, O., & Bull, P. (2012). Understanding audience affiliation in response to political speeches in Japan. *Language & Dialogue, 2*(3), 375–397. https://doi.org/10.1075/ld.2.3.04fel

Freud, S. (1905/1960). *Jokes and their relation to the unconscious*. Norton.

Friedman, H. H., & Friedman, L.W. (2019). Laughing matters: When humor is meaningful. *Journal of Intercultural Management and Ethics, 4*, 55–71. https://papers.ssrn.com/sol3/papers.cfm?abstract_id=3418980.

Functions of humor in conversations of men and w.pdf. (2000). https://www.ffri.hr/~ibrdar/komunikacija/seminari/Hay

Galili, Z. (2017, June 3). Levi Eshkol who turned humor into a political weapon. *Logic in madness*. http://www.zeevgalili.com/2017/06/22003 (in Hebrew).

Gardner, G. C. (1994). *Campaign comedy: Political humor from Clinton to Kennedy*. Wayne State University Press.

Geertz, C. (1963). The integrative revolution: Primordial sentiments and civil politics in the new states. In C. Geertz (Ed.), *Old societies and new states: The quest for modernity in Asia and Africa* (pp. 105–119). Free Press of Glencoe.

Goldman, N. (2013, November). Comedy and democracy: The role of humor in social justice. *Animating Democracy.* http://animatingdemocracy.org/sites/default/files/Humor%20Trend%20Paper.pdf.

Gray, J., Jones, J. P., & Thompson, E. (Eds.). (2009). *Satire TV: Politics and comedy in the post-network era.* New York University Press.

Harris, M. K. (2009). The political application of humor. *Honors Capstone Projects—All, 497,* 1–41. https://surface.syr.edu/honors_capstone/497.

Hey, J. (2000). Functions of humor in the conversations of men and women. *Journal of Pragmatics, 32,* 709–742.

Hoffman, L. H., & Young, D. G. (2011). Satire, punch lines, and the nightly news: Untangling media effects on political participation. *Communication Research Reports, 28*(2), 159–168. https://doi.org/10.1080/08824096.2011.565278

Humoropedia (n.d.). *175 Ronald Reagan quotes.* https://humoropedia.com/175-ronald-reagan-quotes/.

Jones, J. P. (2010). *Entertaining politics: Satiric television and political engagement* (2nd ed.). Rowman & Littlefield.

Katz, M. (2003). *Clinton & me.* Hyperion.

Kazarian, S. S., & Martin, R. A. (2004). Humour styles, personality, and well-being among Lebanese university students. *European Journal of Personality, 18*(3), 209–219. https://doi.org/10.1002/per.505

Kim, H. S., & Plester, B. A. (2019). Harmony and distress: Humor, culture, and psychological well-being in South Korean organizations. *Frontiers in Psychology, 9*(2643). https://doi.org/10.3389/fpsyg.2018.02643.

Kotler-Fux, S. (2018). "Hitler-pants" parodies: Folklore in Israel's virtual sphere. *Jerusalem Studies in Jewish Folklore, 31,* 161–193.

Leshem, B. (2020, February 3). *A choice between two liars.* YNET. https://www.ynetnews.com/article/SkrhymtEL.

Lintott, S. (2016). Superiority in humor theory. *The Journal of Aesthetics and Art Criticism, 74*(4), 347–358. https://doi.org/10.1111/jaac.12321

Mankoff, R. (2012, November 1). *How does satire influence politics? The intersection of politics and satire.* Moment. https://momentmag.com/how-does-satire-influence-politics/.

Martin, R. A. (1998). Approaches to the sense of humor: A historical review. In W. Ruch (Ed.), *The sense of humor: Explorations of a personality characteristic* (pp. 15–60). Walter de Gruyter & Co. https://doi.org/10.1515/9783110804607.15.

Martin, R. A., & Ford, T. (2018). *The psychology of humor: An integrative approach.* Elsevier Academic Press.

Morreall, J. (1983). *Taking laughter seriously.* State University of New York Press.

Morreall, J. (Ed.). (1987). *The philosophy of laughter and humor.* State University of New York Press.

Nakamura, M. (2000, August 11). Rumor: Prime Minister Mori's "Who are you" gaffe!? Truth or false. In *Weekly Asahi* (p. 142) (in Japanese).

Niven, D., Lichter, S. R., & Amundson, D. (2003). The political content of late-night comedy. *Harvard International Journal of Press/politics, 8*(3), 118–133. https://doi.org/10.1177/1081180X03008003007

Patt, A. (2020). Yad Vashem you so fine: The place of the Shoah in contemporary Israeli and American comedy. In D. Slucki, G. N. Finder, & Avinoam Patt (Eds.), *Laughter after: Humor after the Holocaust* (pp. 261–284). Wayne State University Press. https://www.santafejff.org/wp-content/uploads/2020/05/Yad-Vashem_You-So-Fine.pdf.

RBBToday. (2015, January 14). *"There is no control over speech:" On the Bakusho issue and the "NHK strife."* RBBToday.https://www.rbbtoday.com/article/2015/01/14/127317.html (in Japanese).

Ross, A. S., & Rivers, D. J. (2017). Digital cultures of political participation: Internet memes and the discursive delegitimization of the 2016 US Presidential candidates. *Discourse, Context & Media, 16*, 1–11. https://journals.sagepub.com/doi/pdf/10.1177/1461444821989621.

Salamon, H. (2007). The ambivalence over the Levantinization of Israel: "David Levi" jokes. *Humor, 20*(4), 415–442. https://doi.org/10.1515/HUMOR.2007.020

Saroglou, V., & Scariot, C. (2002). Humor styles questionnaire: Personality and educational correlates in Belgian high school and college students. *European Journal of Personality, 16*(1), 43–54. https://doi.org/10.1002/per.430

Shultz, T. R. (1976). A cognitive developmental analysis of humour. In A. J. Chapman & H. C. Foot (Eds.), *Humor and laughter: Theory, research, and applications* (pp. 11–36). Transaction Publishers.

Smuts, A. (2006). Humor. In J. Fieser & B. Dowden (Eds.), *Internet encyclopedia of philosophy*. http://www.iep.utm.edu/h/humor.htm.

Steinberg, J. (2022, October 9). *Israel's favorite sketch comedy show celebrates 20 years of political satire*. The Times of Israel. https://www.timesofisrael.com/israels-favorite-sketch-comedy-show-celebrates-20-years-of-political-satire.

Steir-Livny, L. (2016). Is it OK to laugh about it yet? *The European Journal of Humour Research, 4*(4), 105–121.

Taher, D., Kazarian, S. S., & Martin, R. A. (2008). Validation of the Arabic humor styles questionnaire in a community sample of Lebanese in Lebanon. *Journal of Cross Cultural Psychology, 39*(5), 552–564. https://doi.org/10.1177/0022022108321177

Toshiko. (2022, December 28). *10 Common Japanese jokes (Oyaji Gyagu)*. JW. https://jw-webmagazine.com/common-japanese-jokes/.

Young, D. G. (2016). Humor and satire, political. In G. Mazzoleni (Ed.), *The international encyclopedia of political communication* (pp. 487–494). Wiley.

Yue, X. D., & Hui, A. N. (2015). Humor styles, creative personality traits, and creative thinking in a Hong Kong sample. *Psychological Reports, 117*(3), 845–855. https://doi.org/10.2466/04.17.PR0.117c28z4

Warren, C., Barsky, A., & McGraw, A. P. (2021). What makes things funny? An integrative review of the antecedents of laughter and amusement. *Personality and Social Psychology Review, 25*(1), 41–65. https://doi.org/10.1177/1088868320961909

Ziv, A. (1984). *Personality and sense of humor*. Springer.

Ziv, A. (1988). Humor in Israel. In A. Ziv (Ed.), *National styles of humor* (pp. 113–132). Greenwood Press.

Ofer Feldman is Professor of Political Psychology and Behavior at the Faculty of Policy Studies, Doshisha University, Kyoto, Japan. His research centers on the psychological underpinnings of mass and elite political behavior in Japan. He has extensively published journal articles, books, and book chapters on issues related to political communication and persuasion, political leadership, and political culture. His books include *The Rhetoric of Political Leadership* (2020, edited), *When Politicians Talk* (2021, edited), *Adversarial Political Interviewing* (2022, edited), *Political Debasement* (2023, edited), *and Debasing Political Rhetoric* (2023, edited). In 2021 he was elected Honorary Chair of the Research Committee on Political Psychology, International Political Science Association.

Part I
Humor in Legislative Bodies

Chapter 2
Founding Contradictions, Contemporary Expressions: Political Humor in American Culture

Michael Phillips-Anderson

Abstract This chapter examines the interplay between humor and culture in a time of political polarization and division in the United States. Incongruity is a primary way that humor is enacted in general and all the more so for political humor in America. Rubin's concept of "The Great American Joke" is offered as a lens through which to view comedy in America with a focus on the incongruity between the stated ideals of the country's founding and the lived reality of the people. Americans frequently fail to see that the gap between the ideal and the real in America involves willfully ignoring reality or redefining it to suit a different view. Those seeking to narrow the gap as well as those who want to maintain it can use humor to explore and express this condition. Humor that exploits this gap between the ideal and the real is found in diverse texts of American humor. Examples: The fictional politics of Parks and Recreation depicts an idealized and exaggerated look at local government; the rhetorical use of humor by politicians, particularly Donald Trump, shows how rhetorical humor functions. Finally, an examination of "cancel culture" demonstrates how American comedy wrestles with free speech and accountability.

2.1 Introduction

Twenty-first century American political humor continues a long tradition of American humor, reflecting a wrestling with identity, political access, and community. It is challenging to talk about the interplay between political humor and culture in America (as in every other country) because humor and culture are manifold concepts. America today is one where the dominant narratives are of division and discord. Political polarization is certainly not an exclusively American phenomenon, but the ideologies have become increasingly partisan. A Pew Research study found that Americans were more divided by political party in assessing their government's response to the coronavirus pandemic than other countries (Dimock & Wike, 2020,

M. Phillips-Anderson (✉)
Department of Communication, Monmouth University, West Long Branch, NJ, USA
e-mail: mphillip@monmouth.edu

© The Author(s), under exclusive license to Springer Nature Singapore Pte Ltd. 2024
O. Feldman (ed.), *Political Humor Worldwide*, The Language of Politics,
https://doi.org/10.1007/978-981-99-8490-9_2

para. 5). A majority of Americans think the country is more divided than usual (McKown-Dawson, 2023, para. 1). This claim might be an overstatement, given that there was a civil war in America's history, but "senior U.S. counterterrorism officials assess that the risk of major civil disruption is still salient" (Simon & Stevenson, 2023, para. 6). Resolving differences in a democracy requires discussion and debate, yet a majority of Americans find it stressful to talk about politics with people with different views (Van Green, 2021, para. 1). This chapter explores how comedy meets this moment of political division by examining how Americans are creating and using humor to cope with, understand, and change their communities.

2.2 Political Humor/Political Culture

There might not be such a thing as comedy that is not influenced by the political culture of a community or a country. We laugh about the things we care about and things that make us uncomfortable. To be sure, laughter is neither a necessary nor sufficient indicator of comedy. Most laughter is not even in response to humor (Provine, 2001, p. 42). Someone might tell what they think is a joke, and the audience either does not get it or gets it but does not find it funny. Either way, it is an example of comedy, but without laughter. This distinction is particularly important when examining political humor, as our own beliefs might lead us to miss that the speaker intended a statement to be funny, or in our thinking it is not funny to reject that it could possibly be humor.

When classifying different types of humor, the determiner is often the subject of the humor such as religion, family, and professions. We might think of political humor as a species alongside other subjects, but that would miss the fact that many humor subjects have a political dimension. Most humor requires the audience to have familiarity with the context of the humor that is generally public and, at some level, political. Even with the awareness that there is a political aspect to a great deal of humor, scholars have attempted to identify particular categories of political humor. Young (2017, p. 872) defined political humor as an "umbrella term that encompasses any humorous text dealing with political issues, people, events, processes, or institutions." Baumgartner (2019) further divided political humor into comedy and satire. Political comedy is "a form of political humor that has as its primary goal to make people laugh. Political satire, on the other hand, is more focused on delivering a political message" (Baumgartner, 2019, p. xxii). Parody, as a species of political humor, is linked by Hariman (2008, p. 251) to epideictic rhetoric, that of praise and blame: "Parody is like its natal genre of epideictic speech: the public formalization of language beside itself puts social conventions on display for collective reflection. The parodic imitation simultaneously praises and blames, and one result is to highlight where discourse ends." Whether the primary intention of the political humorist is to make the audience laugh, direct their attention to a political issue, or even change their minds about the political, the fact that politics is part of the comedy means that it differs from other forms of comedy as it is shaped by the political context in which it is delivered.

American political humor can be found on television, in comedy clubs, in newspapers and magazines, and online. It proliferates in non-institutional venues, particularly in the Trump and post-Trump eras (or what might be at the time of this writing, the Trump Interregnum). This humor is found across the political spectrum in memes and short videos in the cacophony of Twitter, Facebook, Instagram, TikTok, and other social media platforms seen as less "mainstream," such as Parler and 4chan. Political comedy can help audiences see the incongruities in the world which might be a first step toward resolving them. Humor can be used to help people of different perspectives understand each other, as seen in comedian W. Kamau Bell's series *United Shades of America*. Not all humor about politics serves to transcend the moment. Sometimes joking, and having an audience appreciate the jokes, is a mark of cultural and social acceptance. A participant at a conservative conference for young women remarked, "It's nice to be here, where you agree with everybody on the conservative issues, I walk around here and I have my filter off. We all agree on the core themes. You can make jokes. It's a really nice sense of community" (Voght, 2023, para. 14). The themes and effects of American humor cut across venues and communities. The roots of it can be identified in the country's founding.

2.3 The Great American Joke

Current trends in American political culture and humor can be examined through the history of the country, particularly its promises and shortcomings. In "The Great American Joke," Rubin (1973) establishes the central paradox of American life as the failure to live up to the country's purported ideal of equality. He argues that American humor "arises out of the gap between the cultural ideal and the everyday fact, with the ideal shown to be somewhat hollow and hypocritical, and the fact crude and disgusting" (Rubin, 1973, p. 12). America has always had an idea of itself that it has never fully realized. The Declaration of Independence proclaims that "All men are created equal," even as the authors enslaved people. Just a few paragraphs after this claim for equality, the Declaration depicts the indigenous people of North America as "merciless Indian Savages." The contradictions and ironies of an America built on the simultaneous ideas of equality and white superiority have shaped American humor since its founding. According to Melton (2017, p. 10),

> Not only is delusion central to American culture (thus providing an inherent and persistent incongruity for jesters to exploit) but it is also intertwined with individual beliefs. Americans at all levels of the social structure maintain (sometimes desperately, sometimes hysterically) the illusion that the incongruity does not exist. This cultural response is similar to laughing at someone slipping on a banana peel while also denying that the banana peel exists, or, at least, that it is in any way slippery.

Even if the contradictions are not acknowledged, many Americans have likely felt some unease about them. The gap between how America thinks of itself and how it is in actuality is similar to how people perceive themselves. Most people believe they make good choices and possess more knowledge than they actually do (see the Dunning-Kruger effect, Dunning, 2011). This tendency may be an evolutionary tool for survival. Perhaps imagining ourselves to be better than we are provides us an ideal, or at least a goal, to strive for. We may not be there yet, but we can try. The founders of America established values in the Declaration of Independence that they did not enact in practice. And yet, these flawed writers claimed those values for a new nation and built in the capacity for change. It only makes sense that there would be strong resistance to such change. Comedian and activist Dick Gregory, on his album *The Light Side: The Dark Side* (1969), said

> America is the only country that lies about what she is. And it should embarrass you because how dirty the rest of the world is they will own up to what they are. We say we about one thing but we do all together something else in this country so I say you youngsters have a big job but thanks to us old fools you waking up right quick.

To not see the gap between the ideal and the real in America is an act of willfully ignoring reality or redefining it to suit a different view. To know that the gap is there but to pretend it does not is the enactment of the Great American Joke. Both those seeking to narrow the gap and those who want to maintain it can use humor to explore and express this condition. It is difficult to see that something we have always believed is, in fact, a lie. But humor can have the power to cut through that illusion. When we find a joke funny, we may also uncover the incongruity between the ideal and the real. Not everyone is going to get the joke or have the same disposition toward it. Young (2017, p. 878) argues that rather than there being a fixed meaning in a humorous text, "it is in the reconciliation of the incongruity which, in turn, is at the mercy of whatever the listener brings to the text." Even if some in the audience fail to understand, the intention of the comedian matters. Krefting (2014, p. 2) argues that

> Some jokes are tears in the fabric of our beliefs. They challenge the myths we sustain about how fair and democratic our society is and the behaviors and practices we enact every day to maintain that fiction [...] Jokesters unmask inequality by identifying the legal arrangements and cultural attitudes and beliefs contributing to their subordinated status—joking about it, challenging that which has become normalized and compulsory, and offering new solutions and strategies.

What does our laughter at our failures and hypocrisies accomplish? Does laughter help us bypass the defenses we employ to navigate American politics and culture, to help us, if even only for a brief moment, to see the problems? Or does it desensitize us, serving as an anesthetic that lets us briefly notice the problem from the corner of our eyes, before pushing it away as the laugh fades and we move on? Rubin's concept that American humor lives in this gap has been used in a variety of scholarly studies including an analysis of women's humor in American culture (Walker, 1988), American animated comedy shows (Ezell, 2016), the Coen Brothers' *Raising Arizona* (Melton, 2017), and Progressive Era comics (Saguisag, 2019).

If Rubin is correct that much of American humor is rooted in the incongruity between the ideal and the real in American life, the question follows: What is the effect of humor in the form of The Great American Joke? Young's (2017, p. 877) review of political humor research found that there is "the potential of political humor to increase viewers' attention to politics, hence indirectly fostering certain kinds of political learning, particularly among those with the least political interest from the start." Beyond garnering attention, some comedians are not convinced that their work changes minds. Tom Lehrer, comedian, musician, and math professor, expressed doubt about the persuasive impact of satire, stating, "I don't think this kind of thing has an impact on the unconverted, frankly. It's not even preaching to the converted; it's titillating the converted" (Thompson, 2000, para. 7). Others are even more skeptical. Comedian Peter Cook, founder of a music and comedy club called "The Establishment," sarcastically compared the power of the satire performed there to the satirical Berlin cabarets of the '30s, "which did so much to stop the rise of Hitler" (Bird, 1995, para. 6). Such direct action might be too tall an expectation for any form of communication.

Key & Peele (2012–2015) was a sketch comedy show, starring Keegan-Michael Key and Jordan Peele. Luther was a recurring character who served as President Barack Obama's "anger translator." In each instance, Obama, portrayed by Peele, would speak in a way familiar to the audience while Luther, portrayed by Key, would provide the subtext to Obama's ideas. The premise was that beneath Obama's cool persona lay passion and anger that he could not directly express. Guerrero (2016, pp. 270–271) explained that

> The performance of that integrated blackness is disallowed in the actual public sphere. Even as rage is projected onto black bodies within the social imaginary (including that of the President of the United States), its actual articulation must continually be denied to black people (*especially* the President of the United States), because an articulated black rage forces the nation out of its post-racial pan and into its racial fire.

In an online sketch, Obama and Luther offered two takes on a holiday (Atencio, 2012):

> Obama: Today is Martin Luther King, Jr. Day. A day in which we celebrate a great leader.
>
> Luther: And all y'all do is remember him one day a year and then name some lame ass streets after him. Fuck y'all.

The Great American Joke in this example is that even though an African-American has been elected to the most powerful position in the country, he was still not free to express himself in any way he would like.

The notion that humor possesses the power to persuade in favor of truth has a longstanding history in American culture. One of the most famous expressions of this idea is attributed to Mark Twain, who wrote in an unfinished novel, *The Mysterious Stranger*, "Against the assault of laughter nothing can stand" (1916, p. 142). In an analysis of the source of this Twain quotation, Kersten argues that the meaning widely ascribed to it, "that humor can function as a social corrective" (Kersten, 2018, p. 64) may not be what Twain intended. First, the work, published posthumously, was not from a completed Twain manuscript, but one compiled by editors (Kersten, 2018, p. 65). In the original work, "there is no example to illustrate in what way exactly humor and laughter might improve the human condition [...] Humor may be a weapon, but humans are definitely incapable of using it to better their lot" (Kersten, 2018, p. 68). The gap between the power of humor and humanity's ability to use it is like the gap in The Great American Joke. Americans seem to live in this space between the ideal and the real. Of course, this is true in other countries, but one sense of American exceptionalism might be the veneration of a founding idea and willfully ignoring the failure to live up to it. Does this mean humanity is forever incapable of using humor to successfully attack injustice? Even if not immediately successful, Webber et al., (2021, p. 420) suggest that political humor could function "through the work it might do in preparing the groundwork—the affective cultural shift—necessary to effect widespread change at some future point in time." To explore the interplay of comedy and political culture in contemporary America, I now turn to examples that use politics as the context and content of comedy, including fictional politics, the use of rhetorical humor by political figures, and the debates around cancel culture in comedy.

2.4 Fictional Politics

Fictional politics can provide insights into a culture's values. Comedic films and television, or dramas with a significant comedic component, that revolve around politics have a long history in America. Examples include *Mr. Smith Goes to Washington* (1939), *Being There* (1979), *Dave* (1993), *The West Wing* (1999–2006), and *Veep* (2012–2019), among many others. Holland (2019) claims that fictional television "has an important and politically consequential role to play, whether in the amplification of dominant discourses or their contestation" (Holland, 2019, p. 88). The American scripted television comedy *Parks and Recreation* (2009–2015) fits into Baumgartner's category of political comedy rather than political satire. This does not mean that the show had nothing to say about American politics, but rather that it did not offer a clear delineation of the complexity of political problems or propose solutions. But it did employ humor that leveraged the idea of The Great American Joke.

Parks and Recreation, created by Michael Schur and Greg Daniels, is centered around the fictional small town of Pawnee, Indiana, and its Deputy Director of the Parks and Recreation Department, Leslie Knope, portrayed by Amy Poehler. Leslie is deeply committed to the belief that civil servants and local government have a crucial role in improving their communities. The award-winning show was a critical success and even featured cameo appearances by American political figures including Joe Biden, Michelle Obama, and John McCain. VanDerWerff (2017) claimed that *Parks and Recreation* was the television show that best reflected the Obama presidency. She argued that the show "exemplified a kind of American optimism about the idea that public service is an ultimate good" (VanDerWerff, 2017, para. 7). The gap between our ideals of government and the reality is the source of much of the show's humor. VanDerWerff (2017, para. 7) observed that "though protagonist Leslie Knope believes she's doing the best for her constituents, they see her as out of touch with their real needs—no matter how ridiculous those 'real needs' might be." In the course of the series, Leslie Knope runs for the city council and eventually works for the National Parks Service. But as the series began, her character often functions to explain the political culture of the town to the viewers.

The Pawnee City Hall is the central setting for Parks and Recreation. Inside the building, there are murals adorning the walls that showcase significant events in the town's history (for pictures of the murals see: Pawnee City Hall, 2022). These murals are likely a reference to real-world murals created by artists as part of the New Deal in the 1930s. Rife argues that the real-world murals sought "to reassure an uneasy populace through rosy depictions of settlers arriving and 'replacing' Native people, bountiful agriculture, and oil extraction" and "worked to shore up settler colonialism" (Rife, 2020, p. 2). Many of the Pawnee murals depict interactions between the indigenous people of the area and the white homesteaders who seized their land and often their lives. An article in the *Anishinabek News*, a publication of the Union of Ontario Indians, praised *Parks and Recreation* for its "vivid and equitable picture of America's relationship with the Indigenous people" and "hilariously honest depictions of Indians" (Corbiere, 2019). In Season 1, Episode 3, Leslie is giving a tour of city hall to local reporter Shauna Malwae-Tweep (portrayed by Alison Becker). During the tour, Leslie points out one of the murals depicting two white soldiers aiming a cannon at a Native American chief from a few feet away.

> Leslie Knope: And this is called 'The trial of Chief Wamapo.' It was painted in 1936 and this is Chief Wamapo and he was convicted of crimes against the soldiers. I am always amazed at his quiet dignity right before he's killed by a cannonball.
>
> Shauna Malwae-Tweep: I'm surprised no one's complained about this.
>
> Leslie Knope: Oh, tons of people have. Yeah, we get letters every day (Goor, 2009, 4:53)

Another mural depicts a battle but it is covered with a poster to shield children from the extremely graphic violent scenes. Perhaps the most offensive mural, The Spirit of Pawnee, is routinely defaced. The mural shows a train, The Spirit of Pawnee, hurtling toward Native Americans lying on the tracks while racist caricatures of Chinese workers who are building the railroad look on. The news of the defacement is treated as a normal enough occurrence that the only question is what was used to vandalize it. In this instance, it was chocolate pudding. When proposing a solution to the problem, no one suggests removing the murals entirely. Leslie says "We really need better security here. We also need better, less offensive history" (Axler, 2009, 0:24). It is not clear from the way that Leslie says this how aware her character is of the humor or importance of what she is saying. She is not laughing, but it is likely that the writers expected the audience to laugh. The Great American Joke provides the perspective that embedded in the humor of the idea that what we need in America is less offensive history is the confusion about how the culture deals with its past. Less offensive history is not something that America can get. Ignoring history is a way that some Americans try to justify their belief that America is living up to its ideals. For those that get the joke, it is clear that while America cannot have a less offensive history, the people can work toward a less offensive future, if only they acknowledge their past.

After soliciting new designs, Leslie said that the city "realized it was going to cost a ton of money to hire a muralist. So, they're just going to restore the old one. They're changing the title to The Diversity Express" (Axler, 2009, 20:42). This example illustrates how humor can draw attention to political problems and the problematic responses they often receive. Leslie claims that the issue lies with history itself. This tension reflects the ongoing debates in contemporary American politics regarding how history should be taught in schools. It is impossible to present an honest and inoffensive history of the United States, and claiming otherwise is to ignore the incongruity between America's founding principles and its actual history. The town's decision to (not) paint over the offensive history and rename the mural to reflect "diversity" highlights the practice of offering cosmetic changes rather than addressing deeper structural issues.

2.5 The Strategic Use of Humor by Elected Officials

American politicians have long employed humor as part of their communication strategies. Humor allows them to win over audiences, deflect criticism, attack opponents, and advance their policy goals. Despite not being widely recognized as such today, Abraham Lincoln might have been one of the funniest American presidents. In his famous debates with Stephen Douglas on the topic of slavery, Lincoln criticized his opponent's argument in favor of maintaining slavery joking that it was "as thin as the homeopathic soup that was made by boiling the shadow of a pigeon that had starved to death" (Lincoln, 1858). Other American politicians known for their humorous approaches include Presidents John F. Kennedy and Ronald Reagan, as well as leaders such as Texas Governor Ann Richards and Representative Katie Porter.

One of the most well-known instances of humor in American political rhetoric comes from President Ronald Reagan. During a debate with Democratic candidate Walter Mondale, Reagan deflected concerns about his age while cleverly contrasting himself with his opponent. Reagan (1984) stated, "I will not make age an issue of this campaign. I am not going to exploit, for political purposes, my opponent's youth and inexperience." This joke, which even made Mondale laugh, effectively stopped the questioning of his age and capacity to continue as president without providing evidence other than his ability to deliver a funny line.

When examining the current state of comedy and political culture, it would be difficult to ignore the peculiar humor of former President Donald Trump. At first glance, Trump is unlikely to be included in lists of intentionally funny presidents. Unlike other presidents who have found self-deprecating humor to be a useful rhetorical tool, Trump does not joke about himself. Michael Cohen, Trump's former lawyer who was convicted of campaign finance violations, remarked that Trump "doesn't have a sense of humor. He doesn't laugh, he doesn't tell jokes, he doesn't have a sense of humor. He means it when he says it" (Garcia, 2020). However, taking a broader perspective on what constitutes humor, Lewis (2019) argues that Trump's style of communication and his use of exaggeration and inflammatory remarks can be seen as a form of humor in the political context. Lewis (2019, para. 16) argues that Trump

> [...] shares with many authoritarians a sense of theatre. Even his worst opponents can't seem to look away. That is probably why Trump won the presidency. If the root of all humour is cruelty, Trump is very funny. Whether it is parody of others or self-parody, the audience shakes its head and laughs. Low-energy Jeb; Little Marco and his water; Pocahontas; his entourage of third-rate goombahs and grifters.

The nicknames are indicative of his frequent use of humor that can be classified as "insult humor," resembling a style often seen in the comedy world. One notable example is Trump mocking the voice and movements of a disabled reporter (Kessler, 2016). While the humorous nature of such instances may be debatable, the fact that the audience responded with audible laughter suggests that they perceived it as humor or had a similar physiological response. However, this type of humor is unlikely to win over Trump's opponents. Its purpose may be to solidify support among his existing followers and capture the attention of those who are not aligned with any specific political movement or party.

In 2015, Trump criticized former Republican presidential candidate Senator John McCain, calling him a loser for not winning the 2008 presidential race. When the moderator countered by highlighting McCain's status as a war hero, Trump responded, "He's not a war hero. He was a war hero because he was captured. I like people who weren't captured" (Neuman, 2015, para. 3). This comment seemingly aimed at humor evoked a mixed response from the audience, with laughter and groans. Other Republicans criticized Trump for the remark, but his campaign persisted. As a contrast, consider the remarks of James Stockdale, the 1992 Reform Party Vice Presidential candidate and Vietnam POW, who humorously said about his captivity, "The best thing I had going for me was I had no contact with Washington for all those years" (The Commission on Presidential Debates, 1992). This statement maintains the seriousness of Stockdale's situation while reframing it into a humorous political critique of government bureaucracy.

Trump appears to lack the ability to take a joke. He frequently criticized late-night hosts and impersonators, reportedly going so far as to have White House staffers contact the Disney corporation in an attempt to get Jimmy Kimmel to "tone down his anti-Trump humor" (Burtt, 2023, para. 3). However, this attempt was ultimately unsuccessful. According to Wickberg (1998, pp. 197–198),

> In today's environment, it is the political leader who refuses humor and laughter that runs the risk of damaging his credibility. No politician wishes to be accused of lacking a sense of humor. The demagogue and the fanatic, the autocrat and the dogmatist, it is widely believed, are without a sense of humor. Humor is a sign of political flexibility, moderation, willingness to see both sides of a question, capacity for compromise.

However, Trump's humor does not typically demonstrate the aforementioned flexibility or moderation. Instead, it tends to be insulting and cruel. Cruelty is often a characteristic of comedy, as seen in the performances of insult comedians like Don Rickles, Jeff Ross, and Lisa Lampanelli. In an interview, Rickles said that he rejected the term insult comedian and said: "What it is, is I don't really insult. I exaggerate all ourselves, our beings. I make fun of everything, of our life and what we are. But I don't tell jokes, really. I just exaggerate life, and it comes out funny" ("Remembering Don Rickles, The Insult Comic Who Made Fun of Everything," 2017). Trump's humor may be perceived by some in his audience in a similar way, as an entertaining exaggeration. However, the ways in which he employs humor inevitably raise questions of appropriateness and effectiveness. The same humor that might delight one audience can cause another to recoil, further driving them away from supporting a politician.

At a Washington Press Club dinner in 2023, Republican Representative Nancy Mace, a frequent critic of other Republicans in non-humorous ways, used political humor to ridicule others in her party. Mace referenced the protracted voting that took 15 ballots to elect Representative Kevin McCarthy to the position of Speaker of the House and the allegations of sex trafficking of a minor by Representative Matt Gaetz when she quipped: "We all knew Matt Gaetz wouldn't let the speaker vote get to 18. I do have a message from Matt—he really wanted to be here tonight, but he couldn't find a babysitter" (Scott & Solender, 2023, para. 13).

In a joke making fun of the serial liar Republican Representative George Santos as well as former President Donald Trump, Mace said: "I mean who lies about playing college volleyball? If you're going to lie make it about something big, like you actually won the 2020 presidential election" (Scott & Solender, 2023, para. 10). When the discourse is so far removed from the ideals of the country and reality, humor functions to highlight the incongruity, and through the affective experience of laughter might give reassurance to the receptive audience that their perspective is shared.

2.6 Comedy and Cancel Culture

Norms and expectations of funniness and acceptability are in a period of flux in American comedy. Comedian Jerry Seinfeld gained attention in 2015 for saying that he refuses to perform at colleges because the students are too politically correct, though he also noted that this is only what he has heard since he does not perform at colleges. Seinfeld continued, "They just want to use these words: 'That's racist;' 'That's sexist;' 'That's prejudice;' They don't know what the hell they're talking about" (Falcone, 2015, para. 3). That some audiences might take issue with a comedian's work is not new, but previously the less powerful would have had limited opportunity to express their views. Now they can "leverage networked collectivity and a sense of immediacy to demand accountability from a range of powerful figures" (Clark, 2020, pp. 90–91). Seinfeld's comments speak to a central tension within comedy and political culture. The views of an older, established, wealthy person can come into conflict with the values of a younger, less powerful community. One manifestation of this conflict has been framed as an explosion of "cancel culture."

The term "cancel culture" came into widespread use in the 2010s and by 2021 it was "inescapable" (Romano, 2021, para. 1). The use of the term is largely a creation of the political right, arguing that the woke mob is "wielding power against innocent victims" (Romano, 2021, para. 18). From another perspective, Clark (2020, p. 88) defines "canceling" as "an expression of agency, a choice to withdraw one's attention from someone or something whose values, (in)action, or speech are so offensive, one no longer wishes to grace them with their presence, time, and money." Clark locates the origins of canceling within queer communities of color, particularly Black Twitter, and the use of the "callout" to voice opinions about offensive conduct (Clark, 2020, p. 89). Roxanne Gay denies the existence of cancel culture and argues that as a culture we have not figured out how to hold people accountable in appropriate ways. She said:

> Cancel culture is this boogeyman that people have come up with to explain away bad behavior and when their faves experience consequences. I like to think of it as consequence culture, where when you make a mistake—and we all do, by the way—there should be consequences. The problem is that we haven't figured out what consequences should be. So it's all or nothing. Either there are no consequences, or people lose their jobs, or other sort of sweeping grand gestures that don't actually solve the problem at hand (Schwartz, 2021, para. 13).

A Pew Research study found that 44% of Americans were familiar with the term and that there were strong differences in perception of its meaning along partisan lines. Democrats and liberals were more likely to think that it referred to "actions taken to hold others accountable" while Republicans and conservatives framed it as a "censorship of speech or history" and "mean-spirited actions taken to cause others harm" (Vogels et al., 2021). These competing framings demonstrate that cancel culture is not a settled idea and that struggles around framing discussions of comedy are contests for power.

The invocation of cancel culture often presents the criticism of comedians as a challenge to free speech. The concept of free speech is enshrined as the second right in the First Amendment of the United States Constitution, following freedom of religion. However, the understanding of how freedom of speech operates reveals a gap in understanding. Americans who face criticism for their speech can argue that they have a First Amendment right to say what they want. Yet, they often overlook the first part of the amendment, which states that "Congress shall make no law respecting [the] enumerated rights." Therefore, if the criticism does not come from Congress, the defense falls flat. Americans might cherish their rights but frequently lack a deep understanding of them. Their freedom of speech must remain intact while criticism of their work is the real outrage. In this attempt to maintain power, Clark argues that cancel culture has morphed into "a tool for silencing marginalized people who have adapted earlier resistance strategies for effectiveness in the digital space" (2020, p. 89). The standards of what is acceptable and interesting in comedy are always changing and that change will be a site of struggle.

Joe Rogan, the comedian and podcaster, faced criticism for anti-Semitic and anti-Black comments, and covid misinformation on his Spotify podcast (Murray, 2022). Several music artists, including Neil Young and Joni Mitchell, and podcasters including Roxane Gay, pulled their catalogs from the Spotify platform in response.

Rogan responded by saying "I'm not trying to promote misinformation, I'm not trying to be controversial. I've never tried to do anything with this podcast other than to just talk to people" (O'Kane, 2022, para. 6). Rogan later opened an "anti-cancel culture" comedy club in Austin, Texas in 2023. Rogan's discourse has continued to include anti-trans, racist, anti-Semitic, and conspiracy theory themes. In the FAQ for the club, they recommend that patrons research comedians before attending a show because "Comedy is subjective and certain comedians are not for everybody" (Comedy Mothership, 2023). A report of the opening night performances found that "Within seconds of the first comic taking the stage, a gay slur was thrown out, followed by jokes about trans people. The audience hooted. For the anti-cancel-culture crowd, this is their new safe space" (Hibberd, 2023). Clearly, Joe Rogan was not canceled.

In 2017, comedian Hari Kondabolu wrote and starred in a documentary, *The Problem with Apu* (Melamedoff, 2017), about *The Simpsons*, comedy, and representation. The idea started as a 2012 segment on Totally Biased where Kondabolu was a writer. While discussing the increased representation of Indian-Americans in comedy, he voiced his frustration with *The Simpsons*' character, Apu, a stereotyped Indian-American convenience store clerk. Kondabolu identified the problem: "Apu—a cartoon character voiced by Hank Azaria, a White guy. A White guy doing an impression of a White guy making fun of my father" (2017, 3:30). The documentary argued that the portrayal of Apu was an example of brownface. *The Simpsons*' creator Matt Groening was not initially persuaded claiming, "I think it's a time in our culture where people love to pretend they're offended" (Keveney, 2018, para. 20). The show responded with a 2018 episode "No Good Read Goes Unpunished" in which a bedtime story is edited to make it less offensive. The character Lisa Simpson says: "Something that started decades ago and was applauded and inoffensive is now politically incorrect. What can you do?" (Rubin, 2018, para 4). Kondabolu criticized the show's response in a tweet: "The Simpsons response tonight is not a jab at me, but at what many of us consider progress" (2018). In 2020, Azaria, after resisting the criticism, said he would no longer voice the character (Variety Staff, 2020, para. 1), and later that year *The Simpsons* pledged to not have White actors voice non-White characters (Thorne, 2020, para. 2). Reflecting on the controversy, Azaria recognized that his first response was to frame it as cancel culture. "I didn't want to cave to so-called 'PC pressure' or 'the woke mob'—whatever you want to call it. On the other hand, I didn't want to continue to engage in a harmful practice if that's what I was doing" (Murray, 2023, para. 14). In this example, the views might have changed because of reflection and growth, or from the recognition of changing audience expectations.

Some comedians who have faced criticism for their performances have responded by attacking "cancel culture." Dave Chappelle, in his 2021 Netflix special *The Closer*, made transphobic jokes and despite complaints of being canceled, the special remains on Netflix (Mier, 2023). Comedian Bill Maher has also complained about "cancel culture" on his HBO show *Real Time with Bill Maher*. He argued that "liberals need a stand your ground law for cancel culture so that when the woke mob comes after you for some ridiculous offense you'll stand your ground. Stop apologizing"

(Maher, 2021). Maher is comparing what liberals should do with speech to the so-called "stand your ground" laws that allow people to use deadly force to defend themselves if they believe their life to be in danger. This is in opposition to the "duty to retreat" which does not allow for the use of violence in self-defense if it is possible to leave the situation. When it comes to speech, who has ground to stand on? Who gets to say "This isn't acceptable?" Throughout most of American history, only the elite (white, male, wealthy individuals) held this power. Historically, the "mob" comprising comedians and their fans joking about oppressed groups, now claims that "cancel culture" is demanding that their speech should be silenced. This argument becomes convoluted, suggesting that one can criticize the speech of those who complain about their own speech, but those critics cannot voice their concerns.

Comedian Katt Williams said that comedians "weren't all that extremely funny back when they could say whatever they wanted to say. At the end of the day, there's no cancel culture. Cancellation doesn't have its own culture" (Budden, 2021). Comedian Sarah Silverman explained that "Comedy is not evergreen! There are jokes I made 15 years ago that I would absolutely not make today, because I am less ignorant than I was. I know more now than I did. I change with new information" (Heawood, 2017). The idealization of a past where any comedian could work without comment or consequence is obviously a fantasy, but one that has significant power. The Great American Joke is that not all Americans have enjoyed equal access to freedom of speech and when it becomes more broadly available, entrenched power might not think it is such a good idea anymore. The ability of comedians to speak is constrained by both law and culture. Laws in America have traditionally favored White men who were also the gatekeepers of the culture. The political and social changes of the twentieth century, which have only accelerated in the twenty-first, have demonstrated that there are voices and audiences for different kinds of comedy.

2.7 Conclusion

Using Rubin's Great American Joke as a lens to examine the influence of American political culture on comedy enables us to see how much of American life revolves around navigating and exploring the gaps between the ideal and the real. However, it also raises the question of whether laughing at our weaknesses indicates a form of strength. Does laughter empower us to strive toward bringing America closer to its professed ideals? Laughter possesses the ability to bypass the strength of our arguments and emotional defenses, exposing what the humor is attempting to reveal. The strength required to effect change then emerges from a different source. Laughter can help us recognize the absurdity in our shortcomings and the attempts to deny their existence. Hariman (2008, p. 258) suggests: "The long-term effect of a public culture alive with parody is an irreverent democratization of the conventions of public discourse, which in turn keeps public speech closer to its audiences and their experiences of the public world." Does comedy assist American culture in thriving as a pluralistic society that embraces diversity while simultaneously constituting itself as a unified whole? Hopefully it can, so that the story does not end as a tragedy.

References

Atencio, P. (Director). (2012, January 13). Obama's anger translator—Martin Luther King Day. In *Key & Peele*. Comedy Central. https://www.youtube.com/watch?v=FZpE5o9NsEk.

Axler, R. (Writer), & Shelton, M. (Director). (2009, November 12). The camel (Season 2, Episode 9). In G. Daniels (Executive Producer), *Parks and Recreation*. Deedle-Dee Productions, Universal Media Studios, Fremulon, and 3 Arts Entertainment.

Baumgartner, J. C. (Ed.). (2019). Introduction. In *American political humor: Masters of satire and their impact on U.S. policy and culture* (pp. xxi–xxv). ABC-CLIO.

Bird, J. (1995, January 10). *Obituary: Peter Cook*. The Independent. https://www.independent.co.uk/news/people/obituary-peter-cook-1567341.html.

Budden, J. (Host). (2021, June 4). *Katt Williams joins the JBP* [Podcast episode]. In *The Joe Budden Podcast*. https://www.youtube.com/watch?v=miVhHsEIqZ0.

Burtt, K. (2023, February 27). *Donald Trump was reportedly so hurt over this one late night comedian's jokes he got the White House involved*. Sheknows. https://www.sheknows.com/entertainment/articles/2726834/donald-trump-jimmy-kimmel-jokes-disney/.

Clark, M. D. (2020). DRAG THEM: A brief etymology of so-called "cancel culture." *Communication and the Public, 5*(3–4), 88–92. https://doi.org/10.1177/2057047320961562

Comedy Mothership. (2023). FAQ. *Comedy Mothership FAQ*. https://comedymothership.com/faq.

Corbiere, K. (2019, December 27). The hilariously honest depictions of Indians in NBC's Parks and Recreation. *Anishinabek News*. https://anishinabeknews.ca/2019/12/27/the-hilariously-honest-depictions-of-indians-in-nbcs-parks-and-recreation/

Dimock, M., & Wike, R. (2020). *America is exceptional in the nature of its political divide*. Pew Research Center. https://www.pewresearch.org/short-reads/2020/11/13/america-is-exceptional-in-the-nature-of-its-political-divide/.

Dunning, D. (2011). The Dunning-Kruger effect: On being ignorant of one's own ignorance (Chap. 5). *Advances in Experimental Social Psychology, 44*, 247–296. https://doi.org/10.1016/B978-0-12-385522-0.00005-6

Ezell, S. K. (2016). *Humor and satire on contemporary television: Animation and the American joke*. Routledge.

Falcone, D. R. (2015, June 8). *Jerry Seinfeld: College students don't know what the hell they're talking about*. Entertainment Weekly. https://ew.com/article/2015/06/08/jerry-seinfeld-politically-correct-college-campuses/.

Garcia, C. (2020, September 9). Cohen: Trump "doesn't have a sense of humor," isn't joking about being POTUS for "12 more years." *The Week*. https://theweek.com/speedreads/936490/cohen-trump-doesnt-have-sense-humor-isnt-joking-about-being-potus-12-more-years.

Goor, D. (Writer) & Blitz, J. (Director). (2009, April 23). The reporter (Season 1, Episode 3). In G. Daniels (Executive Producer), *Parks and recreation*. Deedle-Dee Productions and Universal Media Studios

Gregory, D. (1969). *The light side: The dark side* [LP]. Poppy. https://archive.org/details/lp_the-light-side-the-dark-side_dick-gregory.

Guerrero, L. (2016). Can I live? Contemporary Black satire and the state of postmodern double consciousness. *Studies in American Humor, 2*(2), 266–279. https://doi.org/10.5325/studamerhumor.2.2.0266

Hariman, R. (2008). Political parody and public culture. *Quarterly Journal of Speech, 94*(3), 247–272. https://doi.org/10.1080/00335630802210369

Heawood, S. (2017, November 19). *Sarah Silverman: 'There are jokes I made 15 years ago I would absolutely not make today.'* The Guardian. https://www.theguardian.com/global/2017/nov/19/sarah-silverman-interview-jokes-i-made-15-years-ago-i-wouldnt-make-today.

Hibberd, J. (2023, March 7). *Joe Rogan opens his anti-cancel culture club in Austin.* The Hollywood Reporter. https://www.hollywoodreporter.com/news/general-news/joe-rogan-comedy-mothership-review-austin-club-1235343105/.

Holland, J. (2019). *Fictional television and American politics: From 9/11 to Donald Trump.* Manchester University Press.

Kersten, H. (2018). Mark Twain's "Assault of Laughter": Reflections on the perplexing history of an appealing idea. *The Mark Twain Annual, 16*(1), 64–76. https://doi.org/10.5325/marktwaij.16.1.0064

Kessler, G. (2016, August 2). *Donald Trump's revisionist history of mocking a disabled reporter.* The Washington Post. https://www.washingtonpost.com/news/fact-checker/wp/2016/08/02/donald-trumps-revisionist-history-of-mocking-a-disabled-reporter/.

Keveney, B. (2018, April 27). *"The Simpsons" exclusive: Matt Groening (mostly) remembers the show's record 636 episodes.* USA Today. https://www.usatoday.com/story/life/tv/2018/04/27/thesimpsons-matt-groening-new-record-fox-animated-series/524581002/.

Kondabolu, H. [@harikondabolu]. (2018, April 9). *In "The Problem with Apu," I used Apu & The Simpsons as an entry point into a larger conversation about* [Tweet]. Twitter. https://twitter.com/harikondabolu/status/983211404214714368.

Krefting, R. (2014). *All joking aside: American humor and its discontents.* Johns Hopkins University Press.

Lewis, E. (2019, April 1). *Donald Trump is undeniably funny—And that's why we should be on our guard.* The Independent. https://www.independent.co.uk/voices/trump-funny-dangerous-mueller-report-dictators-europe-right-wing-hitler-mussolini-a8850151.html.

Lincoln, A. (1858, October 13). *Sixth debate: Quincy, Illinois.* National Park Service, Lincoln Home. https://home.nps.gov/liho/learn/historyculture/debate6.htm.

Maher, B. (Writer). (2021, February 26). *New rule: Cancel culture is over party.* Real Time with Bill Maher. HBO. https://www.youtube.com/watch?v=gmXTUSP9a9M.

McKown-Dawson, E. (2023, April 29). *Two-thirds of Americans think the country is more divided than usual.* YouGov. https://today.yougov.com/topics/politics/articles-reports/2023/04/29/americans-think-country-more-divided-united-poll.

Melamedoff, M. (Director). (2017, November 19). *The problem with Apu.* truTV.

Melton, J. (2017). Romancing the American dream: The Coen Brothers' *Raising Arizona. Studies in American Humor, 3*(1), 1–21. https://doi.org/10.5325/studamerhumor.3.1.0001

Mier, T. (2023, January 24). *Dave Chappelle addresses transphobic remarks. He's playing the victim.* Rolling Stone. https://www.rollingstone.com/tv-movies/tv-movie-news/dave-chappelle-addresses-transphobia-protests-1234667521/.

Murray, C. (2022, February 8). *Joe Rogan draws backlash for antisemitic comments—Spotify silent on latest controversy from its biggest podcaster.* Forbes. https://www.forbes.com/sites/conormurray/2023/02/08/joe-rogan-draws-backlash-for-antisemitic-comments-spotify-silent-on-latest-controversy-from-its-biggest-podcaster/.

Murray, T. (2023, June 7). *Hank Azaria: 'I didn't want to cave to so-called PC pressure.'* The Independent. https://www.independent.co.uk/arts-entertainment/tv/features/hank-azaria-the-idol-simpsons-apu-b2352423.html.

Neuman, S. (2015, July 18). *Trump lashes out at McCain: "I like people who weren't captured."* NPR. https://www.npr.org/sections/thetwo-way/2015/07/18/424169549/trump-lashes-out-at-mccain-i-like-people-who-werent-captured.

O'Kane, C. (2022, January 31). *Joe Rogan responds to Neil Young and Spotify's new advisory for podcasts that discuss COVID-19.* CBS News. https://www.cbsnews.com/news/joe-rogan-spotify-response-podcasts-covid-19-advisory/.

Pawnee City Hall. (2022, August 19). *Parks and Recreation Wiki.* https://www.parksandrecreation.fandom.com/wiki/Pawnee_City_Hall.

Provine, R. R. (2001). *Laughter: A scientific investigation*. Penguin Books.
Reagan, R. (1984, October 21). *Debate between The President and former Vice President Walter F. Mondale in Kansas City, Missouri*. The Ronald Reagan Presidential Foundation & Institute. https://www.reaganfoundation.org/ronald-reagan/reagan-quotes-speeches/debate-between-the-president-and-former-vice-president-walter-f-mondale-in-kansas-city-missouri/.
Remembering Don Rickles, the insult comic who made fun of everything. (2017, April 7). *Fresh Air*. NPR.
Rife, M. E. (2020). *Public art, private land: Settler colonialism and environment in New Deal murals on the Great Plains*. Ph.D. dissertation, University of Toronto.
Romano, A. (2021, May 5). *The second wave of "cancel culture."* Vox. https://www.vox.com/22384308/cancel-culture-free-speech-accountability-debate.
Rubin, L. D., Jr. (1973). *The comic imagination in American literature*. Rutgers University Press.
Rubin, R. (2018, April 9). *'The Simpsons' responds to Apu stereotype criticism*. Variety. https://variety.com/2018/tv/news/the-simpsons-respond-apu-stereotype-controversy-1202747506/.
Saguisag, L. (2019). *Incorrigibles and innocents: Constructing childhood and citizenship in progressive era comics*. Rutgers University Press.
Schwartz, M. (2021, March 5). *Roxane Gay says cancel culture does not exist*. Mother Jones. https://www.motherjones.com/media/2021/03/roxane-gay-says-cancel-culture-does-not-exist/.
Scott, E., & Solender, A. (2023, February 9). *Nancy Mace lights up Republicans at Press Club event*. Axios. https://www.axios.com/2023/02/09/nancy-mace-trump-santos-mccarthy-greene-press-club.
Simon, S., & Stevenson, J. (2023, April 21). *The threat of civil breakdown is real*. Politico. https://www.politico.com/news/magazine/2023/04/21/political-violence-2024-magazine-00093028.
The Commission on Presidential Debates. (1992). *October 13, 1992 debate transcript*. https://www.debates.org/voter-education/debate-transcripts/october-13-1992-debate-transcript/.
Thompson, S. (2000, May 24). *Tom Lehrer*. AV Club. https://www.avclub.com/tom-lehrer-1798208112.
Thorne, W. (2020, June 26). *The Simpsons' will 'No longer have White actors voice non-White characters,' producers say*. Variety. https://variety.com/2020/tv/news/the-simpsons-will-no-longer-have-white-actors-voice-non-white-characters-producers-say-1234691910/.
Twain, M. (1916). *The mysterious stranger*. Harper & Bros.
Van Green, T. (2021). *Republicans and Democrats alike say it's stressful to talk politics with people who disagree*. Pew Research Center. https://www.pewresearch.org/short-reads/2021/11/23/republicans-and-democrats-alike-say-its-stressful-to-talk-politics-with-people-who-disagree/.
VanDerWerff, E. (2017, January 19). *The past 10 presidencies, explained by the TV shows that defined them*. Vox. https://web.archive.org/web/20201114234425/, https://www.vox.com/culture/2017/1/19/14288694/presidents-tv.
Variety Staff. (2020, January 17). *Hank Azaria says he will no longer voice Apu on 'The Simpsons.'* Variety. https://variety.com/2020/tv/news/hank-azaria-apu-the-simpsons-1203471153/.
Vogels, E. A., Anderson, M., Porteus, M., Baronavski, C., Atske, S., McClain, C., Auxier, B., Perrin, A., & Ramshankar, M. (2021). *Americans and 'cancel culture': Where Some see calls for accountability, others see censorship, punishment*. Pew Research Center. https://www.pewresearch.org/internet/2021/05/19/americans-and-cancel-culture-where-some-see-calls-for-accountability-others-see-censorship-punishment/.
Voght, K. (2023, June 14). *Inside a conservative confab for young women, where feminism is a lie*. The Washington Post. https://www.washingtonpost.com/lifestyle/2023/06/15/inside-conservative-confab-young-women-where-feminism-is-lie/.
Walker, N. A. (1988). *A very serious thing: Women's humor and American culture*. University of Minnesota Press.
Webber, J., Momen, M., Finley, J., Krefting, R., Willett, C., & Willett, J. (2021). The political force of the comedic. *Contemporary Political Theory, 20*(2), 419–446. https://doi.org/10.1057/s41296-020-00451-z

Wickberg, D. (1998). *The senses of humor: Self and laughter in modern America.* Cornell University Press.

Young, D. G. (2017). Theories and effects of political humor: Discounting cues, gateways, and the impact of incongruities. In K. Kenski & K. H. Jamieson (Eds.), *The Oxford handbook of political communication* (Vol. 1, pp. 871–884). Oxford University Press. https://doi.org/10.1093/oxfordhb/9780199793471.013.29_update_001.

Michael Phillips-Anderson is Associate Professor of Communication at Monmouth University, New Jersey, USA. He is a rhetorical theorist and critic who studies the ways that language, particularly humor and nonviolent communication, constructs, and challenges power. He has published on topics including the rhetoric of Sojourner Truth and Thich Nhat Hanh, the humor of US Presidents, and the comic theory of Lucie Olbrechts-Tyteca.

Chapter 3
Humorous Genres and Modes in Greek Political Discourse

Marianthi Georgalidou

Abstract In the context of Greek political discourse, and various discourses about Greek politics, the present study investigates aspects of humor as well as humorous genres commenting on contemporary political affairs. Based on an overview of research on humor in Greek culture and specifically in Greek politics as a strategy of im/politeness, the aim of this paper is to discuss representative examples of humorous texts, namely political satire, as well as texts pertaining to the sphere of serious discourse, namely parliamentary speeches and media talk that interact with the humorous mode in various ways. The research questions posed concern political humor in the context of Greek cultural trends that favor high degrees of confrontational and combative encounters in private and public/institutional communication. The methodological approach is interactional, seeing texts as locally negotiated communicative acts. It is also critical; effort is made to trace the overall trends in the texts under examination i.e., the macro level of cultural preferences in contemporary Greece.

3.1 Introduction

The present study investigates aspects of the humorous mode as well as humorous genres commenting on political affairs, in the context of contemporary Greek political discourse and various discourses regarding Greek politics. Following an overview of research on humor in Greek culture and specifically in Greek politics as a strategy of im/politeness (Georgalidou, 2021), the aim of this chapter is to discuss representative examples of humor in political texts pertaining to the sphere of serious discourse, namely parliamentary speeches and media talk that employ the humorous mode in various ways (Dynel, 2011; Morreall, 2005; Mulkay, 1988). I also discuss instances of contemporary political satire (Dynel, 2011; Milner Davis, 2017; O'Connor, 2017; Popa, 2011; Rolfe, 2017).

M. Georgalidou (✉)
Department of Mediterranean Studies, University of the Aegean, Rhodes, Greece
e-mail: georgalidou@aegean.gr

In the case of institutional genres such as parliamentary interactions and media talk, the questions posed concern humor as a discourse strategy employed to enable adversaries to attack the "face" of their rivals, striking blows to their adequacy and/ or integrity in a manner that will not induce penalties for breeching parliamentary decorum (Bippus, 2007; Georgalidou, 2011, 2021; Tsakona & Popa, 2011). Another question concerns benefits to the attacker that such witticisms bestow (Nuolijärvi & Tiittula, 2011; Tsakona, 2011). In the case of political satire, questions concern the partisan aspect of humorous/ironic attacks against politicians as a serious case of stance taking (Ödmark, 2021). They also concern the potential of satirical discourse to serve as primary sources of information (O'Connor, 2017), bypassing mainstream news channels. Reactions to satirical political discourse based on publicized comments are also examined.

Analysis in the present chapter focuses on how humor mediates Greek politics. The study takes into consideration aspects of Greek culture correlated to preference for positive politeness strategies (Sifianou, 1992), close-knit social network connections (versus individualism), and the abandoning of typicality (i.e., negative politeness strategies) early on in relationships (Bayraktaroglu & Sifianou, 2001). It also examines how a tendency to undermine authority and contest hierarchy attested to in Greek communities of practice (Hirschon, 2001), is mediated via humor. More specifically, the research questions posed concern political humor as an impoliteness strategy that threatens the face of multiple targets in the context of Greek cultural trends favoring high degrees of confrontational and combative encounters, in private and public/institutional communication (Georgalidou, 2021; Hirschon, 2001; Kakava, 2002; Tsakona, 2008, 2009).

In Sect. 3.2, I discuss humor in Greek culture and specifically in Greek politics (Sects. 3.2.1, 3.2.2), satirical genres as humor with a critical purpose (Sect. 3.2.3), and the data (Sect. 3.3). Section 3.4 summarizes my findings and offers additional research goals to be pursued in the future.

3.2 The Overall Context: Humor in Greek Culture and Politics (2008–2023)

3.2.1 Humor as Positive Politeness—Humor as Impoliteness

Summarizing approximately four decades of research on linguistic humor, Gasteratou and Tsakona (2023, p. 7, and references therein) structurally define humor as the mismatch between how things appear to be and how they should have been i.e., as a case of entertaining semantic/pragmatic incongruity based on the subversion of speakers' expectations. Moreover, looking at humor as a sociolinguistic phenomenon, one of its most important parameters is its target, be they institutions or persons. The targeting of institutions, persons and/or positions and value systems renders them inferior, at the same time enabling humorists to portray themselves as superior (Gasteratou & Tsakona, 2023, p. 7). Target, as an integral component of humorous discourse, brings forth the question of humor as a means of criticism, also discussed in aggression/superiority theories (Attardo, 1994, 2001; Morreall, 2009; Raskin, 1985). As Gasteratou and Tsakona (2023, p. 7) convincingly claim, "humor turns out to be a means of mitigated criticism or even covert aggression against the humorous targets." In this light, humor has been extensively discussed as an indirect im/politeness strategy.

As far as the politeness end of the spectrum is concerned, Brown & Levinson (1987) claim that joking can be used to emphasize shared background and values. Thus, conversational humor has been ascribed a mitigating function in performing face threats (Norrick, 1993), and joking can even serve bonding purposes, a priority for social groups that are positive politeness oriented (Sifianou, 1992). In the Greek sociocultural environment, preference for positive politeness strategies (Sifianou, 1992), close-knit social network connections (versus individualism), and the abandoning of typicality (i.e., negative politeness strategies) early on in relationships have been noted in research (Bayraktaroglu & Sifianou, 2001; Sifianou, 1992). According to Antonopoulou and Sifianou (2002, p. 765), in Greek society, where language is frequently seen as a form of play (Hirschon, 1992; Mackridge, 1992), joking receives further significance. It can serve mitigating, face-saving, and bonding functions. However, the tendency to undermine authority and contest hierarchy that has also been attested to in Greek communities of practice (Hirschon, 2001), favor high degrees of confrontational and combative encounters in private as well as public/institutional communication (Georgalidou, 2021; Hirschon, 2001; Kakava, 2002; Tsakona, 2008, 2009). Thus, face threats, even the ones delivered indirectly via the humor, can be perceived as impoliteness and aggressive conduct.

As I have discussed elsewhere (Georgalidou, 2023, and references therein), impoliteness comprises face-threatening speech acts accomplished by participants through discourse via concrete, interactional communication ostensibly contextualized as aggressive in responses (Arundale, 2010; Culpeper, 2005; Eelen, 2001; Garcés-Conejos Blitvich, 2013; Haugh, 2015; Watts, 2010). Despite apparent playfulness, humor can be deployed by speakers to gain face for themselves (Goffman[, 1955] 1967, p. 24), bypassing/defying requirements for decorum (Tsakona, 2011). It can thus strike a blow to the addressee's face and at the same time threaten the face of collectivities s/he is a member of, and be ostensibly perceived as impolite. On the other hand, aggressive humor can also serve bonding purposes via positive reactions in unison by members of the audience in alignment with the humorist. As a consequence, humor does not have a universally accepted interpretation as a conversational strategy. Responses to structural incongruities vary according to individual or collective positions and agendas—political genres discussed subsequently being a case in point.

3.2.2 Parliamentary Humor as an Impoliteness Strategy

Humor has become a major issue in the analysis of the discourse produced by and about politicians and political affairs (Bippus, 2007; Georgalidou, 2011, 2021; Mulkay, 1988; Tsakona & Popa, 2011). Focusing on political humor produced within humorous and non-humorous genres, such as political satire, stand-up comedy, and institutional political debates in parliament and the media respectively, research has explored the close relations among modes of discourse that could be considered incompatible. Parties interacting via the above-mentioned genres employ humor as a form of positive politeness to mitigate face threats, or as strategic impoliteness to attack political targets (Georgalidou, 2011, 2021, 2023). In this context, despite the fact that due to its inherent or superficial ambiguity, humor has been approached mainly as redressive action (Brown & Levinson, 1987; Norrick, 1993), it can nevertheless serve as a means for constructing and negotiating face threats, as well as striking a blow at the opponent's face and enhancing the face of the attacker (Georgalidou, 2011, 2021; Nuolijärvi & Tiittula, 2011; Tsakona, 2011).

Humor "is never 'innocent' and devoid of emotional impact and social consequences, whether positive or negative ones. On the contrary, it is employed as a tool for testing common ground and shared values, thus bringing interlocutors closer together or driving them further apart" (Chovanec & Tsakona, 2018, p. 6). In political combat, humor and irony, seen as a facet of the same pragmatic devices, set up the target and can be perceived as moving along a spectrum of aggression, therefore also being constructed as relevant inappropriateness (Attardo, 2000). In this analysis, humor results in different outcomes by differently oriented interlocutors. Amusement might be a possible outcome (Nuolijärvi & Tiittula, 2011), especially for the audience affiliated with the humorist, as even covert offensive action has the potential to establish positions of power (Fairclough, 2013) and to strengthen in-group cohesion and ties. However, once the target registers the attack as threatening, the dominant outcome is humor that undermines affiliation among political communities.

What is more, political humor, whether affiliative or non-affiliative, can be indicative of the different ways in which politics is organized in various socio-cultural and political systems. Thus, humor in competitive democracies, such as the Greek, becomes particularly aggressive, mainly promoting polarization and the discrediting of opponents (Archakis & Tsakona, 2011; Georgalidou, 2021; Tsakona, 2009)—all the more so during years of economic crisis (Frantzi et al., 2019). Aggressive humor by rival political parties and collectivities crosses boundaries among contrasting ideologies, attempting to undermine the political image of common opponents (Georgalidou, 2011). Humorous discourse choices, therefore, simultaneously address multiple political audiences and targets. The same is true for professional humorists engaging in political satire.

3.2.3 Political Satire

Political satire is nothing new, as humorously commenting on sociopolitical affairs is found over eons of human political history in various cultures, ancient Greek Aristophanes' comedies being just a case in point. In contemporary western political systems that enlist various media channels to disseminate ideological positions and propaganda, it is an established form of political action. Satirists address vast cross-demographic populations via television (Popa, 2011) and social media (Crittenden et al., 2011), claiming the role of opinion leaders (Ödmark, 2021). According to Popa (2011, p. 140), they provide a metalanguage for discourse produced in the institutional political arena about the social and political order. Satirical texts scrutinize public life and have become a source of political information bypassing, and at times taking the place of, mainstream news agencies as primary sources of news (O'Connor, 2017). At the same time, they function as a medium for protest and critique. Thus, humorous/ironic attacks against politicians in the context of satirical programs have to be examined as a serious case of stance taking with the potential to influence the electorate.

Satirists attempt to mediate politics by offering a partisan outlook on political affairs (Milner-Davis & Foyle, 2017, p. 3), at times producing discourses that construct the radicalization of their agents (Watters, 2011). Despite disclaimers of affiliation with political parties and controversy as an inherent characteristic of humor, political satire is designed to promote and/or undermine political agendas, exhibiting political intent (Ödmark, 2021). In tandem with their politically purposeful intervention, satirists seem to prefer aggressive discourse aimed at destroying an opponent's credibility by making the audience laugh at the victim's expense (Rolfe, 2017, p. 41). In this context, satirical genres encompass humor with a critical purpose (Milner-Davis & Foyle, 2017), daring to speak the unspeakable by momentarily appearing to defy social norms about how one is expected to speak (Chovanec & Tsakona, 2023, p. 91). As Terkourafi and her associates (2018, p. 38) claim in their socio-pragmatic analysis of uncivil Twitter (now "X"), commentators draw a contrast between being refined and speaking one's mind, giving themselves license to say things that are not obscured by the niceties of polite speech, drawing an opposition between "polite" versus "sincere" (Terkourafi, 2011). Similarly, satirical discourse is delivered via absurdities, irreverent behavior, ridicule, and quite often through sexual allusions (Popa, 2011, p. 150). Audiences keep assessing verbal performances, aligning (or not) with non-affiliative, aggressive humor and verbal violence that are contextualized as funny only by in-groups (Dynel, 2011).

In the Greek sociocultural context with its indigenous Greek emphasis on freedom and personal autonomy of action and expression, including tolerance of insults (Hirschon, 2001, p. 34) and resistance to conceding rank, but also on a predilection for democracy (Hirschon, 2001, p. 22), satirical expression can be aggressively face-threatening, as can be seen in the examples discussed in Sect. 3.3 below. Thus, in a continuum of more or less formal political genres, I will ferret out the above-mentioned trends and their potential to interact with contemporary Greek institutional political discourses. In the next section, I discuss indicative examples of parliamentary/political discourse (Sects. 3.3.1 and 3.3.2) and satirical texts (Sect. 3.3.3) in terms of humor as an impoliteness strategy posing threats to face in Greek political confrontations.

3.3 Data Analysis: Humor as an Impoliteness Strategy in Greek Political Genres[1]

The present analysis focuses on the humorous targeting of Greek politicians in genres of political discourse, as facework. The examples come from (a) sexist humor in the era of economic crisis and beyond[2]; (b) the pre-election period of 2019 and (c) the comparable context of July/August 2022[3]; (d) political satire in the pre-election period during the first half of 2023. The issues discussed in the analysis are twofold. First, instances of humorous personal attacks against adversaries in the Greek Parliament as well as in satirical programs are structurally examined as discursive practices in the context of political combat. Second, we examine humor in terms of the political culture dominating political confrontations in Greece, as this has evolved within a long history of political divisions between the (far)right and left-wing political polarities (Boukala, 2014; Kostopoulos, 2021).

The analytic approach is predominantly emic, based on the analysis of discourse units as there-and-then social actions. Moreover, a combination of interactional and critical frameworks is applied so that complicated distinctions between expected political rivalry and verbal abuse can be approached in terms of external, etic cultural parameters for the negotiation of preferences in political combat.

---

[1] Part 3.3.1 is based on my previous work cited in the analysis.

[2] As I discussed elsewhere (Georgalidou, 2023, p. 176), after a period of aggravated social turmoil and intense parliamentary conflicts in 2008, the Greek financial crisis was officially acknowledged at the end of 2009. New Democracy (ND) called a snap general election that was followed by successive governments unable to complete the four-year term in office designated by the Greek constitution. The sharp deterioration of the economy and the adoption of austerity measures dictated by the second memorandum (MoU) with the IMF and the EU led to weakening of the previously powerful parties PASOK and ND. On the 25th of January 2015 a snap election was called for the fourth time in five years. The election was won by SYRIZA, that after four and a half years in office, called another snap election won by the ND in July 2019. In May and June 2023, double general elections were also won by the conservative party (ND), surpassing the loyal opposition party of SYRIZA by approximately 22% and scoring an impressive 40.56% of the votes despite harsh criticism against its administration that had to do with the illegal tapping of politicians and journalists by the National Intelligence Service under the auspices of Prime Minister Kyriakos Mitsotakis himself (Georgalidou, 2023). Harsh criticism was also addressed to the ruling party due to its economic and health policy, and a terrible train accident with 57 casualties that highlighted the shortcomings of public security provisions. Wiretapping fellow and opposition politicians and journalists, in addition to the train accident (the focal point of both the opposition and satirical discourse), went unnoticed or were not evaluated as crucial by the majority of the electorate.

[3] Rumors of early elections were widespread in the second half of 2022, leading to aggravated oppositional strategies in the political debate.

3.3.1 Sexist Humor

Example 3.1 (June 29th, 2015, Official Proceedings).

Basileios Keggeroglou: But I have explained [things] and I have handed the documents to Mrs. Fotiou many times, not just once. Because she forgets. Thus, I have jokingly told her that she has Alzheimer's.[4]

[*Alla eho exigisi ke eho dosi eggrafa stin kyria Fotiou polles fores, ohi mia. Giati xehna. Tis eho pi malista haritologontas oti ehi Alzheimer*].

Theano Fotiou: Do not accept this kind of [small, minor] joke. I do not accept them because this is scurrilous. I do not accept them.

[*Den dehome astiakia tetiou typou. Den ta dehome, giati afto ine hideotis. Den ta dehome*].

In Example 3.1, Keggeroglou, a PASOK[5] Member of Parliament (MP) in 2015, claims that the then Undersecretary of Employment and Social Welfare, Theano Fotiou (SYRIZA),[6] continually forgets things (turn 1). He goes on to suggest that she suffers from Alzheimer's, an illness that induces memory loss mainly in the elderly, indirectly invoking her identity as a senior MP. His comment is directly categorized by him as jesting. However, the alleged mitigative function of employing the humorous mode is rejected by Fotiou, who in her responsive turn assesses the comment as a hideous insult (*scurrilous*, turn 2) (Georgalidou et al., 2019, p. 115). Keggeroglou's attack activates stereotypes of female incompetence based on mental illness connected to old age, directly contextualized as offensive by the recipient.

Example 3.2 is a sexist attack delivered as humorous, this time in a media context. Gerasimos Giakoumatos (MP-ND)[7] is invited to the night entertainment TV program "The Kardasians" on the Antena TV Channel. He is encouraged by one of the hosts of the program, Grigoris Arnaoutoglou, to comment on Konstantopoulou's (SYRIZA) parliamentary discursive style, perceived as unfeminine, followed by a comment by the hostess, Maria Bekatorou, "*Look now how he* [i.e. Giakoumatos] *is going to be pissed off* [laughter]," contextualizing the event as humorous.

Example 3.2 (Newsbomb, 2015).

Gerasimos Giakoumatos: I say a—(.) in my prayers at night among the other things I say, I who understand her and loves her very much, I say God [he crosses himself], when is the beloved husband of hers the sailor going to disembark.

[*Ego kano mia—(.) stin prosefhi mou to vradi mesa ap' t' alla pou leo pou tin katalaveno ke tin agapo para poli leo Thee mou* ((he crosses himself)) *pote tha xebarkari o agapimenos mas naftikos o andras tis*].

---

[4] Humorous attacks are underlined.

[5] PASOK, the Panhellenic Socialist Movement that ruled Greece for almost 40 years starting in 1982. Its political power diminished during the years of the economic crisis.

[6] SYRIZA, the Coalition of the Radical Left that ruled Greece during 2015–2019.

[7] ND, New Democracy, the conservative party ruling Greece since 2019.

Sexist humor is produced by indirectly presupposing a sexually deprived woman (*in my prayers* [...] *I say God, when is our beloved husband of hers the sailor going to disembark*), as a cause for unfeminine, hysterical behavior on her part, again indirectly invoking mental illness. The hostess's and the participating audience's laughing reactions highlight sexist verbal attacks against women parliamentarians as media spectacles (Georgakopoulou, 2013) and as an acceptable form of entertainment. The fact that the incident was uploaded and circulated by numerous news sites and blogs on the internet further reinforces this interpretation. However, assessments by several media of the incident as a *xydaia*—a hideous attack confirm the non-universal interpretations of similar attacks against politicians as benevolently humorous.

Attacks as the ones discussed above, recycle—and as a consequence, attempt to legitimize disguised as humor—sexist discourse against female parliamentarians. As excerpts 1 and 2 show, female politicians become the targets of humorous insults and aggression by attackers who resort to indirect verbal means invoking sexist i.e., subversive, stereotypes of alleged sexual or mental inadequacies, to undermine them as legitimate political counterparts (Georgalidou, 2017; Georgalidou et al., 2020).

3.3.2 Humor as Strategic Rudeness

Greek political divisions for most of the 20th and the first two decades of the 21st century form the overall context for employing impoliteness in Greek parliamentary discourse pertaining to right- and left-wing parties (Georgalidou, 2023). The following examples are excerpts of discursive events within extended speeches. They are selected as instances of strategic impoliteness/rudeness (Keinpointer, 1997) conveyed via humor, representative of targeting the competence and ethos of one's rival. The questions posed concern the verbal mechanisms that produce humorous impoliteness. Responses by verified addresses (not included in the examples)[8] confirm the perceived interpretation of the attacks as aggressive. The episodes involve male parliamentarians, members of adversary political parties participating in sittings that discuss a vote of confidence prior to the May 2019 national elections, when the the left-wing SYRIZA was still in office (Example 3.3), and the phone tapping of politicians and journalists by the National Intelligence Service under the auspices of the right-wing ND (August 2022, Example 3.4). They are representative of verbal combat between the leaders of the two biggest parliamentary parties i.e., right-wing New Democracy and left-wing SYRIZA.

Example 3.3 (May 8th, 2019, Official Proceedings).
Kyriakos Mitsotakis (President of ND):

[...] Your moral high ground, Mr. Tsipra, sank in the turquoise Ionian waters.

---

[8] Discussed in Georgalidou, 2023.

3 Humorous Genres and Modes in Greek Political Discourse   57

[Applause by ND.] You laugh, Mr. Tsipra. Indeed, it would be funny because once people cheered 'here comes the prime-minister', whereas now they will be cheering here comes Tsipras the yacht-cruise-maker. This is how Greek society will remember you! From the Left of the squats to the Left of the yachts!

[[…] *To ithiko sas pleonektima, kyrie Tsipra, vouliakse sta galazoprasina nera tou Ioniou.* ((Applause by ND)) *Gelate, kyrie Tsipra. Pragmati, tha ine astio, dioti eki pou sas fonazan kapote "na tos, na tos, o Prothypourgos!", tora tha lene "na tos, na tos, o Tsipras o skafatos!" Etsi tha sas thymate I elliniki kinonia! Apo tin Aristera ton katalipseon, stin Aristera tou koterou!*]

[Applause by ND]

[Noise—protests by SYRIZA]

Mitsotakis launched successive attacks against Tsipras via humor and irony. In the first jab line, the speaker referred to Tsipras' personal ethos. Mitsotakis used the metaphor of it having "*sunk in the turquoise Ionian waters.*" In the next utterance we are informed that Tsipras' reaction to the attack was laughter. Responding to Tsipras' dismissive reaction, Mitsotakis escalated the attack, this time by means of the mock chant, "*here comes Tsipras the yacht-cruise-maker,*" echoing the pre-electoral chant, "*here comes the prime minister,*" by which supporters welcome party leaders. The pun refers to a three-day cruise Tsipras and his family went on, in August 2018, three weeks after a destructive fire in Attica which led to about one hundred casualties. The pun portrays Tsipras as cynical and indifferent to the people's suffering. Mitsotakis' attack concluded with another humorous pan, "*From the Left of the squats to the Left of the yachts!*", referring to Tsipras' young past as an activist of the Left and his alleged political transformation. Banter against the adversary has an affiliative effect within ND MPs expressing applause, whereas it is contextualized as offensively non-affiliative by SYRIZA MPs who protest vociferously.

Example 3.4 (August 26th, 2022, Official Proceedings).

Alexis Tsipras (President of Syriza): […] Even if we accept this, if we accept that is, that you were not ruling, you were just presiding [over the government], that your nephew was the [actual] prime minister, this is what you are telling us, you were not ruling. […]. But Mr. Mitsotakis, you know something? The evasions and the lies are over. You cannot keep hiding behind the finger of your nephew, of your deputy until the day before yesterday, Mr. Dimitriadis, and of your emissary in the National Intelligence Service, Mr. Kontoleon. And if half of your speech today was audacity, the other half was cowardice. The gravest cowardice is not assuming political responsibility[9] and claiming that "it is not my fault; it is my nephew's fault." Not even primary school children do that! "It is not my fault; it is my nephew's fault"! […].

[[…] *Akomi ke afto an to dehtoume, na dehtoume diladi oti den kyvernousate esis, esis apla proedrevate, oti Prothypourgos itan o anipsios sas -afto mas lete, den kyvernousate esis.* […]. *Omos kyrie Mitsotaki, kserete kati? I ypekfyges kai ta psemata teliosan. Den borite na kryveste pia piso apo to dahtylo tou anipsiou sas ke mehri prohthes ant' aftou sas, tou kyriou Dimitriadi, ke tou eklektou sas gia tin EYP, tou kyriou Kontoleonta. Ke an to miso*

---

[9] Denying accountability for the National Intelligence Service tapping political adversaries and journalists.

tis paremvasis sas simera itan thrasos, to allo miso itan dilia. I megalyteri dilia ine na min analamvanete tin politiki efthyni ken na lete <u>"den fteo ego, ftei o anipsios mou"</u>. Oute pedia tou dimotikou den to kanoun afto! <u>"Den fteo ego, ftei o anipsios mou"</u>! [...].

[Applause by SYRIZA]

Tsipras' humorous attack is structured as a sequence of hypothetical scenarios attributing limited capacity and lack of control over governmental executives who answered directly to the prime minister Kyriakos Mitsotakis himself. Conditional structures introduced (*"Even if we accept that"*) and asserted administrative inadequacy (*"you were not ruling* [...] *your nephew was the* ((actual)) *prime minister"*). Ownership of the claims is attributed to Mitsotakis himself: *"you are telling us you were not ruling."* Tsipras escalates ridicule by paraphrasing a popular metaphor (*"You cannot keep hiding behind the finger of your nephew"*), portraying the prime minister as hiding behind the index finger of his nephew who served as the head of Mitsotakis personal office at the time. He uses first person reported, direct speech to establish ownership of the claims of ignorance by Mitsotakis himself (*"It is not my fault; it is my nephew's fault"*), whom he compares to *"primary school children"* i.e., minors. He thus instrumentalizes the humorous mode to activate debasing implicatures, presenting them as Mitsotakis's own claims (*"you are telling us / you are claiming"*).

Examples 3.3 and 3.4 confirm the employment of humor in institutional parliamentary discourse as a weapon enabling adversaries to become implicitly aggressive (Georgalidou, 2011, p. 105). What is more, as Nuolijärvi and Tiittula (2011, p. 580) point out, opposition leaders tend to use more attacking humor and irony as opposed to prime ministers in office. As Examples 3.3 and 3.4 exhibit, both Mitsotakis and Tsipras as opposition leaders, use humor to offend. They thus bypass possible repercussions of overt aggression, while at the same time scoring marks as witty and eloquent orators. Here we see how impoliteness masked as humor provides invaluable rhetorical weapons in political power games. In the next section, I examine analogous trends in Greek political satire.

3.3.3 *Political Satire in the Context of Contemporary Greek Politics*

If freedom of speech is a crucial right in western democracies, then "a right to offend" (Winston, 2012) is part of the freedom to express criticism and even rejection of political actions and persons. Exercising this right is part and parcel of offensive acts performed by satirists. In the following examples, I discuss three comedians engaging in political satire, representing different generations and political stances in contemporary Greek politics.

Christoforos Zaralikos, a comedian affiliated with the Greek Communist Party (KKE), in his popular weekly YouTube satirical program, reviews current affairs and critically comments on the way the news is presented by mainstream news media.

3 Humorous Genres and Modes in Greek Political Discourse

He also regularly refers to prominent politicians from major parliamentary parties, using offensive terms/phrases under the pretext of satire to target them. For example, he has humorously referred to Tsipras as "the little prick of our heart" [*To kavlaki tis kardias mas*] and to Mitsotakis as "the moron of the family" (Mitsotakis family) [*To zavo tis ikogenias*].

In Example 3.5,[10] Zaralikos targets a prominent minister of the conservative government, Adonis Georgiadis, bringing forth his political past as a member of the far-right Popular Orthodox Rally (LAOS). He systematically referred to Georgiadis by the substitute name "male Eva Brown," alluding to the German Nazi party in World War 2, as Brown was Hitler's mistress. Despite the fact that Zaralikos customarily referred to Georgiadis as the "male Eva Brown," on this occasion Georgiadis reacted to the satirical content by threatening Zaralikos with a lawsuit, categorizing the attack as hate speech, contextualizing it as a direct threat to his persona:

Example 3.5 Political satire by Christoforos Zaralikos (ZaraleaksTV (n.d.), 25:00–25:52, and response to it by Adonis Georgiadis (Proto Thema, 2023).

Christoforos Zaralikos: If you want to have even more people [in your pre-election gatherings] than you've had this year, make an announcement that you are going to cut your throat on live streaming, in the presence of the audience. You will fill OAKA [the biggest Atehnian stadium] to its full capacity. Really, I am drawing a [mental] picture for you. *Follow your leader* [projecting the image of Hitler committing suicide in the background]. If you also find a way to resurrect yourself, you will manage twelve successive *sold out* OAKA concerts.

[*An thelis tou hronou na eheis akoma perissotero kosmo apo oti ihes fetos, vgale anakinosi oti tha kopsis se zontani syndesi, ke parousia kinou, ton lemo sou. Tha gemisis to OAKA. Pragmatika, sto eho ke ikona.* Follow your leader. *An vris ki enan tropo na anastithis, tha kanis kollita dodeka synavlies* sold out *OAKA*].

Adonis Georgiadis: I have always favored satire and well-meaning criticism. Quite often, I have uploaded excerpts on my social media accounts. I never expected a comedian to express himself in such a hideous way referring to my face. Whoever has seen the video of Mr Zaralikos in question, realizes that such characterizations reinforce hate speech and toxicity in which some invest, pursuing personal or party gain. Not having other means of defense, I will fully exercise my legal rights as a citizen, and specifically as a father and consequently I am taking the matter to Court.

[*Anekathen imoun yper tis satiras ke tis kaloproeretis kritikis. Polles fores malista eho anevasi o idios stous logarasmous mou sta mesa kinonikis diktyosis shetika apospasmata. Pote den perimena enas komikos ithopios na ekfrasti me tetion hydeo tropo sto prosopon mou. Osi ehoun dei to shetiko video tou kyriou Zaralikou, antilamvanonte oti tetiou idous haraktirismi enishioun ti ritoriki misous ke to toxiko klima sto opio kapii ependyoun, epidiokontas prosopika i kommatika ofeli. Min ehontas alli dynatotita amynas, asko sto akereo kathe nomimo dikeoma mou os politis ke idietera os pateras ki os ek toutou prosfevgo sti Dikeosyni*].

Zaralikos used aggressive humor to strike a blow at politicians that he considered as covertly representing fascist ideology. He exercised what he perceived as his right to offend in the name of a political ethos breached by the said politician. Implicatures of a repulsive political identity as well as the incongruous proposal to organize a

---

[10] Appeared on February 14th, 2023. 142.000 views, 299 comments, mostly positive, until February 28th, 2023.

suicide/resurrection show to maximize attendance at his political campaigns, aggravating implicit aggression, led Georgiadis to threaten with a lawsuit. Bypassing the contextualization of the program as satirical, Georgiadis focused on the threatening implicatures of the text that he interpreted as hate speech, establishing grounds for legal action.

The next two examples are related to the aftermath of the national elections in May and June 2023, in which the major party of the left, SYRIZA, was soundly defeated by the conservative ND by a margin of 22%. In both examples, satirists made use of humorous sexual connotations depicting the victory by ND as an act of anal rape in which Alexis Tsipras, the leader of SYRIZA, is portrayed as the victim.

Example 3.6 Political satire by Lakis Lazopoulos (2023)[11]

> Lakis Lazopoulos: Opopopo. What has just happened? Twenty centimeters, twenty centimeters, it went up its throat [that of SYRIZA/TSIPRAS]. Houhag [an exclamatory expression imitating drowning]. Did you know that Kyriako had twenty centimeters? Did you? Oh my mother!
>
> [*Opopopopo. Ti 'tan afto pou egini. Ikosi pontous, ikosi pontous, sto lemo tou eftase. Houhag* ((an exclamatory expression imitating drowning)). *To 'xires esi oti ihe ikosi pontous to Kyriako? To 'xires? Oh manoula mou!*].

Example 3.7 Political satire by Nefeli Meg (2023)[12]

> Nefeli Meg: [...] And rumor has it that a:fterwards, because eh eh Alexis it took him a long, long time to appear in Koumoundourou [SYRIZA headquarters] a:nd, as everybody knows, he probably stopped wi:th, I am guessing now, by Evaggelismos [one of the biggest hospitals in the center of Athens] for stitches. For stitches. He didn't take it [laughing].
>
> [*Ke fimes lene oti me:ta:, giati eh o: Alexis tou pire para poli ora na emfanisti stin Koumoundourou ke:, os gnoston, mallon perase me::, leo go tora, apo ton Evaggelismo gia rammata. Gia rammata. Den antexe*] (laughing).

Sexual allusions are systematically used in Greek satirical programs, rendering sexist humorous attacks debatable as far as the right to offend within democratic norms is concerned. However, in Example 3.6, reactions to Lazopoulos' humorous choices are mostly positive, whereas Nefeli Meg's comparable allusions (Example 3.7) are met with criticism connected to her female gender, young age, and her alleged political affiliation with the conservative party. The fact that Kyriakos Mitsotakis chose to be interviewed by the young blogger as part of his electoral campaign sparked intense reaction against her rhetoric, even by government friendly media such as Skai TV, which uploaded excerpts of a lifestyle program discussing the incident, with the title *"Nefeli Meg: The indecent comment of the youtuber against Alexis Tsipras after the results of the elections,"* contextualizing her satirical intervention as an act of indecency.

---

[11] May 24, 2023, Episode 21st, 140.000 views and 250 comments, mostly positive, until July 6, 2023.

[12] May 23, 2023, 2:43–2:59, 7.300 views, 83 comments, mostly rejective, until July 6, 2023.

3 Humorous Genres and Modes in Greek Political Discourse

Lazopoulos, on the other hand, one of the most prominent contemporary comedians with a career of more than four decades in Greek sociopolitical satire, indiscriminately attacks all major political actors in his shows. For example, in excerpt 8, he referred to Mitsotakis's commitment to have a public debate on television with the leader of the loyal opposition, Alexis Tsipras, and his refusal to abide by this commitment after the outcome of the first election on May 21st 2023, that turned out victorious for him. Lazopoulos makes use of a quite common, Greek pun/rhyme, rizo/gyrizo, targeting Mitsotakis' inconsistency. As a result of his choosing targets from all political parties, his sexist comment did not activate public reproach.

Example 3.8 Political satire by Lakis Lazopoulos (Newsbreak, n.d.)

Lakis Lazopoulos: My name is Rizos and I do as I please!

[*Me lene Rizo ki opos thelo ta gyrizo!*]

The excerpts of political satirical texts discussed confirm the tendency in Greek political culture to undermine authority and contest hierarchy (Hirschon, 2001), as attacks to political personnel exhibit irreverence and are frequently assessed as breaching civility. What is more, satirical attacks threaten the face of political targets and allow for high degrees of confrontational and combative encounters in public and institutional communication as predicted in both anthropological and discourse analytic research (Georgalidou, 2021; Hirschon, 2001; Kakava, 2002; Tsakona, 2008, 2009).

3.4 Conclusion

After winning the general elections, on May 30th, 2023 in a public speech in Athens (New Democracy, 2023), Kyriakos Mitsotakis, leader of the conservative party in office, claimed that:

Something happened that I consider very important. The citizens turned their back to toxicity, to hatred, to political passions, to divisions. Divisions have been defeated and unity won. Toxicity has been defeated and civility won.

[*Alla egine ke kati akoma to opio theoro poly simantiko. I polites gyrisan tin plati stin toxicotita, sto misos, stin empathia, ston dihasmo. Ittithike o dihasmos ke kerdise i enotita. Ittithike i toxikotita ke kerdise i efprepia*].

Defining what constitutes civility in political rhetoric, as opposed to incivility, which in turn is sometimes equated with toxicity, is no easy endeavor, as exhibited in the discussion on humor and im/politeness in political genres. Political discourse entails criticism and conflict through overt and covert aggression. As far as the latter is concerned, humor is instrumentalized to bypass demands for decorum and ideally avoid the institutional or even legal consequences of offensive acts. However, when direct and implicit offense is registered by participants in *political* events, it constitutes sociopolitical action that renders offense undeniable. The "right to be offended" (Serafis et al., 2023) is exercised in reaction to vitriolic political humor and contextualizes impoliteness on the part of the primary target(s) of the offense. Thus, rejective evaluations of attacks structured as humorous, and categorization of satirical comments as impropriety, incivility, and even as hate speech, is common in real time interactions. Analogous responses to vitriolic humor also form part of dialogic media networks reacting to the satirical targeting of political action and actors.

Consequently, in the context of Greek political rhetoric, the role of humor as a strategy for mitigating face-threats is controversial. First, the examined incidents containing humorous/satirical political attacks against adversaries attest to debasing discursive practices masked as humor in the context of Greek political combat. Despite utterances having more than one interpretation allowing interlocutors to disclaim face threats (Brown & Levinson, 1987; Sifianou, 1997), off-the-record statements have proven to be a controversial strategy for mitigating offense as seen by rejective reactions to the examples discussed. Second, in a macro-level analysis of political culture dominating confrontation in contemporary Greece, as Antonopoulou and Sifianou (2002, p. 766) predict, humorous utterances have the potential to actually reinforce offense as they address the target in an aggressive, albeit indirect manner.

Thus, in positive politeness cultures such as the Greek, in which the tendency for undermining authority and contesting hierarchy (Hirschon, 2001) is frequently mediated via the humorous mode, political humor is mostly employed as an impoliteness strategy that threatens the face of multiple targets. Despite pleading humor to disclaim offensive acts, Greek cultural trends that favor a high degree of confrontational and combative encounters, in private and public/institutional communication (Georgalidou, 2021; Hirschon, 2001; Kakava, 2002; Tsakona, 2008, 2009), disprove the affiliative function of humor, at least as a weapon in political combat. As a result, political encounters in contemporary Greece, either in institutional or media domains, raise the question of what is and what is not tolerated as legitimate political confrontation, contrary to claims of incivility and toxicity having been defeated. As a result, research on humor and offense in Greek politics continues to be a work in progress.

References

Antonopoulou, E., & Sifianou, M. (2002). Conversational dynamics of humour: The telephone game in Greek. *Journal of Pragmatics, 35*(5), 741–769. https://doi.org/10.1016/S0378-2166(02)00150-9

Archakis, A., & Tsakona, V. (2011). Informal talk in formal settings: Humorous narratives in Greek parliamentary debates. In V. Tsakona & D. E. Popa (Eds.), *Studies in political humor: In between political critique and public entertainment* (pp. 61–81). John Benjamins. https://doi.org/10.1075/dapsac.46.06arc.

Arundale, R. B. (2010). Constituting face in conversation: Face, facework and interactional achievement. *Journal of Pragmatics, 42*(8), 2078–2105. https://doi.org/10.1016/j.pragma.2009.12.021

Attardo, S. (1994). *Linguistic theories of humor*. Mouton de Gruyter.

Attardo, S. (2000). Irony as relevant inappropriateness. *Journal of Pragmatics, 32*(6), 793–826. https://doi.org/10.1016/S0378-2166(99)00070-3

Attardo, S. (2001). *Humorous texts: A semantic and pragmatic analysis*. Mouton de Gruyter.

Bayraktaroglu, A., & Sifianou M. (2001). Introduction. In A. Bayraktaroglu & M. Sifianou (Eds.), *Linguistic politeness across boundaries: The case of Greek and Turkish* (pp. 1–16). John Benjamins. https://doi.org/10.1075/pbns.88.02bay.

Bippus, A. (2007). Factors predicting the perceived effectiveness of politician's use of humour during a debate. *Humour, 20*(2), 105–121. https://doi.org/10.1515/HUMOR.2007.006

Boukala, S. (2014). Waiting for democracy: Political crisis and the discursive (re)invention of the 'national enemy' in times of 'Grecovery.' *Discourse & Society, 25*(4), 482–499. https://doi.org/10.1177/0957926514536961

Brown, P., & Levinson, S. C. (1987). *Politeness: Some universals in language usage*. Cambridge University Press.

Chovanec, J., & Tsakona, V. (2018). Investigating the dynamics of humor: Towards a theory of interactional humor. In V. Tsakona & J. Chovanec (Eds.), *The dynamics of interactional humor: Creating and negotiating humor in everyday interactions* (pp. 1–26). John Benjamins.

Chovanec, J., & Tsakona, V. (2023). "The girl is on fire!": Interactional humour in YouTube comments on the Notre Dame disaster. In E. Linares (Ed.), *The pragmatics of humour in interactive contexts* (pp. 87–107). John Benjamins. https://doi.org/10.1075/pbns.335.04cho.

Crittenden, V. L., Hopkins, L. M., & Simmons, J. M. (2011). Satirists as opinion leaders: Is social media redefining roles? *Journal of Public Affairs, 11*(3), 174–180. https://doi.org/10.1002/pa.400

Culpeper, J. (2005). Impoliteness and entertainment in the television quiz show: The weakest link. *Journal of Politeness Research, 1*(1), 35–72. https://doi.org/10.1515/jplr.2005.1.1.35

Dynel, M. (2011). Entertaining and enraging: The functions of verbal violence in broadcast political debates. In V. Tsakona & D. E. Popa (Eds.), *Studies in political humour: In between political critique and public entertainment* (pp. 109–133). John Benjamins. https://doi.org/10.1075/dapsac.46.08dyn.

Eelen, G. (2001). *A critique of politeness theories*. Jerome Publishing.

Fairclough, N. (2013). *Critical discourse analysis: The critical study of language*. Routledge.

Frantzi, K., Georgalidou, M., & Giakoumakis, G. (2019). Greek parliamentary discourse in the years of the economic crisis: Investigating aggression using a corpus-based approach. In E. Zakaza (Ed.), *Argumentation and appraisal in parliamentary discourse* (pp. 1–30). IGI Global. https://doi.org/10.4018/978-1-5225-8094-2.ch001.

Garcés-Conejos Blitvich, P. (2013). Introduction: Face, identity and im/politeness. Looking backward, moving forward: From Goffman to practice theory. *Journal of Politeness Research, 9*(1), 1–33. https://doi.org/10.1515/pr-2013-0001.

Gasteratou, S., & Tsakona, V. (2023). Deconstructing imagined identities and imagined communities through humor: Evidence from adult L2 learners' humorous narratives. *Pragmatics and Society, 14*(3), 461–483. https://doi.org/10.1075/ps.20079.gas

Georgakopoulou, A. (2013). Building iterativity into positioning theory: A practice-based approach to small stories and self. *Narrative Inquiry, 23*(1), 89–110. https://doi.org/10.1075/ni.23.1.05geo

Georgalidou, M. (2011). "Stop caressing the ears of the hooded": Political humor in times of conflict. In V. Tsakona & D. E. Popa (Eds.), *Studies in political humour: In between political critique and public entertainment* (pp. 83–108). John Benjamins. https://doi.org/10.1075/dapsac.46.07geo.

Georgalidou, M. (2017). Addressing women in the Greek parliament: Institutionalized confrontation or sexist aggression? *Journal of Language Aggression and Conflict, 5*(1), 30–57. https://doi.org/10.1075/jlac.5.1.02geo

Georgalidou, M. (2021). Negotiating im/politeness via humor in the Greek parliament. *Estudios de Lingüística del Español, 43*, 99–122. https://doi.org/10.36950/elies.2021.43.8432 (in Spanish).

Georgalidou, M., (2023). Greek political discourse, 2019–2022: Instrumentalizing impoliteness and aggression. In O. Feldman, (Ed.) *Political debasement: Incivility, Contempt, and Humiliation in Parliamentary and Public Discourse* (pp. 173–189). Springer. https://doi.org/10.1007/978-981-99-0467-9_9.

Georgalidou, M., Frantzi, K., & Giakoumakis, G. (2019). Addressing adversaries in the Greek parliament: A corpus-based approach. In M. Chondrogianni, S. Courtenage, G. Horrocks, A. Arvaniti & I. Tsimpli (Eds.), *Proceedings of the 13th international conference on Greek linguistics* (pp. 106– 116). University of Westminster.

Georgalidou, M., Frantzi, K., & Giakoumakis, G. (2020). Aggression in media-sharing websites in the context of Greek political/parliamentary discourse in the years of the economic crisis. *Journal of Language Aggression and Conflict, 8*(2), 321–350. https://doi.org/10.1075/jlac.00039.geo

Goffman, E. ([1955] 1967). *Interaction ritual: Essays on face-to-face behaviour*. Pantheon.

Haugh, M. (2015). Impoliteness and taking offense in initial interactions. *Journal of Pragmatics, 86*, 36–42. https://doi.org/10.1016/j.pragma.2015.05.018

Hirschon, R. (1992). Greek adults' verbal play, or, how to train for caution. *Journal of Modern Greek Studies, 10*(1), 35–56. https://doi.org/10.1353/mgs.2010.0250

Hirschon, R. (2001). Freedom, solidarity and obligation. The socio-cultural context of Greek politeness. In A. Bayraktaroglu & M. Sifianou (Eds.), *Linguistic politeness across boundaries: The case of Greek and Turkish* (pp. 17–42). John Benjamins.

Kakava, C. (2002). Opposition in modern Greek discourse: Cultural and contextual constraints. *Journal of Pragmatics, 34*(10–11), 1537–1568. https://doi.org/10.1016/S0378-2166(02)00075-9

Kienpointner, M. (1997). Varieties of rudeness: Types and functions of impolite utterances. *Functions of Language, 4*(2), 251–287. https://doi.org/10.1075/fol.4.2.05kie

Kostopoulos, C. (2021). A tale of two prime ministers: The influence of Greek culture in post-crisis political speech. In O. Feldman (Ed.), *When politicians talk: The cultural dynamics of public speaking* (pp. 129–148). Springer. https://doi.org/10.1007/978-981-16-3579-3_8.

Lazopoulos. L. (2023, May 24). *Out of Lakis mouth: Now you are crying, why are you crying. Episode 21[Video]*. YouTube. https://www.youtube.com/watch?v=S__PUorxlsw (in Greek).

Mackridge, P. (1992). Games of power and solidarity-commentary. *Journal of Modern Greek Studies, 10*(1), 111–120. https://doi.org/10.1353/mgs.2010.0137

Milner Davis, J. (Ed.). (2017). *Satire and politics: The interplay of heritage and practice*. Palgrave Macmillan.

Milner Davis, J., & Foyle, L. (2017). The satirist, the larrikin and the politician: An Australian perspective on satire and politics. In J. Milner Davis (Ed.), *Satire and politics: The interplay of heritage and practice* (pp. 1–35). Palgrave Macmillan. https://doi.org/10.1007/978-3-319-56774-7_1.

Morreall, J. (2005). Humour and the conduct of politics. In S. Lockyer & M. Pickering (Eds.), *Beyond a joke: The limits of humour* (pp. 193–225). Palgrave Macmillan. https://doi.org/10.1057/9780230236776_4.

Morreall, J. (2009). Comic relief: A comprehensive philosophy of humor. *Wiley-Blackwell*. https://doi.org/10.1002/9781444307795

Mulkay, M. (1988). *On humor: Its nature and its place in modern society*. Basil Blackwell.

Nefeli Meg #69. (2023, May 23). *President, come backwards!. Boukla 99 [Video]*. YouTube. https://www.youtube.com/watch?v=D6N8gIvbxoc (in Greek).

Newsbomb. (2015, April 3). *Giakoumatos' hideous attack against Zoe Konstantopoulou*. Newsbomb. https://www.newsbomb.gr/bomber/parapolitika/story/573526/xydaia-epithesi-giakoymatoy-kata-tis-zois-konstantopoyloy#ixzz3dj7RELWf (in Greek).

Newsbreak. (n.d.). *Out of Lucky's mouth—They set the brakes on fire (Episode 22) (Video)*. You Tube. https://www.youtube.com/watch?v=LyFqn_qVvVs (in Greek).

New Democracy. (2023, May 30). *Mitsotakis speech in Peristeri [Video].* https://www.google. com/search?q=mitsotakis+peristeri&rlz=1C1GCEA_enGR950GR950&oq=mitsotakis+perist eri&aqs=chrome..69i57.7850j0j4&sourceid=chrome&ie=UTF-8#fpstate=ive&vld=cid:6b9bf2 51,vid:-xiub9RDILQ (in Greek).

Norrick, N. R. (1993). *Conversational joking: Humor in everyday talk.* Indiana University Press.

Nuolijärvi, P., & Tiittula, L. (2011). Irony in political television debates. *Journal of Pragmatics, 43*(2), 572–587. https://doi.org/10.1016/j.pragma.2010.01.019

O'Connor, A. (2017). The effects of satire: Exploring its impact on political candidate evaluation. In J. Milner Davis (Ed.), *Satire and politics: The interplay of heritage and practice* (pp. 193–225). Palgrave Macmillan.

Ödmark, S. (2021). De-contextualisation fuels controversy: The double-edged sword of humour in a hybrid media environment. *The European Journal of Humour Research, 9*(3), 49–64. https:// doi.org/10.7592/EJHR2021.9.3.523

Popa, D. E. (2011). Political satire dies last: A study on democracy, opinion formation, and political satire. In V. Tsakona & D. E. Popa (Eds.), *Studies in political humour: In between political critique and public entertainment* (pp. 137–166). John Benjamins. https://doi.org/10.1075/dap sac.46.10pop.

Proto Thema. (2023, February 21). *Georgiadis suing comedian Christoforos Zaralikos expressing himself hideously.* Proto Thema. https://www.protothema.gr/politics/article/1342452/georgi adis-minusi-ston-komiko-hristoforo-zaraliko-ekfrazetai-me-hudaio-tropo/ (in Greek).

Raskin, V. (1985). *Semantic mechanisms of humor.* Reidel.

Rolfe, M. (2017). The populist elements of Australian political satire and the debt to the Americans and the Augustans. In J. Milner Davis (Ed.), *Satire and politics: The interplay of heritage and practice* (pp. 37–71). Palgrave Macmillan. https://doi.org/10.1007/978-3-319-56774-7_2.

Serafis, D., Asimakopoulos, S., & Piata, A. (2023, July 9–14). Using humour to call out racism: Political satire, the right to offend and take offense. In *Paper presented in the 18th International Pragmatics Conference,* Brussels.

Sifianou, M. (1992). *Politeness phenomena in England and Greece: A cross-cultural perspective.* Clarendon Press.

Sifianou, M. (1997). Politeness and off-record indirectness. *International Journal of the Sociology of Language, 126,* 163–179. https://doi.org/10.1515/ijsl.1997.126.163

Skai.gr. (2023, May 26). *Nefeli Meg: The youtuber's inappropriate comment about Alexis Tsipras after the election results [Video].* YouTube. https://www.youtube.com/watch?v=u8mgZ-3LVW0.

Terkourafi, M. (2011). From politeness1 to politeness2: Tracking norms of im/politeness across time and space. *Journal of Politeness Research, 7*(2), 159–185. https://doi.org/10.1515/jplr.201 1.009

Terkourafi, M., Catedral, L., Haider, I., Karimzad, F., Melgares, J., Mostacero-Pinilla, C., Nelson, J., & Weissman, B. (2018). Uncivil twitter: A sociopragmatic analysis. *Journal of Language Aggression and Conflict, 6*(1), 26–57. https://doi.org/10.1075/jlac.00002.ter

Tsakona, V. (2008). Parliamentary discourse: A linguistic analysis. In *Proceedings of the 28th annual meeting of the Department of Linguistics, School of Philology, Aristotle University of Thessaloniki, "Language and Society,"* (pp. 391–401). IMGS (in Greek).

Tsakona, V. (2009). Humour and image politics in parliamentary discourse: A Greek case study. *Text and Talk, 29,* 219–237. https://doi.org/10.1515/TEXT.2009.010

Tsakona, V. (2011). Irony beyond criticism: Evidence from Greek parliamentary discourse. *Pragmatics and Society, 2*(1), 57–86. https://doi.org/10.1075/ps.2.1.04tsa

Tsakona, V., & Popa, D. (2011). Humour in politics and the politics of humour. In V. Tsakona & D. E. Popa (Eds.), *Studies in political humour: In between political critique and public entertainment* (pp. 1– 30). John Benjamins. https://doi.org/10.1075/dapsac.46.03tsa.

Watters, C. (2011). Being Berlusconi: Sabina Guzzanti's impersonation of the Italian prime minister between stage and screen. In V. Tsakona & D. Popa (Eds.), *Studies in political humor: In between political critique and public entertainment* (pp. 167–189). John Benjamins. https://doi.org/10.1075/dapsac.46.11wat.

Watts, R. J. (2010). Linguistic politeness theory and its aftermath: Recent research trails. In M. A. Locher & S. L. Graham (Eds.), *Interpersonal pragmatics* (pp. 43–70). Mouton de Gruyter. https://doi.org/10.1515/9783110214338.1.43.

Winston, B. (2012). *A right to offend: Free expression in the twenty-first century.* Bloomsbury Academic.

ZaraleaksTV (n.d.) UFO EVERYWHERE !!! [Video]. YouTube. https://www.youtube.com/watch?v=2kMjC9Rg7Xw (in Greek).

Marianthi Georgalidou is Professor in Linguistics/Discourse Analysis in the Department of Mediterranean Studies, University of the Aegean, Greece, where she teaches Discourse Analysis, Pragmatics, and Sociolinguistics. She has published articles on the pragmatics of code-switching and minority discourse, on child discourse, gender, and im/politeness. She has investigated sexist language in Greek parliamentary discourse. Her recent research focuses on aggressive and derogatory forms of speech that attack the integrity, the gender, or other aspects of the identities of political adversaries.

Chapter 4
British Phlegm and Individualism in Humorous Political Advertising

Kostoula Margariti, Leonidas Hatzithomas, and Christina Boutsouki

Abstract This chapter delves into the role of humor within the context of the U.K. political landscape, exploring how it is influenced by cultural factors. The past two decades have witnessed significant upheaval in British national policy and politics, marked by events such as the Iraq invasion, the 7/7 London bombings, and Brexit. Throughout these historical moments, the British people have often responded with a unique blend of excitement and humor. Known for its distinctiveness, British humor is characterized by a penchant for biting and self-deprecating forms of humor, particularly satire. British phlegm, a somewhat dismissive and frequently ironic comedic understatement, showcases the ability of the humorist to maintain a composed demeanor in challenging situations. Examining these elements through the lens of the individualistic cultural orientation of the British people, this chapter explores various instances of humorous political speeches and electoral campaigns that have emerged in response to historical events. By doing so, it provides valuable insights into British humor and presents a structured framework that can be applied by advertisers, political parties, and academics alike.

4.1 Introduction

According to Booth-Butterfield and Booth-Butterfield (1991) humor can be described as the "intentional verbal and nonverbal messages which elicit laughter, chuckling, and other forms of spontaneous behavior taken to mean pleasure, delight, and/or surprise in the targeted receiver" (p. 206). In the framework of social (superiority)

K. Margariti (✉) · L. Hatzithomas
Department of Business Administration, University of Macedonia, Thessaloniki, Greece
e-mail: kostmar88@gmail.com

L. Hatzithomas
e-mail: hatzithomas@uom.edu.gr

C. Boutsouki
School of Economics, Aristotle University of Thessaloniki, Thessaloniki, Greece
e-mail: chbouts@econ.auth.gr

theories, humor is viewed from the perspective of superiority, ridicule, and aggression, as suggested by Hatzithomas et al. (2021). This perspective suggests that humor often involves making fun of someone and can boost the self-esteem of those who understand and find the joke amusing. Incongruity theories define humor based on cognitive dimensions (Mandler, 1982). An incongruent event occurs when the expectations are unmet, or the rules are not followed leading to the emergence of surprise and humor.

Humor is a form of communication that is shaped by cultural contexts and is acquired and cultivated over time, primarily through imitation, in conjunction with other societal values, norms, and attitudes. As prior studies suggest, perceptions and use of humor differ among cultures. For instance, Chen and Martin (2007) demonstrated that individualistic cultures are more inclined to self-enhancing humor, while in collectivist ones self-deprecating humor prevails.

Humor isn't solely a spontaneous reaction to fearful or stressful situations; instead, it can be a consciously chosen strategy for dealing with challenging situations, such as those involving aggression or competition. An illustrative example of intentionally deployed humor can be found in the realm of politics. Paletz (1990) mentions that democracies by nature encourage humor being publicly expressed and pointed at the authority-holders. The issues handled with humor in political contexts range from gaffe and minor mistakes to scandals, blunders, and corruption. Two distinctive examples of political humor are satire and parody. Satire (i.e., cartoons and caricatures) seeks to make sociopolitical judgments, while parody involves mimicking the style of individuals (e.g., politicians) or events that are being referenced. Davis et al. (2018) argue that the rise of enhanced humorous political commentary, increased engagement on social media (Vaccari et al., 2015), and the flourishing cyber-culture that expects and values humor all contribute to the interconnectedness between politics and humor, particularly in the realm of social media.

In this chapter, humor is broadly defined to encompass all forms of humorous content found in literature. In pursuit of this objective, we embrace the conceptualization put forth by Eastman in 1922, which characterizes humor as the "instinctual inclination to confront discomfort with a playful attitude." Our study delves into the application of political humor within the context of the United Kingdom, examining its connection with the country's cultural traits, including individualism and uncertainty avoidance. By retracing the political milestones throughout the history of the U.K., the current study aims to present a comprehensive overview of British political humor, applied by front-line politicians (from Tony Blair to Rishi Sunak in public speeches, electoral political campaigns, posts on social media etc.), expertise comedians (e.g., TV presenters, cartoonists, graphic designers etc.), comedic journalists and columnists, as well as citizens (through personal social media accounts, amateur memes etc.).

4.2 Theoretical Framework

4.2.1 The Individualistic Society of the U.K. and its Effect on the Use of Humor

Individualism has been recognized as a distinctive national characteristic that has shaped the ideologies and cultural values of the English populace. Initially, individualism denoted the documented shift from a "feudal-peasant" society to an "industrial-capitalist" one, a transformation chiefly observed between 1350 and 1650. This evolution ultimately sought to address the breakdown and fragmentation of society. The individualistic conceptualization of western societies is attributed to Christianity, the Renaissance, the Enlightenment, Romanticism, the growth of capitalism, and Protestantism among others (Swart, 1962). Individualism emphasizes personal development, freedom, and accomplishments; thus, characteristics that are closely linked to democracy, and collectively impact free capitalist economies. (Gorodnichenko & Roland, 2012; Ham, 2000), such as the U.K. one. Moreover, religion has had an impact on the political landscape in the U.K. Protestantism and its corresponding ethical principles played a central role in molding capitalism, nurturing economic well-being, and playing a part in the rise of democracy in Western societies, including the U.K. (Bruce, 2004). In the 20th century, Protestant organizations spearheaded the establishment of diverse social moralities and institutions that promoted liberal democracy (freedom in one's decisions, personal autonomy, etc.), thus highlighting the deliberate, significant connection between religion and democracy.

Hofstede (1984) determined that, among others, the dimension of individualism vs. collectivism is a key driver of cultural variance. The U.K. stands as an individualistic society the highest score (89) in Europe (Hofstede, 2001). In individualistic cultures, people prefer direct and explicit communication, while in collectivistic ones, individuals maintain and respect hierarchy, conform to rules, avoid conflict, and use polite and implicit communication. Collectivism or individualism affects peoples' tendency to dissent and disagree. In collectivist cultures individuals oppose less than in individualistic ones (Croucher et al., 2018).

Western cultures, such as British culture, tend to exhibit a higher inclination towards humor compared to Eastern cultures, like Chinese culture (Chen & Martin, 2007). Western societies generally view humor as a positive aspect of one's personality, while Asian cultures, prioritizing propriety, and formality, often have a lower regard for humor as a personality trait. In a similar context, Kazarian and Martin (2004) investigated the connection between culture and humor types. They argued that collectivist cultures that emphasize unity and selflessness in interpersonal relationships tend to favor affiliative or self-deprecating humor. Vertical individualistic cultures that embrace competitiveness tend to use aggressive humor. Kuiper et al. (2010) showed that aggressive humorous comments negatively affect people in individualistic cultures, leading to the exertion of negative emotions (e.g., ridiculing and sadness), and lower levels of the urge to socially interact. Prior research also demonstrates that humor, and particularly satire and disparagement humor, is extensively used in individualistic countries compared to collectivist ones (Hatzithomas et al., 2009, 2011).

According to Hofstede's (2001) theory of cultural dimensions, uncertainty avoidance is another significant dimension that sheds light on national differences. The U.K. constitutes a culture rated low in uncertainty avoidance (35), meaning that the British are tolerant towards ambiguous, unknown, and challenging conditions. Particularly, uncertainty avoidance refers to the extent to which individuals become nervous when subjected to unstructured, unknown, or unpredictable conditions, and the extent to which they try to avoid such situations. When a society is rated high in uncertainty avoidance, it means that this society does not easily embrace change and is very risk adverse. On the contrary, uncertainty acceptance is attributed to cultures (such as the British one) that are more willing to acknowledge different opinions, consent to as few rules as possible, and are more open-minded. Individuals within societies with high uncertainty acceptance are more phlegmatic and thoughtful, not easily expressing their emotions even when they are subjected to stressful situations (Hofstede, 2001).

4.2.2 Beyond the Cultural Aspect: The "British Phlegm" and the "British Humor"

Both high individualism and low uncertainty avoidance that characterize British culture are projected in another, distinct, British, cultural trait, that is known as "British phlegm." The euphemism "British phlegm" reflects the sense of calmness in the face of threatening situations and events (Thompson, 1994). The concept of phlegm has roots in the theory of Hippocrates (the "Father of Medicine," 460–377 BC) for the four temperaments or four humors. Hippocrates' theory revolved around the concept of four bodily fluids found in humans, among others the phlegm. Hippocrates suggested that an individual's personality traits, behaviors, and moods are influenced by the dominance of one of these fluids in their body, leading to distinct temperaments, such as the phlegmatic one. A phlegmatic personality is slow, balanced and calm, with emotions not easily manifested or expressed (Akmal, 2022). Rakhmanina et al. (2020) mention that a phlegmatic individual is the one that wants to keep a distance from problems, lives a balanced and peaceful life, and is hard to anger. Importantly, phlegmatic characters are friendly, good listeners, and prefer negotiation over conflict. Mahusay-Baria (2015) examined the type of temperaments with respect to public speaking performances. According to that study, the phlegmatic speaker is peaceful, calm, and relaxed, yet sometimes appears dull and uninteresting to the public.

Along a similar vein, British people are often associated with several clichés, including being polite, respectable, and gentle. The expression "British phlegm" succinctly embodies the attributes associated with the British population, including traits like hospitality, moral values, proper etiquette, cleanliness, and religiosity

(Murray, 1870). According to Sigelman et al. (1996), the notion of British phlegm encompasses qualities such as poise, logical reasoning, and skill in handling difficult or uncomfortable situations. It represents characteristics like self-control and modesty. Therefore, contrary to the notion of the British personality being exclusively defined by self-control and aloofness, it is enriched by emotions, fervor, and vitality.

Noteworthy here is that this British cultural characteristic is also expressed through British humor that can be ironic, sarcastic, and self-deprecating. When British individuals use humor, they are driven by a sense of calmness, mildness, and peacefulness, even when they are subjected to tough or awkward situations. Always motivated by British kindness and gentleness, the Brits use humor to control and cope with a situation that is annoying and uncomfortable.

4.3 Historical Milestones and the Utilization of Political Humor in the U.K.: an Examination of Prime Ministers from 1997 to 2023

Over the last twenty years, the U.K. has encountered numerous challenges and faced various political crises. These include the global rise of terrorism following the September 11th attacks on the U.S. in 2001, the joint U.S. and U.K. invasion of Iraq in 2003, and the tragic "7/7 attacks" in 2005, marking the U.K.'s first Islamic suicide attack resulting in the tragic loss of 52 lives. These events triggered substantial political turbulence in the U.K.

The global financial crisis from 2008 until the U.K.'s financial recovery in 2014 resulted in high unemployment, lower wages, and inflation in the country. In the decade spanning from 2010 to 2020, there was a pronounced political struggle, driven by the multicultural landscape and transformations within the U.K., seen as challenges to the nation's identity and contributing to the growth of Euroscepticism. Ultimately, this led to Brexit in 2020. The 2016 referendum resulted in three prime ministers (David Cameron, Theresa May, and Boris Johnson) stepping down within a five-year span.

Additionally, the U.K. was profoundly affected by impactful occurrences such as the terrorist attacks on London's Westminster Bridge and the Manchester Arena during an Ariana Grande concert in 2017. Furthermore, the onset of the Coronavirus pandemic crisis in 2020 had devastating consequences, leading to the loss of nearly 230,000 lives in the U.K.

For years, humor has been extensively used in the context of British political communications, in politicians' public speeches, political campaigns, and social media posts, to effectively manage challenging circumstances, as previously mentioned. British politicians commonly utilize humor in their communication (Brassett, 2021) to foster a distinct and more expansive mode of thinking. This approach not only boosts creativity in addressing problems but also conveys an image of authorities as approachable, affable, and relatable. The incorporation of parody and humor in the political context of British society represents a type of communication often characterized as "public diplomacy" (Chernobrov, 2022). Humor has been established as a potent tool in House of Commons debates, where certain members of parliament employ more assertive humor than their colleagues. During the economic crisis, the inclination of U.K. citizens towards humor became evident in various forms, such as a surge in stand-up comedies at bars and theaters (Collinson, 2011). Furthermore, internet-based humor has gained traction to either encourage individuals align themselves with politicians or satirize their opponents (Yarwood, 2001).

In general, humor serves as a universally favored communication approach, and in the U.K. it plays a central role as highlighted by Weinberger and Spotts (1989). Notably, nearly 36% of television advertisements in the country incorporate comedic elements (Wang et al., 2019). In their study, Hatzithomas et al. (2011) underscore the distinctive advertising approach employed in the U.K. This approach prioritizes the elicitation of emotions and entertainment value over the mere conveyance of information. It is characterized by its straightforwardness, lucidity, and refinement, incorporating techniques like soft-sell messaging, satirical components, and wordplay. Drawing from Speck's taxonomy (1991), they note that aggressive humor is more prevalent in the U.K. compared to Greece, and notably it is remarkably effective in capturing the audience's attention.

Political challenges faced by U.K. Prime Ministers during their terms were often approached with humor affecting the public perception of their policies, and most notably, how these leaders were depicted. Analyses of portrayals by individuals such as comedian experts, amateur meme creators, columnists, as well as social groups who employ varying degrees of humor in their perspectives constitute characteristic examples of these depictions.

4.3.1 Tony Blair

During his tenure as the Prime Minister of the United Kingdom from 1997 to 2007 as a member of the Labour Party, Tony Blair frequently employed humor in his public speeches and addresses. He was characterized by remarkable communication and presentation skills, was able to excite, impress and persuade the public, promoting the party's ideas and values with honesty and straightforwardness (Theakston, 2011). Recognizing the importance of humor, Tony Blair enlisted the expertise of qualified comedians and consultants to enrich the humor in his speeches. Through the value and advantages of jokes and laughter, Blair aimed to enhance the appeal and impact of his public speeches (Seldon, 2007).

During a public address to his Sedgefield constituency, Tony Blair injected some humor into his speech by recounting amusing anecdotes from his past experiences. One such anecdote involved his encounter with the Emir of Kuwait at Buckingham Palace. Blair humorously shared that he was informed he had to wait to speak with the Emir because the latter held royal family status. However, what he hadn't initially realized was the custom where all the princes waited for others to initiate conversation. Reflecting on the encounter, Blair quipped: "It was quite an interesting meeting...a moment of complete silence." Feeling the need to break the ice, he decided to ask, "How is Kuwait?" to which the Emir responded: "After the Gulf war, it has been challenging." Blair humorously noted, "And then, there was yet another prolonged period of silence" (New Labour, 2022). Arguably, even though Blair might have felt uncomfortable and embarrassed by his own question, due the U.K.'s involvement in the Gulf war (1990–1991), he turned to be self-sarcastic and humorized the awkward moment with the Emir of Kuwait.

Tony Blair participated in a humorous promotional video in support of the Comic Relief charity. The Prime Minister messes up his serious and inapproachable image, while he communicates his gentleness and patience during a nerve-racking conversation. In a video clip from The Catherine Tate Show, the fictional character Lauren Cooper, famous for her catchphrase "Am I bovvered?" (a mispronunciation of "Am I bothered?") used when she's annoyed or offended, visits 10 Downing Street to gain work experience. Upon her arrival, she encounters Tony Blair engaged in a telephone conversation. Notwithstanding his busy schedule, Lauren is determined to inform Tony Blair about the most famous person she has ever encountered. To her astonishment, Tony Blair responds by ironically asking if she is "bovvered" and instructs her to leave the room. This prompts her to exclaim that the most famous person she ever encountered was Ross Kemp, the actor known for portraying the lead character, Grant Mitchell, in the television show EastEnders, which depicted the lives of fictional community members and their everyday experiences. Despite Lauren's storm of questions, Tony Blair appeared even-tempered and remained polite until the end of their conversation. It's noteworthy that this program tackles subjects that are considered forbidden or taboo within British society and culture.

Throughout the 2005 U.K. election, political parties employed humor in their campaigns, although with caution. Instead, net activists were quick to detect and utilize satirical campaigns, through traditional and modern media channels (e.g., websites, viral email) (Coleman, 2001). In their research, Shifman et al. (2007) examined four distinct categories of websites during the electoral campaigns of 2005. These categories included party websites, viral email websites, satirical and humorous websites focusing on news and current events in a comical manner, and ad hoc websites dedicated exclusively to election-related content (e.g., "BackingBlair"). These websites featured parody videos that utilized discrepancies between spoken words and visual elements to convey a message suggesting that Blair was aligned with Bush and posed a risk to the democracy of the U.K.

Taking a more aggressive tone, videos like "The Iraq war in 30s" depicted Tony Blair naked, embraced by George Bush and covered with the US flag, while the song of the U.K. pop band, Spice Girls, played in the background. The site included, among others, three flash videos about Blair with humorous elements, such as irony and obscenity. Tony Blair was also targeted by the Green Party and the Liberal Democrats, with e-postcards, depicting him either as chameleon or a cartoon, declaring their opposition towards the war in Iraq. Because of the absence of evidence supporting the existence of weapons of mass destruction in Iraq, the print media criticized Blair, often referring to him as "Bliar" and depicting him in a manner reminiscent of Pinocchio (Downs, 2020).

4.3.2 Gordon Brown

Gordon Brown was the U.K.'s Labour Party Prime Minister between 2007 and 2010. The Brown government was heavily impacted by scandals and failures, such as doubts, and criticism raised about lawmakers' and politicians living expenses that led to the resignation of five government ministers. Brown had to manage the declining economy amidst the global financial crisis and face a growing Conservative opposition led by David Cameron (Cumming, 2009).

It is generally accepted that Gordon Brown lacked the communication skills and the ability to effectively connect with and persuade the public. When facing the media, he often appeared uneasy and nervous. Brown acknowledged his deficiency in political, public speech and communication, stating: "I'm good at what politics used to be about, about policies [...] But now people want celebrity and theatre" (Mandelson, 2010, p. 14). Nevertheless, knowing that humor enhances creativity in political speech, Brown was detected having sarcastic moments as a way to thoughtfully amplify his weakness in communication. Humor can be very popular and influential with the public, as for example, students. Jokes, comic and irony, sarcasm, funny analogies and so forth can create a relaxed, intimate environment that attracts attention, increases interest, and builds trust (Jeder, 2015). In this vein, in his first public speech after his resignation Gordon Brown appeared in a college in his constituency. Employing self-deprecating humor, Brown humorously informed the students that he believed the purpose of his visit to the college that day was to enroll in the "Communication Skills" course. He went on to say: "Then I thought I might do Public Relations or maybe Media Management or even Drama and Performance," eliciting some laughter from the audience (On Demand News, 2010).

At times, Brown displayed a humorous side, as seen during Nelson Mandela's visit at 10 Downing Street when he attempted to explain to Mandela who Amy Winehouse was. Brown kept sharing the story, even when Winehouse concluded her concert in tribute to Mandela singing "Free Blakey my fella" instead of "Free Nelson Mandela" (Daily Mail reporter, 2008). The Conservative party noted that over the course of a year, Brown frequently employed the same joke in his public appearances. This particular jest revolved around the time when Ronald Reagan, the 40th President of the United States, was on the verge of meeting Olaf Palme, who served as the Prime Minister of Sweden from 1969 to 1976 and again from 1982 to 1986. Brown reminisced Reagan asking his team, "Isn't that man a communist?" with his aides responding: "No, sir, he's an anti-communist." To which Reagan replied, "I don't care what kind of communist he is" (Freeland, 2009).

4.3.3 David Cameron

David Cameron led the Conservative party from 2005 to 2016 and served as Prime Minister between 2010 and 2016. Cameron had his fair share of amusing moments during his tenure, such as when he humorously likened himself to Arnold Schwarzenegger, the renowned Hollywood actor and former governor of California. While visiting California, Cameron playfully remarked in a newspaper interview "Look at me, look at me" adding, "and think of Arnold Schwarzenegger"? Making fun of oneself can be very risky since it endangers one's own safety and comfort zone. However, self-deprecating humor can be used to communicate one's confidence and competence by neutralizing the negatives, and in turn lead to higher perceived status. In this vein, Cameron was not afraid to be compared with another politician and in fact, he was confident enough to compare himself with Schwarzenegger, in order to help the Americans understand "what kind of Conservative he is." Also, one might say, that with his statement he became sarcastic about the fact that he and Schwarzenegger are so dissimilar in their appearance, that actually no one could "look at him, and think of Schwarzenegger" (Bull & Wells, 2012).

Back in 2012, during his visit in the White House, David Cameron and Barack Obama gave an interesting and amusing public speech referring to the shared history of the U.K. and the US. Obama: "It's been 200 years that the British came here, to the White House, under different circumstances. They made quite an impression. They literally lit up the place." In the shake of the old Blitz spirit, to overcome the awkward moment, Cameron responded to Obama's comment in a carefully manipulated, ironic manner, by praising the U.S.'s current protection and defense against the U.K. "I am a little embarrassed. As I stand here to think that 200 years ago, my ancestors tried to burn this place down. Now looking around me, you've got the place a little better defended today. You're clearly taking no risks with the British this time" (Tau, 2012). Aligned with the "British phlegm," Cameron's joke, about the shared history of the U.K. and the U.S., was thoughtfully manipulated in a way that was smart and defensive, but not offensive or inappropriate for the given context: Cameron's visit in the White House.

In a less formal exchange with schoolchildren from Warrington in 2015, Cameron brought up the topic of junior martial arts. Specifically, he inquired of the students whether he could employ jiu-jitsu in that evening's debate against his political adversary, Nigel Farage, prompting some laughter from his youthful audience. Trying to seem confident and competent, while at the same time managing to interact with his young audience, Cameron's ironic comment about his political enemy was more of an "inside joke" that made schoolchildren feel close, intimate, and thus satisfied by his argument. Later, when a reporter questioned him about his remark concerning Farage, he clarified that it was merely a jest and emphasized that the evening's debate would entail no physical contact, but rather a presentation of the long-term economic plan. However, he reiterated his stance to discuss concrete actions, not mere words (Dathan, 2015), thereby emphasizing his commitment to capturing the audience's attention and bolstering their trust.

Prime Minister Questions is a weekly session in the House of Commons where members of Parliament can question the Prime Minister. It often features exchanges filled with wit and sarcasm. David Cameron was known for his witty retorts during PMQs. On one occasion, when Jeremy Corbyn asked a question about tax avoidance, Cameron responded, "He talks about tax, but what he hasn't told us is that he supports a tax on jobs—his leadership election."

4.3.4 Boris Johnson

Back in 2016, the Italian Minister, Carlo Calenda, accused Boris Johnson of insulting Italy by suggesting that he should either support Johnson's Brexit deal or face a decrease in sales of the Italian wine, Prosecco (BBC News, 2016). During his address to the House of Commons' Foreign Affairs committee in response to the Prosecco insult being raised, Johnson stated:

> I think, actually, telling jokes is a very effective way of getting a diplomatic message across…- Sometimes people greatly appreciate that you're speaking to them in that informal way while subtly getting your point across—and actually, it can be a little bit condescending to think that they don't get the point (Errett, 2019).

Prof. John Street, in 2004, examined the concept of celebrity politician, a label that could be fairly attributed to Boris Johnson, who held the position of Prime Minister of the U.K. and served as the leader of the Conservative party from 2019 to 2022. According to Street (2004), the celebrity politician is one who adopts the air and posture of celebrities, e.g., movie or rock stars. The term "populist" could also be attributed to Johnson due to his communicative power. Populists, people who are in touch with public, sometimes even use offense to achieve their goals. In most cases, they use humor to appeal and communicate in the political context (Kefford et al., 2022).

Populism stands out for its capacity to resonate with the general population, its focus on crises, disruptions, and perceived threats, and its utilization of brash or impolite conduct. Boris Johnson is an emotional, expressive, and a politically incorrect speaker that uses slang language to attract the audience (Beck, 2023). Influenced by popular culture, Johnson deviated from the conventional political spectacle, instead infusing his public speeches with elements of "gesture, form, personality, and humor" (Brassett & Sutton, 2017, p. 246).

Johnson often uses his bright and mild humor to tackle inconvenient questions or difficult situations. For instance, he redirected blame toward the U.K.'s European counterparts, seeking to make them responsible for their actions by stating, "some of the urgency you direct at me I would radiate backwards and ricochet it to our friends and partners in Brussels" (Errett, 2019). During the Brexit negotiations in 2019, Johnson with humor communicated the sense of a populist, yet serious, clown.

One of the more sarcastic moments featuring Johnson occurred during his visit to the JCB factory in Uttoxeter. On this occasion, he made a grand entrance by driving a digger, symbolically expressing his determination to overcome his political adversaries in the upcoming election. "Today, he employed a potent visual metaphor, using a piece of heavy machinery adorned with his 'Get Brexit Done' slogan, complete with a Union flag paint job. He drove it through a Styrofoam wall to emphasize his central message to the voters," emphasized his spokesperson (Maidment, 2019). On the one hand, Johnson's action was creative and funny, albeit not easy to digest by everyone, and on the other hand a strong statement about his dedication to get Brexit done.

Johnson occasionally used self-deprecating humor. In an "unconventional approach to foreign diplomacy," when he entered the 2009 G7 summit in Bavaria, greeting the other leaders he mocked bare-chested Russian president, Vladimir Putin, saying "Jackets on? Jackets off? Can we take our clothes off'? We have to show that we're tougher than Putin," he said in a sarcastic, confident manner, implicitly comparing himself and his physical appearance, condition, and strength with that of Putin. His comment elicited laughter from the other world leaders and served as a display of their unified response to the invasion in Ukraine (Sky News, 2022).

Boris Johnson's 2019 election campaign advertisement, titled "Vote Conservative Actually," that parodied the movie "Love Actually," emphasized that the Conservatives required an additional nine seats to secure a majority and complete Brexit (Conservatives, 2019). It is an exceptional example of humor in U.K. politics. The advertisement is a remake of the iconic Christmas-carol scene with Andrew Lincoln holding cards telling Keira Knightly that he loves her. Instead, Johnson holds up cards ("with any luck, by next year," "we will have Brexit done", "and we can move on […]," "your vote has never been more important […]," "the other guy could win […]," "so you have a choice to make […], "arguing about Brexit," "until I look like this," showing a picture of a hairy little puppy satirizing his haircut, ("it's closer than you think") to convince a woman to vote the Conservatives and underline that her vote is more important than ever before. Towards the end of the video, Johnson declares: "Enough, enough. Let's get this done," just before the message "Vote conservative actually" is displayed (Frias, 2019). The participation of Johnson in this romantic comedy-style video signaled that he was not afraid to demonstrate a more emotional, friendly image, especially in the middle of the stressful pre-election period. He was confident enough to present his arguments in a cool, funny, yet reliable manner, while his political enemies would present them in a more straightforward and serious way.

On numerous occasions, Johnson has been the face of funny memes. In one such incident during the pandemic crisis in 2020, he apologized for a party taking place at Downing Street. The Prime Minister became the target of amusing memes and comical videos on social media when he admitted that he hadn't realized he was attending a backyard party; instead, he believed it was a work-related gathering (Sharman, 2022).

Arguably, Boris Johnson is an influential character and a fashionable, humorous, media persona, with his image being crucial for promoting policies, himself, and the party he represents. Back in 2016, Alice Foster in the *Daily Express*, commented about Johnson: "The former London Mayor was the figurehead of the Brexit battle and is thought to have widespread popular support […] the Prime Minister is seen to have the common touch thanks to his genial manner and sense of humor." According to *The Daily Telegraph* in 2017, Johnson's effect relies on his entertaining personality (Honeyman, 2023). Shirbon (2016) from *Reuters* claimed Johnson was the most "colorful" and charming politician whose tenure was marked by numerous gaffes. He rarely uses diplomatic language, whereas his wit and bizarre style helped him handle numerous scandals. Ian Hislop, chief of *Private Eye* notably argued: "He's our Berlusconi, but somehow, it's funny. He's the only feel-good politician we have, everyone else is too busy being responsible."

4.3.5 Elizabeth Truss

Elizabeth Truss was the shortest-serving Prime Minister in the history of the U.K. (September and October 2022). She promised to shake up the U.K. economy, but the market shrank, the British pound took a dive, and after a mere 45 days of service Truss announced her resignation.

From a communication standpoint, Truss was the exact opposite of the popular and entertaining Johnson—a serious and formal public speaker (The Hindu, 2022). During her short service as Prime Minister there were very few funny and informal moments to which Truss was subjected. During her electoral campaign, she openly acknowledged switching her loyalty from the Liberal Democrats to the Conservative party with the controversial statement: "We all had teenage misadventures. Some people had sex, drugs, and rock 'n' roll. I had the Liberal Democrats" (Smith & Talmazan, 2022). It appears that Truss needed to justify her choice of joining the Liberal Democrats in the past. Interestingly, she used a self-deprecating comment and cleverly compared her support of the Liberals during that period with what was considered rebellious, extreme, and out-of-the ordinary.

In another humorous incident back in 2014, Truss referred to the amount of imported cheese in the country, exclaiming: "That is a disgrace!" – a phrase that triggered public uproar. Elaborating on her argument, she claimed that her intention was to emphasize the strength of the U.K.'s food industry and promote the consumption of more British food. Notably, she often talked about cheese in public. In a conference speech during 2018, taking a self-sarcastic pose, she said that she was refraining from referring to cheese (Belam, 2022).

4.3.6 Rishi Sunak

Rishi Sunak, U.K.'s Prime Minister since the 25th of October 2022, hasn't had much time to disclose his tendency towards using humor. In a funny moment during his campaign, he sarcastically referred to people complimenting his "tan." "I have been having the time of my life over the last week…talking to all of you […]. The weather has been fantastic, and we've been in so many people's gardens, the sun has been shining. So much so that someone even said to me the other day: 'Wow, you've got a great tan'" (The Independent, 2022). This was admittedly an awkward moment for the prime minister. In such a phlegmatic approach, he managed to transform another person's awkward, offensive, even to some extent racist comment into a lighthearted humorous moment that he shared with the public, conveying a sincere, tranquil, and gentle personality.

4.4 Conclusion

Most of the time, humor constitutes a characteristic highly valued in a partner or a friend (i.e., "he has a great sense of humor", or "this girl makes me laugh"). However, it is not a trait usually associated with, and highly appreciated in, a leader. Nevertheless, studies show that humor could be an influential communication tool if it is used properly in the right context (i.e., the cultural one) (Bitterly & Brooks, 2020).

Aristophanes was the pioneer in utilizing humor as a rhetorical means of communication during theatrical performances dedicated to the worship of Dionysus in the Athenian theater. Those performances were ingeniously crafted to serve as a satirical veil for political criticism (Hartnoll, 1968). In the contemporary era of mass media and images, conceptualizing and facing politics as a kind of (inter-)play, humor can essentially add to an effective communication strategy and contribute to voters' decision making (Collinson, 2011). Politicians use humor in their electoral campaigns, public speeches, and social media posts, to effectively communicate, persuade, and strive for a more relatable and approachable image. Humor finds expression through late-night comedy programs, stand-up comedies, cartoons, caricatures, and even movies, influencing individuals' perceptions, attitudes, and behaviors.

This chapter discussed the impact of culture on political humor. It focused on the use of humor in the U.K.'s political environment, considering some of the fundamental cultural traits of the nation, such as individualism and its openness to uncertain and ambiguous situations. It is the *old Blitz spirit* i.e., a key dimension of British identity, culture, and history that signals the strength and resilience of the British during hard times and crises, also affecting British humor in politics. "We don't have blood running through our veins, we have phlegm, that mysterious substance that makes us, well... phlegmatic" (Thomas, 2003).

The above discussion emphasized how politicians serving as prime ministers of the U.K., between 1997 and 2023, tackled difficult and embarrassing situations with humor and sarcasm. At the same time, it highlighted how politicians have been met with humor, irony, and parody by skilled comedians, cartoonists, and everyday enthusiasts. As argued, it is a British trait to combine humor and politics (Brassett, 2021).

A distinct reflection of the "keep calm and carry on" in British society is British phlegm, constituting a cultural dimension associated with reason, tranquility, good manners, and cleanliness that is reflected in British political communication to handle stressful situations and move forward (Sigelman et al., 1996). Politicians who are (more or less) funny, such as Boris Johnson or Gordon Brown, appear to embrace sarcastic, ironic, or self-deprecating comments in their political speech to seem peaceful, controlled, and reliable in difficult moments. It is the *stiff upper lip culture*—stoicism that defines and drives British politicians and enables self-restraint in their emotional expressions, even when they must deal with a disastrous event. For instance, while occasionally seen as idiosyncratic, Boris Johnson was undeniably a political figure who extensively utilized humor in his speeches and left a substantial impact on the political landscape (Mauro, 2022). He possesses exceptional communication skills and charisma, enabling him to captivate audiences through positive portrayals and a plethora of amusing moments.

Overall, an effective joke can generate cheerfulness, increase intimacy, and build trust between the joker and his/her audience. Yet, flat, or offensive jokes could be harmful to politicians' image, making them appear less smart and competent. Among other types of humor, sarcasm, irony, and self-deprecating humor, that usually accompany an argument, should be carefully applied so that the audience will not be lost in translation or be offended.

The phlegmatic temperament of Britons is associated with the predominance of "phlegm humor." People with a phlegmatic temperament are thought to have an excess of phlegm, leading to certain personality traits and characteristics. Although the theory of the four temperaments, including the phlegmatic temperament, is largely regarded as an historical and unscientific concept today, it is overly accepted that phlegmatic people are calm, introverted, observant, patient, passive, and easygoing.

British political humor, often characterized by its dry wit, irony, and understatement, can exhibit phlegmatic traits. British comedians are known for their *deadpan delivery*, where they maintain a calm and serious demeanor while delivering absurd or humorous content. Their humor often relies on *sarcasm and irony*, where the true meaning is the opposite of what is said. They also often use *self-deprecating humor* in their public appearances. They are occasionally placed in *absurd or surreal situations* while they maintain a sense of calm and nonchalance. British comedians and politicians seem skilled at making *dry, observational humor* about everyday life. They frequently use *incongruity* by placing unexpected or contradictory elements together in a way that highlights the absurdity of a situation. British political humor often incorporates *wordplay*, puns, and clever use of language.

Finally, British humor seems to have a rich tradition of *satirizing* social, political, and cultural issues, often bringing a calm and composed approach to critiquing and ridicule. These characteristics capture some of the elements commonly associated with British phlegmatic humor. However, it's important to note that while British politics has its share of phlegmatic humor, political humor can vary widely in style and tone. Some politicians and political commentators embrace dry wit and sarcasm, whereas others might prefer more direct or passionate forms of humor.

References

Akmal, N. (2022). Kinds of temperament of human beings. *Web of ScienTist: International Scientific Research Journal, 3*(1), 321–324.

BBC News. (2016, November 16). *Boris Johnson attacked over 'Prosecco insult'*. https://www.bbc.com/news/uk-37995606.

Belam, M. (2022, July 22). *Loves cheese, hates her first name: 10 things you may not know about Liz Truss*. https://www.theguardian.com/politics/2022/jul/29/liz-truss-cheese-karaoke-10-things-you-may-not-know.

Beck, D. (2023). Humorous parodies of popular culture as strategy in Boris Johnson's populist communication. *The British Journal of Politics and International Relations*. https://doi.org/10.1177/13691481231174165

Bitterly, B., & Brooks, W. A. (2020). Sarcasm, self-deprecation, and inside jokes: A user's guide to humor at work. *Harvard Business Review, 98*(4), 96–103.

Booth-Butterfield, S., & Booth-Butterfield, M. (1991). Individual differences in the communication of humorous messages. *Southern Journal of Communication, 56*(3), 205–218. https://doi.org/10.1080/10417949109372831

Brassett, J. (2021). *The ironic state: British comedy and the everyday politics of globalization*. Bristol University Press.

Brassett, J., & Sutton, A. (2017). British satire, everyday politics: Chris Morris, Armando Iannucci and Charlie Brooker. *The British Journal of Politics and International Relations, 19*(2), 245–262. https://doi.org/10.1177/1369148117700147

Bruce, S. (2004). Did Protestantism create democracy? *Democratization, 11*(4), 3–20. https://doi.org/10.1080/1351034042000234503

Bull, P., & Wells, P. (2012). Adversarial discourse in Prime Minister's questions. *Journal of Language and Social Psychology, 31*(1), 30–48. https://doi.org/10.1177/0261927X11425034.

Chen, G. H., & Martin, R. A. (2007). A comparison of humor styles, coping humor, and mental health between Chinese and Canadian university students. *Humor, 20*(3), 215–234. https://doi.org/10.1515/HUMOR.2007.011

Chernobrov, D. (2022). Strategic humour: Public diplomacy and comic framing of foreign policy issues. *The British Journal of Politics and International Relations, 24*(2), 277–296. https://doi.org/10.1177/13691481211023958

Coleman, S. (2001). The transformation of citizenship. In B. Axford & R. Huggins (Eds.), *New media and politics* (pp. 109–126). Sage.

Collinson, D. (2011). Critical leadership studies. In A. Bryman, D. Collinson, & K. Grint (Eds.); The *Sage handbook of leadership* (pp. 181–194). Sage.

Conservatives. (2019). *Boris Johnson's funny Love Actually parody|Our final election broadcast* [You Tube channel]. YouTube. https://www.youtube.com/watch?v=nj-YK3JJCIU.

Croucher, S., Kelly, S., & Chen, H. (2018). Cross-cultural issues on organizational dissent and humor orientation. *Business Communication Research and Practice, 1*(2), 102–105. https://doi.org/10.22682/bcrp.2018.1.2.102.

Cumming, J. (2009, June 4). *Brown's U.K. government teeters near collapse*. News. https://www.nbcnews.com/id/wbna31103004.

Daily Mail Online. (2008, October 23). *Heard the one about Gordon Brown telling a joke? Prime Minister sparks laughter with Amy Winehouse story*. https://www.dailymail.co.uk/news/article-1079921/Heard-Gordon-Brown-telling-joke-Prime-Minister-sparks-laughter-Amy-Winehouse-story.html.

Dathan, M. (2015, April 2). *General election TV debates: Shall I use jiu jitsu to put Nigel Farage on the floor?* Independent. https://www.independent.co.uk/news/uk/politics/generalelection/general-election-tv-debates-shall-i-use-jiu-jitsu-to-put-nigel-farage-on-the-floor-10152834.html.

Davis, J. L., Love, T. P., & Killen, G. (2018). Seriously funny: The political work of humor on social media. *New Media & Society, 20*(10), 3898–3916. https://doi.org/10.1177/1461444818762602

Downs, S. (2020). *Representing leaders in Britain: The portraits of Winston Churchill, Harold Wilson, Margaret Thatcher and Tony Blair*. Loughborough University. https://hdl.handle.net/2134/11823003.v1.

Eastman, M. (1922). *The sense of humor*. Charles Scribner's Sons.

Errett, B. (2019, July 4). *The wit of Boris Johnson: How humour can work as a secret political tool*. The Globe and Mail. https://www.theglobeandmail.com/opinion/article-the-wit-of-boris-johnson-how-humour-can-work-as-a-secret-political/.

Freeland, J. (2009, June 11). *Gordon Brown and the value of a good joke*. The Guardian. https://www.theguardian.com/politics/2007/jun/11/labourleadership.gordonbrown.

Frias, L. (2019, December 10). *UK Prime Minister Boris Johnson released an awkward parody of 'Love Actually' as a major election looms*. Insider. https://www.businessinsider.com/boris-johnson-parodied-love-actually-in-campaign-ad-supporting-brexit-2019-12.

Gorodnichenko, Y., & Roland, G. (2012). Understanding the individualism-collectivism cleavage and its effects: Lessons from cultural psychology. In M. Aoki, G. Roland, & T. Kuran (Eds.), *Institutions and comparative economic development* (pp. 213–236). Palgrave McMillan.

Ham, C. B. (2000). The cultural challenge to individualism. *Journal of Democracy, 11*(1), 127–134. https://doi.org/10.1353/jod.2000.0012

Hartnoll, P. (1968). *A concise history of the theatre*. Thames and Hudson.

Hatzithomas, L., Boutsouki, C., & Zotos, Y. (2009). The effects of culture and product type on the use of humor in Greek TV advertising: An application of Speck's humorous message taxonomy. *Journal of Current Issues & Research in Advertising, 31*(1), 43–61. https://doi.org/10.1080/10641734.2009.10505256

Hatzithomas, L., Voutsa, M. C., Boutsouki, C., & Zotos, Y. (2021). A superiority–inferiority hypothesis on disparagement humor: The role of disposition toward ridicule. *Journal of Consumer Behaviour, 20*(4), 923–941. https://doi.org/10.1002/cb.1931

Hatzithomas, L., Zotos, Y., & Boutsouki, C. (2011). Humor and cultural values in print advertising: A cross-cultural study. *International Marketing Review, 28*(1), 57–80. https://doi.org/10.1108/02651331111107107.

Hofstede, G. (1984). *Culture's consequences: International differences in work-related values*. Sage.

Hofstede, G. (2001). *Culture's consequences: Comparing values, behaviors, institutions and organizations across nations*. Sage.

Honeyman, V. (2023). The Johnson factor: British national identity and Boris Johnson. *British Politics, 18*(1), 40–59. https://doi.org/10.1057/s41293-022-00211-0

Jeder, D. (2015). Implications of using humor in the classroom. *Procedia-Social and Behavioral Sciences, 180*, 828–833. https://doi.org/10.1016/j.sbspro.2015.02.218.

Kazarian, S. S., & Martin, R. A. (2004). Humour styles, personality, and well-being among Lebanese university students. *European Journal of Personality, 18*(3), 209–219. https://doi.org/10.1002/per.505

Kefford, G., Moffitt, B., & Werner, A. (2022). Populist attitudes: Bringing together ideational and communicative approaches. *Political Studies, 70*(4), 1006–1027. https://doi.org/10.1177/00323217211997741

Kuiper, N. A., Kazarian, S. S., Sine, J., & Bassil, M. (2010). The impact of humor in North American versus Middle East cultures. *Europe's Journal of Psychology, 6*(3), 149–173. https://doi.org/10.5964/ejop.v6i3.212

Mahusay-Baria, R. (2015). The "talker", "doer", "thinker", and "watcher"*: Analysis of the four temperaments in relation to public speaking performances. *Humanities and Social Sciences Review, 4*(01), 121–126.

Maidment, J. (2019, December 10). *Boris Johnson comes in like a wrecking ball! PM is let loose in a 'Get Brexit Done' JCB and smashes through a wall marked 'gridlock' as he tries to regain momentum—After polls show he could face ANOTHER hung parliament*. Mail Online. https://www.dailymail.co.uk/news/article-7777109/Boris-Johnson-let-loose-Brexit-JCB-smashes-wall-marked-gridlock.html.

Mandelson, P. (2010). *The third man: Life at the heart of New Labour*. Harper Press.

Mandler, G. (1982). The structure of value: Accounting for taste. In H. Margaret, S. Clarke, & S. T. Fiske (Eds.), *Affect and cognition: The 17th annual Carnegie symposium on cognition* (pp. 3–36). Lawrence Erlbaum.

Mauro, M. (2022, July 22). *Analysing 6 UK Prime Ministers' leadership styles*. Michael Mauro. https://www.michaelmauro.co.uk/thought-leadership/uk-prime-ministers-leadership-styles.

Murray, J. C. (1870). On the nervous, bilious, lymphatic, and sanguine temperaments: Their connection with races in England, and their relative longevity. *The Anthropological Review, 8*(28), 14–28. https://doi.org/10.2307/3024933

New Labour. (2022). *Tony Blair does some stand-up in Sedgefield* [You Tube channel]. YouTube. https://www.youtube.com/watch?v=bIPxnbDmFa0.

On Demand News. (2010). *Brown jokes with students at first public event* [You Tube channel]. YouTube. https://youtu.be/UFdMHJzwJ6Q?si=93rPo-JtqfH-lzx2.

Paletz, D. L. (1990). Political humor and authority: From support to subversion. *International Political Science Review, 11*(4), 483–493.

Rakhmanina, L., Martina, F., & Jayadi, N. (2020). The comparison study on two-types of students' personality: Sanguine and phlegmatic toward their English speaking ability. *Professional Journal of English Education, 3*(4), 443–452.

Seldon, A. (2007). *Blair's Britain, 1997–2007*. Cambridge University Press.

Sharman, L. (2022, January 12). *Hundreds mock Boris Johnson's 'I thought it was a work event' party scandal apology*. Mirror. https://www.mirror.co.uk/news/politics/hundreds-mock-boris-johnsons-i-25925405.

Shifman, L., Coleman, S., & Ward, S. (2007). Only joking? Online humour in the 2005 UK general election. *Information, Communication and Society, 10*(4), 465–487. https://doi.org/10.1080/13691180701559947

Shirbon, E. (2016, July 13). *Known for jokes and insults, Boris Johnson takes helm of British diplomacy*. Reuters. https://www.reuters.com/article/us-britain-eu-johnson-idUSKCN0ZT2FV.

Sigelman, L., Martindale, C., & McKenzie, D. (1996). The common style of common sense. *Computers and the Humanities, 30*, 373–379. https://doi.org/10.1007/BF00054020

Sky News. (2022, June 26). *Ukraine war: G7 leaders show united front against Russia as Boris Johnson jokes about group being 'tougher' than Vladimir Putin*. https://news.sky.com/story/ukraine-war-g7-leaders-show-united-front-against-russia-as-boris-johnson-jokes-about-group-being-tougher-than-vladimir-putin-12640738.

Smith, P., & Talmazan, Y. (2022, October 20). *British Prime Minister Liz Truss resigns after disastrous economic plan*. NBC News. https://www.nbcnews.com/news/world/british-prime-minister-liz-truss-resign-economic-plan-turmoil-rcna52946.

Speck, P. S. (1991). The humorous message taxonomy: A framework for the study of humorous ads. *Current Issues and Research in Advertising, 13*(1–2), 1–44. https://doi.org/10.1080/01633392.1991.10504957

Street, J. (2004). Celebrity politicians: Popular culture and political representation. *The British Journal of Politics and International Relations, 6*(4), 435–452. https://doi.org/10.1111/j.1467-856X.2004.00149.x

Swart, K. W. (1962). "Individualism" in the mid-nineteenth century (1826–1860). *Journal of the History of Ideas, 23*(1), 77–90. https://doi.org/10.2307/2708058

Tau, B. (2012, March 14). *Obama: British really 'lit up' the White House back in the day*. Politico. https://www.politico.com/blogs/politico44/2012/03/obama-british-really-lit-up-the-white-house-back-in-the-day-117432.

The Hindu. (2022, October 20). *Liz Truss promised U.K. a shakeup — but was forced out instead*. https://www.thehindu.com/news/international/liz-truss-promised-uk-a-shakeup-but-was-forced-out-instead/article66037313.ece.

The Independent. (2022). *Rishi Sunak jokes about people complimenting his 'tan' while on campaign trail* [You Tube channel]. You Tube. https://youtu.be/dpEo7SD3JA8?si=xgPmcCU_zg71J-bc.

Theakston, K. (2011). Gordon Brown as prime minister: Political skills and leadership style. *British Politics, 6*, 78–100. https://doi.org/10.1057/bp.2010.19

Thomas, D. (2003, February 16). *British phlegm is an excuse for sheer apathy*. The Telegraph. https://www.telegraph.co.uk/comment/personal-view/3587694/British-phlegm-is-an-excuse-for-sheer-apathy.html.

Thompson, M. (1994). Blood, sweat and tears. *Waste Management & Research, 12*(3), 199–205. https://doi.org/10.1177/0734242X9401200302

Vaccari, C., Valeriani, A., Barberá, P., Bonneau, R., Jost, J. T., Nagler, J., & Tucker, J. A. (2015). Political expression and action on social media: Exploring the relationship between lower-and higher-threshold political activities among Twitter users in Italy. *Journal of Computer-Mediated Communication, 20*(2), 221–239. https://doi.org/10.1111/jcc4.12108

Wang, Y., Lu, S., Liu, J., Tan, J., & Zhang, J. (2019). The influence of culture on attitudes towards humorous advertising. *Frontiers in Psychology, 10*.

Weinberger, M. G., & Spotts, H. E. (1989). A situational view of information content in TV advertising in the US and UK. *Journal of Marketing, 53*(1), 89–94. https://doi.org/10.1177/002224298905300108

Yarwood, D. L. (2001). When Congress makes a joke: Congressional humor as serious and purposeful communication. *Humor, 14*(4), 359–394. https://doi.org/10.1515/humr.2001.010

Kostoula Margariti is a post-doctoral researcher in Marketing, in the Department of Business Administration at the University of Macedonia, Greece. Her academic interests lie in advertising and website design, visual aesthetics, visual metaphors, and minimalism in advertising. She is also interested in cross-media advertising and luxury branding. Her work has been published in several journals including the *International Journal of Advertising, Visual Communication Quarterly, Journal of Promotion Management*, and *Journal of Global Fashion Marketing*.

Leonidas Hatzithomas is an Assistant Professor in the Department of Business Administration at the University of Macedonia, Greece. His research interests include humor, visual metaphors, gender issues in advertising, cross-media advertising, and social media communications. He has published in several journals, including the *International Journal of Advertising, International Marketing Review, Psychology & Marketing*, and *HUMOR: International Journal of Humor Research*.

Christina Boutsouki is a Professor of Marketing at the School of Economics, Aristotle University of Thessaloniki, Greece. Her research interests lie in the areas of humor, gender issues in advertising, visual metaphors, sustainable advertising, neuromarketing and social media advertising. She has published her work in several journals including the *International Journal of Advertising, Journal of Consumer Behavior, Visual Communication Quarterly*, and *Journal of Promotion Management*.

Chapter 5
"*Kapwa*" and Filipinos' Fixation with Presidential Jokes

Rogelio Alicor L. Panao and Ronald A. Pernia

Abstract When does humor work for a public figure and when does it not? We contend that the effect of political humor varies with citizens' collective predisposition and its compatibility with the leadership typology projected by the speaker. To validate our conjecture, we examine the rhetorical practices of Philippine presidents from 1987 to the present and show that Filipinos rarely find jokes offensive if they are carried out by someone who conforms to their popular expectation of what a leader should be: sincere, caring, giving, pro-people and anti-elitist. This is rooted in a national character that finds a premium on leadership based on the idea of "*kapwa*," a Filipino term widely understood as not simply establishing a relationship but a connection with the collective. Conversely, citizens generally view jokes objectionable when they are performed by leaders who they think are insincere, technocratic, and elitist. No matter how funny the jokes actually are and how well they may have been delivered, they will fail if citizens find the leader politically undesirable. We ultimately illustrate how leaders can engage in comedic diversions as part of their governance toolkit.

5.1 Introduction

A president quips in jest about Filipinos' uncanny resilience to withstand typhoons. He draws flak. And as if this wasn't enough his presidential nominee loses the election. A few years later, at the height of the COVID19 pandemic, another president joked that public officials who "lacked women" are likely to die of the virus. Unlike his predecessor, however, he ends his term with the highest approval rating among

---

R. A. L. Panao (✉)
Department of Political Science, College of Social Sciences and Philosophy, University of the Philippines Diliman, Quezon City, Philippines
e-mail: rlpanao@up.edu.ph

R. A. Pernia
Political Science Program, College of Social Sciences, University of the Philippines Cebu, Cebu, Philippines

© The Author(s), under exclusive license to Springer Nature Singapore Pte Ltd. 2024
O. Feldman (ed.), *Political Humor Worldwide*, The Language of Politics,
https://doi.org/10.1007/978-981-99-8490-9_5

presidents in recent history. When does humor work for a public figure and when does it not?

Anchored in literature on political humor and cultural dynamics in illiberal democracies, we argue that leaders exploit humor to tap into citizens' cultural sensibilities and bolster legitimacy. In this chapter, we demonstrate that Filipinos rarely find jokes offensive if they are told by someone who conforms to their popular expectation of what a leader should be: sincere, caring, giving, pro-people, and anti-elitist. This is rooted in a national character that finds a premium on leadership based on the idea of "*kapwa*." *Kapwa* is a Tagalog term widely understood as not just simply establishing a relationship but a connection with the collective. A *kapwa*-infused leader strategically employs comedic and satirical remarks in specific circumstances to gain acceptance for their controversial policies and sometimes disagreeable personal decorum. Conversely, citizens generally view jokes objectionable when they are performed by leaders who they think are insincere, technocratic, and elitist. No matter how funny the jokes actually are and how well they may have been delivered, they will fail if citizens find the leader politically undesirable. We ultimately illustrate how leaders might engage in comedic diversions as part of his or her governance toolkit.

Our chapter proceeds as follows. First we expound briefly on the concept of political humor and its importance as a rhetorical device for chief executives. Next, we discuss the concept of "*kapwa*" as a core Filipino value and as an emotional framework for understanding politician-audience rapport. Afterwards, we analyze rhetorical practices utilizing political humor among Filipino presidents, and show that citizens' reception of jokes depends not just on the context but also on the perceived sincerity of the speaker. The chapter concludes with a summary of important findings and some comments as to why comedians exercise prudence in their portrayals of popular presidents.

5.2 Presidents, *Kapwa*, and Political Humor

Scholars often differentiate political humor into three main types. The first two classifications—political comedy and political satire – are very closely related and at the same time subtly distinct regarding their intended effects. Political comedy refers to comedic content that revolves around political topics, figures, or events. Its primary aim is to entertain and amuse audiences by employing humor, wit, and jokes related to politics. Political satire, on the other hand, employs humor, irony, sarcasm, and exaggeration to critique or ridicule political systems, institutions, figures, and ideologies. It aims to expose and criticize societal and political flaws, hypocrisy, or corruption through clever and often biting commentary. Whereas all political satire is political humor, according to Young (2016), *not* all political humor is satire. A joke that mocks a political leader's physical attributes, but does not criticize or challenge policy or the substance of politics, is humorous, but not satirical. By contrast, a joke that ridicules a politician's honesty or transparency in their political dealings would constitute satire, as it challenges factors relevant to politics.

5 "*Kapwa*" and Filipinos' Fixation with Presidential Jokes

However, there is a third type of political humor popular among Filipino politicians. Self-mockery, also known as self-deprecating humor, is a form of humor in which the politicians deliberately makes jokes or humorous remarks about themselves, their flaws, or their perceived shortcomings, to establish connection or empathy with their audience. Self-mocking humor often involves acknowledging personal weaknesses, embarrassing moments, or humorous aspects of one's own personality or appearance.

The conventional notion is that self-deprecation allows politicians to humanize themselves, bridge the gap between themselves and the electorate, and convey an image of relatable individuals who understand the challenges faced by ordinary citizens. In the Philippines, however, the effectiveness of self-deprecation can vary based on a range of factors, including the president's personality, communication style, cultural context, audience, and the content and delivery of the jokes. To understand why, it is important to revisit the Filipinos core value known as *kapwa*.

The concept of *kapwa* is a central and complex concept in Filipino culture. It encompasses the idea of shared identity, interconnectedness, and recognizing the humanity in others. The closest English equivalent to the word *kapwa* is the word "others." However, according to Filipino sociologist Virgilio Enriquez (1986), it is still very different because the Filipino *kapwa* is the unity of the "self" and "others." Enriquez (1986, p. 12) explains that:

> A person starts having a *kapwa* not so much because of a recognition of status given him by others but more so because of his awareness of shared identity. The *ako* (ego) and the *iba-sa-akin* (others) are one and the same in kapwa psychology: *Hindi ako iba sa aking kapwa* (I am no different from others). Once *ako* starts thinking of himself as different from *kapwa*, the self, in effect, denies the status of *kapwa* to the other.

Within *kapwa* there are two categories to which an individual in a Filipino social interaction is immediately placed: the *ibang-tao* (outsider) and the *hindi-ibang-tao* (one-of-us) (Pe-Pua & Protacio-Marcelino, 2000). Interaction with someone regarded as an outsider might range from simple civility (*pakikitungo*), to conformity (*pakikibagay*), or being along with (*pakikisama*). If one is regarded as *hindi-ibang-tao*, however, interaction can range from understanding and acceptance, to getting involved (*pakikisangkot*) and being one with the speaker (*pakikiisa*).

Reyes (2015) believes *kapwa* is better construed as being "together with the person" as it serves as one of the pillars of cardinal Filipino virtues that are not individualistic but all directed towards the forging and maintenance of human relationships. Because the default intention in *kapwa* is to build a connection, politician-audience rapport based on *pakikipagkapwa* (being one with others) tends to go beyond social roles and status and allows for a more community-oriented disposition.

It is important, however, to distinguish *pakikipagkapwa* from *pakikisama*, a related, indigenous, cultural concept with which it is often confused. Saito (2010) describes *pakikisama* as a typical Filipino trait of getting along or being friendly with others, whether in the private or public workplace, by adapting to group norms and dynamics. This involves yielding to a leader figure or a group in order to legitimize a decision or to make it unanimous (Andres, 1994). Unless everyone conforms, a group cannot have a uniform decision and there is always risk of division. One who gets along well with a group at the expense of personal duty or principles is *magaling makisama* (easy to get along with). Such a person earns public approval. On the other hand, one who finds it hard to conform or (*walang pakisama*) because of an underlying conflict of values or principles is *mayabang* or self-important.

As Enriquez (1986) puts it, while *pakikisama* is a form of *pakikipagkapwa*, the reverse is not the case. "The barkada (peer group) would not be happy with the walang pakisama but Philippine society at large cannot accept the walang kapwa tao" (p. 7). This is because beyond the socio-psychological dimension, *pakikipagkapwa* has a moral dimension that is incompatible with exploitative human interactions. Whereas *pakikisama* puts a premium on the ability to get along or maintain harmonious relationships, *pakikipagkapwa* promotes a sense of shared humanity and recognizes the inherent worth and dignity of every individual.

With *kapwa* as the emotional framework, the politician is then able to use humor as a cultural and rhetorical device to divert, to alleviate, to reconstitute accepted beliefs, and even to render moot fractured social and political realities. If the president is perceived as genuine, relatable, and most importantly, exudes a sense of *pakikipagkapwa*, jokes are more likely to resonate with the audience. However, if the jokes come across as forced or insincere, they may fall flat and fail to connect with the public.

Presidents then must be sensitive to how they are perceived publicly. The public's perception of presidents and their overall public image can influence how jokes are received. If a president is already well-liked, trusted, or viewed positively, even jokes that cross acceptable boundaries may still be warmly embraced by the public. Conversely, if a president is facing public skepticism or criticism, jokes may be met with cynicism or suspicion. Consequently, if the joke is perceived to be maliciously motivated as when, for instance, the speaker is distrusted, the Filipino response is to interpret the act not as banter but rather taking advantage (Enriquez, 1986).

5.3 Presidents as Comedians

Given the contextual nature of where and when presidential speeches are delivered, jokes are not at all uncommon. Even in the Philippines it is well known that humor provides presidents with an extended rhetorical space as an opportunity to connect directly with citizens and tone down expectations, as well as to deflect issues that are likely to attract immediate public criticism (Waisanen, 2015).

5.3.1 *Corazon Aquino*

Corazon Aquino, the former President of the Philippines, was known for her serious and dignified demeanor during her time in office, particularly as she led the country through a challenging period of political change. She was not known for making jokes or humorous statements during her presidency, or at least not with the Filipino public as audience. Her leadership was marked by her commitment to democracy and her role in the People Power Revolution. While there may be anecdotes or instances of humor attributed to her personally, they are not widely known or documented as part of her public persona.

Corazon Aquino ushered in the restoration of democracy in 1986, coming to power at a time of great political turmoil and facing the big challenge of reconstituting the government and establishing social order. She was known to be simple and modest, quite unlike the public's typical perception of one who wields the nation's highest political office. Unfortunately, her modest demeanor was not enough to guarantee a strong government. Her six years in office were marked by coups and destabilization efforts coming from factions within her own military as well as from insurgent groups operating in the countryside. People also quickly began to feel disenchanted, particularly those who perceived her as ill-equipped for the position. Aquino, for instance, started with a +53 satisfaction rating in May 1986 (based on the index by the *Social Weather Stations*) and even got as high as +72 in public approval (October 1986), but saw her approval rating plummet over time. Part of the disenchantment was because her immediate family represented the traditional political and economic elite. It was common knowledge that Aquino was far from the image of a plain housewife that broadsheets tried to portray. As Anderson (1988) noted, Aquino was unabashedly a member of one of the wealthiest and most powerful dynasties within the Filipino oligarchy. "For thirteen years she had served as treasurer of the Cojuangco family holding company, which controls a vast financial, agricultural, and urban real estate empire" (p. 292).

Moreover, she had always been regarded as belonging to the conservative elite. As Rocamora (1991) explained, Aquino failed to effect genuine democratic transformation because throughout her term she was unable to transcend her own class interests. An earlier report just a few months after the elder Marcos was ousted, also described her as being "largely aloof from her people, keeping to her office in a guest house beside the presidential palace, receiving foreign ambassadors and meeting with a handful of her top advisers, most of them close relatives or trusted friends of her late husband, Benigno S. Aquino Jr." (Fineman, 1986).

Aquino ended her tenure with a mere +7 net satisfaction. This figure is lower than Estrada's net satisfaction rating of +9 around the time when he was ousted in December 2000.

One of the more memorable instances in which Aquino tried to be humorous was when she spoke before a crowd of entrepreneurs a few days before she left Malacanang to resume her private life:

> And now for the final joke of the evening. When the matter of pensions of former Presidents was brought to my attention, I had my legal advisers prepare the appropriate Executive Order so that I could at least increase the pension of former President Macapagal from P3,500 a month to P8,000—as much as what widows of former Presidents get. Out of delicadeza, I included a colatilla that this E.O. shall not apply to me. Don't feel sorry for me. I understand former Presidents can charge honoraria for their speaking engagements. So, the next time

you invite me, you'd better have something more than the dinner. The plaques are good, but former Presidents will need the money. End of Joke" (Aquino, 1992).

While the audience had a giggle to cap the night, arguably this would have been unthinkable years earlier. Cory was known for many things, but exchanging and enjoying banter were the least of them. For instance, an obviously miffed Cory Aquino who had been trying to ward off the public perception of weakness sued a widely read columnist who wrote that she hid under the bed during the August 1987 coup led by Gregorio Honasan (Richburg, 1987). According to the Social Weather Stations (SWS), Aquino's satisfaction rating on October 1987 nosedived to +36 from +69 three quarters earlier (Agatep, 2018). Reports say she was most unpopular with the poor who felt she had not made much of a difference (Sanger, 1992). The human rights situation in the country also deteriorated rapidly due to the government's failure to prosecute and convict suspected military violators. For one journalist, Aquino's lukewarm pursuit of human rights violators reflected her inclination toward political survival while minimizing the risk of a coup (Jones, 1990).

The beleaguered columnist, along with his editor, consequently got a two-year sentence and was ordered to pay two million pesos in moral damages. Although the conviction was eventually reversed by the appellate court, the president's lawsuit had a chilling effect and was widely criticized as an attack on press freedom (Tuquero, 2020).

5.3.2 Fidel Ramos

Fidel V. Ramos, Aquino's chief of staff, succeeded as the first elected post-EDSA[1] president in 1992. Ramos' early years in *Malacañang* Palace (the official residence and principal workplace of the president) was a period of political stability and economic growth. Economic indicators were performing well and for the first time the country showed promise of becoming "Asia's next economic tiger." However, unlike Aquino the plain housewife, Ramos hailed from a politically influential family. He and former strongman Marcos were second cousins. As a former military officer, Ramos had the support of the uniformed personnel, and thus was able to insulate his administration from coup attempts. Moreover, unlike his predecessor, Ramos was highly regarded by the press despite his military background (Center for Media Freedom & Responsibility, 2022). FVR was known for being accessible, allowing ambush interviews, volunteering scoops, and interacting personally with reporters. He also loved chatting and sharing jokes with journalists, calling them by their first names (Cal, 2022). Ramos was known for cracking corny jokes during news conferences, and for his openness to media criticism.

---

[1] EDSA is short for Epifanio de los Santos Avenue, which is a major thoroughfare in Metro Manila and the staging ground of the protests that transpired i.e., the first people power movement that overthrew the authoritarian regime of Marcos Sr., restoring the Philippines' formal, liberal democratic regime (Garrido, 2020).

5 "*Kapwa*" and Filipinos' Fixation with Presidential Jokes

Unlike his predecessor, Ramos was regarded as a media darling. At an annual gridiron of the National Press Club in 1996, for instance, he quipped:

> There are a few unpleasant appointments that I have to keep once a year. Two of them are my visits to (1) my doctor and (2) my dentist for my annual checkup which, as many of you senior citizens know to the marrow of your bones, are never a laughing matter. But this annual Gridiron Night of the National Press Club (NPC) is not one of them—for I do look forward to exchanging a few blows without being castigated the following day by the media—for one day out of the year, anyway. I am told that the price of a dinner tonight is P1,500—the same as during the past three Gridirons, which means that prices are stable under the Ramos Administration (Ramos, 1996).

All throughout, Ramos was consistent with his treatment of the media. Even during the last year of his administration, he still relished exchanging banter with the press. One of his more iconic jokes was interestingly about journalists, part of a speech delivered during the Annual Gridiron presentation of the National Press Club of the Philippines in 1997.

> Of the many qualities that journalism claims for itself, none perhaps is more emphasized than its ability to compress events and reams of copy into column inches. This is well illustrated in the story of a newspaper editor who was testing an applicant for rewrite man. "All right," said the editor, "fix this and cut it short." And he handed the fellow the ten commandments. The young man gave the copy one glance, stepped over to the desk, took out his pen, quickly scribbled something—and then returned the page to the editor. Surprised that the applicant worked so fast, the editor looked at the rewritten copy—and then quickly said: "You're hired." The new rewrite man had crossed out all the ten commandments and replaced them with one word: "don't" (Ramos, 1997).

Ramos' SWS satisfaction rating on April 1996 rebounded to +17 from its December 1995 figure of +2. He enjoyed a +19 public satisfaction score when he left Malacanang in 1998. This is decent by all accounts considering that by institutional design single-term Filipino presidents are bound to lose their political capital by the time of their exit.

Villacorta (1994, p. 87) explained that in the Philippines a leader does not really have to be a messiah, a visionary, or an intellectual. "He needs only be a sincere and determined person who means and does what he says. What is needed is someone who has the moral ascendancy to elicit popular trust and support, and because he has the support of the majority of the people, the capability to ward off overwhelming pressures from big politicians and oligarchs." Interestingly, these are characteristics consistent with the Filipinos' notion of *pakikipagkapwa*. Villacorta believed that during his presidency Ramos exuded these qualities. As noted above, Ramos was a distant relative of former President Marcos, but his immediate family did not belong to the traditionally landed and politically entrenched. His professional experience as a civil engineer and as a military officer typified the career prospects of those in the middle class. Ramos was also the country's first non-Catholic president and as such was perceived as anti-establishment, non-conservative, and iconoclastic.

5.3.3 Joseph Estrada

Joseph E. "Erap" Estrada, Ramos' vice president, won by a wide margin of votes during his election in 1998. An accomplished actor, Estrada starred in more than 100 films and thrived in a stunning career spanning almost 33 years on the silver screen. He typically portrayed the role of a poor antihero or a modern-day Robin Hood forced to take the cudgel on behalf of the weak and the powerless. A few months after assuming office in 1998, Estrada enjoyed a +60 SWS satisfaction rating. By December of that year, however, public satisfaction plummeted to just +5. Experts and pundits attributed this to media exposure of his questionable private dealings and failure to address rising fuel prices (Batalla, 2016). Barely halfway through his term, Ilocos Sur governor Chavit Singson who was a close friend of Estrada, alleged that he had given the president P400 million as a payoff from an illegal grassroots numbers game known as jueteng. Singson's exposé prompted the filing of an impeachment complaint by the House and a full-blown trial by the Senate. Estrada was said to have amassed between 78 and 80 million dollars and blamed for undermining global recovery amid the Asian Financial Crisis (Hodess, 2004).

Due to the controversies that hounded his administration, Estrada was constantly the object of comedic sketches and spoofs. Interestingly, instead of openly lashing out at critics, Estrada capitalized on the rumors of his womanizing, his shady dealings, his lack of sterling academic credentials, and his seeming difficulty communicating in the English language.[2] For a time, the so-called Erap[3] jokes even became synonymous with political satire in the Philippines. An example of a well-known Erap joke reads:

> Miriam Santiago, has challenged the "least" intelligent presidentiable to a televised debate. To make things interesting, Miriam is said to have told Erap that for every question he won't be able to answer, Erap has to pay Miriam five pesos. But if it's Miriam who fails to answer Erap's question, the former has to give Erap five thousand pesos. Miriam asks the first question: "What's the distance from the earth to the moon?" Erap doesn't say a word, reaches for his wallet, pulls out a five-peso bill and hands it to Miriam. Now, it's his turn. He asks Miriam: "What goes up a hill with three legs?" After over an hour, she admits defeat and hands Erap five 1,000-peso bills. Erap says nothing, politely accepts the P5,000, and turns away to go home. Miriam is a poor sport and demands from Erap, "Well, so what is the answer?" Without a word, Erap pulls out his wallet and gives Miriam another five pesos [...] (Philippine Entertainment Portal, 2007).

This kind of joke became a household conversation piece and catapulted Estrada's popularity even further. Estrada himself did not appear to mind being the butt of jokes as he himself would occasionally refer to these jokes in his public speeches. For example, while still a senator speaking before a crowd of Cebu-based businessmen and entrepreneurs, he teased:

---

[2] Estrada did fire a former top aide for suggesting in jest during a press forum that government policies were discussed over drinking sessions with Estrada's so-called midnight cabinet. For the full story, see Villanueva et al. (2000).

[3] In the 1998 presidential election, Estrada won by a landslide, riding on the slogan "*Erap para sa mahirap*" (Erap for the poor). Estrada was popularly known as "Erap," the reversed spelling of "pare," Filipino slang for friend or buddy (Reuters, 2007).

"Your invitation has asked me to dwell on many areas, especially the program of government of our party and our position on various issues. I shall address major concerns, hopeful that the rest will be covered during the open forum. I hope that my English will pass your standards, and if it does not, then maybe you can add to your collection of Erap jokes Estrada, Joseph E.Erap joke" (Estrada, 1991).

One scholar contended that despite Estrada's eventual ouster and conviction of plunder, the poor still loved him so much that he was able to place second in the 2010 presidential race (Garrido, 2017). The reason, suggested one sociologist, is that his persona encompassed in the "Erap jokes"—seemingly dimwitted, womanizing, and inarticulate—are the same qualities that endeared Estrada to the poor who regarded him as sincere and sharing their struggles (Karaos, 2006). For supporters among the impoverished, Estrada is *hindi ibang tao* (one-of-us). Hedman (2001, p. 42) believed Estrada's cinematic persona created an image that "he knows, or could know, 'the real people who lived, laboured, and suffered nearby, round the corner', rather than any would-be constituency or ought-to-be class, or, more generally, 'the people', invoked in such ways as to be useful for either (liberal) electoral or (radical) revolutionary mobilization."

Estrada continued to capitalize on these humorous anecdotes even long after his presidency. The jokes were usually self-deprecating and occasionally make reference to matters that are supposedly already public knowledge. For example, before a Rotary Club meeting he told his amused audience: "This will be the first time you will have an ex-convict as your guest speaker…As you know, I am a member of the X-Men in this country—ex-mayor, ex-senator, ex-vice president, ex-president and ex-convict" (Sauler, 2012).

5.3.4 Gloria Macapagal-Arroyo

Gloria Macapagal-Arroyo, who was sworn into office after Estrada's "resignation," had already left the cabinet as early as October 2000 when reports of government corruption began to surface. Arroyo ran in the presidential election campaign of 2004 despite announcing previously that she would no longer seek the presidency after her term as Estrada's constitutional successor. Arroyo won by a margin of just over a million votes against her closest rival actor Fernando Poe Jr., amid allegations of election rigging. In 2005, a former deputy director of the National Bureau of Investigations revealed wiretapped conversations between Arroyo and a high ranking official of the Commission on Elections (COMELEC).[4]

The recordings suggested that the results of the election had been manipulated to secure Arroyo's electoral victory, triggering massive protests from interest groups and former Estrada allies. By October 2004, Arroyo's public satisfaction had dipped to -6. It did not help that Arroyo was not a fan of the media to begin with. Throughout

---

[4] COMELEC commissioner Virgilio Garcillano. The fiasco would later be dubbed the Hello Garci controversy.

her term, she was known to have shied away from the prying eyes of journalists (Macaraig, 2011). Just a few months after succeeding Estrada, for example, she greeted the media:

> I am pleased to pretend to be happy to join you tonight. Actually, I hate going to things like this. But I am sure that unlike me, you are genuinely happy that I am here because you do need me to make hakot[5] for you…Paying guests like this are paying for the tickets not because they like me, it's just that the National Press Club after all these years now knows who are the usual milking cows: the government agencies who are afraid the press will be mean to them if they don't buy a table, or those who want to be promoted and therefore, they need a good press to advocate for them when promotion time comes. And the business groups who are afraid the government will be mean to them if they don't buy a table in an affair where the president is the guest of honor (Arroyo, 2002).

Journalists decried what they described as a "legacy of bloodshed and repression" during her administration. For instance, her husband filed at least 40 criminal libel suits against journalists after a scoop that the first gentleman abetted and aided Arroyo in rigging the 2004 presidential election (Philippine Daily Inquirer, 2021). Raids against media outfits also became frequent, with government security forces openly labelling the media as "enemies of the state" (National Union of Journalists of the Philippines, 2009). On June 2010, just about three months before leaving office, Arroyo's satisfaction rating slid to a record low of -53. Although it is typical for presidents to suffer a drop in popularity around the end of their term (Panao, 2014), Arroyo appears to be the only post-EDSA president who ended her term with a negative public satisfaction rating.

5.3.5 Benigno Simeon Aquino III

President Benigno Aquino III, during his presidency from 2010 to 2016, also incorporated self-deprecating humor in his speeches and public appearances. He would make light-hearted remarks about his personal life, fashion sense, or lack of prowess in certain areas. This self-deprecating style aimed to portray him as a relatable and down-to-earth leader. In one speech before a crowd of public relations practitioners, he quipped: "My love life, I said, was just like Coke: once, it was "regular"; after some time, it became a little "light," and now, finally, it is approaching "zero" [Laughter] (Aquino III, 2014).

Aquino III began his term with a high public satisfaction of $+60$. However, his popularity began to slide down after a series of crises swept his administration. After typhoon Haiyan ravaged Eastern Visayas, in particular, the once funny Aquino III started to lose his composure over criticisms of the inadequate government response. He started to appear arrogant and insensitive, especially during his visits to disaster-stricken areas (Pilling, 2013). At one point, he was even accused of downplaying the disaster's aftermath after he told the Cable News Network (CNN) in an interview that

---

[5] *Hakot* translates roughly to "bring in a crowd.".

the typhoon likely killed about 2,500 only, and dismissed the larger figure reported by the local governments as due to "emotional trauma" (Nery, 2014).

There were also moments when he came across as indifferent. For example, while speaking before the Filipino community in New Zealand in 2012, Aquino III cracked a wheelchair joke purportedly targeted at former president Arroyo:

> We need to demonstrate that we are not stupid. We are a forgiving lot but we need to exact obligations too. We cannot just allow those who are accountable to make excuses. For this reason, I cannot help but be amused by this joke. They say that the corrupt in the Philippines drive fast and have fancy cars. However, when they want to flee the law, they take the wheelchair
>
> [*So kailangan nating ipakita naman: Tayo'y hindi mangmang. Pasensyoso tayong mga tao, pero may obligasyon sa atin ang mga taong nangako sa atin. At ngayon nga ho, maski ano pa ang pagandahan ng palusot—alam n'yo, I-share ko lang po sa inyo: Tawang-tawa ako sa narinig kong joke eh. 'Yung mga kababayan daw po nating kurap sa Pilipinas, kagagara ng kotse, kamamahal, katutulin. Pero 'pag ginustong tumakas, ang ginagamit wheelchair*] [Laughter and applause] (Aquino III, 2012).

After she was charged with election fraud in 2011, former President Arroyo was never seen in public without looking pitiful in a wheelchair and a neck brace. Some believe this was part of a masterful spin to court public sympathy and to spare the former president apparent jail time (Philippine Daily Inquirer, 2014). Although Aquino III's banter drew cheers and laughter from the crowd, Filipinos back home did not seem to be amused. A spokesperson of Aquino III immediately clarified that the joke did not really come from the president and that he merely quoted from a text message (Burgonio, 2012). Persons with disabilities and their supporters, however, were not buying any of it. They lambasted the former president for making fun of their condition and suggested he leave the wisecracks to the comedians (Esguerra, 2012).

Aquino insists that the hate had been misdirected. "Ako [I], I don't think our people will be mad at me. I think they will be mad at those pretending to be ill. And I think they will side with me who will ask those who are pretending to be ill to fess up to the truth, 'di ba' [right?], and not pretend they're ill," he said in a news report (Cheng, 2012).

5.3.6 Rodrigo Duterte

Of the post-EDSA presidents, it was probably Duterte who took humor to a completely different level. Duterte, known for his brash and controversial rhetorical approach, occasionally employed self-deprecating humor. He would make jokes about his appearance, age, or unconventional language. By using self-mocking humor, he aimed to establish a connection with the public and present himself as an approachable leader despite his tough image. Unlike his predecessors, however, Duterte was not coy about making jokes about controversial or taboo subjects –the rape of women, the killing of criminals, and the assassination of bishops:

> I am aware of the intrigues because we started that. Bodies in bags—that is torture—but not our doing. Believe me. De La Rosa cannot even brush his hair, where would he find time to wrap bodies?[6] You just shoot the guy and throw him there. Why do you have to--? How many hours would that take? That is somebody else's handiwork. That is there torture method. You cannot pin everything to government. That's the drama that's being played out to you.
>
> [*Bright na ako diyan sa intriga and we started that. Kaya 'yung mga balot-balot, it's torture, that's not ours. Maniwala ka. Ang intention ko lang, panahon ni Dela Rosa. Hindi nga niya masuklay 'yung buhok niya.* [Laughter] *Tapos, magbalot pa siya ng tao? You just shoot the guy and throw him there. Why do you have to—? Ilang oras gawin mo 'yan? 'Yan ang trabaho ng kabila. 'Yan 'yung torture nila. So hindi lahat ng… baka government, government, lahat na lang government. That's the drama that's being played out to you*] (Duterte, 2016).

Of course, human rights groups do not find any of this funny. But what is more interesting is that citizens do not seem to mind, as demonstrated by Duterte's consistently high approval ratings and the resounding victory of the administration's slate in the 2019 midterm elections. Some contend that Duterte drew public legitimacy not by peddling policies that work but by capitalizing on a performative communication strategy that invoked elite-mass signaling and conveying to the public a semblance of responsiveness (Panao & Pernia, 2022; Pernia & Panao, 2023).

Although media and scholarly literature depicts Duterte as exploiting humor to insult or ridicule enemies, a closer look at his speeches show that jokes are there more often to establish connection than to sow fear. Neither is a resort to humor as a rhetorical device exclusive to occasions where there is opportunity to peddle the government's war on drugs. Consider how Duterte appeared before victims of typhoon Odette in Dinagat Islands in December 2021:

> I was able to scrape up 100—oh you have 100 million for the repairs of […] This will be divided among you so you will have a share of it and you can't say that the government just left you on your own to survive […] Next time, I'll bring some cars so you can all roam around no matter where you pass through. But you seem to have only one—do you only have one road? Are there no other roads apart from this?
>
> [*Naay natilok 100—oh naa mo'y 100 million, dako nga kwarta na pang-repair daw sa kuan* […] [applause] *Bahin-bahinon na ninyo. So naa—naa gyud moy ma. Di gyud mi ka—di mo kaingon nga gipasagdan mo sa gobyerno.* [applause] […] *Sunod balik nako, magdala na ko'g mga auto* [laughter] *para kamong tanan haron magsuroy-suroy na mo ngari og asa muagi.* [laughter] *Murag usa ra gyud—usa ra may kabuok inyong dalan? Wa nay lain?*] (Duterte, 2021).

Interestingly, this remark was never regarded as insulting or condescending. It was probably because the whole speech was delivered spontaneously and in the local vernacular. Likewise, although jokes would be employed to break the monotony of the speech, there was neither attempt to downplay the magnitude of the damage nor divert blame elsewhere. Duterte's parting bid to the typhoon victims almost hints at why his banters had been widely received.

---

[6] De La Rosa served as Duterte's Chief of the Philippine National Police from July 1, 2016, to April 19, 2018. De La Rosa is bald.

I'll go now because your nails are already flying off your fingers because you're clapping so hard. I made some jokes earlier because looking at your faces and seeing how much you're suffering makes me want to cry. So I was joking around to make you happy.

[*Sige na kay inyong kuko nanglagpot na na sige'g pakpak diha. [laughter] Katong akong mga kuan—katong akong mga tiaw yaga-yaga lang na para—para lang mo ma... Kita ko sa nawong ninyo, kahilakon ko sa... Makita gyud nimo ang kapait ba. Mao na sige lang ko'g tiaw para malingaw mo og kuan*] (Duterte, 2021).

5.4 Concluding Remarks

In this chapter, we show that Filipinos have a rich tradition of political humor where public figures such as presidents are creators and objects of political commentary. Using snapshots of Filipino presidents' rhetorical practices, we demonstrate how self-deprecating humor is conventionally resorted to establish a culturally rooted politician-audience rapport based on the concept of "*kapwa.*" We also show that the success of humor as a rhetorical device depends on the president's authenticity and likeability. Despite being offensive, jokes resonate as endearing or humorous if the speaker is perceived as sincere and approachable. In the same vein, jokes, no matter how innocent, offend sensibilities if the speaker is perceived as arrogant, elitist, and deceitful. Hence, we showed how leaders are likely to engage in comedic diversions as part of their governance toolkit.

When presidents are popular, even comedians exercise prudence and hold back. The late master impersonator Willie Nepomuceno, known in the Philippine entertainment industry for his patented caricatures and parodies of Philippine leaders, once quipped that he would stop parodying Duterte not only because he finds Duterte "funnier" but because satires only "add to the political noise and divert attention to the real issues that need to be addressed" (Felongco, 2018; Policarpio, 2018). As Nepomuceno puts it, "You can't just *ridicule*; there still needs to be some *respect* for the subject."

Notwithstanding the analytical assertions of this chapter (which sit primarily on the "supply side"), there is a need to supplement them with further narratives and evidence on the ground ("demand side"). Future studies therefore must validate and examine people's sentiments *empirically* to fully establish the positive effect of presidential comedic strategies towards public opinion. How, and to what extent, citizens sift through the humor to distinguish what (and who) is funny and trustworthy would bring a much nuanced lens to the whole comedic enterprise of presidents.

References

Agatep, C. A. (2018, May 12). The SWS presidential surveys. *INQUIRER.Net*. https://opinion.inquirer.net/113116/sws-presidential-surveys.

Anderson, B. (1988). Cacique democracy and the Philippines: Origins and dreams. *New Left Review, I/169*, 3–31.

Andres, T. Q. D. (1994). *Dictionary of Filipino Culture and Values*. Giraffe Books.

Aquino, C. (1992). *Reflections on our development*. Delivered at the Peninsula Hotel. https://www.coryaquino.ph/index.php/works/article/7d5e8202-f2df-11df-b3cf-001617d76479.

Aquino III, B. S. (2012, October 22). *Speech of President Aquino at the Filipino Community Event in Auckland, New Zealand, October 22, 2012*. Official Gazette. https://www.officialgazette.gov.ph/2012/10/22/speech-of-president-aquino-at-the-filipino-community-event-in-auckland-new-zealand-october-22-2012/.

Aquino III, B. S. (2014, July 15). *Speech of President Aquino at the Daylight Dialogue*. GOVPH. Official Gazette of the Republic of the Philippines. https://www.officialgazette.gov.ph/2014/07/15/speech-of-president-aquino-at-the-daylight-dialogue/.

Arroyo, G. M. (2002, April 30). *Speech of President Arroyo during the National Press Club's Gridiron Night*. Official Gazette. https://www.officialgazette.gov.ph/2002/04/30/speech-of-president-arroyo-during-the-national-press-clubs-gridiron-night/.

Batalla, E. V. C. (2016). Divided politics and economic growth in the Philippines. *Journal of Current Southeast Asian Affairs, 35*(3), 161–186. https://doi.org/10.1177/186810341603500308

Burgonio, T. J. (2012, November 23). *Aquino praises NGOs*. INQUIRER.Net. https://newsinfo.inquirer.net/311525/aquino-praises-ngos.

Cal, B. (2022, August 7). *Newsmen remember FVR as "media darling."* Philippine News Agency. https://www.pna.gov.ph/articles/1180786.

Center for Media Freedom and Responsibility. (2022, August 1). *Press freedom champion: Journalists pay tribute to Former President Ramos*. CMFR. https://cmfr-phil.org/chronicle/obit/press-freedom-champion-journalists-pay-tribute-to-former-president-ramos/.

Cheng, W. (2012, October 26). *PNoy on wheelchair joke: Get mad, but not at me*. ABS.CBN News. https://news.abs-cbn.com/nation/10/26/12/pnoy-wheelchair-joke-get-mad-not-me.

Duterte, R. (2016, August 29). *Speech of President Rodrigo Roa Duterte during the 18th founding anniversary of volunteers against crime and corruption*. Official Gazette. https://www.officialgazette.gov.ph/2016/08/29/speech-president-rodrigo-roa-duterte-during-the-18th-founding-anniversary-of-volunteers-against-crime-and-corruption/.

Duterte, R. (2021, December 22). *Speech of President Rodrigo Roa Duterte during his visit to victims of typhoon "Odettte" in Dinagat Islands*. Presidential Communications Office. https://pco.gov.ph/presidential-speech/speech-of-president-rodrigo-roa-duterte-during-his-visit-to-victims-of-typhoon-odette-in-dinagat-islands/.

Enriquez, V. (Ed.). (1986). KAPWA: A core concept in Filipino social psychology. In *Philippine Worldview* (pp. 6–19). ISEAS Publishing. https://doi.org/10.1355/9789814379021-005.

Estrada, J. E. (1991, April 26). *Speech of Senator Joseph Ejercito Estrada before the Cebu Chamber of Commerce and Industry*, April 26, 1991, Delivered at the Casino Español de Cebu. https://www.officialgazette.gov.ph/1991/04/26/speech-of-senator-joseph-ejercito-estrada-before-the-cebu-chamber-of-commerce-and-industry-april-26-1991/

Esguerra, C. V. (2012, October 25). Disabled, netizens don't find Aquino 'wheelchair' joke funny. INQUIRER.Net. https://technology.inquirer.net/19454/angry-netizens-feel-aquino-went-too-far-with-wheelchair-joke.

Fineman, M. (1986, January 23). *'Opposite of what a woman should be': Imelda says Aquino is 'obsessed.'* LA Times. https://www.latimes.com/archives/la-xpm-1986-01-23-mn-27897-story.html.

Felongco, G. (2018, June 30). *"No" to spoofing Duterte, Willie Nep says*. Gulf News. https://gulfnews.com/world/asia/philippines/no-to-spoofing-duterte-willie-nep-says-1.2244318.

Garrido, M. (2017). Why the poor support populism: The politics of sincerity in Metro Manila. *American Journal of Sociology, 123*(3), 647–685. https://doi.org/10.1086/694076

Garrido, M. (2020). A conjunctural account of upper-and middle-class support for Rodrigo Duterte. *International Sociology, 35*(6), 651–673.

Hedman, E.-L. (2001). The Philippines: Not so military, not so civil. In M. Alagappa (Ed.), *Coercion and governance: The declining political role of the military in Asia* (pp. 165–186). Stanford University Press.

Hodess, R. (2004). *Global corruption report 2004: [Special focus: political corruption]*. Pluto Press/Transparency International.

Jones, S. (1990). Aquino's tarnished track record. *Index on Censorship, 19*(2), 5–7. https://doi.org/10.1080/03064229008534776

Karaos, A. M. (2006). Populist mobilization and Manila's urban poor: The case of SANAPA in the NGC East Side. In: A. Fabros, J. Rocamora, & D. Velasco (Eds.). *Social movements: Experiences from the Philippines*. Institute for Popular Democracy.

Macaraig, A. (2011, September 4). *Arroyo's fortress and the nosy press*. RAPPLER. https://www.rappler.com/nation/110-arroyo-s-fortress-and-the-nosy-press/.

National Union of Journalists of the Philippines. (2009, August 7). *The media under Arroyo: A legacy of bloodshed and repression*. Davao Today. https://davaotoday.com/opinion/the-media-under-arroyo-a-legacy-of-bloodshed-and-repression/.

Nery, J. (2014, February 17). *The Amanpour interview: Framing Aquino*. INQUIRER.Net. https://opinion.inquirer.net/71691/the-amanpour-interview-framing-aquino.

Panao, R. A. L. (2014). Beyond roll call: Executive-legislative relations and lawmaking in the Philippine House of Representatives. *Philippine Political Science Journal, 35*(1), 59–77. https://doi.org/10.1080/01154451.2014.903554

Panao, R. A. L., & Pernia, R. A. (2022). Fear and loathing or strategic priming? Unveiling the audience in Duterte's crime rhetoric. *Journal of East Asian Studies, 22*(1), 77–98. https://doi.org/10.1017/jea.2022.1

Pe-Pua, R., & Protacio-Marcelino, E. A. (2000). Sikolohiyang Pilipino (Filipino psychology): A legacy of Virgilio G. Enriquez. *Asian Journal of Social Psychology, 3*(1), 49–71. https://doi.org/10.1111/1467-839X.00054

Pernia, R. A., & Panao, R. A. L. (2023). The cuss that cares? Paternalistic cussing in Philippine President Rodrigo Roa Duterte's rhetoric. In O. Feldman (Ed.), *Debasing Political Rhetoric* (pp. 89–105). Springer Nature Singapore. https://doi.org/10.1007/978-981-99-0894-3_6.

Philippine Daily Inquirer. (2021, July 7). *Weaponizing the law*. INQUIRER.Net. https://opinion.inquirer.net/141818/weaponizing-the-law-3.

Philippine Daily Inquirer. (2014, July 12). *The wheelchair set*. INQUIRER.Net. https://opinion.inquirer.net/76479/the-wheelchair-set.

Philippine Entertainment Portal. (2007, September 12). *Erap, and everything "Erapting" about him*. PEP.Ph. https://www.pep.ph/lifestyle/13775/erap-and-everything-erapting-about-him.

Pilling, D. (2013, November 14). *Philippines typhoon knocks Benigno Aquino's reputation*. Financial Times. https://www.ft.com/content/a1e5062a-4d11-11e3-9f40-00144feabdc0.

Policarpio, A. (2018, June 30). *Willie Nep bares why he won't impersonate Duterte*. INQUIRER.Net. https://entertainment.inquirer.net/281389/willie-nep-bares-wont-impersonate-duterte.

Ramos, F. (1996, April 22). *Speech of President Fidel V. Ramos at the Annual Gridiron Night of Philippines*. Official Gazette of the Republic of the Philippines. https://www.officialgazette.gov.ph/1996/04/22/speech-of-president-ramos-at-the-annual-gridiron-night-of-the-national-press-club-of-the-philippines/.

Ramos, F. (1997, April 21). *Speech of President Fidel V. Ramos at the Annual Gridiron presentation of the National Press Club of the Philippines*. Official Gazette of the Republic of the Philippines. https://www.officialgazette.gov.ph/1997/04/21/speech-of-president-ramos-at-the-annual-gridiron-presentation-of-the-national-press-club-of-the-philippines/.

Reuters. (2007, September 12). *FACTBOX: Key facts on Philippines' former leader Estrada*. Reuters. https://www.reuters.com/article/us-philippines-estrada-factbox-idUSMAN32465120070912.

Reyes, J. (2015). *Loób* and *Kapwa*: An introduction to a Filipino virtue ethics. *Asian Philosophy, 25*(2), 148–171. https://doi.org/10.1080/09552367.2015.1043173

Richburg, K. B. (1987, October 13). *AQUINO sues Philippine journalist for libel*. Washington Post. https://www.washingtonpost.com/archive/politics/1987/10/13/aquino-sues-philippine-journalist-for-libel/d6977cd8-5452-4a1b-a843-d70f351579f5/.

Rocamora, J. (1991). Discontent in the Philippines. *World Policy Journal, 8*(4), 633–661.

Saito, I. (2010). *Pakikisama: A Filipino trait*. Institute of Psychology Rissho University. https://core.ac.uk/download/pdf/268585067.pdf.

Sanger, D. E. (1992, June 8). *Her term about to end, Aquino "hasn't made much difference" to the poor*. The New York Times. https://www.nytimes.com/1992/06/08/world/her-term-about-to-end-aquino-hasn-t-made-much-difference-to-the-poor.html.

Sauler, E. (2012, October 18). *Estrada drops 'Edsa 2' jokes in speech before Rotary members*. Inquirer.net. https://newsinfo.inquirer.net/291532/estrada-drops-edsa-2-jokes-in-speech-before-rotary-forbes-members.

Tuquero, L. (2020, June 20). *FALSE: Cory Aquino's libel suit vs Beltran was not deemed press freedom issue*. RAPPLER. https://www.rappler.com/newsbreak/fact-check/264304-cory-aquino-libel-suit-vs-beltran-not-deemed-press-freedom-issue/.

Villacorta, W. V. (1994). The curse of the weak state: Leadership imperatives for the Ramos government. *Contemporary Southeast Asia, 16*(1), 67–92.

Villanueva, M. A., Araneta, S., & Arquiza, R. (2000, March 23). *Estrada fires Laquian over drinking joke*. Philstar.Com. https://www.philstar.com/headlines/2000/03/23/87207/estrada-fires-laquian-over-drinking-joke.

Waisanen, D. (2015). Comedian-in-Chief: Presidential jokes as enthymematic crisis rhetoric: Comedian-In-Chief. *Presidential Studies Quarterly, 45*(2), 335–360. https://doi.org/10.1111/psq.12190

Young, D. G. (2016). Humor and satire, political. In G. Mazzoleni (Ed.), *The international encyclopedia of political communication* (1st ed., pp. 1–7). Wiley. https://doi.org/10.1002/9781118541555.wbiepc100.

Rogelio Alicor L. Panao, is an Associate Professor in the Department of Political Science, University of the Philippines Diliman. He is also a member of the Philippine Bar.

Ronald A. Pernia, is an Assistant Professor in the Political Science Program of the College of Social Sciences, University of the Philippines Cebu.

Chapter 6
Holocaust Humor in Israel as a Political Tool of the Left-Wing

Liat Steir-Livny

Abstract As part of the narrative in the last few decades that seeks to reevaluate how the collective memory of the Holocaust is conveyed to the Israeli public, left-wing scholars and intellectuals have claimed that Holocaust memory was and is politically manipulated by the right-wing to intensify a siege mentality, present Israel as an eternal victim, and elicit constant fear and paranoia to justify violent policies against the Palestinians in the occupied territories, and block opportunities for a peace treaty. Based on the literature in the fields of Holocaust commemoration, political agendas in Israel, and studies on humor, satire, and parody, this chapter traces how since the 1990s, Israeli Holocaust humor, satire, and parody have been a part of the left-wing struggle against the right-wing that has governed Israel (with a few exceptions) since 1977. The analysis shows how speeches and declarations by right-wingers who use the Holocaust to characterize threats to the State of Israel prompt the left-wing to produce Holocaust humor, satire, and parodies that castigate these attitudes and beliefs as false and manipulative.

6.1 Introduction

The Holocaust was and remains a major trauma in Israel's national consciousness. The memory of the trauma has not faded over the years. Surveys consistently indicate that since the end of WWII and across generations, most Jewish-Israelis have viewed the Holocaust as a defining event. Studies show that Israeli media, education, and culture frame the Holocaust as a current, ongoing local trauma rather than an event that ended decades ago in another place (Bar-Tal, 2007; Meyers et al., 2014; Steir-Livny, 2014).

A siege mentality is defined as a state of mind or behavior in which an individual or group perceives an external threat and feels emotionally and psychologically

---

L. Steir-Livny (✉)
Sapir Academic College, Sderot, Israel
e-mail: liatsteirlivny@gmail.com

Open University of Israel, Ra'anana, Israel

isolated, defensive, and fearful. It often results in an "us vs. them" mentality and an aggressive or paranoid response toward perceived threats, whether real or imagined (Ben-Shaul, 1997, 2006). The Holocaust, as a pivotal memory in Israeli life, impacts how the Israeli-Palestinian conflict is perceived and represented in Israeli culture. The decades-long, Jewish-Israeli-Palestinian conflict, the threat of annihilation, and the continuing terrorist attacks and intifadas, have created an atmosphere of constant vigilance and anxiety that is shaped by the trauma of the Holocaust in the Israeli collective memory.

From the late 1940s until the late 1970s, direct parallels between Arabs and Nazis were a key feature of Israeli culture. Israel's wars against Arab nations were seen as a way to prevent a second Holocaust, and Arab leaders were depicted as Nazi successors. Demonizing the Arabs and forging links between the past and the present helped consolidate the ranks in Israel and created immediate empathy for Zionism in the Western world. The implication was that just as the Allied forces had fought the Nazis in the past, today it was their duty to subjugate the Arabs (Bar-Tal, 2007; Evron, 2011; Steir-Livny, 2009). Politicians and public figures from both the right and the left used the Holocaust to account for crises in present-day Israel, thus strengthening the siege mentality of a hunted, unwanted people, constantly intimidated by Arab states, continually on the verge of another extermination, that must defend itself from its enemies or be destroyed (Zertal, 1993).

Ever since the right-wing has controlled successive governments in Israel, left-wingers have gradually abandoned and condemned the victimization-siege scenario. This evolution is directly linked to local political and social changes. The decade spanning the late 1960s to the late 1970s was a period of crisis for the left-wing Labor movement that governed Israel since its founding. The 1967 war that initiated the ongoing moral and legal debate about the occupied territories, the *Yom Kippur War* (1973) and the commission of inquiry that followed it, the illegal dollar account held by Leah Rabin (the wife of then Prime Minister Yitzhak Rabin) that was discovered in Switzerland, were all emblematic of the fall of the moderate left. The rise to power of the right-wing Likud movement in 1977 constituted the first time the left had been ejected from hubs of political power. In conjunction with the growing endorsement of right-wing attitudes, new militant groups emerged from the nationalist religious right.

From 1977 onward, the chasm between the right and left wings deepened. The right-wing continued to recycle the idea that Arabs are the equivalent of Nazis (Steir-Livny, 2014). As part of a left-wing narrative since 1977 that sought to reevaluate how the collective memory of the Holocaust is conveyed to the Israeli public, left-wing scholars and intellectuals have claimed that Holocaust memory was and is politically manipulated by the right-wing to present Israel as an eternal victim. Ophir (2001) argued that Holocaust memory in Israel underwent a process of "sanctification." Avraham Burg (2007) referred to this evolution as "the religion of trauma," and in Gan's (2014) view, it created a "victimization discourse" with "victimized awareness" shaping the Israeli identity. In the left-wing view, this victimization elicits constant fear and paranoia that is mustered to justify violent policies against the

Palestinians in the occupied territories, as well as efforts to block opportunities for a peace treaty.

Based on research in the fields of Holocaust commemoration, political agendas in Israel, as well as studies of humor, satire, and parody, this chapter shows how since the 1990s, Israeli Holocaust humor, satire, and parody have been an integral part of the left-wing struggle against what they perceive as a siege mentality orchestrated by the right-wing. The analysis shows how speeches and declarations by right-wingers who use the Holocaust to characterize threats to the State of Israel prompt left-wingers to produce Holocaust humor, satire, and parodies that castigate these attitudes and beliefs as false and manipulative. Whereas the right-wing tries to generate more of a chasm between Jewish Israelis and Palestinians, Arabs, and Muslims, left-wingers use satire to protest and reveal these tactics. The analysis below illustrates the ways in which Holocaust humor targets right-wingers in general but also specific politicians. It also shows that even though the left-wing uses humor, satire, and parody to criticize the politicization of the Holocaust by the right wing, sometimes left-wingers do the same and tap into Holocaust humor, satire, and parody to advance their own political and social agenda.

6.1.1 Holocaust Humor and Black Humor as a Left-Wing Political Weapon

For many years, Holocaust humor, satire, and parody were considered borderline blasphemy in Israeli culture. Official agents of Holocaust memory still adhere to this doctrine. However, as of the 1990s, a new unofficial and subversive trajectory of memory began taking shape with texts that treated the Holocaust with humor, satire, and parody. The emergence of Holocaust humor is part of a broader pattern of changes since the 1980s in Holocaust awareness in Israel in numerous cultural fields (Pinchevski & Brand, 2007; Pinchevski & Liebes, 2010; Yablonka, 2011), which have been examined extensively in research (Ne'eman Arad, 2003; Ofer, 2013; Porat, 2011). Despite the growing acceptance of Holocaust humor, it remains controversial and continues to spark anger and debate (Rosenfeld, 2013, 2015; Steir-Livny, 2014, 2017). The left-wing has utilized Holocaust-related satire since the 1990s to counter the right wing's siege mentality. Satire, in particular, is used to slam the right-wing's attempts to exploit the Holocaust in the present to instill constant fear and anxiety that will permanently block dialogue between Jews and Palestinians.

Freud considered humor to be a key defense mechanism. He believed that when people use humor in situations that elicit fear and anxiety, they can acquire a new perspective that helps ease negative emotions. People can deal with difficult situations through humor and reduce emotional suffering and grief (Freud, 1990). More recent studies have argued that humor can alleviate stress, enable people to cope with negative feelings and challenging situations, mitigate suffering, temporarily dissipate anxiety, and gain some sense of power and control in situations of helplessness. This can often take the form of black and self-deprecating humor (Ziv, 1996; Cramer, 2000; Ostrower, 2009, 63–104; Berger & Berger, 2011). Black (or alternatively sick or gallows) humor is deliberately used to cope with challenging situations where the harshness of reality cannot be changed. However, the attitude toward this reality can be inflected (Ziv, 1996).

Holocaust humor is used by the left to help cope with its political inferiority, with the dominance of right-wing siege narratives in Israel that are fueled with Holocaust memory. Left-wing satire works against victimization, protests against the amalgamation of the past with the present, and dismantles fear. In this sense, Holocaust humor in Israel also enables people to vent their frustration as well as serving as a mechanism for social cohesion (Ziv, 1996). Holocaust humor, satire, and parody challenge the way Israeli society lives the trauma in the present by deconstructing the fear factor. Paradoxically and probably unwittingly, it also simultaneously strengthens the dominance of trauma in the present by integrating it even more into everyday life and popular culture. Although the fear factor is much less frightening it becomes more salient through humor i.e., this contradictory process involves elimination and assimilation at the same time. The vignettes below illustrate this dual phenomenon.

6.2 Prime Minister Benyamin Netanyahu and Holocaust-Related Satire

TV Holocaust-related satire aims at a range of right-wing figures. However, the most vilified politician is Binyamin ("Bibi") Netanyahu, who has served longer than any other prime minister in Israel. Netanyahu constantly uses the Holocaust when discussing the Jewish-Israeli-Palestinian conflict, the Jewish-Israeli-Arab conflict, and the Jewish-Israeli-Muslim conflict. In his fifteen years at the helm, he has frequently equated Arabs with Nazis, Palestinians with Nazis, and the nuclear threats of Iran with Hitler's goal of exterminating the Jewish people. Netanyahu has repeatedly argued that a nuclear Iran would happily commit a second Holocaust. Left-wing Israelis express their outrage at these analogies and ridicule his attempts to conjure up atavistic fears.

For example, during the 2012 Purim holiday, Netanyahu held a series of meetings with U.S. President Barack Obama to discuss Iran's nuclear threat and whether Iran should be preemptively attacked. Netanyahu found it appropriate to give Obama *The Book of Esther* [*Megilat Esther*],[1] that relates how the ancient Persian vizier Haman set out to exterminate the Jews and how his plans were ultimately foiled. In his speech to Obama, Netanyahu also produced an historical document dating from the Second World War in which Jewish-American representatives pleaded with the American government to bomb Auschwitz. Netanyahu hinted that in a similar situation the Jews would handle matters themselves and not wait for an American green light.

---

[1] *Megilat Esther*—one of the five scrolls in the Writings [*Ketuvim*] section of the Jewish *Tanakh* (the Hebrew Bible). The Megillah forms the core of the Jewish festival of *Purim*.

The skit "Remembrance Day for Shushan and Heroism" [*Yom ha'zi'karon la'shushan ve'la'gvuran*] on the satire show *It's a Wonderful Country* (*Eretz Nehedert*; Keshet Productions, Channel 2-Keshet, 2003–2023) was aired on Purim 2012. The skit satirized the political links between the Holocaust, ancient Persia, and modern-day Iran. It depicted employees at a nuclear reactor in Iran, marking "Remembrance Day for Shushan[2] and Heroism Day," thus renaming the ceremonial hallmarks of Israel's Holocaust and Heroism Remembrance Day. In Israel's first decades, survivors were sometimes criticized for having gone to their death in the Holocaust "like sheep to the slaughter." In the skit, the master of ceremonies says that the downtrodden Persians went like "sheep to the slaughter" under Ahasuerus, the ancient Persian ruler. The phrase "and these are the names of the fallen," intoned during observances of Holocaust and Heroism Remembrance Day in Israel, is used in the skit to eulogize Vizier Haman's murdered sons.[3] The two-minute siren that is sounded throughout Israel on Holocaust and Heroism Remembrance Day is replaced by shaking a rattle.[4] The skit also depicts a well-known emotional reaction in Israel when people struggle to stifle their laughter during the two-minute memorial siren rather than stand silently at attention. Here, an Iranian reactor employee cannot stop laughing during the ceremony.

On Holocaust Remembrance Day in Israel, the regular TV schedule is canceled and replaced by programs dealing solely with the Holocaust and its memory. Dirges are played throughout the day on Israeli radio. In the skit, we learn that the TV program schedule in Iran has also been changed, and the radio plays songs from "good old Iran." The Iranian nuclear reactor employees slander the Israeli Zionists who stuck to their usual schedules that day as "Purim-deniers" (vs. "Holocaust deniers"). The role-switching in the skit ridicules Netanyahu's attempts to represent the Israelis as eternal victims. By deconstructing the behavioral patterns of Holocaust Remembrance Day, the writers showed how easy it is to manipulate memory.

Left-wing satire also criticized Netanyahu's political use of the Holocaust in his speech to the World Zionist Congress in Jerusalem on October 20, 2015, in which he stated that Hitler did not want to murder the Jews but only expel them and that it was the Arab Mufti, Haj Amin El-Husseini, who advised him to murder the Jews. The subtext was clear: at a troubled time in Israel (October–November 2015), sometimes called "The third Intifada," Netanyahu claimed that all Arabs—from the past to the present— were Nazis. This subtextual comparison turned Jewish–Israelis into eternal victims, trapped in a repetitive Holocaust by the Nazis and the Palestinians combined.

Israeli right-wingers took quick advantage of his speech to anchor their claim that Palestinian terror is not related to the Jewish settlements in the West Bank but, in fact, existed long before the 1967 war. Right-wing public figures claimed that historically, the Arabs in *Eretz Yisrael* (the Land of Israel) wanted to obliterate the Zionist entity

---

[2] *Shushan* was the capital city of ancient Persia.
[3] The King's advisor *Haman* plotted to kill the Jews but, in the end, after Queen Esther interceded with Ahasuerus, he and his sons were executed instead.
[4] A rattle or noisemaker is used during readings of the *Book of Esther* on Purim, every time the name of *Haman* appears in the text.

and the Jews in Palestine, and the fact that Israel still controls the West Bank and that there are Jewish settlements in the West Bank is not and was never the reason for Arab terror.

Left-wingers responded through serious commentary but also with humor. Many made it clear that Netanyahu had committed a historical mistake, reminding their audiences that the Mufti, a Nazi sympathizer, did not represent all the Arabs in Eretz Israel. Thus, the speech was nothing more than another example of attempts by the Israeli right-wing to fuel hatred and racism, strengthen its siege mentality, and undermine opportunities for dialogue. Netanyahu's speech was criticized and dismantled through satire and parody. Left-wingers released memes titled "The Mufti made me do it" on the internet, mocking his statement on Israeli social media.

An analysis of "The Mufti made me do it" memes suggest they can be divided into several main groups. The first is political memetic photos. Meme-based political discourse often begins with a single memetic photo that relates to political actors and controversies. The memetic responses to these photos expose their use as inauthentic, flawed, and manipulated (Shifman, 2013). The famous picture of the Mufti meeting Hitler is known and genuine and was not disputed. Left-wingers added to the photo Netanyahu's image as though he had been there to listen to the conversation or added ridiculous subtitles explaining how a fairly naïve Hitler does not want to hurt the Jews. However, the Mufti persuades him to do so. For example, in one, Hitler wants to punish the Jews by denying them ice cream, but the Mufti replies, "No. Kill them."

The second group is comprised of memes drawing on pop culture to create a comic effect to discuss politics. Numerous memes depicted figures from popular culture on TV shows, sitcoms etc., blaming Haj Amin El Husseini for their misfortunes. For example, in a famous episode of the sitcom *Friends*, Ross and Rachel decide to separate for a while and Ross kisses someone else. This episode caused turmoil amongst Friends fans, and other episodes discussed this kiss at length. The caption under a picture of Ross and Rachel in the meme says that Ross did not want to kiss her; the Mufti made him do it. In another meme, under a picture of Gargamel, the villain in *The Smurfs*, the caption says that he actually liked the little blue creatures, but one day the Mufti convinced him otherwise. A caption under a picture of Jerry Seinfeld says that numerous Israelis wanted to go to Seinfeld's gala performance in Israel, but the Mufti bought all the tickets. The caption to a picture of Biff Tannen, the villain in the film *Back to the Future* (directed by Robert Zemeckis in 1985), explains that the Mufti is the vicious power that turned innocent Biff into the bad guy. In yet others, the Mufti's head is placed on iconic pop culture heroes, suggesting that he was the cause of their tragedies. For example, the Mufti's head was positioned on one of the Beatles, thus "explaining" who really caused their breakup.

The third group comprises videos based on the "Hitler rants" YouTube parodies that began appearing in August 2006. A Spanish web surfer took a scene from the film *Downfall*, showing Hitler yelling at his staff as the end of WWII approaches—but added subtitles in Spanish to make it seem that Hitler is upbraiding Microsoft's flight simulator. An English-speaking surfer uploaded the English subtitles version, thus making the joke accessible to the rest of the flight simulator fans on YouTube. Since then, hundreds of parodies have been produced in English, Spanish,

Chinese, Japanese, and many other languages (Ben-Ari, 2020) that engage with politics, economy, sports, technology, gaming, culture and everyday trivialities, topical events, and trivial news or gossip.

Hitler rants parodies started appearing in Hebrew in 2009 and have become hugely popular. In Israel, they are used to protest political issues, Israeli wars, military service, religious coercion, etc. In one video, Hitler is presented as a Judeophile who wants to help "the poor Jews" but is driven to killer behavior by the evil Mufti. In the second one, he gets angry because Netanyahu took the credit away from him for killing the Jews.

Netanyahu, who as mentioned, uses Holocaust memory numerous times in his rhetoric, sometimes criticizes other politicians who use Holocaust associations. One of the ways left-wingers use to respond to this is satire. For example, in May 2016, Deputy Chief of Staff Yair Golan gave a speech on Holocaust and Heroism Remembrance Day in which he said that Jewish-Israelis must look reflexively at Jewish-Israeli society and acknowledge its tendencies toward racism and violence: "What is frightening me in the memory of the Holocaust is to recognize disheartening processes that happened in Europe and especially in Germany then, and finding evidence of them here in 2016." His speech caused turmoil and was criticized by Netanyahu and others, who stated that Golan had "cheapened the Holocaust" (Efraim & Azulay, 2016).

Left-wingers turned against the fact that the prime minister who uses the Holocaust so often is seemingly appalled when a left-wing politician uses Holocaust equivalencies. Satirist Asaf Harel, for example, in his late-night *Asaf Harel* (Channel 10, 2015–2016), created a skit called "Mr. Holocaust." This skit was a take-off on Charles Roger Hargreaves' famous children's book series, *Mr. Men*. In the skit, Harel is holding a book that looks like it is from the series, but instead of Mr. Happy, Mr. Tickle, or any of the other childish protagonists, Harel reads from a book entitled Mr. Holocaust. The protagonist resembles Hargreaves' images (a monochromatic round image of a head with a small body) but is still identifiable as a depiction of Netanyahu with purple hair. Harel reads the story as though he is talking to children:

> Mr. Holocaust lived in a big house with a dog and many servants […] From morning till night, he kept comparing, frightening, and warning: "it might come back. This is the reason you should vote for me."

On the following pages, Netanyahu has a yellow star coming out of his mouth, which looks like the yellow badge Jews were forced to wear on their clothes. Harel continues:

> And as Mr. Holocaust repeated these messages, he got reelected again and again. […] One evening he met Mr. Security, who stood on stage, compared and warned and even dared to alert. Mr. Holocaust became so upset: 'the Holocaust is mine! You have no right!! If somebody else talks about the Holocaust, it is cheapening!'

The camera focuses on Yair Golan's cartoon image in the book, looking sad and lying in bed, while through the window violence rages. Harel ends: "Mr. Security returned to his home sad and upset and thought that from now on he would not compare the Holocaust to socio-political phenomena in Israel. Moreover, since that day, everybody understood that only one man can warn, frighten, compare." The camera shows Netanyahu's image in the book embracing the yellow badge as though he owns it. The moral, as though taught to children, emphasizes the hypocrisy in Netanyahu's statements against Golan but also alerts the public to Netanyahu's constant use of the Holocaust as a political tool and his interest in fanning constant fear and anxiety to get reelected.

6.3 Lampooning the Siege Mentality and the Holocaust-Based Victimization Narrative

In recent decades, right-wing circles have broadened the purview of groups that can be compared to Nazis, including people expressing left-wing positions and/or those willing to give up the occupied territories (or parts of them) for a peace treaty. Both are often represented as collaborators with the Arabs and as Nazis. For example, a photograph of Yitzhak Rabin, doctored so that he appears to be wearing a Gestapo uniform, was brandished at a right-wing demonstration in Jerusalem's Zion Square in 1995. This photo became a major symbol of right-wing resistance to the Oslo Accords and ultimately played an integral part in the demonization process that ended with Rabin's assassination in November 1995. When Jewish settlements in the (Gaza-area) *Gush Katif* bloc were evacuated in August 2005, IDF soldiers and the government that sent them (a right-wing government headed by Ariel Sharon) were sometimes called Nazis. Holocaust survivors living in *Gush Katif* were dispatched to the media to relate how the evacuation reminded them of their expulsion during the Second World War. The settlers called the evacuation "an expulsion," wore orange stars (reminiscent of the Nazi-era yellow star), and frequently compared the disengagement to the expulsion of European Jews from their homes.

Left-wing satirists responded to these trends by ridiculing them. For example, during the Gush Katif evacuation the satirists Goldstein and Rephael (2005) wrote a short column in the *Ma'ariv* newspaper entitled "The same as in the Holocaust." They ridiculed the political manipulation of those who were evacuated from *Gush Katif*:

> The settlers are right. What's happening now really resembles the Holocaust […] In the Holocaust, it was hot. Now it's also hot. Now it is exactly like in the Holocaust. In the Holocaust, there were flies. In Tel Aviv there are also flies. Tel Aviv is like the Holocaust […] In the Holocaust, there were six million. In the lottery, there are also six million. The lottery is like the Holocaust […]

Left-wing skits also criticized the victimization narrative of the right-wing in general. They turned against using Holocaust memory to gain favors in the world (by playing the victim card) or in Israel (intimidating voters by reminding them of the past and/or the problematic security situation).

For example, a skit in *It's a Wonderful Country* in 2004 was broadcast after a terror attack in a Sinai desert resort at a time when warnings about travel to the Sinai were issued in the Israeli media. In the skit, a travel agent counsels a couple worried about flying to dangerous places to consider flying to a concentration camp memorial site. When they arrive, the woman comments that she feels safe because of the watchtowers and the electrified fence: they have come to the Auschwitz-Birkenau Museum. This skit criticized the "industry of fear" in Israel (Feldman, 2008; Zertal, 2010), which feeds off recurrent warnings about the likelihood of terrorist attacks. It sparked numerous complaints to Israel's Channel 2, the Television Broadcasting and Radio Authority, as well as to Yad Vashem. Keshet, the show's production company, responded that there had been no intention to ridicule the Holocaust or use its memory as entertainment. Its spokesperson pointed out that *It's a Wonderful Country* is a satirical program whose skits are intended not solely to provoke laughter but also to warn and sometimes shock. He insisted that the skit was an allegory for the state of fear after the recent terror attack in Sinai and warnings regarding overseas travel, which added to the sense of siege (Holler, 2004).

Other satirical texts have expanded the debate on the misuse of Holocaust memory by addressing the instrumentalization of the Holocaust by public figures. A well-known skit by *The Chamber Quintet*, "Feldermaus at the Olympics" [*Feldermaus baolimpyada*], is set in Stuttgart, Germany, during the Olympic Games. Two Jewish-Israeli wheeler-dealers have managed to get onto the track. In broken English spiked with Hebrew and Yiddish, they demand that the official poised with his starting pistol let the Israeli runner start before the other athletes to reduce the "historic injustice" and "to reduce the humiliation." The Israeli athlete, is short and scrawny; he has "legs like toothpicks." Since the Israeli runner seems incapable of competing with the other participants (who are non-Jews) in terms of his physical strength, the wheeler-dealers use a stereotypic Jewish tactic of bargaining, which is accompanied by the quintessentially Israeli quality of chutzpah by tapping into the historical injustice of the Holocaust. They operate in the Jewish *schnorrer* (supplicant/beggar asking for handouts) tradition, combining their dealing with Israeli aggressiveness that soon devolves into curses and threats but ultimately manages to convince the starter to do their bidding.

Uzi Weil, a screenwriter for *The Chamber Quintet* noted that these manipulations of the Holocaust have become unpleasant and disproportional: "Somebody says 'Holocaust,' and everyone shuts up." His view is that the Holocaust has become a mechanism for forcing people to stand at attention whenever the word is spoken mentally; he links this to the "Holocaust industry" that includes the de-rigueur school trips to Poland, the selling of right-wing politics in the guise of sensitivity to the Holocaust, etc. Weil says that using humor to highlight the Holocaust's instrumentalization can counter hypocrisy and close the gap between people's words and genuine emotions (Shifman, 2008). By confronting the pathos-ridden, political exploitation of the Holocaust, the satirists of the "Feldermaus at the Olympics" skit were holding up a mirror to emphasize, through humor, how ridiculous and wrong it is.

In another example, a skit entitled "This Terrible Place" [*Ha'makom ha'nora ha'zeh*] by *The Chamber Quintet* depicts an Israeli prime minister and his entourage who are touring Poland with a crew of security guards and photographers and decide to use the site of mass murder as a photo opportunity. The prime minister asks to be photographed next to a specific tree "in this terrible place." He is not sad or touched while the camera is not on; instead, he is all smiles, cracks jokes, and is entirely detached from the site's significance. When the photographers start filming, he puts on a serious face. All he can do is repeat the mantra, "In this terrible place, in this horrible place, Jews were slaughtered."

In broken English, he mumbles a series of clichés along the lines of "Look at this tree. This holy tree was watered with blood." His movements are ludicrous: he pushes his wife aside and tries to find a place in the center frame above the heads of the still photographers crowding around him. As he is swept away by the metaphor of a tree symbolizing the Jewish people, its roots emblematic of the roots of the Jews whose ancestors were killed next to that tree, a security guard steps away and discovers that they are standing next to the wrong tree and that the right one is a few yards away. The prime minister's embarrassed advisors ask the delegation and photographers to move to the right tree and start again; the politician's wife smiles hypocritically. The politician resumes the same cliché-ridden and detached speech when they reach the right tree. With the very same pathos, he repeats his speech about what happened "in this terrible place."

This skit did not refer to a specific prime minister. It did not name names or use mannerisms to signal a specific individual; instead, the pathetic prime minister in the skit is a synecdoche for politicians who have no real feeling about the trauma and use it as a political instrument. Ami Meir, the producer of *The Chamber Quintet*, maintained that skits citing the Holocaust are intended to show how it has been twisted to respond to a manipulative need to justify actions in the present. In his view, satire is aimed to make the audience realize that the exploitation of the Holocaust is pathetic (Blau, 2004). "When it comes to jokes, the question is always who is being laughed at," says Uzi Weil. "Humor may be a weapon, so who are we actually fighting against? In my skits, I attack the contrast between the bland language we use and how we exploit the emotion surrounding the Holocaust for reasons far from being high-minded" (Blau, 2004).

6.4 Right-Wing Politicians as Nazis

The sections above showed how left-wingers use Holocaust-related humor, satire, and parody to protest right-wingers' statements, policies, and culture of siege. However, left-wingers sometimes use the Holocaust to criticize right-wing politicians and public figures' nationalistic and racist stances.

The examples illustrate how they tackle specific politicians based on his/her statements. In the second season of their TV satire show, *This is our Country [Zu Arzenu]* (Channel 2; Reshet, 2001), satirists Sahi Goldstein and Dror Rephael created a skit criticizing the right-wing's attempts to use the Holocaust to impart nationalistic ideas to Israelis. In the skit, Likud minister Limor Livnat gives Raphael a lesson in Zionism which quickly turns into a lesson in racist nationalism, while acknowledging her with a semblance of a Nazi salute.

In 2006, Knesset (Israeli Parliament) member Avigdor Lieberman suggested exchanging territory with the Palestinian Authority and transferring the Arab citizens of Israel to the Palestinian territory and then compared members of *Yesh Gvul* (a human-rights anti-occupation movement) to Kapos in the Nazi extermination camps. He became the focus of a controversial *It's a Wonderful Country* skit in December 2006. Each time Lieberman's character appeared in the skit, he was greeted with "Heil Lieberman!" and a right-arm salute.

In March 2010, right-wing Knesset member Yaakov Katz circulated a memorandum calling for African asylum seekers who had entered Israel through Egypt to be relocated to a 'distant city' that they would build from scratch through "workfare." Paying homage to the opening sequence of *Inglorious Basterds* (directed by Quentin Tarantino in 2009), an *It's a Wonderful Country* skit (March 2010) addressed the theme of the right-wing's persecution of refugees and illegal migrant workers. It showed Katz, depicted by the actor Tal Friedman, as the Nazi officer, Col. Hans Landa, who hunted down Jews in occupied France. In the skit, Katz is shown going from house to house, evicting asylum seekers and foreign workers. Several of Friedman's lines also repeated memorable quotations from the film.

In May 2012, during a demonstration in South Tel Aviv protesting authorizations to allow African refugees to live, work and stay in Israel, right-wingers attacked African bystanders, shop windows were shattered, and goods were stolen. As part of the left-wing counter protest which extended to the right-wing's attitude toward the refugees from Africa in general, left-wingers posted numerous comparisons to Kristallnacht and caricatures comparing the protestors and their supporters to Nazis on social media. For example, Miri Regev (at the time a Knesset Member), who attended the demonstration, referred to the African refugees and foreign workers as a "cancer in our body." Caricaturist and illustrator Mysh Rozanov published a caricature entitled Kristallnacht, in which Regev approaches a group of Ku Klux Klan members who are saying, "Thanks for coming to complete our minyan, Miri'leh." The Facebook group *Entrecotes from Holy Cows* [*Entrecote mi'parot kdoshot*] uploaded a photograph of a protester wearing a T-shirt with the words "Death to the Sudanese" glued next to a picture of Hitler talking on the phone, giving the illusion that the protester was calling him. They both seem happy with the conversation, and the caption, "No, you hang up," illustrates their loving relationship.

In December 2013, following the refusal of African asylum seekers to be sent to the *Holot* detention facility, a formal document was published in which the asylum seekers were not mentioned by name but given numbers. Many respondents compared the numbers to those tattooed by the Nazis on the arms of Jewish prisoners in Auschwitz. A photograph uploaded to the Facebook page of *It's a Wonderful Country* presented former Minister of Interior Gideon Sa'ar getting ready to tattoo a number on the arm of an anonymous refugee. The photograph caused turmoil and received mixed responses ranging from horrified objections to support. The image was removed from the program's Facebook page a day later.

In October 2022, the most right-wing government in Israel's existence was elected. Among the new politicians given prominent ministries in the new government was Itamar Ben-Gvir, a radical, highly controversial figure who heads the *Jewish Force* [*Otzma Yehudit*] party. For years he supported *Kach*, a racist movement whose key platform is the transfer of Arab Israelis, while displaying a photograph in his living room of Baruch Goldstein, a settler and *Kach* supporter who massacred 29 Palestinians in the Cave of the Patriarchs in Hebron in February 1994. For years Ben Gvir publicly said he adored him. Since the elections and Ben-Gvir's ministerial appointment, left-wingers have frequently compared him to Nazi leaders on social media. For example, in January 2023, Zehava Galon, the former head of the left-wing party *Meretz*, whose party failed to pass the electoral threshold in the last elections, tweeted a picture of Ben Gvir raising his hand in what resembles a Nazi salute with the caption "Heil Kahane" (Meiri, 2023). She later deleted the tweet.

The satirical show *It's a Wonderful Country* has addressed his racist, semi-Nazi traits in many shows. The most obvious comparison to a Nazi appeared in a skit entitled "*It's the Ben-Gvir Time*," perhaps one of the show's most daring skits since it made an obvious comparison between Ben-Gvir and Hitler. In the skit, Netanyahu introduces his "winning card" to escape his pending corruption trial, and then Ben Gvir appears. Ben-Gvir sings and dances as he explains his agenda, accompanied by a chorus wearing T-shirts with the *Kach* logo.

The effect is a grotesque combination of racist violence set to a jaunty song and dance routine. He sings about burning Arab villages and tells Netanyahu that Baruch Goldstein deserves to have his own official day of mourning, that the Jew who deliberately set a fire that incinerated an Arab family should have a pool installed in his cell, and that Yigal Amir, who assassinated left-wing prime minister Yitzhak Rabin, should rapidly be pardoned and released from jail where he is currently serving a life sentence. He promises to transfer all the Arabs, left-wingers, and judges from Israel (as the chorus sings, "the train is leaving" with its clear association to the death convoys). He promises to flatten the Al-Aqsa Mosque and return the LGBTQ community "to the closet." The Netanyahu character explains that Ben-Gvir "has become moderate, no longer extreme and delusional." However, the satire goes much deeper.

The comparison is blunter for those who recognize the tune since it is a satirical homage to "Springtime for Hitler and Germany" from the film *The Producers* (directed and produced by Mel Brooks in 1968), a song and dance routine where the Hitler character describes all the good he will do for Germany. In the film, the audience loves it, and it becomes a tremendous hit to the dismay of the producer characters hoping to claim bankruptcy by producing a flop. In Israel's reality, *It's a Wonderful Country* clarifies that the voters got what they deserved: an imitation of Hitler in the Israeli government.

6.5 Conclusion

Left-wing satirical use of the Holocaust tries to fight what left-wingers perceive as right-wing siege mentality by ridiculing three themes: Prime Minister Netanyahu and his constant use of Holocaust jargon, right-wing politicians' racist stances, and the domestic and international manipulation of Holocaust memory for political purposes. Alongside, this chapter has shown that left-wingers use Holocaust-related associations many times when they want to strengthen their agenda—for example, by creating comparisons between right-wing politicians and Nazis.

There is ample evidence that humor can enable individuals to feel that they are part of a larger group. Humor increases group cohesion and relieves stress within the group. It boosts the group's morale and strengthens the bonds between its members, thus strengthening consensus and minimizing the distance between its members. Humor also creates a common language that emphasizes the group's uniqueness. Aggressive humor mocking other groups emphasizes the superiority of the group using it (Ziv, 1996). The left-wing's political and social Holocaust satire and parody give the defeated left-wing a sense of power. It is used not only to vent frustration but also to create social cohesion and as a political tool to protest against right-wing narratives, and what left-wingers see as distorted connections between the Israeli-Palestinian-Arab conflict, and the manipulation of Holocaust memory for political profit.

References

Bar-Tal, D. (2007). *Living with the conflict.* Carmel (in Hebrew).
Ben-Ari, G. (2020, February 26). *Hitler found a parking place.* Yediot Aharonot (in Hebrew).
Ben-Shaul, N. (1997). *Mythical expressions of siege in Israeli films.* Edwin Mellen.
Ben-Shaul, N. (2006). *Israeli persecution films, traditions in world cinema.* Edinburgh University Press.
Berger, A. L., & Berger, N. (2011). *Second generation voices: Reflections by children of Holocaust survivors and perpetrators.* Syracuse University Press.
Blau, S. (2004, April 22). Did somebody say Holocaust? *Haaretz.* http://www.haaretz.co.il/news/health/1.961589 (in Hebrew).
Burg, A. (2007). *Defeating Hitler.* Yediot Aharonot (in Hebrew).
Cramer, P. (2000). Defence mechanism in psychology today: Further processes for adaptation. *American Psychologist 55,* 637–646.
Efraim, O. & Azulay, M. (2016, May 8). *Netanyahu against the deputy chief of staff: "Injustice, indignities of the Holocaust."* YNET.https://www.ynet.co.il/articles/0,7340,L-4800636,00.html (in Hebrew).
Evron, B. (2011). *Athens and Oz.* Nahar. (in Hebrew).
Feldman, J. (2008). *Above the death pits, beneath the flag: Youth voyages to Poland and the performance of Israeli national identity.* Berghan Press.
Freud, S. (1990). *Jokes and their relation to the unconscious* (The Standard ed.). W. W. Norton & Company.
Gan, A. (2014). *From sovereignty to victimhood: An analysis of victimization discourse in Israel.* The Israel Democracy Institute (in Hebrew).

Goldstein, S., & Rephael, D. (2005, July 29). *Like in the Holocaust*. Ma'ariv. https://www.makorrishon.co.il/nrg/online/1/ART/964/558.html (in Hebrew).

Holler, R. (2004, November 10). *Eretz nehederet pagu berigshot nizolei hashoa [Eretz Nehederet Hurt Holocaust Survivors]*. YNET. https://www.ynet.co.il/articles/0,7340,L-3002314,00.html (in Hebrew).

Meiri, G. (2023, January 25). *Former Meretz chief blasted for tweet comparing Ben-Gvir to Nazis*. YNET. https://www.ynetnews.com/article/skzcwcaoi (in Hebrew).

Meyers, O., Neiger, M., & Zandberg, E. (2014). *Communicating awe: Media memory and Holocaust commemoration*. Palgrave Macmillan.

Ne'eman Arad, G. (2003). Israel and the Shoah: A tale of multifarious taboos. *New German Critique, 90*, 5–26.

Ofer, D. (2013). We Israelis remember, but how? The memory of the Holocaust and the Israeli experience. *Israel Studies, 18*(2), 70–85.

Ophir, A. (2001). *Working for the present: Essays on contemporary Israeli culture*. Hakibbutz Hameuhad (in Hebrew).

Ostrower, H. (2009). *Without humor we would have killed ourselves*. Yad Vashem (in Hebrew).

Pinchevski, A., & Brand, R. (2007). Holocaust perversions: The Stalags pulp fiction and the Eichmann trial. *Critical Studies in Media Communication, 24*(5), 387–407.

Pinchevski, A., & Liebes, T. (2010). Severed voices: Radio and the mediation of trauma in the Eichmann trial. *Public Culture, 22*(2), 265–291.

Porat, D. (2011). The smoke-scented coffee: The encounter of the Yishuv and Israeli society with the Holocaust and its survivors. Yad Vashem & Am Oved (in Hebrew).

Reshet. (2001). *This is our country* (in Hebrew).

Rosenfeld, A. (2013). *The end of the Holocaust*. Indiana University Press.

Rosenfeld, G. D. (2015). *Hi Hitler: How the Nazi past is being normalised in contemporary culture*. Cambridge University Press.

Shifman, L. (2008). *Televised humor and social cleavages in Israel, 1968–2000*. Hebrew University Magnes Press (in Hebrew).

Shifman, L. (2013). *Memes in digital culture*. MIT Press.

Steir-Livny, L. (2009). *Two faces in the mirror: The image of Holocaust survivors in Israeli cinema*. Eshkolot-Magnes (in Hebrew).

Steir-Livny, L. (2014). *Let the memorial hill remember*. Resling (in Hebrew).

Zertal, I. (1993). *The nation and death*. Dvir (in Hebrew).

Ziv, A. (1996). *Personality and sense of humor*. Papyrus (in Hebrew).

Liat Steir-Livny is an Associate Professor at Sapir Academic College and the Open University of Israel. She teaches in the Department of Culture at Sapir Academic College and in the Department of Literature, Language, and the Arts at the Open University of Israel. Her research focuses on Holocaust commemoration in Israel from the 1940s until the present. It combines Holocaust studies, memory studies, cultural studies, trauma studies, and film studies. She is the author of many articles and six books.

Part II
Ethno-National Humor in Religion, Art, and Popular Culture

Chapter 7
Cultural Wars in Polish Political Humor

Dorota Brzozowska and Władysław Chłopicki

Abstract This chapter focuses on the rich tradition of political humor in Poland. The aim of the chapter is to point out how Polish culture, in the broad sense of the term, is reflected in different genres of political humor. The discussion and examples will concern the sources of political humor, including religion, class system, literary tradition, art, film, and popular culture in general. A distinct source of humor is socio-political polarization that currently takes the shape of conservative and liberal sides of the political debate, but the opposing sides of the political scene used to vary over the course of history of Poland, with the main vectors remaining similar (e.g. traditional, patriarchal/progressive, Christian/atheist, patriotic-nationalist/cosmopolitan, Polish/Western, Polish/Russian-Soviet, communist/anti-communist, and generally high/low stature), and it is these that have inspired political humor. In recent decades new genres have appeared, forcing a change of style, although rhetorical techniques have remained largely the same—irony, parody, allusion, or intertextuality have prevailed. We will draw on the Discourse Humor Theory to analyze particular instances of humor in the public sphere.

7.1 Introduction: Historical Overview

Political humor in Poland has a very rich tradition that we have described e.g., in the volume on Polish humor (Brzozowska & Chłopicki, 2012). There is little room here to discuss it in great detail, but we can point out what can be considered milestones.

The 16th century was the golden age of Poland, the time of political stability and economic development, but also the time when political and social satire thrived. The court of King Sigismund I (reigned 1507–1548) is associated with the presence of the court jester by the name of Stańczyk, who became known as a sage hiding under the

---

D. Brzozowska (✉)
Institute of Linguistics, University of Opole, Opole, Poland
e-mail: dbrzozowska@uni.opole.pl

W. Chłopicki
Institute of English Studies, Jagiellonian University, Kraków, Poland
e-mail: w.chlopicki@uj.edu.pl

© The Author(s), under exclusive license to Springer Nature Singapore Pte Ltd. 2024
O. Feldman (ed.), *Political Humor Worldwide*, The Language of Politics,
https://doi.org/10.1007/978-981-99-8490-9_7

guise of a clown. His characteristic figure, wearing a red cloak and jester's hat, was immortalized by painters and became the icon of wisdom, but also a sarcastic sense of humor (Matejko, 1862, see Fig. 3). He was apparently the only person who could rebuke the all-powerful king, without suffering any consequences. For example, when one day the king fell ill and was treated with leeches, as was the custom of the day, Stańczyk compared leeches stuck onto his body to courtiers. Noticing that leeches dropped off when full, he said, "Behold, friends of lords! They hold while they drink blood, they fall off, as they are filled with it" (Krzyżanowski, 1958, p. 343; quoted after Lemann, 2012, p. 21; clearly a high-low stature opposition). On another occasion, he complained to the king that he was assaulted, and his cloak was stolen. The king scolded him for losing it, whereupon the jester retorted (referring to the recently lost battle with Muscovy at Smolensk): "You have been robbed worse: Smolensk was robbed of you, and you are quiet" (Lipiec, 2017).

The best-known example of political satire in the 17th century were the memoirs of Hieronim Pasek (written in 1690–1695), where "he portrays the nobility and its many vices, such as squabbling, drunkenness, gambling, autocracy and aversion to any authority or manic litigation and demanding satisfaction for every damage to the honour by duelling" (Lemann, 2012, p. 24). The 18th century, as the age of Enlightenment, witnessed the publication of the first Polish novel written by Ignacy Krasicki, entitled "The Adventures of Mikołaj Doświadczyński" (Krasicki, 1776/1910); the last name of the protagonist translates as "Experiencer"). The key line of the plot was his escape from Poland to the island of Nipu, because "[t]he gentry society was corroded with an incurable disease of brawling, selfishness, drunkenness and pursuit of self-interest instead of the purpose of the state, and an honourable man like Mikołaj could implement the educational achievements of Nipu only among his family and serfs" (Lemann, 2012, p. 28).

The novelist and Nobel prize winner Henryk Sienkiewicz (1846–1916), author of well-known Polish historical novels, created the iconic character of a 17th-century nobleman, Jan Onufry Zagłoba (sometimes compared to Shakespeare's Falstaff), who preferred drinking over fighting, and was the master of cunning and wit, too. Some of his quotes entered the repertoire of Polish sayings, such as: "The devil put on the chasuble and is ringing for the mass with his tail"—a comment on somebody's hypocrisy. His sayings were often comments on the events he was taking part in, posing for general truths to achieve the desired effects e.g., "When father is missing, there you will obey the uncle, as the scriptures say" (Sienkiewicz, 1866: 34; our translation), a (successful although deceitful) way to convince his rather dim-witted guard that they were relatives (which they were not), and that he should be let free (which he was; evoking another clear example of high-low stature opposition).

Witold Gombrowicz (1904–1969) was the *enfant terrible* of Polish literature during the interwar period, but at the same time a brilliant satirist, unmasker of pomposity especially among Polish nobility, intellectuals, teachers, or the middle class. In his novels, he did not refrain from a colloquial style and ridiculed the patriotic habits of the Polish school. Gombrowicz's (1937) novel *Ferdydurke*, for instance, included the scene where a frog is slipped down the blouse of "an ideal Polish girl," or one where pupils engage in a face-making duel. Teachers are mocked, too e.g.,

Professor Pimko (a humorous name, perhaps a wordplay on *piwko*—a diminutive for beer), a highly cultured philologist from Krakow, short and thinly built, with prominently yellow nails, who forced into his students' heads that "Słowacki[1] was a great poet" (Lemann, 2012, p. 117).

Sławomir Mrożek (1930–2013) followed Gombrowicz in his love of absurd humor. In his short stories and mock dramas, he brilliantly reflected the difficult circumstances of everyday life that Polish society experienced under the communist system. For example, in the classical short story "The Elephant" (Mrożek, 1957/1962), he created the figure of a progressive director of a zoological garden who wanted to save money for the country and thus decided not to import an elephant but rather install its rubber dummy. When a group of school children arrived at the zoo and listened to the fact-filled talk on elephants as the largest and heaviest land animals, the gust of wind blew the dummy into the air and the lie was exposed (very much like clumsy lies of communist propaganda). Children were left to cope with the aftermath, and their lives were derailed as a result.

At the time of communism in Poland (1945–1989), political humor thrived, with thousands of political jokes being told in private conversations as a way of getting at communist officials, as usurpers who were not democratically elected (cf. Davies, 1990). Dymel (1994, pp. 183–184) distinguished six categories of targets of political jokes circulating in Poland before 1989:

(1) all leaders and communist party activists;
(2) official institutions, such as the communist party, the police, the paramilitary force;
(3) the oppressive character of the regime and its totalitarian nature;
(4) communist slogans;
(5) shortages of basic products on the market;
(6) the Russian people and the U.S.S.R.

An example of the latter: "Why do we call the U.S.S.R. 'our brother' and not 'our friend?' Because you can choose a friend" (Świątkowicz-Mośny, 2012, p. 433).

Political humor at the time could be considered a sort of defense strategy. Political jokes tried to explain the reality in a way that was different from official propaganda and thus "constituted the oasis of freedom. Today, part of the jokes is not understood by young citizens of the free Poland, others may still be funny without historical context, and some have been adapted to new conditions and, for example, instead of stupid militiamen we now have stupid blondes" (Świątkowicz-Mośny, 2012, p. 434). Describing political humor in Poland, one notices that after the year 1989, it "lost a little of its attractiveness of the 'forbidden fruit.' A political situation in which everything can be said does not foster sophisticated form, craftily hidden prohibited content from the eye of censorship in the thicket of innocent words or 'smuggling' information in a brilliant and smart way" (Dymel, 1994, p. 186).

One other Polish tradition that is very characteristic, although somewhat elusive, is the artistic poster style not lacking in humor. The term "The Polish School of

---

[1] 19th century Romantic poet, see below.

Poster Art" was coined in 1960 by Lenica (1960, quoted in Schubert, 2008, p. 55), who wrote in *Graphis*, a prestigious Swiss journal devoted to graphic design that:

> The poster has become to Poland what the woodcut of Espinal was to France and the contemporary woodcut to Mexico: it has achieved the rank of a distinct Polish school due to its universality and quantity[…]. [overall, its unifying feature is that] the Polish poster is romantic and this romanticism is displayed in an entire gradations of tones: from lyrical to the pathetic-heroic.

Here are just a few examples of the political posters from very different periods and famous in very different ways. The first one played on the style of Bolshevik posters, usually presenting enemies as disgusting and grotesque, blood-thirsty, sometimes ape-like, but on other occasions ridiculing them as small and clumsy. An example is "the work of an unknown author, 'And don't creep inside, you bastard!'… that quite comically portrays a Bolshevik slammed by a door. Here the aggressor is represented as a troublesome neighbour whose trespass can be handled with humour, by quickly shutting the door in his face" (Libura & Kiełbawska, 2012, p. 317).

The related poster authored by Włodzimierz Zakrzewski (1945/2023) visualized the abusive label of the enemy of communism, that of a "reactionary dwarf spitting on himself," which was virtually ever present in the 1940s and 1950s. The furious but essentially helpless dwarf (the somewhat comic incongruity), which spits everywhere, including on the large and powerful communist soldier and himself, was to symbolize the Polish underground Home Army: it had fought against the German occupation and remained loyal to the legal Polish government in London after the Soviet-installed government had taken power in Poland in 1945. Zakrzewski allegedly regretted having designed the poster in the face of the communist government's ruthless policies, including the persecution of Home Army soldiers, torture, executions, and deportations to Siberia.

Another poster was designed by Sarnecki (1989), then a student of the Academy of Fine Arts, and became the symbol of the first free elections in Poland after five decades of communist oppression. The image on the poster is a clear visual allusion to the western film "High Noon" by Fred Zinnemann, which stars Gary Cooper as the brave sheriff Will Cane who fearlessly walks alone to face an uneven fight against bandits. In the poster, he is recontextualized (see the next section for explanation of the term) and placed against the background of the Solidarity trade union banner (the symbol of anti-communist opposition at that time); he also wears the Solidarity badge above his sheriff star and holds a ballot card in his hand. The clash of contexts obviously had a humorous but primarily persuasive effect.

The poster was recontextualized at least twice in recent years, once for women's strike (Humour in the European public sphere, n.d.) and once for the sake of the political opposition's march on June 4, 2023. The latter poster (Fig. 7.1) features Donald Tusk, the former President of the European Council and present leader of the largest opposition party in Poland; the same film title has been turned into an election slogan, and in a humorous twist, it is accompanied by the eight stars, which in the Poland of 2020s came to symbolize the opposition against the populist government of Law and Justice (PIS) party: they stand for the five-letter and three-letter words

Fig. 7.1 "High Noon", June 4, 2023. *Source* Opposition march poster, 2023

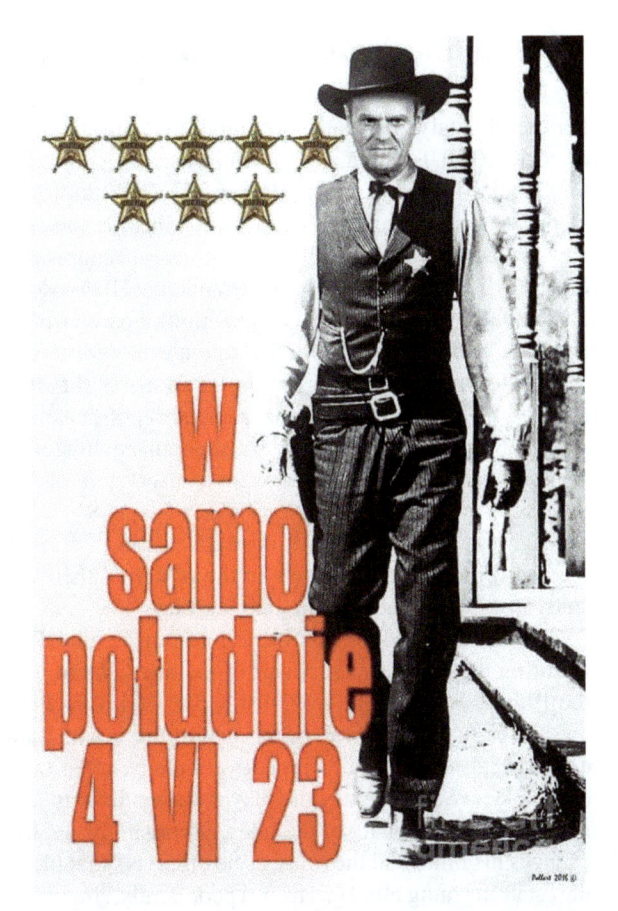

forming the slogan—*Jebać Pis* (Fuck PIS). The fact that the latter slogan made such an impact (at some point it even gave rise to the "8-star movement") is significant in itself. The type of humor considered acceptable by the intellectual public (a large part of the opposition electorate) does not normally include obscenities, thus replacing each letter of the slogan with a star is a pragmatic solution to the problem. It also reminds one of the strategies of struggle against the communist regime (not only in Poland), where the symbolism was a highly successful strategy (e.g. in 1982 after the martial law was declared, a lot of people wore resistors [ ] attached to their coats or lapels).

7.2 Cultural Sources and Inspirations of Political Humor

In order to analyze instances of humor to be discussed below, the Discourse Humor Theory (DTH; Tsakona, 2020) will be used as a point of departure. DTH is based on the General Theory of Verbal Humor (GTVH; Attardo & Raskin, 1991). The analysis of the text according to GTVH should include the following elements: language, narrative strategy, target, situation, logical mechanism, and script opposition. DTH broadens the GTVH by adding three analytical foci—sociocultural assumptions (with contextually based humorous opposition), genre (with typical narrative strategies), and text, bringing to the fore the notion of humor as a form of recontextualization. These are important factors in our analysis, as the discussion below concerns the recontextualization of traditional sources of political humor, including religion, class system, literary tradition, art, film and popular culture in general, as well as the current socio-political polarization between conservative and liberal sides of the political divide.

We first present four short illustrative cases of current visual political humor that are based on specific conflicts of the past, and then will present an extended case study inspired by most of these as a group.

The first example uses a screen shot from the film "Barrel Organ" (Jędryka, 1967), featuring the barrel organ player of the title. The film was the screen adaptation of the 19th century novella by Polish writer Bolesław Prus. The plot tells the story of the player who is banned from visiting the internal yard of a Warsaw residential estate because the organ's repetitive melody, often out of tune, irritates the owner of the place. Still, one day the player makes his way into the yard, because the new gatekeeper is not aware of the rules. Surprisingly, the owner does not scold him and changes his mind and the rules, as he discovers that the tunes make a new resident of the estate, a young blind girl from a poor family, singularly happy. The meme achieves a sophisticated metaphorical effect by cleverly superimposing the smiling head of Jarosław Kaczyński, leader of a political party called Law and Justice, on the head of the original player, even retaining the original beret on his head. The two photos at the bottom of the meme represent the heads of the former Prime Minister, Beata Szydło (2015–2017), and populist President Andrzej Duda (from 2015 onwards). They look like they are singing, while Kaczyński is playing false tunes on his barrel organ and smiling at the success of his cunning plan. Thus, the sociocultural context evokes the oppositions populist/progressive, democratic/autocratic, contributing to the interpretation of the meme: the carrier of populist values plays false, repetitive tunes that please the public, but they are generally harmful.

Another meme example features a similar humorous superimposition of the head of a current conservative politician upon that of Marshal Józef Piłsudski. During World War I, he was a commander of Polish military units (called Legions), and then leader of the Polish State in the years 1918–1935, who won the war against Soviet Russia of 1920. The meme is based on a painting by Kazimierz Sichulski (1917, see Fig. 7.2), where Piłsudski (in the foreground) is portrayed as a strong military leader wearing a uniform and holding a sword, with two figures flanking him: The

Fig. 7.2 "Piłsudski with Stańczyk and Wernyhora." *Source* Sichulski, 1917

jester Stańczyk on the left, and Wernyhora—the 17th-century Ukrainian bard and visionary, on the right. The Wernyhora figure is meaningful too, as he prophesied the future of the Ukraine and the independence of Poland and perhaps could be taken to symbolize Piłsudski's attempt to unite both nations within one democratic state during World War I. Wernyhora was also a protagonist of Polish 19th century Romantic literature (especially Juliusz Słowacki's epic poems), where he became the symbol of resurrected Poland.

Notably, Piłsudski was popularly and affectionately, and also somewhat jocularly nicknamed *Dziadek*—Grandpa (see the case study section below). The painting itself earned the related nickname too: "'The Grandpa' in the company the jester and the prophet" (Łanuszka, n.d.). Due to the presence of the two side figures, the painting is more of a powerful allegory than a caricature, especially that at the time when it was painted Piłsudski was a legendary figure held in prison by the Germans, only to be released in November 1918, taking power in Poland.

The politician whose head replaces Piłsudski's in the meme is the highly controversial Antoni Macierewicz, former anti-communist, democratic, opposition activist in the 1970s, then minister of the interior and defense in consecutive right-wing governments. He became notorious in the 1990s by pressing for the vetting of active politicians against (dubious) communist police archives to discover any connections with the communist system and possibly remove them from public life. Then he caused another major controversy in the 2010s by pushing the groundless claim that the Smolensk plane crash in 2010 was actually a willful assassination of the Polish leaders by the Russians. During his term as minister of defense, he insisted on a public reading of the list of the "assassination victims" during every public commemoration ceremony, regardless of what it was, as well as on the exhumation of all the victims even against their families' wishes. Overall, he is seen as a strong-willed nationalist politician who is obsessed with fixed ideas and willing to achieve them at any cost and regardless of the potential effect. Thus, his portrayal in the meme as a country leader is deeply ironic and more caricature-like than the original. This context evokes the humorous oppositions communist/ anti-communist, nationalist/ democratic, or Polish/Soviet, and enables the interpretation of the key figure as being an impostor.

The third example is a meme featuring Stańczyk again as he was portrayed by Jan Matejko (see Fig. 7.3). This time it is a backdrop for a verbal recontextualization of the original scene, where the jester is concerned about the future of the country. The three captions refer to three different but equally worrying situations that occurred in 2022/2023 in Poland. The first one (a Russian rocket flying towards Bydgoszcz) is a worry related to the military, connected to the stray Russian[2] rocket which flew over Poland from Belarus in December 2022 and landed unnoticed in a forest in a central part of the country, near the city of Bydgoszcz. It was not discovered until April 2023 when a horse rider noticed it on his ride through the forest (Kmiecik & Makarewicz, 2023). It was followed by a big political row and calls for dismissal of Minister of Defense as incompetent, as the fact that the rocket over which apparently the Russians had lost control was able to fly into Poland undetected raised justified worries of how well Poland airspace is protected.

The second concern is a social one. The second caption (Ball in the opera with [Minister] Czarnek) alludes to the lavish birthday party organized for a friend and collaborator of the controversial Minister of Science and Education, Przemysław Czarnek (in government since 2020) (Fakt.pl, 2023). The party was organized in Wrocław Opera House in February 2023 and was accompanied by a banquet held on stage of the opera house, following the performance of the opera "La Boheme," with the Minister and his retinue not paying for tickets and for the party. The caption is also an intertextual reference to the famous satirical poem by Julian Tuwim (1894–1953; a well-known and highly talented poet, writer, and satirist of Jewish origin) entitled "Ball in the Opera," written in 1936 (not published as a whole until 1982). The poem deals with the debauchery and corruption of Polish social and political elites (including the clergy) in the 1930s. The caption in the meme is intended to emphasize the applicability of the pre-war poem to the current situation.

---

[2] Notably, in the meme the adjective *ruska* is used for the comic effect, stereotypically implying primitivism or bad construction. (such lexical choices constitute the Text focus in Tsakona's (2020) DTH system).

7 Cultural Wars in Polish Political Humor   125

Fig. 7.3 Stańczyk's concerns 2023. *Source* Kwejk.pl, 2023a

The third caption (Lex [Donald] Tusk) refers to the new law passed by the ruling party in the Polish Parliament in May 2023, ostensibly in an effort to establish a state commission with the powers of a court that would investigate Russian influence in the Polish state over the last two decades. The aim of the commission was to deny civil rights for up to ten years to the public figures found guilty of treason. The new law was dubbed "lex Tusk," since this was the election campaign period, elections to be held in October, and Donald Tusk as the leader of the largest opposition party and candidate for the next Prime Minister had been publicly accused by government politicians and media of having pursued pro-Russian policies when he was in office as Prime Minister (2007–2014). Both the European Parliament and the European Commission, as well as the US government, expressed their concern over the new law that could influence the democratic process in Poland.

As can be seen, this meme evokes past-present, Polish-Russian, Polish-European oppositions, and in addition raised the issue of the corruption/abuse of power (the same problems raised in early Polish political satires mentioned at the outset). Stańczyk as a clown character and comic figure in an old-fashioned trickster suit triggers a humorous reading especially when set in a contemporary political context. Envisaging 21st century politicians as courtiers in the supposedly democratic and not monarchist country, altogether with all the clever hints to recent scandalous events bring at least smile on the viewers' faces. Skillfully combining the old painting with three different current stories, the meme is an example of sophisticated, highly contextual, witty, even if slightly pessimistic type of humor, culturally characteristic for Polish intellectuals.

Finally, the last example is a cartoon by renowned Kraków cartoonist Andrzej Mleczko (2021) with the caption: "Find ten details that make these drawings distinct." There we can see two similar scenes—on the right there's a group of three Polish workers marching along the street protesting against the West, shouting "Away with Western decay," carrying the red flag with hammer and sickle, portraits of Lenin, the communist newspaper *Trybuna Ludu* in hand, coursebooks on Marxism in the pockets, and the names of Marx, Engels, and Lenin on their T-shirts. On the right, the same workers in the same poses protest against the EU, shouting "Away with the European Union," carrying the Polish flag, the religiously inspired newspaper *Nasz Dziennik* in hand, prayer books in pockets, and the slogan "God, honor, fatherland" (in the same font as before) on their T-shirts. This obviously ironic humor draws attention to the old dichotomies of tradition and progress, democracy and religion, populism and mature democracy having taken a new shape, although the workers seem to have acquired better boots (compared to the original wellies).

Thus, to conclude this section, it is worth drawing attention to sources of inspiration of political humor, including the dichotomies: tradition/progress, communism/anti-communism, democracy/autocracy-nationalism, corruption/honesty, Poland-Russia/Soviet Union, Poland-Europe, Christianity/atheism, democracy/religion, populism/mature democracy. The genres of humor included internet memes and cartoons recontextualizing cultural resources such as film or painting (evoking various sociocultural assumptions discussed above). We focused on mainly literary rhetorical techniques such as irony, parody, allusion, intertextual reference, and on targets of humor who were mainly political figures.

7.2.1 Case Study—Dziad(y)

Taking into account Wierzbicka's (1997) idea that cultures can be understood through their key words, we will look more closely at one particular key word that we find important for Polish culture, that of *dziad(y)*, in order to show the interplay between political humor and various cultural concepts that draw on Polish tradition. In the humorous material connected with concept of *dziad(y)*, one can find all the major Polish dichotomies, in which the country was always entangled: Positivist/Romantic; Christian/atheist, communist/anti-communist, Soviet/Western, pro-European/anti-European, patriotic/cosmopolitan, patriarchal/progressive.

7.2.1.1 Definition

Literally, *dziad* (pl. *dziady*) is a slightly obsolete term for an ancestor, grandfather, that when used today could be taken as an augmentative, since the contemporary form is *dziadek*. But it also means a loser, beggar, or tramp, with the related adjective *dziadowski* meaning poor and shabby, and the verb *dziadować* as well as the phrase *zejść na dziady* both meaning leading a miserable life or losing the status/

lowering quality. *Dziady* (Forefather's Eve) is also a title of the most popular literary work of Mickiewicz (1823).

7.2.1.2 Adam Mickiewicz (1798–1855)

Mickiewicz is considered to be the top Romantic poet and first bard of the nation during the time of foreign partitions as well as a symbol of the Polish language and identity. The poet, who wrote literature even in exile and was also an ardent columnist, political activist, and visionary, had an interesting life spent in many countries. Thus, even though he is a symbol of Polishness and patriotism he could also be called cosmopolitan as well as drunkard and womanizer. There is probably no town or city without a street that bears his name. His monuments are erected in central places, and he is treated as a sacred national treasure. His works are mandatory reading in schools as part of the canon literature, so it is little wonder that he is a target of humorous material. For example, the ironic memes say: "Adam Mickiewicz. Born in Belarus, he wrote his most famous book in France, and in it he wrote in Polish that Lithuania was his homeland" (Jeja.pl, n.d.), or "Please do not point out my youth errors. I did not know you would discuss all this in school. I was stoned. I swear" (Stejk.org, 2021).

The dichotomies characteristic of Polish culture are visible also in the "duel" between the heritage of Mickiewicz and his younger colleague and rival Juliusz Słowacki (1809–1849). What is interesting, even when the two represent the same literary trends—they are both Romantic poets—they still tend to split the audience into two separate groups of supporters. The animosity of the two main poets is a topic of multiple allusive memes (see e.g., Fig. 7.4 where Mickiewicz himself ironically uses the word *dziad* (loser) in reference to Słowacki (who was a posh youngster and used drugs to support inspiration), thus evoking the high-low stature dichotomy). Humor here lies in the contrast between highly elaborated style of the poet, perceived as skillful creator of the sublime language and user of Polish alexandrine verse lines, and vicious and offensive language not fitting his authority and role-model status. This type of language makes him easier for regular teenagers to identify with him, when they have to learn Mickiewicz's complicated verses by heart and have a good reason not to like him for creating them. Contemporary sun-glasses make him look like a spy or gangster, which adds an extra flavor to the humorous perception of his sad face image. Mickiewicz is a quintessence of Polishness, and as such he also is a political figure. His importance for Polish identity was acknowledged also by those who wanted to destroy it, e.g. Germans during World War II (on August 17, 1940) purposefully demolished his monument in Krakow's central square, which they renamed Adolf-Hitler-Platz.

Fig. 7.4 "Słowacki? Even I have not seen such a loser." *Source* Demotywatory.pl, 2023

7.2.1.3 Dziady

In *Dziady*, Adam Mickiewicz describes pre-Christian traditions connected with celebrations of ancestors' ghosts. This drama is actually a trilogy, a cornerstone of Polish religious and Romantic mythology. The poet compared the historical trauma of Poland's loss of independence, its oppression and struggle to regain it, to the sacrifice of Jesus, thus giving Polish history a metaphysical, religious meaning. The common motif of all three plays is contact between humans and their ancestor spirits, particularly during the special celebration of the ancestors which took place on the eve of November 1- All Saints Day (especially in today Belarus, where the poet was born) and was referred to as Dziady. The rituals described in the drama are seemingly Christian, but in fact, they come from a much older, pagan heritage, the relics of which have been retained (cf. Zembaty, n.d.).

This opposition between Christianity and paganism has been enhanced by the addition of the previously uncelebrated holiday, Halloween, on the same night of the eve of November 1, and is widely seen as a result of the Americanization and globalization of Polish culture. Thus, it is a common topic of memes, cartoons and demotivational posters appearing mostly around the October 30 each year. In Fig. 7.5, the female teacher of religion (saying: "In my time, Halloween was not celebrated.") is irritated by the student implication that she is old—as old as Dziady ("In your time, Dziady was celebrated."), her vulgar reaction ("Are you fucking kidding me?") evoking the religion/obscenity opposition. This is a highly political issue related to the strong division of Polish people into those who accept and admire the West and are eager to be part of the global, American-like culture, and those who are more traditional—often religious Catholics. An extra layer of this heated political discussion is also about teaching religion at public schools. Some see it as an achievement introduced after the fall of communism in Poland, a return to pre-war traditions, while others see it as an imposition of church power over the state politics. Also

7 Cultural Wars in Polish Political Humor

Fig. 7.5 Religion teacher. *Source* M.komixxy.pl, 2023

some religious people see the negative side of teaching religion at schools (and not in parish halls); there religion is perceived as one more ordinary and often boring course—the drowsy student in Fig. 7.5 ostentatiously shows his lack of interest in the subject, even if he then wakes up to make a critical comment.

The cartoon by Iskra (2022) entitled "Dziady" uses the same tradition/modernity opposition in the new context of the war in Ukraine. It consists of two panels depicting a scene from the life of a man during the shortages of electricity: the first is a closeup of his head where we can see him talking on the phone and claiming he does not celebrate Halloween but Dziady, like a true Pole. In the second panel, it turns out he is lying on the couch. In a punchline, he explains to his interlocutor: "I am sitting at home, with the power switched off," thus alluding to the above-mentioned poverty implied by *dziady* in the other sense of the word.

7.2.1.4 *Dziad* and *Spieprzaj Dziadu*

Dziad as a traditional figure is also a contemporary derogative term. The "*spieprzaj dziadu*" phrase (Please piss off, old geezer) entered the repertoire of Polish idioms, and became a reference to the later Polish President (in office 2005–2010) Lech Kaczyński's actual reaction to an insistent heckler in 2002, when he was campaigning as a candidate for the Mayor of Warsaw. This phrase experienced a comeback with the series of sick disaster jokes (cf. Brzozowska, 2010) after the presidential airplane crashed on April 10, 2010, killing him, his wife, and many prominent politicians. It reappears in anti-government protests and is now often used in relation to Lech Kaczyński's twin brother Jarosław, emphasizing the high/low stature dichotomy.

The cartoon by Mosor (2021), which features the phrase, represents the scene on November 1 when money is collected for the renovation of old tombs in the old Powązki Cemetery in Warsaw, where many famous Poles are buried. The collector apparently encounters a contingent of Dziady celebrators from the preceding night who interrupt his efforts, resembling more vagrant beggars than pagans. The donation collector wants to dismiss them and for the purpose, he uses the phrase in the imperative: *Spieprzać dziady*!!! (Piss off, geezers) thus evoking the humorous tradition/modernity opposition as well as referring to the late president's infamous behavior.

7.2.1.5 *Dziady* as Basic Knowledge Resource

Lack of knowledge and ignorance about national literature (including the *Dziady* drama) among politicians is also a subject of numerous memes. An example is the meme (Kwejk.pl, 2023b) where Prime Minister Mateusz Morawiecki, well known for the intentional inaccuracies he serves to the public, meets with some local folk group in traditional outfits, in characteristic surroundings of religious symbols: the portrait of Pope John Paul II and the cross on the wall. Morawiecki makes an emotional speech: "I love folk culture, my favorite book is "The Wedding" by Rejtan, or maybe it was Rejent. In any case, he nicely described the Dziady ritual" in which he makes a fool of himself, by nonchalantly mixing up three canonical literary works: the drama *The Wedding* by Stanisław Wyspiański (1901), where folk culture was indeed central, comedy *The Revenge* by Aleksander Fredro (1838), where one of the protagonists involved in the central feud was Rejent (Lawyer), and *Dziady*.

7.3 *Dziady* in the Theater

7.3.1 Background—Warsaw 1968

The story of *Dziady* performances is interesting, especially during the communist period. Then the play was considered to express anti-Russian or anti-Soviet as well as pro-religion sentiments, and thus its performances were looked upon with suspicion by the authorities. One particular performance went down in history as uniquely important: the staging by Kazimierz Dejmek from 1967. "His staging of 'Forefather's Eve' was loyal to Mickiewicz's original… though he embellished these with a highly personal interpretation" (Raszewski, 1981). The play was performed 14 times, but then was publicly criticized by the Central Committee of the Polish United Workers' Party, and finally the performances were called off on January 30, 1969. The public was enraged and protested. As one of the participants of the protests recalled: "Our actions were nothing out of the ordinary, were simply the reaction of young people […] to yet another instance of censorship in the theater world" (Holoubek & Dziewulska, 1999, p. 5). The protests precipitated a series of unexpected events: Dejmek was sacked as director of the National Theater in Warsaw, and soon after, the nation-wide students protests of March 1968 started, followed by an anti-intellectual and anti-Semitic smear campaign by the authorities; the ban on *Dziady* was widely regarded as the stimulus for all these events (cf. Culture.pl, n.d.).

7.3.2 Kraków 2021

History likes to repeat itself, and so the Law and Justice authorities reacted negatively to the new staging of *Dziady* in the Juliusz Słowacki theater in Kraków, directed by Maja Kleczewska in 2021, on the 120th anniversary of the first performance of the play. The official message on the theater website was bound to evoke reactions, as it argued that:

> Two Polands are [part of] our daily life—two nations fighting against each other. And poets stand lonely between the warring sides. Nobody needs poets. […] Like in a ghastly nightmare, we dream the same story over and over again, and we fail as humans. Conservative Poland wants to appropriate poets. To shut their mouths. It wants to appropriate national history, to rewrite it. It wants to write an idyllic, heroic, and innocent story. You can suffocate from this innocence. Drawing-room Poland, conformist, without ideas for the future, wants only abundance and peace. This repetitive drama seems to have no end. Today it is clearly visible.

We are blinded by it. Not seeing a solution. The poet's voice sounds distinct and tragic in this world (Dziady in Słowacki Theater, 2021; our translation).

This announcement was supported by specific stage decisions, such as casting an actress to play the main male character, Konrad (although the character came out as unisex, rather than female), as well making specific references to contemporary life: the Dziady ceremony at the cemetery features a confrontation between throng of right-wing militants and religious fanatics on the one hand, and an LGBTQ person, Jew, and prostitute, on the other hand, with the Polish flag being used as a weapon (cf. the Mosor cartoon described above).

The performance caused nationwide outrage, with the local Superintendent for Education calling for school groups not to attend the play. The Minister of Culture followed suit: he called the performance a *dziadostwo* (here meaning rubbish, an obvious pun on the play's title, invoking the high-low stature dichotomy), called for the theater director's resignation and initiated the procedure for his replacement (this has not been effective, though, and the play continued with packed houses). As a not unexpected result, the tickets for the performances were sold out for months.

In the discussion of the whole affair, associations with 1968 were emphasized, as in Fig. 7.6. In the meme, the main protagonists of the American box office hit from 1985, "Back to the Future," are reading the headline from the newspaper they have found on having arrived in 2021 in Poland ("I recommend not to organize school trips to see the performance of *Dziady* by Mickiewicz. In my assessment, it is disgraceful to use the work of the national bard for the sake of political struggle of the contemporary, anti-government opposition against the Polish national interest," wrote the Superintendent for Education of the Małopolska Region) and conclude that they must have mistakenly arrived in 1968 ("My God, Marty! We are not in 2021, but in 1968!!"). The meme also evokes the oppositions between Poland and the West as well as generally between local and global events.

The cartoon by Mario Niepoważnie (2021), in turn, plays on the popularity of the play condemned by the government. We can see the office of the Superintendent with appropriate decorations: a big cross in the middle of the wall against the huge Polish flag flanked by two significant portraits: the Pope (probably Pope Francis, but he looks more like Bart Simpson), and Jarosław Kaczyński with his pet cat. A representative of a rival Krakow theater comes to ask the Superintendent for the favor of condemning a play (saying: "Good morning, Madam Superintendent. I come from Stary Theater. Would you mind publicly denouncing something from our repertoire? I will pay if necessary").

Regarding the role of the above-mentioned city of Kraków, the former capital of Poland (still proud of it) and the place of the coronation and burial of most Polish kings, as a cultural resource in Polish humor, two brief examples from recent political demonstrations in Kraków will be illustrative. Both draw on the distinct dialect spoken in Kraków and the surrounding area, its best known expression being "*na pole*" (lit. into the field), meaning outside, while the equivalent, spoken elsewhere in Poland, particularly in Warsaw the seat of government, is "*na dwór*" (it is often misunderstood as meaning "to the manor," although it actually literally means "into

7 Cultural Wars in Polish Political Humor 133

Fig. 7.6 "Back to the Future" in Poland: Michael Fox and Christopher Llyod. *Source* Mistrzowie.org, 2021

the yard"). This difference is often used and is subject of jokes on these two centers, each considering the other as inferior, politically and linguistically (the high-low stature dichotomy). In Fig. 7.7, the despondent demonstrator denounces the political situation using the above-mentioned 8-star slogan to frame the justification of his presence at the demonstration: if a Krakow resident had to leave his own safe dialect and speak the Warsaw one (he used the expression *na dwór*), the situation must be really bad.

The other example features the banner saying: "Kraków's sovereign [people] express their will: Jarosław [Kaczyński, the Warsaw resident] '*na dwór*', and Jędrek

Fig. 7.7 "It is so bad that Krakow had to leave *na dwór* (outside)." *Source* Jbzd.com.pl, 2023

[President Andrzej Duda, originally from Kraków] *'na pole'*" (Rusinek, 2023). It makes a reference not only to government propaganda that speaks of the people as "sovereign" to enforce decisions (usually in the context of defending the government's own right to decide on behalf of the people), but also to the fact that Kraków has a greater right to be "a sovereign" due to being the royal necropolis. The slogan is rhymed in Polish; and the second line of the banner is highly allusive and ambiguous: the will of the Krakow people it voices can be interpreted as wanting both the party leader and the president to step down, although each of them is addressed in the language he understands—the dialect of Warsaw and Kraków, respectively.

7.4 Feminism, Liberal Movements and Language Policy

The final brief section of this chapter illustrates further the resonance of the *dziad(y)* reference in the current political discourse. Both of the examples relate to the current political conflict between the right-wing government and the feminist movement over the restrictive abortion law and generally over women's rights. In the political protests, it is quite common to see the placards where the *Spieprzaj dziadu* (piss off, old geezer) slogan is used in reference to Jarosław Kaczyński in the sense of demanding his resignation and insulting him as *dziad*, but also referring in this way to his general perception by the public as an old, physically unfit man in a disheveled outfit, and wearing two unmatching shoes (the ultimate high-low stature dichotomy again; Galeria.trójmiasto.pl, 2020; see also Sect. 2.1.1.). The meaning of *dziad* is extended here to refer to a male in general, which generally fits the radical feminist rhetoric. The example, a humorous one, is provided in Fig. 7.8, where an angry radical protester expresses her disgust with the celebration of Dziady, probably because the concept seems alien to her and she would like to celebrate "Baby" (old women).[3] This is only a potential equivalent to Dziady, since Dziady was in fact a celebration of ancestors' spirits without regard for their gender, although one could argue that this generic use of male form suggests omission and disregard of the role of female ancestors.

Both examples serve to demonstrate the process of increasing radicalization and vulgarization of the public sphere in Poland (e.g., with the use of the word *dziady* in its offensive sense). They are also illustrative of the increasing visibility of women in public spheres and in language—by using and promoting female forms of language.

---

[3] The character in the picture is a radical Canadian feminist Chanty Binx, who became a living meme. For more information about her cf. NateTalksTo You, 2019.

Fig. 7.8 "You celebrate *Dziady*? Why not *Baby* [old women]?" *Source* Galnor, 2023

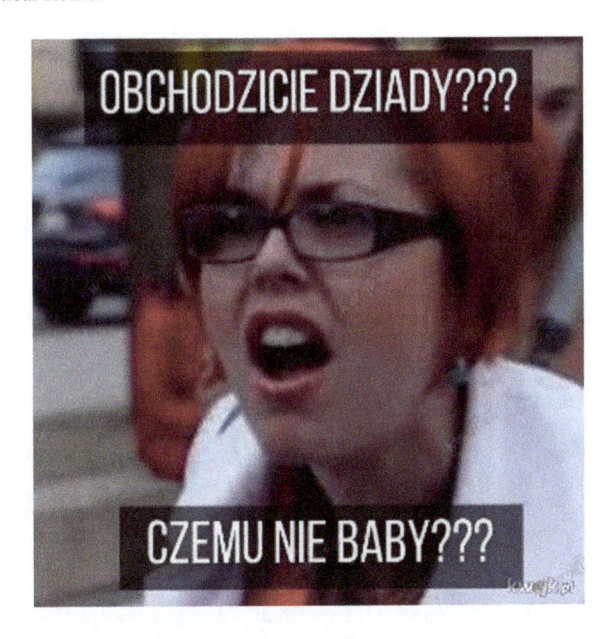

7.5 Conclusions

In the article, we claim that the inspirations for the use of political humor have remained similar over the centuries, with the dichotomies such as traditional/patriarchal versus progressive, Christian versus atheist, nationalist versus cosmopolitan, Poland versus the West/Russia, corruption versus honesty (and generally high-low stature) recurring, even though under various guises; still, new genres have appeared too, forcing change of style. The rhetorical techniques, however, such as irony, parody, allusion, intertextual reference, remained stable too as well as targets of humor, who were mainly political figures. We also drew attention to the new processes of the commercialization and vulgarization of humor, paralleling the populist tendencies in contemporary Polish politics.

To show the strong relationship between humor and culture, the leitmotif of this volume, we have deliberately chosen the examples based on "tropes" from the past. They gave us a good reason to focus on a few key concepts and patterns of Polish culture, but this choice had also some disadvantages, as references to other texts existing in the cultural circulation of the source language, even if recognized, are not possible to reproduce in the translated language if the source work is unknown to the target reader. Brigitte Schultze calls this situation "squaring the circle" (Schultze, 1999, p. 243). It is also very difficult, if at all possible, to translate culturally specific humor because what is very humorous in one culture might be only mildly (or not at all) humorous in another. What's more, an old saying is still valid here: "Explaining a joke is like dissecting a frog—you learn a lot from it, but they're both dead in the end."

Obviously, we assure the readers that there are also examples of more universal humor circulating in Poland. All things considered, it is amazing to observe how traditional, cultural themes are strongly rooted, preserved, and recycled in contemporary political discourse. The same topics are continuously passed down to succeeding generations. Circumstances change, but the seeds of culture seem to be strong and grow new branches with a usual variety of fruits: some sour and some sweet.

References

Attardo, S., & Raskin, V. (1991) Script theory revis(it)ed: Joke similarity and joke representation model, *Humor,* 4(3/4), 293–347.

Brzozowska, D. (2010). Jokes and media: The first cycle of sick-disaster jokes. *Stylistyka, XIX,* 119–134. (in Polish).

Brzozowska, D., & Chłopicki, W. (Eds.), (2012). *Polish humour.* Tertium.

Culture.pl (n.d.) *Kazimierz Dejmek.* https://culture.pl/en/artist/kazimierz-dejmek (in Polish).

Davies, C. (1990). *Ethnic humour around the world.* Indiana University Press.

Demotywatory.pl (2023, June 7). *The great internet conflict Mickiewicz vs Słowacki becomes a hit of the Polish internet* [Meme]. https://demotywatory.pl/4596653/Wielki-internetowy-konflikt--Mickiewicz-vs-Slowacki-staje-sie-hitem-polskiego-internetu?galleryPage=3 (in Polish).

Dymel, R. (1994), Forbidden laughter: On selected scripts in Polish political humor. In M. Abramowicz, D. Bertrand, & T. Stróżyński (Eds.), *European humor.* Uniwersytetu Marii Curie-Skłodowskiej. (in Polish).

Dziady in Słowacki Theater. (2021, December 21). *Magiczny Kraków.* https://www.krakow.pl/aktualnosci/254966,33,komunikat,_dziady__w_teatrze_slowackiego.html (in Polish).

Fakt.pl (2023, February 28). *Czarnek went to the opera accompanied by state security bodyguards. He had fun with an important priest, the Bayer Full band, and TVN celebrity.* https://www.fakt.pl/polityka/przemyslaw-czarnek-na-imprezie-z-waznym-ksiedzem-celebryta-i-gwiazdami-disco-polo/ptsylwm (in Polish).

Galeria.trójmiasto.pl (2020, October 24). *The manifestation under the slogan This is war* [Placard]. https://galeria.trojmiasto.pl/Manifestacja-pod-haslem-To-jest-wojna-Blokowanie-Huciska-864034.html?tag=To&pozycja=22 (in Polish).

Galnor (2023, June 27). *Dziady versus baby* [Meme]. https://kwejk.pl/obrazek/3277173/dziady-kontra-baby.html (in Polish).

Gombrowicz, W. (1937) *Ferdydurke.* Tow. Wydawnicze „Rój." (in Polish).

Holoubek, G., & Dziewulska, M. (1999). On Dejmek's "Forefather's Eve." *Teatr,* 5, 9–11. (in Polish).

Humour in the European public sphere. (n.d.). *Maggie Smith gets politely vulgar—Poland 2021* [Poster]. https://humorinpublic.eu/project/maggie-smith-gets-politely-vulgar/.

Iskra (2022, October 31). *Dziady* [Cartoon]. https://twitter.com/SmutneHistorie/status/1587153862183587842 (in Polish).

Jbzd.com.pl (2023, June 4). *It is so bad that Krakow had to leave* "outside" [Photo of a banner]. https://jbzd.com.pl/obr/3084120/marsz-4-czerwca (in Polish).

Jędryka, S. (1967). *Barrel organ* [Film]. Zespół Filmowy Rytm. https://freedisc.pl/malysmok18,f-1766706,katarynka-avi= (in Polish).

Jeja.pl (n.d.), *Adam Mickiewicz* [Meme]. https://memy.jeja.pl/192101,adam-mickiewicz.html (in Polish).

Kmiecik, P., & Makarewicz, N. (2023, May 2). *Did the Russian rocket infringe Polish airspace? The commentary of the Prime Minister.* [Press article]. Radio RMF

24. https://www.rmf24.pl/fakty/polska/news-czy-rosyjska-rakieta-naruszyla-przestrzen-powietrzna-polski-,nId,6753307#crp_state=1 (in Polish).
Krasicki. I. (1776/1910). *The adventures of Mikołaj Doświadczyński*. Gebethner i Spółka. (in Polish).
Krzyżanowski, J. (1958). The old king's clown. Stańczyk in the history of Polish culture. In *In the century of Rej and Stańczyk. Sketches from the history of the Renaissance in Poland*, (pp. 328–406). PWN.
Kwejk.pl (2023a, June 6). *Stańczyk* [Meme] In the public domain. https://kwejk.pl/obrazek/3981442/stanczyk.html (in Polish).
Kwejk.pl (2023b June 6). *Morawiecki* [Meme] In the public domain. https://kwejk.pl/obrazek/3448501/morawiecki.html (in Polish).
Łanuszka, M. (n.d.). *"The Grandpa" in the company of the jester and the prophet. Caricatures of Józef Piłsudski according to Kazimierz Sichulski*. https://historiaposzukaj.pl/wiedza,obiekty,311,obiekt_jozef_pilsudski.html (in Polish).
Lemann, N. (2012). Humour in prose literature from the Middle Ages to 1918. In D. Brzozowska & W. Chłopicki (Eds.), *Polish humor* (pp. 15–38). Tertium.
Lenica, J. (1960). The Polish school of poster art. *Graphis, 88*, 136–143.
Libura, A., & Kiełbawska, A. (2012). Humour in posters. In D. Brzozowska & W. Chłopicki (Eds.), *Polish humor* (pp. 311–352). Tertium.
Lipiec, P. (2017). *Were Stańczyk's jokes really funny?* [Press article] https://kurierhistoryczny.pl/artykul/czy-zarty-stanczyka-naprawde-byly-smieszne,237. (in Polish).
Mario niepoważnie (2021, November 26). *This time the lamp of enlightenment shone exceptionally strongly, so strongly that tickets for Dziady at the Słowacki Theater sold like hotcakes* [Cartoon]. https://www.facebook.com/Mario.niepoważnie/ (in Polish).
Matejko, J. (1862). *Stańczyk* [Fragment of the painting]. https://artsandculture.google.com/asset/sta%C5%84czyk/4AHFtRqeObzoRw?hl=pl (in Polish).
Mickiewicz, A. (1823). Forefather's Eve. In *Poems* (pp. 89–214). Józef Zawadzki. Wilno. (in Polish).
Mistrzowie.org (2021, November 24). *Dziady forbidden again* [Meme]. In the public domain. https://mistrzowie.org/782684 (in Polish).
M.komixxy.pl (2023, June 6). *Religion teacher [Meme] In the public domain.* https://m.komixxy.pl/548803 (in Polish).
Mleczko, A. (2021, August 13), *Rotten West* [Cartoon]. https://muzeum4rp.iq.pl/wiki/index.php?title=Zgni%C5%82y_zach%C3%B3d (in Polish).
Mosor, M. (2021, October 29). *Piss off, geezers* [Cartoon]. https://galeriawidgeta.pl/rysunek-sprzed-lat-dziady-prezes-cmentarz-poganie-rodzimowiercy-rodzimowierstwo/ (in Polish).
Mrożek, S. (1957/1962). *The elephant* [trans. K. Syrup]. Grove Press (in Polish).
NateTalksTo You (2019, June 25). *WHO IS BIG RED?—The Story of Chanty Binx* [Youtube movie]. https://www.youtube.com/watch?v=_a2Umgioia0.
Opposition march poster (2023, June 6). *High Noon 4 June 2023* [Poster]. https://opowiecie.info/jedziesz-warszawy-4-czerwca-sa-zapisy/ (in Polish).
Raszewski, Z. (1981). Dejmek. *Pamiętnik Teatralny, 3–4*, 229–258. (in Polish).
Rusinek, M. (2023, June 5). *Banner slogans are interesting, but better not to be needed* [Press article]. https://wyborcza.pl/7,175992,29838535,jaroslaw-na-dwor-a-jedrek-na-pole-rusinek-przyglada.html (in Polish).
Sarnecki, T. (1989, June 4). *Solidarity: High noon—4th June 1989* [Poster]. https://muzeum-niepodleglosci.pl/aktualnosci/w-samo-poludnie-obchody-30-rocznicy-wolnych-wyborow/ (in Polish).
Schubert, Z. (2008). *Poster masters and pupils* [trans. J. Holzman]. Przedsiębiorstwo Wydawnicze Rzeczpospolita SA. (in Polish).
Schultze, B. (1999). *Polish studies and comparative perspectives*. Universitas. (in Polish).
Sichulski, K. (1917). *Piłsudski with Stańczyk and Wernyhora* [Painting]. https://mnwr.pl/pilsudski-ze-stanczykiem-i-wernyhora/ (in Polish).
Sienkiewicz, H. (1866). *The deluge*. Noskowski. (in Polish).

Stejk.org, (2021, April 23). *Adam was stoned* [Meme]. https://memsekcja.pl/mem/adam-sie-nae bal/jk7ZqQj (in Polish).

Świątkowicz-Mośny, M. (2012). Political humour in the period of People's Republic of Poland. In D. Brzozowska & W. Chłopicki (Eds.), *Polish Humor* (pp. 425–436). Tertium.

Tsakona, V. (2020). *Recontextualising humour. Rethinking the analysis and teaching of humor*. De Gruyter Mouton.

Wierzbicka, A. (1997). *Understanding cultures through their key words: English, Russian, Polish*. Oxford University Press.

Zakrzewski, W. (1945/2023, June 6). *Giant and reactionary dwarf spitting on himself* [Poster]. https://ipn.gov.pl/ftp/wystawy/proces_krakowski/html/plansza01-07a.html (in Polish).

Zembaty, W. (n.d.) *Forefathers Eve—Adam Mickiewicz*. https://culture.pl/en/work/forefathers-eve-adam-mickiewicz.

Dorota Brzozowska is a Full Professor at the Institute of Linguistics of the Opole University, Poland. Her scholarly research interests comprise research on humor, stylistics, discourse analysis, intercultural communication, and semiotics. She authored books e.g., *On Polish and English Jokes: A Linguistic and Cultural Analysis* (2000), *Polish Ethnic Jokes: Stereotype and Identity* (2008); and *Chinese Traces in Polish Contemporary Discourse* (2018) (in Polish), and co-edited books on different aspects of humor. She is a co-editor of *The European Journal of Humour Research* and *Tertium Linguistic Journal*.

Władysław Chłopicki is Professor of Linguistics at the Jagiellonian University in Kraków, Poland. His academic interests include interdisciplinary humor research in the context of cognitive linguistics, linguistic pragmatics, narratology, and cultural studies (most recently humor in the public sphere—humorinpublic.eu). He has published extensively on humor related issues, including a Polish language volume on humor studies (1995), as well as volumes co-edited with Dorota Brzozowska on *Polish Humour* (2012), *Culture's Software: Communication Styles* (2015), and *Humorous Discourse* (2017). He is co-editor of *The European Journal of Humour Research* and *Tertium Linguistic Journal*.

Chapter 8
Jewish Humor as a Survival Tool and a Bridge to Social Justice

Linda Weiser Friedman and Hershey H. Friedman

Abstract Social justice attempts to make the world a better place, a place where everyone counts, where we treat everyone equitably, and all people have the same opportunity to achieve success. By its very definition, then, social justice *humor* is political in nature. Like many powerful tools, humor can be used for both good and evil. It can perpetuate stereotypes; it also can redress a wide variety of prejudices and preconceptions. This chapter investigates how Jewish humor—going all the way back to the Hebrew Bible—can serve as a prism through which to examine the political and cultural oppression of this enduring people, including some of the worst moments in Jewish history. The modern genre of stand-up comedy is at its most poignant and razor-sharp when used in the service of social justice. Many oppressed groups practice this sort of humor including African-Americans, women, Muslims, and the disabled, among others. Historical examples discussed here include humor of the conversos, Jewish victims of the blood libel, that of enslaved African-Americans, anti-Nazi humor, and humor in the former Soviet Union. Social justice humor can be a tool for educating bigots, for promoting the self-esteem of the oppressed, or for simply getting even.

8.1 Introduction

Social justice attempts to make the world a better place, a place where everyone counts and is treated equitably, and where all people have the same opportunity to achieve success. By its very definition, then, social justice *humor* is political in nature. And, of course, funny. In addition, social justice humor contains shadows of

---

L. W. Friedman (✉)
Faculty in Business and Jewish Studies, Baruch College, City University of New York, New York City, USA
e-mail: prof.friedman@gmail.com

H. H. Friedman
Koppelman School of Business, Brooklyn College, City University of New York, New York City, USA
e-mail: x.friedman@att.net

hostility towards those who cause strife—the racists, the bigots, the unaware, and the uneducated. The objective of this type of humor is to educate, to counter stereotypes, and if all else fails, to get even.

In examining what a people laugh at, we come close to learning what they value. The Jewish people—oppressed throughout most of its history as a disenfranchised minority in a hostile host country, aka The People of the Book, always needing to live by their wit(s)—drew upon their traditions from the *Scriptures*, the *Talmud*, and the *Midrash*. In fact, in a recent Pew survey: 34% of U.S. Jews see having a good sense of humor as essential to their Jewish identity, more than *halacha* (Jewish law) which was 15% (Pew, 2021).

Humor is a powerful tool and can be used for good or for evil. Sometimes humor is employed as a tool to facilitate prejudice or to mask a verbal (or written) attack, a subtle way to put down, delegitimize, and provide "psychological cover to avoid the appearance of bias" (Hodson & MacInnis, 2016, p. 63). Conversely, humor can serve to bond together those oppressed by others outside the group and build self-esteem.

This chapter investigates how Jewish humor can serve as a prism through which to examine the political and cultural oppression of this enduring people, as well as a bridge to social justice humor in general and, of course, to social justice itself.

8.2 Why We Laugh

While many theories hypothesize why people laugh, three major theories of humor predominate: incongruity, relief/release, and superiority. Many of the others can be shown to be variants. These theories are expounded on in many articles (e.g., Keith-Speigel, 1972), so that this paper will only briefly address them.

Incongruity theory posits that humor results from a contrast between what is logically expected and what actually takes place or what is said. A related theory focuses on surprise and/or suddenness i.e., being presented with the unexpected. Still another, ambivalence or conflict mixture theory, asserts that laughter results from someone simultaneously experiencing opposite or incompatible emotions. This is similar to incongruity theory, but it stresses incompatibility between emotions/feelings rather than ideas.

The relief/release theory of humor focuses on laughter's role as a socially acceptable way to release pent-up tension and nervous energy, and thus relieve stress. This theory, first developed by Spencer (1860), was made famous by Freud (1905/1960). Many people may fear or find it difficult or uncomfortable to discuss certain subjects—for example: rape, impotence, homosexuality, violence, racism, and incest. Humor gives these people a socially acceptable way to relieve their tension about these sensitive areas. Laughter can be used as a substitute for violent behavior and thus help people avoid conflict. Relief/release theory might explain why people often need to tell jokes at funerals or why teenagers enjoy sexual humor. Relief/release theory may best explain the importance of humor in healing (e.g., medical clowns).

Superiority theory suggests that the purpose of humor is to demonstrate one's superiority, dominance, or power over others. Mocking humor that belittles the stupidity, infirmities, or weaknesses of other groups is a clear way to demonstrate one's "superiority"—or the supposed superiority of one's reference group—and thus boost one's ego. Racist and sexist humor falls in this category, often used to perpetuate stereotypes about women and minorities and keep them "in their place."

Ford and Ferguson (2004, p. 79) define disparagement humor as "humor that denigrates, belittles, or maligns an individual or social group." They observe that it "can function as a potential tool of prejudice, stereotyping, and discrimination" (ibid., p. 305). Appalling examples of this kind of humor are provided by Hodson and MacInnis (2016, p. 63), including: "What's the difference between football and rape? Women do not like football."

Disparagement humor is a tool used by bigots and workplace bullies to create a hostile work environment (Murphy, 2018) and to spread harmful views of vulnerable people such as women, Blacks, Asians, and Jews (Ford, 2016). It is not easy to deal with disparagement humor because one who responds to it in a forceful manner might be accused of having no sense of humor. This may be the reason that many victims simply ignore it, instead of trying to respond appropriately (Kuipers, 2011, pp. 72–73).

Ford (2016) discusses the consequences of disparagement humor, jokes whose purpose is to belittle marginalized groups such as women, Blacks, or Jews. It is a subtle way of expressing and spreading harmful views of vulnerable people. These are not harmless jokes because they often dehumanize others. Humor targeting women or gays (for example), sends a message that it is safe and acceptable to express hostile feelings towards those groups. Pro-Nazi newspapers (e.g., Der *Stürmer*) used hate-filled comics and cartoons to depict Jews as outsiders, subhuman, depraved, and a threat to the world. Posters were also used for this purpose. The drawings typically showed Jews as being ugly, short, and with grotesque noses (Land, 2022).

The kind of humor which mocks outsiders goes back as far as ancient Europe, according to Cynthia Merriwether-de Vries, a sociology professor. She notes that there were court minstrels who mocked the Visigoths for their stench. There are also memos from Medieval Europe warning that the jokes of a particular jester regarding the Hapsburgs went too far and could affect diplomatic relations (Cohen & Richards, 2006).

The primary function of what Friedman and Friedman (2003) call "bonding humor" appears to be the creation of a feeling of belongingness and togetherness. This category of humor covers a wide variety of comic endeavors, including the humor of various ethnic groups, racial groups, religions, professions, scientific disciplines, and, indeed, any group of individuals who share a body of knowledge, rituals, experience, lore and, of, course, a sense of humor. For example, this gem pulled from social media:

10 ways to tell if you are a chemo patient (with apologies to Jeff Foxworthy):

1. If you can wow your friends with a weight loss of 30 lbs. in a month, without even trying… you might be a chemo patient.

2. If you are delighted with all the money you save on shampoo... you might be a chemo patient.
3. If you are delighted as well with the time and money you save on hair coloring, waxing, and laser hair removal services... you might be a chemo patient.
4. If you take three times longer than you should getting dressed in the morning, and then need to take a nap... you might be a chemo patient.
5. If you have created an album on your phone with pictures of your medical insurance cards... you might be a chemo patient.
6. If you think that lifting your cell phone and texting should be part of your daily exercise regimen ... you might be a chemo patient.
7. If your Google/Amazon search history contains keywords like "mouth sores," "ice packs," large knee bandages," "survival rate," "relapse rate," "mouth sores," "can I survive on ice cream," "what does near remission mean," "help with buttons and zippers," and—oh, yes—"mouth sores" ... you might be a chemo patient.
8. If you take on a project that you think you should be able to do, only to drop it in the mid.

Some humor may be hermetic; that is, the listener must bring some kind of specialized knowledge to the joke-telling enterprise, or the joke is meaningless or at least not funny. This can occur in tightly knit groups or with groups that share similar experiences or knowledge; for example: musicians, mathematicians, computer scientists, or even families (Friedman & Friedman, 2003; Ziv & Gadish, 1989).

Schutz (1989, 1995) feels that ethnic humor plays an important social function by helping ingroups bond and reinforce their values. While humor can be used to deride others (e.g., racist jokes, lawyer jokes), it can also be used to enhance the image of a group. Of course, one joke can sometimes do both jobs at the same time: mock one group while at the same time making another group appear smarter than everyone else. The jokes of victims and oppressed groups very often have this dual purpose. Certain kinds of ethnic humor can simultaneously strengthen the rapport among the insiders and disparage the outgroup (Lowe, 1986; Martineau, 1972).

The various theories of humor are not necessarily incompatible with each other. Some jokes may be explained by two or more different theories. And the same joke may operate under different theories, depending on the identity of the teller and the audience.

Freud (1905/1960, p. 103) made the following observation about hostile jokes that he believed served the purpose of aggressiveness or defense: "By making our enemy small, inferior, despicable or comic, we achieve in a roundabout way the enjoyment of overcoming him." Davies (1998) asserts that all ethnic groups tell "put-down" jokes, whose goal is to show scorn and belittle a member of another group. This is especially true when the other group is known to be prejudiced to the first group and/or is seen as a rival. Thus, Blacks will tell jokes about White supremacists, women will tell jokes about male chauvinists, and Jews will tell jokes about antisemites. It is an ideal way for those that are oppressed, abused, or taken advantage of to "get even" with their oppressors. Comeback jokes and put-down humor can be an instrument of self-respect and a way to get even with oppressors. Moreover, they are the weapon of the oppressed, who can use it as a way to bond with others who are persecuted.

Humor is important and pervasive among Jews, serving as a common language. The body of Jewish humor can be used to teach a seminar on Jewish history or certainly on antisemitism. We can find examples of political humor and yes, mocking humor, that are quite ancient if we go to the Hebrew Scriptures. How far back does Jewish humor go?

8.3 An Historical Perspective of Jewish Humor

The Jewish people—oppressed throughout history, dispersed to all parts of the globe, for most of its history a disenfranchised minority in a hostile host country, the People of the Book, always needing to live by their wit—drew upon its traditions from the Scriptures, the *Talmud*, and the *Midrash* (Friedman & Friedman, 2014).

Over many centuries, Jews have been dispersed to practically every corner of the globe. Today, as the world gets smaller, we see that wherever Jews settled, they took on elements of the culture of the lands in which they were immersed. When Jews can be Ashkenazi, Sephardi, Bukharan, Iranian, Russian, Brazilian, Argentinian, Mexican, etc., how do they recognize their "own" when everyone is so different? What do they have in common? Not dress, daily language, or food. Certainly, there is much the Jews all over the world still have in common: rituals, prayer, holidays, the *Torah* and other Scriptures, the Hebrew language, the *Talmud*, a communal history centered on the land of Israel, and, of course, humor. They ultimately have in common the *Torah* as the bedrock of their existence. Of all the commonalities evidenced by Jews from seemingly different cultures, one that is arguably the most important—to identity, to survival, to bonding with fellow Jews—might be humor.

There are those who believe that the Bible and the *Talmud* are devoid of humor, that Jewish humor is a modern manifestation not in evidence before 19th century Europe. In fact, the Hebrew Bible does include humor—lots of it. However, to truly appreciate much of this humor, one must be well versed in the Hebrew language. Language-based humor—like puns, alliteration, and wordplay—does not translate very well.

Davies (1998, p. 80) notes that Jewish jokes are especially unique because Jews have always "faced much greater danger from hostile outsiders than almost any other ethnic group; what was at stake was not merely national prestige, pride or even independence, but sheer survival." Moreover, these types of Jewish jokes directed against outsiders tend to be more "subtle, clever, and indirect" than "put-down" jokes told by other groups.

Andrew Silow-Carroll, a journalist and expert on Jewish humor, said he could summarize all of Jewish history in ten jokes (Lipman, 2014). Another way of looking at this, of course, is that since their humor has helped Jews survive as a people, they can possibly use examples of humor as a way to teach about antisemitism throughout much of recorded history. Some of the worst moments in Jewish history (both ancient and more recent) are memorialized in Jewish humor. Some examples follow. [The timeline used in this chapter accords with traditional Jewish sources (Kantor, 2020).]

8.3.1 From the Hebrew Bible

8.3.1.1 1556 BCE

Biblical humor is often political in nature even, or especially, when it is used to mock idolatry. One example of this is in the story of the matriarch Rachel. When Rachel's husband Jacob took his family and fled from his father-in-law Laban, Rachel had (unbeknownst to Jacob), stolen her father's *teraphim*, small personal statues used for idolatry and divination. When Laban caught up with Jacob, he asked (Genesis, 31:30): "Why have you stolen my gods?" The reader is certain to realize that a god that can be stolen cannot be much of a god. Even worse, Rachel hid her father's deities by sitting on them. These idols did not get much respect; nor did they speak up, and shout, "Hey, we're over here!".

8.3.1.2 1313 BCE

We learn much about the character of the newly freed Israelites from their sarcastic way of asking Moses for help only seven days after their triumphant exodus from Egypt. The people, when seeing Pharaoh's massive army approaching behind them with only the sea in front of them, exclaim (Exodus, 14:11): "Was there a lack of graves in Egypt, that you [Moses] took us away to die in the wilderness?" This may be the first instance of sarcasm combined with gallows humor.

8.3.1.3 874–853 BCE

Queen Jezebel, the wife of King Ahab, murdered the prophets of God, and she and her husband became followers of Baal. The prophet Elijah exposed the prophets of Baal as frauds and challenged them to get their god to accept their offering by sending fire from heaven. The prophets called out in the name of Baal from morning until evening, but nothing happened. Elijah mocked them sarcastically, saying (I Kings, 18:27): "Call with a loud voice, for he is a god. Perhaps he is talking, or he is pursuing enemies, or he is relieving himself, or perhaps he is sleeping and will awaken."

8.3.1.4 355 BCE

Mordechai and Esther declare a new holiday, Purim, to commemorate the survival of the Jews living in the ancient Persian empire. The Book of Esther tells this story, filled with humor. There are two especially funny episodes in the Book of Esther, one in which the king asks Haman how to honor who is worthy of being praised. Haman, believing that the king must mean to honor Haman himself, responds with how he would like to be honored—to be dressed in the "royal robe that the king has worn, and the horse upon which the king has ridden, and on whose head a royal turban has been placed" (Esther 6:8) and to be paraded around the city with the announcement: "This is what is done for the man whom the king is delighted to honor!" (ibid., 6:7). Unfortunately for Haman the king wishes to honor Mordechai, Haman's most bitter enemy. The king tasks Haman with parading Mordechai around town in this way. The second humorous scene is when Haman falls on Esther's couch, trying to plead for his life. The king walks in and says: "Will you actually assault the queen while I am in the house?" (Esther 7:8).

Even the very name of the holiday—Purim, which means lots, as in lottery—is humorous. Yes, Haman used lots to select the ideal day to exterminate the Jewish people, but why name a holiday after that? The modern equivalent might be to call a holiday "Roulette Wheel."

8.3.2 The Medieval Period

Abraham Ibn Ezra (1089–1164 C.E.), in his commentary, uses sarcasm to mock several of the interpretations of Ben Zuta, a Karaite exegete. Karaism, a medieval Jewish sect, saw the Hebrew Bible as the sole source of religious law and rejected the oral tradition of the Talmud and Rabbinic Judaism. The sect was relatively strong towards the end of the eleventh century.

In his commentary on the verse "If one man's ox injures his friend's (*rey'ehu*) ox and it dies [...]" (Exodus 21:35), Ibn Ezra quotes the opinion of Ben Zuta that "his friend's ox" does not refer to a human but rather to a fellow ox i.e., the goring ox and the gored ox are the "friends." Ibn Ezra's characteristically caustic remark about this explanation is that the only "friend" an ox has is Ben Zuta himself.

8.3.3 Spanish Inquisition: 1478–1834

According to Kaplan (2021), there were two types of conversos, Jews who converted to Christianity. Some were sincere Christians, while others were crypto-Jews, forced to convert but who continued to observe Jewish practices. Indeed, many were probably waiting to return to Judaism when possible. This might explain why there was a great deal of suspicion of all conversos who were discriminated against and persecuted. The purpose of the Inquisition was to root out and punish the crypto-Jews. Funny, huh?

Indeed, there were converso poets who used humor to mock themselves and other conversos (Kaplan, 2008). Gutwirth (1990, p. 223) sees this type of humor as "black humor" that reveals a "tragic sense of life." In a poem, Juan Alfonso de Baena declares that he has only eaten two types of fish (salmon and meagre) and refrained from eating unclean fish. With this distinction, he alludes to Jewish dietary laws; the only fish that are kosher have fins and scales. De Baena mocks another converso who keeps the *Torah* rather than accepts the Holy Trinity (Kaplan, 2021). Conversos responded to being marginalized in much the same way Jews do it today. The humor underscores that it is impossible to escape from the second-class status of being a Jew, even after adopting the religion of the persecutor.

8.3.4 Blood Libels: 12th Century—Present

The Blood Libels were based on the antisemitic myth that Jews use the blood of Christian children for their rituals, especially to bake matzo for Passover. This ugly rumor spread all over Europe, especially in the 12th century after the First Crusade with the growing strength of Christianity. This myth was used to justify pogroms and eventually found its way into 20th century Nazi propaganda and anti-Jewish mythology in the Middle East today. The infamous Beilis trial in Czarist Russia in 1911 involved the false accusation that Menachem Mendel Beilis had kidnapped a Christian child. He was acquitted in 1913. The Kielce pogrom of July 1946 in Poland resulted in the death of 42 Jews and was triggered by a missing Christian boy supposedly kidnapped by Jews for ritual purposes. The boy returned home two days later. A 2003 television series broadcast in Syria and Lebanon depicted Jews as kidnapping Christian children and draining their blood for matzos (US Holocaust Memorial Museum, 2023). And yet, Jews tell the following classic joke:

> In a small village in Ukraine, a terrifying rumor was spreading: A Christian girl had been found murdered. Realizing the dire consequences of such an event, and fearing a pogrom, the Jewish community instinctively gathered in the synagogue to plan whatever defensive actions were possible under these circumstances. Just as the emergency meeting was being called to order, in ran the president of the synagogue, out of breath and all excited. "Brothers," he cried out, "I have wonderful news! The murdered girl is Jewish!" (Novak & Waldoks, 1981, p. 73).

This odd joke/not-a-joke can almost be considered to be hermetic i.e., an in-joke. Jews laugh at it; non-Jews, not so much.

This very important piece of humor teaches history, culture, and morality. We might also consider this as being pogrom humor. Lipman (2020), an expert on Jewish humor, asks: "Who tells jokes about pogroms? Or about possible pogroms?" Jews know the answer. Jews! The victims of many pogroms. For that matter, who tells jokes about surviving the Holocaust? Um, well.

8.3.5 The Holocaust: Mid-20th Century

> Two elderly Holocaust survivors die and go to heaven, where they tell each other Holocaust jokes. God happens by, sees them laughing, and tells them He did not find the jokes funny; in fact, He found them to be offensive. They just look at God, look at each other, shrug, and say: "I guess you had to be there."

The Nazis did not much like humor; they especially disliked humor that mocked Nazis. Between 1933 and 1945, as many as 5,000 people were sentenced to death for being involved in anti-Nazi humor (Morreall, 2001). Gordon (2012, p. 99) analyzes what the two quasi-sociologists, Keller and Andersen (1937), attempted to accomplish in their antisemitic book, *The Jew as Criminal*. It was important for the two authors to find ways to malign Jewish humor as an evil tool and thereby dehumanize Jews and make it acceptable to exterminate them. Thus, they claimed that the Jewish talent to make people laugh had an insidious purpose. It enabled Jews to appear harmless when in actuality they had wicked and destructive intentions and were trying to further the selfish interests of international Jewry at the expense of the German people. They saw self-deprecating humor as one of the most potent Jewish weapons. This is exactly what makes social justice humor so effective – it allows the comic to get under the audience's protective barriers.

The Nazi propagandists felt that humor was specifically Nordic, not Jewish. They felt that Jews, being an inferior race, could only create cynical, corrosive, and subversive humor. Jewish humor had the ability to corrupt German culture and was, therefore, a threat. This was consistent with the opinion of the Nazis that Jews were an uncultured people (Kaplan, 2020, pp. 164–166).

Siegfried Kadner, Nazi propagandist and author of *Race and Humor*, ranked various races on their sense of humor. Germans, of course, ranked first and Jews ranked last. The fact that Germans, not known as a humorous people in Europe, ranked first was in itself a good joke. That Jews were in last place also made no sense given that "The humor industry of pre-Nazi Weimar Berlin (1919–1933) was almost exclusively Jewish. In fact, it was more demographically Semitic than the Borscht Belt during its heyday" (Gordon, 2012, p. 97).

> A teacher asked his pupil, "Tell me, my little one, why did we lose World War I?"
>
> The child answered, without hesitation, "Because of the Jewish generals, sir."
>
> "But there weren't any Jewish generals in the German army," the teacher said.
>
> "That's why we lost" (Lipman, 1991, p. 174).

Lest we think that Holocaust humor is only acceptable today due to the passage of time since those atrocities, the interested reader is directed to Ostrower (2014), who interviewed Holocaust survivors and captured their contemporary humor. In the notorious concentration camp of Treblinka, where the prisoners were employed to carry the gassed corpses of inmates to the crematorium, prisoners who ate too much would be told by their fellows, "Oy, Moishe, don't overeat! Think of those of us who will have to carry you!" (Ostrower, 2014, p. 91).

Robin Williams tells the story of the time he was interviewed on German radio:

I was once on a German talk show, and this woman said to me, 'Mr. Williams, why do you think there is not so much comedy in Germany?' And I said, 'Did you ever think you killed all the funny people?' (Williams, 2009, 0:10)

In a similar vein, the folks of Monty Python were invited to come to Germany to write a comedy show because apparently there were no funny writers in Germany. They were picked up from the airport and taken directly to visit the Dachau concentration camp. Along the way, no one could give them directions. "Everyone kept denying they knew where it was." (Subtle, right?) They were late, and the camp was about to close for the day. How did the group get in? Graham Chapman suggested: "Tell them we're Jewish" (Idle, 1998).

And this is Israeli comic Shahar Hason's response to a German woman in the audience who remarked that she did not like Israelis because they do not know how to wait in line politely:

We don't stay in lines because the last time we stood in line, look what happened. The minute you Germans say stay in line, we are going to run. We are not going to fall into that trap again (Sponder, 2017, 3:40).

We cannot let this topic go without presenting one of the true classics of Holocaust humor:

Freudenheim was walking down the street in Nazi Germany in 1934 when suddenly a large black limousine pulled up beside him. Freudenheim looked up in astonishment and terror as Hitler himself climbed out of the car.

Holding a gun to Freudenheim, Hitler ordered him to get down on his hands and knees. And pointing to a pile of excrement on the curb, Hitler ordered the Jew to eat it.

Freudenheim, putting discretion before valor, complied. Hitler began laughing so hard that he dropped the gun. Freudenheim picked it up and ordered Hitler to undergo the same humiliation. As Hitler got down on the sidewalk, Freudenheim ran from the scene as fast as he could.

Later that day, when Freudenheim returned home, his wife asked him, "How was your day?"

"Oh, fine, dear," he answered. "By the way, you'll never guess who I had lunch with today!" (Novak & Waldoks, 2006, p. 82)

The question of the appropriateness of Holocaust humor is addressed in documentary filmmaker Ferne Pearlstein's film "The Last Laugh" (Artsy, 2017). One doubts that other ethnic groups have much humor revolving around them being slaughtered. Lipman (1991) and Ostrower (2014) show how victims of the Holocaust used humor to cope with the horrors of the Nazis. Jewish humor has helped the Jewish people deal with the hostility, ugliness, and hatred they faced in their everyday life. It is unique because it does more than poke fun at the failings and weaknesses of the Jewish people, but also asserts that the Jews will survive regardless of all the suffering and frightening situations that confront them (Abrami, n.d.).

8.3.6 Assimilation

Jews often try to blend into the culture of the land in which they reside, some more and some less successfully. A large portion of the assimilation-related Jewish humor is especially poignant, and yes, humorous to the wandering Jew who periodically is forced to lay down roots in a new and alien land.

> Three Jewish converts to Christianity are having drinks in an exclusive country club. "I converted out of love," says one. Seeing the dubious looks on his friends' faces, he adds, "Not for Christianity but for a Christian girl. My wife insisted that I convert."
>
> "And I converted in order to succeed in law," the second one says. "I would never have been appointed a federal judge if I hadn't become an Episcopalian."
>
> The third says, "I converted because I think the teachings of Christianity are superior to those of Judaism." To which the other two respond indignantly. "What do you take us for, a couple of goyim [non-Jews]?" (Friedman & Friedman, 2014, p. 303)

No matter how diligently a Jew tries to assimilate, much humor arises from the difficulty of sloughing off the old skin. For example, this classic attributed to Groucho Marx:

> In the 1920s, two friends of the Marx Brothers were walking along 5th Avenue. The first was Otto Kahn, a patron of the Metropolitan Opera. The second was Marshall B. Wilder, a hunch-backed script writer. As they walked past a synagogue, Kahn turned to Wilder and said, "You know I used to be a Jew." And Wilder said, "Yeah, and I used to be a hunchback" (Lee, 1998, p. 179).

And this one from the former Soviet Union:

Telephone rings. "Hello."

"Hello. May I please speak to Moshe?"

"There is no Moshe here."

"Really? There is no one called Moshe there?"

"No Moshe here." Hangs up.

Ring. "Hello."

"Hello. Is Mischa there?"

"Just a moment." Calls out, "Moshe! It's for you!"

8.3.7 Neo-Nazis and Other Modern Antisemites

But wait, there's more. Unfortunately, even today, antisemitism is still a problem in much of the world.

Comedian David Finkelstein, one of three stand-up comics whose fledgling careers are portrayed in the film *Standing Up* (Miller, 2017), has a very funny bit about a "Captioned Swastika":

> Recently there was a swastika spray-painted in my neighborhood. I'm a comedian, so I totally got the joke. But what really tickled me was that next to the swastika someone wrote "kill the Jews." It was like a little caption explaining the swastika. Like the guy felt like he had to explain. He didn't want anyone to take it the wrong way. Someone would come along, "Oh, that's just a symmetrical design." No! Kill the Jews! That's what this is all about (Comedy Time, 2013, 1:30).

From comedian Mordechai (MODI) Rosenfeld:

> Cancel culture is antisemitic. If you say something against somebody who's Asian, a Latino person, gay, trans—you're finished. You got to get a lawyer, a new job, change Twitter, you're done. DONE! If somebody says something bad against Jews, the worst that can happen to them is they make them visit a Holocaust Museum, which is the stupidest idea in the world. You're taking someone who hates Jews into a Holocaust Museum. They come out of there, 'Wow! Holy Cow! That was amazing! 'Get me a T-shirt, a poster, something to remember this place!' (MODI, 2022).

8.4 Social Justice Humor

The good news is that humor can also be used to fight back against bigots and their humor (Friedman & Friedman, 2020) and, in fact, can be a powerful weapon for good. Some researchers have been examining the use of comedy as a way to get people to pay closer attention to social justice issues (Chattoo, 2019; Chattoo & Feldman, 2020; Feldman & Chattoo, 2019). It appears that comedy is more likely to engage and persuade people than simple facts.

Positive humor—unlike negative humor, whose goal is to demean, humiliate, and destroy the spirit of people—has the ability to heal by laughing at the foibles people tend to share; it is meaningful, warm, and compassionate. Fosco (2018) asserts that humor is changing and focuses on how various vulnerable groups have been mistreated by those in power. The goal of this humor is to mock the oppressors and demonstrate how ridiculously they behave. Bigots, ageists, body shamers, appearance mockers, and sexists have no reason to feel superior. Some types of humor may be seen as a form of resistance. It allows those who are oppressed to defend themselves against the oppressor by using humor as a weapon and a means of protection. This is often accomplished by turning the humor around and making the oppressor the butt of the joke (Reay, 2015; Weaver, 2010).

As noted above, the relief/release theory of humor views humor as a socially acceptable way to release pent-up tension and thereby relieve stress. Laughter can be used as a substitute for violent behavior and thus help people avoid conflict. Theodor Reik, a disciple of Sigmund Freud, saw humor as a way of dealing with the misfortunes and tragedies of life. By joking about adversities, one can rise above and handle the cruelties of life (Abrami, n.d.).

Mel Brooks says that *The Producers* (Brooks & Glazier, 1967) was his way of getting even with Hitler (Beier, 2006). Brooks states: "Of course it is impossible to balance the scales for six million murdered Jews. But by using the medium of comedy, we can try to rob Hitler of his posthumous power and myths."

> Several stormtroopers enter an Evangelical Church during a Sunday morning service. "My fellow Germans," begins their leader. "I am here in the interest of racial purity. We have tolerated non-Aryans long enough and must now get rid of them. I am ordering all those here whose fathers are Jews to leave this church at once." Several worshipers get up and leave.
>
> "And now I am ordering out all those whose mothers are Jewish."
>
> At this, the pastor jumps up, takes hold of the crucifix, and says, "Brother, now it's time for you and me to get out." (Morreall, 2001)
>
> A Jew in czarist Russia falls into a lake, and, not knowing how to swim, he frantically screams, "Help, save me!" But his calls are totally ignored by all present, including a number of soldiers standing nearby. In desperation, the Jew yells out, "Down with the czar!" At that moment, the soldiers immediately jump in, yank the Jew out of the water, and haul him off to prison (Abrami, n.d., para. 8).

Jokes about outwitting an oppressor are quite common among many oppressed people. In many jokes, the Jew, using his "superior" intelligence, outwits the oppressor *du jour*.

> During the Second World War, a southern matron calls up the local army base.
>
> "We would be honored," she tells the sergeant who takes her call, "to accommodate five soldiers at our Thanksgiving dinner."
>
> "That's very gracious of you, ma'am," the sergeant answers.
>
> "Just please make sure that they're not Jews."
>
> "I understand ma'am."
>
> Thanksgiving afternoon, the woman answers the front doorbell and is horrified to find five black soldiers standing in the doorway.
>
> "We're here for the Thanksgiving dinner, ma'am," one of the soldiers says.
>
> "But,… bu…but your sergeant has made a terrible mistake," the woman says.
>
> Oh no, ma'am," the soldier answers. "Sergeant Greenberg never makes mistakes"
>
> (Friedman & Friedman, 2014, p. 6)

Of course, this sort of humor is by no means limited to Jews. Sadly, there is plenty of oppression to go around.

Dance (1977) points out that the African-American slaves used humor as a tool to maintain their dignity. They would make fun of the so-called superior, "smart" master and joke about his foolishness and gullibility. One suspects that, much like Nazis in our own time, the slave owners felt very much like members of the "master race."

> Forced to suffer at the hands of a formidable and often brutal foe [...] was able to attack him in his humor and thus secure some measure of revenge and victory [...] derived much satisfaction and revenge in observing the ignorance of the so-called superior white man, and they delighted in accounts of his stupidity, his ineptness as a businessman, his fear of conjuration, and his gullibility (Dance, 1977, p. 128).

They observed the hypocrisy of the slaveholder who professed to be a good Christian but treated his slaves with great cruelty. Much of the humor in slave narratives deals with the way slaves outsmarted their masters; indeed, one collection of slave narratives has the title, "Puttin' on Ole Massa" (Osofsky, 1969).

Unquestionably, a consideration of the slave narratives indicates that the Black American slave's sense of humor was often his salvation, or as James Weldon Johnson has his narrator in The Autobiography of an Ex-Coloured Man assert: "It [his humor] had done much to keep him [the American Negro] from going the way of the Indian" (Johnson, 1912, p. 56). Faced with the ambiguous situation of having to live as a slave within a "democratic," "Christian" country, the Black American slave was able to ridicule the ludicrousness of that situation and thus secure some relief from his frustrations (Dance, 1977, p. 132).

> I was walking down the street and I punched a white guy and then I was arrested for assault. The next day after I got out, I punched a black guy and I was arrested for impersonating a police officer. Mark Bolton (Laugh Factory, 2022).

Who else tells this sort of humor? Well, just about any oppressed people. For example,

> If women can do everything men can, how come they have never successfully oppressed an entire gender?

> Question: What is that insensitive bit at the base of the penis called?

> Answer: The man.

> Question: What did God say when He created Adam?

> Answer: I can do better than this.

When someone called comedian Margaret Cho a "Chink," she looked the guy straight in the eye and said, "I'm Korean, I'm not a chink, I'm a gook. If you're going to be racist, get your insults straight!" (Korff, 2017, para. 8).

Muslim comic Shazia Mirza talks about boarding a plane, and the fearful woman who refused to sit next to her. Says Mirza:

"Yes, I'm gonna sit on this plane and blow it up… And do you think you're going to be safer, three rows back?" (StockholmLive, 2009, 1:49).

When was the first Soviet election? When God put Eve in front of Adam and said, "Go ahead, choose your wife" (Davies, 2011, p. 273).

Social justice comedy combines humor with social activism. It attempts to make the world a better place, using humor as a tool to change society. Ziv (1984) cites Charlie Chaplin, who stated that "the function of comedy is to sharpen our sensitivity to the perversions of justice within the society in which we live." Ziv asserts that people are afraid of being laughed at.

Moreover, the fear of becoming a target for mockery should be sufficient to prevent a person from again committing the deed that has led to a punitive reaction. Thus, laughter should have the power to change not merely the personal behavior of one individual but also the behavior of institutions and even whole societies (Ziv, 1984, para. 3).

This is why humor may be a powerful social justice tool.

Goebel (2018) maintains that humorous texts work better than serious literature in teaching young students about social justice. He cites Native American comic Don Kelly, who observed that if you keep people laughing, they will listen to what you have to say. Many social justice stand-up comics see their role as pushing social boundaries and neutralizing stereotypes that hurt minority groups and prevent them from being part of an unbiased, egalitarian society (Chattoo & Feldman, 2020). Stand-up comedy can cause transformation in a way that leaves many audience members wanting more. In our own study of social justice humor, we note: "[V]iolence doesn't educate, and there is no lasting cultural change. With humor, on the other hand, you have a chance of actually doing some good for society" (Friedman & Friedman, 2020, p. 38).

When humor is employed in the service of social justice, it has the opportunity to educate, to bond together members of an oppressed group and help them cope, target their oppressors, and to heal both the oppressed and the oppressor if they are willing to be educated.

Humor has been used by countries under occupation without the ability to militarily fight back and gain their freedom e.g., countries that were part of the Soviet Union. This kind of humor "is an instrument of self-respect and the spirit of freedom" (Ziv, 1984). The joke below was told in Czechoslovakia when it was occupied by the Nazis.

"Did you hear that the Germans have decided to lengthen the day to 29 hours?"

"No, why?"

"Because the Fuhrer has promised them that by the spring they'll be in Moscow!" (Ziv, 1984, para. 14).

The oppressors in a dictatorship may imprison or execute those who mock them, but while keeping alive the spirit of hope and freedom, there is no evidence that humor can topple a totalitarian regime (Davies, 2011, p. 247). The Soviet Union remained a powerful dictatorship despite all the jokes about communism. Humor provides victims with psychological empowerment and enables them to rise above despair and hopelessness.

Humor can sometimes influence voting behavior. There is evidence that President Jimmy Carter was helped in his quest for the presidency by Chevy Chase skits on the *Saturday Night Live* television show that regularly portrayed incumbent President Ford as a bumbling fool. No one wants a fool for president. Similarly, the 2008 election, which John McCain and Sarah Palin lost, was also influenced by *Saturday Night Live* (Goldman, 2013).

Evan Mecham, elected to a four-year term as Governor of Arizona in 1986, was extremely unpopular, especially after he canceled what was then a state holiday to honor the birthday of Rev. Martin Luther King, Jr. (the holiday has since become a U.S. federal holiday). According to Nilsen and Nilsen (2019, pp. 282–288), anti-Mecham jokes had a huge impact on his reputation and contributed to his impeachment. For example:

> Did you hear that Mecham ordered the University of Arizona School of Agriculture to develop chickens with only right wings and all-white meat?
>
> Why did Mecham cancel Easter? He heard the eggs were going to be colored.
>
> What do Mecham and an untrained puppy have in common? They both cringe at the sight of a newspaper (Nilsen & Nilsen, 2019, pp. 285–288).

Much can be learned from the situation with the government by examining the political humor of the time. Many of these jokes shed light on the political environment of the time.

8.5 Conclusion

Humor has the ability to perpetuate and preserve stereotypes and even mock those who have a physical or mental disability. On the positive side, it can also redress preconceptions and biases. Humor can be a bonding tool that reduces stress and make people receptive to learning about the importance of social justice. It can provide victims with psychological empowerment and enables them to rise above despair and hopelessness. Of course, the wrong kind of humor can be a negative tool and cause irreparable harm to people. The acid test to determine whether humor is healing or harmful requires that one answers what were the consequences of the humor. Did it enhance the self-esteem of groups subject to humiliation and degradation? Did it bring disparate people together?

Gibson (2016, para. 3) underscores that

> [H]umor can be used to *make others feel good*, to *gain intimacy*, or to *help buffer stress*. Along with gratitude, hope, and spirituality, a sense of humor belongs to the *set of strengths* positive psychologists call transcendence; together they help us forge connections to the world and provide meaning to life.

In a nutshell, humor should be taken seriously. Perhaps, after all, humor is not a laughing matter.

References

Abrami, L. M. (n.d.). *Jewish humor and psychoanalysis.* Academia.edu. https://www.academia.edu/27929208/JEWISH_HUMOR_AND_PSYCHOANALYSIS.

Artsy, A. (2017, March 10). *Finding humor in Hitler and the Holocaust.* Jewish Journal. https://jewishjournal.com/culture/arts/hollywood/216253/finding-humor-hitler-holocaust/.

Beier, L. O. (2006). *Spiegel interview with Mel Brooks: With comedy, we can rob Hitler of his posthumous power.* Spiegel Online. http://www.spiegel.de/international/spiegel/spiegel-interview-with-mel-brooks-with-comedy-we-can-rob-hitler-of-his-posthumous-power-a-406268.html.

Brooks, M. (Director) & Glazier, S. (Producer) (1967). *The Producers.* Embassy Pictures.

Chattoo, C. B. (2019). A funny matter: Toward a framework for understanding the function of comedy in social change. *Humor, 32*(3), 499–523. https://doi.org/10.1515/humor-2018-0004

Chattoo, C. B., & Feldman, L. (2020). *A comedian and an activist walk into a bar: The serious role of comedy in social justice.* University of California Press.

Cohen, R., & Richards, R. (2006). *When the truth hurts, tell a joke: Why America needs its comedians.* Humanity in Action. https://www.humanityinaction.org/knowledgebase/174-when-the-truth-hurts-tell-a-joke-why-america-needs-its-comedians.

Comedy Time (2013, February 1). *Brief nudity (Funny Videos).* [Video] YouTube. https://youtu.be/kLhF478q3g8?t=90.

Dance, D. C. (1977). Wit and humor in the slave narratives. *Journal of Afro-American Issues, 5*(2), 125–134.

Davies, C. (1998). Jewish jokes, anti-Semitic jokes, and Hebredonian jokes. In A. Ziv (Ed.), *Jewish humor* (pp. 75–96). Transaction.

Davies, C. (2011). *Jokes and targets.* Indiana University Press.

Feldman, L., & Chattoo, C. B. (2019). Comedy as a route to social change: The effects of satire and news on persuasion about Syrian refugees. *Mass Communication and Society, 22*(3), 277–300. https://doi.org/10.1080/15205436.2018.1545035

Ford, T. E. (2016, September 6). *Psychology behind the unfunny consequences of jokes that denigrate.* Conversation. https://theconversation.com/psychology-behind-the-unfunny-consequences-of-jokes-that-denigrate-63855.

Ford, T. E., & Ferguson, M. A. (2004). Social consequences of disparagement humor: A prejudiced norm theory. *Personality and Social Psychology Review, 8*(1), 79–94. https://doi.org/10.1207/S15327957PSPR0801_4

Fosco, M. (2018, December 11). *The last laugh: How comedy had enough of self-deprecation.* Ozymandias. https://www.ozy.com/fast-forward/the-last-laugh-how-comedy-had-enough-of-self-deprecation/90948.

Freud, S. (1905/1960). *Jokes and their relation to the unconscious* [Trans. J. Strachey]. W. W. Norton (Original work published in 1905).

Friedman, L. W., & Friedman, H. H. (2003). *I-get-it as a type of bonding humor: The secret handshake.* SSRN.com. https://ssrn.com/abstract=913622, https://doi.org/10.2139/ssrn.913622.

Friedman, H. H., & Friedman, L. W. (2014). *God laughed: Sources of Jewish humor.* Transaction.

Friedman, H. H., & Friedman, L. W. (2020). The pen is mightier than the sword: Humor as a social justice tool. *Review of Contemporary Philosophy, 19*, 26–42. https://doi.org/10.22381/RCP1920202

Gibson, J. M. (2016, October 5). *A good sense of humor is a sign of psychological health.* Quartz. https://qz.com/768622/a-good-sense-of-humor-is-a-sign-of-psychological-health/.

Goebel, B. (2018). What's so funny about social justice? *English Journal, 107*(6), 48–53. https://www.jstor.org/stable/26610193.

Goldman, N. (2013, November). *Comedy and democracy: The role of humor in social justice.* Animating Democracy.http://animatingdemocracy.org/sites/default/files/Humor%20Trend%20Paper.pdf.

Gordon, M. (2012). Nazi "proof" that Jews possessed the worst humor in the world. *Israeli Journal of Humor Research, 1*(2), 97–100. https://www.israeli-humor-studies.org/page34.php.

Gutwirth, E. (1990). From Jewish to Converso humour in fifteenth-century Spain. *Bulletin of Hispanic Studies, 67,* 223–233. https://doi.org/10.1080/1475382902000367223

Hodson, G., & MacInnis, C. C. (2016). Derogating humor as a delegitimization strategy in intergroup contexts. *Translational Issues in Psychological Science, 2*(1), 63–74. https://doi.org/10.1037/tps0000052

Idle, E. (1998). World's best one-liner. Graham Chapman on how to get into Dachau; anecdote retold by Eric Idle in this clip from the *Live in Aspen* show (1998), [Video] YouTube. https://youtu.be/5VH4c0-p-CY.

Johnson, J. W. (1912). *The autobiography of an ex-colored man.* Sherman, French, & Company.

Kantor, M. (2020). *Timeline of Jewish history: Adapted from the Codex Judaica, a chronological index of Jewish history covering 5764 years of Biblical, Talmudic, & post-Talmudic history.* https://www.chabad.org/library/article_cdo/aid/3915966/jewish/Timeline-of-Jewish-History.htm#q4.

Kaplan, G. B. (2008). Jewish tendencies in converso humor: A psychoanalytical approach. *Cuaderno Internacional De Estudios Humanísticos y Literatura, 10,* 33–45.

Kaplan, L. (2020). *At wit's end: The deadly discourse of the Jewish joke.* Fordham University Press.

Kaplan, G. B. (2021). The psychology of converso humor. *Academia Letters,* Article 674. https://doi.org/10.20935/AL674.

Keith-Speigel, P. (1972). Early conceptions of humor: Variety and issues. In J. H. Goldstein & P. E. McGhee (Eds.), *The psychology of humor* (pp. 3–39). Academic Press.

Keller, J., & Andersen, H. (1937). *The Jew as criminal.* Nibelungen-Verlag.

Korff, J. (2017, May 11). *How to deal with racist people.* Creative Spirits. https://www.creativespirits.info/aboriginalculture/people/how-to-deal-with-racist-people.

Kuipers, G. (2011). The politics of humour in the public sphere: Cartoons, power and modernity in the first transnational humour scandal. *European Journal of Cultural Studies, 14*(1), 63–80. https://doi.org/10.1177/1367549410370072

Land, G. (2022, June 13). *5 examples of anti-Jewish propaganda in Nazi Germany.* Historyhit.com. https://www.historyhit.com/culture/anti-jewish-propaganda-in-nazi-germany/.

Lee, C. P. (1998). "Yeah and I used to be a hunchback": Immigrants, humour and the Marx brothers. In S. Wagg (Ed.), *Because I tell a joke or two: Comedy, politics and social difference* (pp. 165–179). Taylor & Francis.

Lipman, S. (1991). *Laughter in hell: The use of humor during the Holocaust.* Jason Aronson.

Lipman, S. (2014, November 4). *4,000 years, 10 jokes.* JTA. https://www.jta.org/2014/11/04/ny/4000-years-10-jokes.

Lipman, S. (2020). *Finding light in the darkness: The art of Jewish humor.* Jewish action. https://jewishaction.com/religion/jewish-culture/finding-light-in-the-darkness-the-art-of-jewish-humor/.

Lowe, J. (1986). Theories of ethnic humor: How to enter laughing. *American Quarterly, 38*(3), 439–460. https://doi.org/10.2307/2712676

Martineau, W. (1972). A model of the social functions of humor. In J. H. Goldstein & P. E. McGhee (Eds.), *The psychology of humor* (pp. 101–125). Academic.

Miller, J. (Director). (2017). *Standing up.* United States: Fancy Squid Productions/Lucky 8 Films.

MODI (2022, April 30). *Modi at Comedy Cellar on cancel culture & antisemitism.* [Video] YouTube. https://youtu.be/R90_EeRP2wc.

Morreall, J. (2001). Humor in the Holocaust: Its critical, cohesive, and coping functions. In *1997 annual scholars' conference on the holocaust and the churches, hearing the voices: Teaching the holocaust to future generations.* http://oystory.org/Oy_Story!_Blog/Entries/2011/7/29_Humor_in_the_Holocaust_Its_Critical%2C_Cohesive%2C_and_Coping_Functions.html.

Murphy, H. (2018). *When 'jokes' go too far: Confronting workplace bullying.* Forbes.com. https://www.forbes.com/sites/forbescoachescouncil/2018/03/07/when-jokes-go-too-far-confronting-workplace-bullying/#7a62c5671055.

Nilsen, A. P., & Nilsen, D. L. F. (2019). *The language of humor.* Cambridge University Press.

Novak, W., & Waldoks, M. (2006). *The big book of Jewish humor.* Collins.

Osofsky, G. (Ed.). (1969). *Puttin' on ole massa: The slave narratives of Henry Bibb, William Wells Brown, and Solomon Northup.* HarperColins.

Ostrower, C. (2014). *It kept us alive: Humor in the Holocaust.* Yad Vashem.

Pew. (2021). *Jewish identity and belief.* Pew Research Center. Washington, DC. https://www.pewresearch.org/religion/2021/05/11/jewish-identity-and-belief/.

Reay, M. (2015). Using "wild" laughter to explore the social sources of humor. *Social Forces, 93*(3), 1241–1265. https://doi.org/10.1093/sf/sou106

Schutz, C. (1989). The sociability of ethnic jokes. *Humor: International Journal of Humor Research, 2*(2), 165–177. https://doi.org/10.1515/humr.1989.2.2.165.

Schutz, C. (1995). The sociability of ethnic jokes. *Australian Journal of Comedy, 1*(1), 89–102.

Spencer, H. (1860). The physiology of laughter. *Macmillan's Magazine, 1*, 395–402.

Sponder, Y. (2017). *Funny Monday 9—Hason, Sponder and friends [Video].* YouTube. https://youtu.be/R9oV5vGF1lQ.

StockholmLive (2009, August 26). Shazia Mirza. [Video] *YouTube.* https://youtu.be/QIsY6z8FmF8?t=108)

US Holocaust Memorial Museum. (2023). Blood libel. In *Holocaust Encyclopedia.* https://encyclopedia.ushmm.org/content/en/article/blood-libel.

Weaver, S. (2010). The "other" laughs back: Humor and resistance in anti-racist comedy. *Sociology, 44*(1), 31–48. https://doi.org/10.1177/0038038509351624

Williams, R. (2009). *Weapons of self-destruction—German comedy [Video] (Uploaded by Robin Williams Official YouTube Channel Jan 14, 2021). From HBO Special: Weapons of Self Destruction, 2009.* YouTube. https://youtu.be/Sq1y_YVG99s.

Ziv, A. (1984). *Personality and sense of humor.* Springer. https://msu.edu/~jdowell/ziv.html.

Ziv, A., & Gadish, O. (1989). Humor and marital satisfaction. *Journal of Social Psychology, 129*(6), 759–768. https://doi.org/10.1080/00224545.1989.9712084

Linda Weiser Friedman is Professor of Information Systems and Statistics in the Baruch College Zicklin School of Business; affiliated faculty in the Baruch College Jewish Studies Center; on the doctoral faculties in Business and Computer Science of the Graduate Center; all of the City University of New York. Her scholarship includes humor studies, Jewish studies, computer information systems, higher education, and simulation. She has published scholarly articles, books, fiction, and poetry.

Hershey H. Friedman is Professor of Business Management in the Koppelman School of Business, Brooklyn College of the City University of New York. His research and teaching interests include business statistics, leadership, marketing, humor studies, Jewish business ethics, Biblical leadership, and online education. He has more than 300 publications. Many of his papers are available at the SSRN.com website: http://papers.ssrn.com/sol3/cf_dev/AbsByAuth.cfm?per_id=638928 as well as the Researchgate.net website: https://www.researchgate.net/profile/Hershey_Friedman/publications. His most recent book: *God Laughed: Sources of Jewish Humor* by Hershey H. Friedman and Linda Weiser Friedman (2014).

Chapter 9
Humor and Cynical Political Parody in Italian Movies and Newspaper Cartoons

Benedetta Baldi

Abstract Italian cinematographic comedy is poised between an indulgent picture of Italian society and its recent history, and the denunciation of responsibilities and compromises. Movies such as the *saga of Peppone* [The Communist Mayor] and *Don Camillo* [The Parish], respond to a comforting representation of the common feeling whereby Italians, also in war or in political struggle, remain "good people," sensitive to human values. However, in the post-war period we find a more crude and cynical satire of politics, typically in the form of social criticism, generally inspired by left-wing thinking, gradually more effective in denouncing the problems of an increasingly consumerist and individualistic society. Social satire has been able to interpret the widespread mistrust towards politicians, reflecting the long impasse of civil and social rights in Italian democracy and the growing cultural changes in society during the forty-year government of the Christian Democracy [*Democrazia Cristiana*] party. Different semiotic and rhetorical tools are used by films and other media to create desecrating and provocative satire, such as social alienation and hypocritical conformism, vulgar language as difference, and the hidden and petty faces of power.

9.1 Introduction

The goal of this chapter is to investigate Italian political parody as an expression of the cultural universe of society. I will focus on one of the fundamental traits of Italian culture: the deep and atavistic distrust of politics and its inability to foster social progress. My analysis takes into consideration the basic tools of satire, its special way of communicating aspects of reality through a surreal narrative. Just going beyond the known is the goal of satire, whereby "The real comedian is the one who goes to unknown borders, who goes to risk zones, where none has ever dared" (Lagioia, 2015, p. 11).

B. Baldi (✉)
Department of Humanities and Philosophy, University of Florence, Florence, Italy
e-mail: benedetta.baldi@unifi.it

© The Author(s), under exclusive license to Springer Nature Singapore Pte Ltd. 2024
O. Feldman (ed.), *Political Humor Worldwide*, The Language of Politics,
https://doi.org/10.1007/978-981-99-8490-9_9

Italian political satire has been first and foremost a social satire, as an expression of political forces and power. In other words, a society subject to conservative laws, rules, and attitudes, has generally fueled a satirical representation and critique of the political world and its representatives. The overlapping of political and social satire depends on several historical and cultural factors, including the fact that for forty years the same party had been in government. Social satire was a way, clear and understood by all, to attack the government and politicians from time to time. As we will see in the following sections, it finds its main expression in the cinema, where great directors and great actors were able to manifest the contradictions of a society emerging from a destructive war, and based on strong cultural and economic contrasts, social tensions, and ideological oppositions, not completely overcome (Gotor, 2019).

Italian collective imagery seems to seek a kind of redemption from a complex of unedifying memories, historical experiences, and inherited beliefs. It is well-known that Italian society in different moments has been responsive to populist discourse, where abstract ideals cover irrational and incomplete political and social aspirations—from fascism to the period of terrorism in the seventies and eighties, and of judicial investigations of *"Mani Pulite"* (Clean Hands). The end of the so-called first republic (Gotor, 2019), coincided with cultural and economic discrepancies in society that strengthened a conservative sensibility in people. In this regard, it should be remembered that often an almost caricatural representation of Italian society and its history emerges in public opinion, filtered through the stereotype "mandolin and pizza." This is a misleading and wrong vision, but it has some influence on historical and social approaches, especially in some elements of Anglo-Saxon culture. In fact, nothing in the Italian historical landscape is particularly funny, a landscape that the cinema has represented in a dramatic and complex way.

Schematically, here are some of the main types of socio-political satire and comedy:

(1) A fundamental message of political satire concerns society and the contrast between the ruling class and the conditions of economic backwardness or social exclusion of the masses. This type of satire characterizes the first decades after World War II and is also fueled by the ideological struggle between the Left parties and the government.
(2) In the forty years of uninterrupted *Christian Democracy* [*Democrazia Cristiana*] government, forms of corruption, opportunism, and prevarication ended up characterizing the management of power, by the governing parties and in part by those in opposition.
(3) The latter showed a kind of continuity with the fascist organization of the state, such as censorship of artistic expression, substantially in line with a traditionalist and moralistic approach to human life and social relations.
(4) We find a self-absolutory and indulgent attitude to political faults and errors, based on a populist and consoling/comforting representation of society.
(5) This contrasts with a satire based on cynical and provocative irony able to destroy any reliability and accountability of institutional communication and political actors.

As well-known, Jakobson (2009[1933]) sees the poetic function as a crucial property of the organization of linguistic messages. In poetic texts, sounds, words, and sentences are combined according to specific principles of similarity and equivalence (rhymes, alliterations, repetitions, etc.) that create a special code, an interpretive level different from the literal one. Can we apply this idea to film? In what sense, one wonders, is poetry connected to satire? Films become more effective in grasping the cognitive sphere of the individual as their formal aspects become more prevalent. In other words, satire is all the more evident and powerful the less narrative it contains.

Cinematographic texts obey the same principles of other semiotic systems, insofar as they convey meaning through signs coinciding with reality: individuals, objects, behaviors, and events. Thus, acoustic and visual reality, and the language itself, are transformed into signs (Jakobson, 1933/2009). According to Lotman (1973/2019, pp. 77–78) a film text is a semiotic process, with an interesting difference from a text based on language. In the linguistic text, "the sign is a primary datum, pre-existent to the text: the text is composed of signs." In the case of a film "the primary datum is the text." The figurative arts generate a narrative interpretable exactly as in poetry, where the verbal text "is composed as a unique and indivisible iconic sign-text."

The iconic nature of the visual process of films has the tendency to be interpreted as a system of metaphors. Metaphor is part of the visual sequence of scenes and shots of the film to the extent that the reality portrayed serves to express something else. In fact, the ability of metaphoric uses to project a system of semantic relations has the effect of creating new meanings by substituting for the old ones (Lakoff & Johnson, 1999). According to Bowdle and Gentner (2005) and Gentner and Bowdle (2008), metaphor is the result of a cognitive process that establishes correspondences between the partially isomorphic conceptual structures associated with two terms. In this sense, metaphor is a source of polysemy, as it generates an additional abstract meaning in addition to the literal meaning of a term, with the result that this new category can be conceptualized separately from the original ones. The multiplicative effect of metaphor is pointed out by Sperber and Wilson (1986/1995) whereby, like the poetic and stylistic effect, an expansion of the meaning is obtained by means of implicatures triggered by metaphorical discourse.

9.2 A Difficult Balance: Satire Between Nostalgia and True Criticism[1]

Given the conservative ethos mentioned above, Italy had a wide scope of censorship that worked in a few directions:

(1) Defense of public morality, by blocking images with sexual content and allusions and any criticism or derision of the traditional Catholic family and its values;

---

[1] In addition to the original Italian title, the films are listed here in the English name with which they were distributed and are known on the international market.

(2) Avoidance of criticism, irreverent allusions and satiric representations of the Government, specifically the Christian Democracy party;
(3) Evisceration of Communist symbols and ideology.

It is within this state of affairs that political parody has been exercised.

Since the 1940s the main and most popular tool of parody has been found in film. The problems faced by the directors concerned censorship applied by the bureaucrats, and in fact many films were censored by cutting scenes or replacing the sound (Brunetta, 2009). In addressing this type of satire, I think that the cinema of Totò, the stage name of actor Antonio De Curtis, is an extraordinarily significant and profound example of subversive and derisory satire of most commonplace Italian social and political conformism in the Fifties and Sixties. In his first movies after the war, his aim was not to provide hope or a synthesis of social and cultural discrepancies but rather to desecrate the "customs and institutions of fascist Italy: martial rhetoric, patriotic rhetoric, bigoted Catholicism, religious hypocrisy" (Tirino, 2017, p. 10). In a famous scene of *The Two Colonels* [*I due colonnelli*] (1963), directed by Steno, Totò, dressed as a colonel, mimics the movements and rhetoric of the Duce, mocking their dark and insipid grandeur.

His film character was able to introduce all the themes of an impoverished society without illusions, in the framework of a cynical and tragic view of the world. He was a man affected by an age-old and atavistic hunger for food, sex, and social advancement, a man always at risk of a catastrophic end. His individual solitude was the metaphor for the inextinguishable social insecurity that no government was able to eradicate, neither fascism nor the new democracy. He impersonated the greedy underclasses or petty bourgeois concerned to maintain their status in a society always in critical status, with unbalanced and uncertain social rules. It is interesting to note that the intolerant rebelliousness personified by Totò is fully manifested in the films with the other great comedian Peppino de Filippo. As highlighted by Tirino (2017, p. 25), as a couple, Totò abuses, offends, and lies to Peppino, but these forms of sadism are a special application of the criticism of conformism:

> But, more than the protagonist who torments his sidekick, Totò in the couple is configured as the tempter who seeks the complicity of Peppino and frees him from his worries (the avarice, the provincialism) to lead him to enjoyment, to freedom (Anile, 2001, p. 31).

Thus, in *Totò, Peppino and the Hussy* [*Totò, Peppino e... la malafemmina*] (1956) directed by Camillo Mastrocinque, Totò is not only the sadistic leader of the couple but also the tempter, inducing the restive and parsimonious companion to a final revelry. Every worry fades away: Totò and Peppino spend, eat, and have fun with beautiful girls. This is freedom! The Italian society is, thus, pessimistically depicted through the continuous implacable irony regarding political power, its representatives, its symbols, and social differences. His jokes, the expression on his face, and his way of gesturing translate the representation of society into surreal imagery, into an uninterrupted teasing that makes any value or symbol devoid of trustworthiness.

In a famous sketch, the scene of the wagon lit in *Totò in Color* [*Totò a colori*] (1952), directed by Steno, Totò meets a parliamentarian, the Honourable Trombetta, literally "small Trumpet." The expressive, pragmatic, and linguistic behavior of Totò gives rise to a lunatic conversation: Totò appoints the station master *colonel in plain clothes*, says he has the profession of "Free citizen [...] [which] professes a doctrine [...] [he] frees citizenship" [*Libero Cittadino* [...] *professa una dottrina* [...] *libera la cittadinanza*], he appoints the Honourable Trombetta as *Trombone*, in Italian an expressive name for a pompous and opinionated person. The satire of political rhetoric was systematic, mixed with a general irony about the bombastic language of politicians and the archaic forms of bureaucracy. In many cases, it used lexical elements or expressions taken from a high style or a specialized language, such as *meco* (*with me*, archaic and literary), *sponsali* (*wedding*, archaic and literary), (*è/fa*) *d'uopo* (*it is necessary*, literary), etc. with the interesting consequence of discriminating between educational and cultural levels of the characters (Rossi, 2002). He inserted these forms in usual conversational contexts, where they obviously clashed. This satirical use of archaic forms reflects the distance between power and populace, historicizing the difference in the terms of Butler (1997), with ridiculous but anxiety-producing effects. Thus, the surreal world of Totò is a product of the metaphorical tools adopted: his language and behavior, attitudes, relationship with Peppino, and so on.

As expected, the films of Totò were often targeted by censorship, regarding sexual allusions as well as expressions evoking political and social distrust or cynical and tragic views of the world. This is the case in movies such as *Totò and the King of Rome* [*Totò e i re di Roma*] (1952), *Totò and Carolina* [*Totò e Carolina*] (1955) directed by Mario Monicelli, *His Excellency Stopped to Eat* [*Sua Eccellenza si fermò a mangiare*] (1961), directed by Mario Mattoli, which among other problematic aspects, represented institutional figures. *Totò and Carolina* is the story of a policeman, a poor widower with a child and an old father, induced by the superintendent to keep with him a pregnant orphan girl found in Villa Borghese, a place frequented by prostitutes. Everything in this story contrasts with the common morality and the honor of the institution, specifically the police, defended by the Christian Democracy and its government. The film underwent more than 50 cuts, with some scenes distorted. For instance, a procession of protesters singing The Red Flag, the communist anthem, is transformed into a procession that sings a patriotic song, and so on. But what is not acceptable is that the decorum of the police, the bulwark of public morality, is being questioned by a policeman who takes an adolescent mother to his house!

Let's consider some indulgent approaches first. This frame included the movies of the famous saga of Peppone [the communist mayor] and Don Camillo [the parish priest] of the same village, Brescello, in the Emilian plain. The saga took place in five films, produced from 1952 to 1965, (freely) based on the tales of Giovannino Guareschi, a convinced anti-communist intellectual and journalist. The tales were published in several collections as well as in *Candid* [*Candido*], the humorous weekly directed by the same Guareschi (cf. Sect. 9.4). In the films *Don Camillo* 1952 and *The Return of Don Camillo* [*Il ritorno di Don Camillo*] (1953), directed by Julien Duvivier, *Don Camillo's Last Round* [*Don Camillo e l'onorevole Peppone*] (1955) and *Don Camillo: Monsignor* [*Don Camillo monsignore... ma non troppo*] (1961), directed by Carmine Gallone, and finally *Don Camillo in Moskow* [*Il compagno Don Camillo*] (1965) directed by Luigi Comencini, two excellent actors satirized the two protagonists: Fernandel as Don Camillo; Gino Cervi as Peppone. The tales, although told through different events, stories, figures, and vicissitudes, evoked the same deep narrative scheme: the fight between freedom and communism, even if the fight is transfigured in the kindly and generous friendship between two real members of the after-war Italy. Peppone and Don Camillo participated together in the war of liberation, they are old friends (even if they try to avoid manifesting it), esteeming and when possible helping each other. In this narrative, Don Camillo is the true hero on whom the story depends: he is often aggressive and grumpy with Peppone, often severe and rigid, thus highlighting the ambiguous and dangerous populism of the left-wing party.

An interesting example of this semantic core was the fifth movie, *Don Camillo in Moskow*, where Don Camillo manages to be part of a representative of the communist section of Brescello in the trip to the Soviet Union for the twinning with a small Russian town. During the journey, the economic difficulties, the poverty, and the lack of people's freedom are gradually brought to light in a merciless way by the behavior of Don Camillo, thus showing the contradictions between Soviet politics and the normal life and feelings of people. The help that Don Camillo gives to his fellow citizen from Brescello, the comrade 'il Brusco' to find his brother's tomb, which fell during the Russian Campaign, suggests a reconciled vision of Italy, based on the memory of a common homeland and history.

Although the stereotype of "Italian good people" has been unmasked by historians (Del Boca, 2005), this mythical representation of Italian soldiers inspired a film on the Italian occupation of Greece, *Mediterraneo* (1991), directed by Gabriele Salvatores, in which eight Italian soldiers are assigned to a small island in the Aegean Sea. Their relationship with the population is peaceful and friendly. A rhetorical nostalgia diminishes the satirical intent, hiding the most disturbing aspects of Italian responsibility in the Greek campaign. The paradoxical result is that the military occupation of the island becomes an aesthetic object and justified by the loss of the illusions of a freer and fairer Italian society.

9.3 A Different Code for a Cynical, Sometimes Debasing Approach

In the Sixties and Seventies, cinema depicted a grotesque fresco of Italian society, its contradictions, and a political class that wields power often far from the changes of custom that people go through. Those were the years of the so-called Center-Left governments, in the midst of the Cold War, afflicted by an underground clash between extreme right-wing forces and extreme left-wing forces and by the communist opposition anchored in the dogmas of real socialism and proletarian ethics. In this cultural frame, television was under government control. Newspapers and magazines, except for a few exceptions, reflected the official positions of right and left, and their values and beliefs. Only films, directed by able and creative investigators of society could offer a critical analysis of social tensions and power.

An example of this was the multifaceted, satirical production, partly in the wake of Neorealism, that characterized the long post-war period (Brunetta, 2009), such as the numerous comedies with Alberto Sordi portraying many characters displaying Italian society afflicted by conformism and social climbing in a continuous struggle for social advancement and individual enrichment. The cynic and careerist Doctor Guido Tersilli, in the film *Be Sick… it's Free* [*Il medico della mutua*] (1968) directed by Luigi Zampa, and the urban policeman Otello Celletti who had to adapt to the interests and prevarications of city mayors in *The Traffic Policeman* [*Il vigile*] (1960) directed by Luigi Zampa, interpret the development of cultural poverty and class differences of Italian society emerged from the war. *I vitelloni* (literally *The Slackers*) (1953), directed by Federico Fellini, shows the irresponsible and empty life of provincial youth, mother's pets within the petty bourgeoisie, without ideals, finding its emblematic expression in the scene of the fuck-off gesture that Alberto (Sordi) gives to some workers, by which he is then chased.

The power of Christian Democrats is subject to strong sarcasm and parodies that reveal its underlying hypocrisy. An interesting example is the film of Lucio Fulci *The Eroticist* [*Nonostante le apparenze… e purché la nazione non lo sappia… all'onorevole piacciono le donne*] (1972), starring Lando Buzzanca. The film was blocked by censorship, both for some scenes of a sexual nature, and mainly for the dark and subversive representation of political events, the parliament, and the ruling party. In particular, the parliamentarian obsessed with uncontrollable sexual libido was a clear reference to the then prime minister Emilio Colombo. In addition, the film alluded to the coup attempt on the night of December 7–8, 1970 by Prince Junio Valerio Borghese and the extreme-right organization National Vanguard, the plot involving the figure of a cardinal. The sexual obsession and the disturbing nature of the characters created a satirical representation of the political and civil condition of Italian society, its hypocrisy, and conformist moralism. We see a society where ideological control by the government was undermined by extremist movements, terrorism, and the strategy of tension.

Persons Unknown [*I soliti ignoti*] (1958), directed by Mario Monicelli, starring Vittorio Gassman, Marcello Mastroianni, Totò among others, is a famous comedy that portrays the city of Rome in the years of urban expansion and social change. A group of unemployed loafers from the suburbs try to rob a pawnshop by breaking a wall of an adjacent apartment. The robbery, prepared in a laughable and unrealistic way, ends in failure: the broken wall is the wrong one, actually the wall of the kitchen, so that the thieves are reduced to eating the pasta and beans they find there. Monicelli represented Italy in a phase of transformation, where the great urban suburbs were being born and the economic boom of the Sixties began to give rise to social changes and internal migrations, as suggested by the different origins and dialects of the characters. As noticed by Brunetta (2009, p. 311), "The linguistic mixture is the sign of a new social mobility in place at the end of the Fifties, recorded with the greatest possible timing. It is an Italy, facing the threshold of the boom, not yet unified and hegemonized by that national Italian created and broadcast by Rai-TV […]." But the film left a light nostalgia for the past that began moving towards a social fabric ever more based on conformism and social climbing (as denounced by Pasolini, 2008 [1975]).

The backwardness of Italian laws, still based on the Rocco code of the fascist era and inspired by a still patriarchal conception of women and the family, is the subject of a famous film directed by Pietro Germi, *Divorce Italian Style* [*Divorzio all'italiana*] 1972, starring Marcello Mastroianni and Stefania Sandrelli. In Italy, the act of honor [*delitto d'onore*] still existed, whereby the husband could take revenge on his wife caught in adultery, risking a reduced penalty. Although the Divorce Act was introduced in 1970, honor attacks and the so-called shotgun marriage were abolished in 1981. The reform of family law, which recognized equal rights for women and men, was approved in 1975. The film narrated the story of a provincial Sicilian nobleman who tries to get rid of his wife by creating the conditions of her adultery. In the end, after several paradoxical events, he catches her red-handed and shoots her. His young and beautiful ex-lover now becomes his wife, but in the last scene appears quite ready to be unfaithful to him. Germi narrated a provincial world, where discrimination ends up hitting those who exercise it, the unconfessed fear of a patriarchal and male-dominated society.

The subculture of the marginalized classes and its relationship with the Italian Communist Party led by the charismatic leader Enrico Berlinguer are addressed in the film *Berlinguer, I Love You* [*Berlinguer ti voglio bene*] (1977), directed by Giuseppe Bertolucci and starring Roberto Benigni. The film reflected a particular moment in Italian politics when newspapers begin to talk about the so-called 'historical compromise' i.e., a government also including the Italian Communist Party. The film, shot on the outskirts of Prato, near Florence, and spoken in Florentine dialect, depicted the irreparable social alienation of the lower class. Mario Cioni, played by Roberto Benigni, his mother, and his friends are frequenters of the People's House, meeting place of the Communist Party. They are a people without any prospect of improving their social status, awaiting the orders of Berlinguer, but without hope. They continuously talk and think about sex, with a systematic use, deliberately exasperated, of sexist and scurrilous expressions and behaviors. This use is their only available subversion and it created a surreal way of interpreting reality and social relations by demolishing and debunking bourgeois taboos of the right-thinkers. In a crucial scene, Bozzone (played by Carlo Monni), a friend of Mario, bringing him on the bicycle, recites a poem that synthesizes the hopelessness of this marginal world[2]:

> We are that race
>
> that is not too well
>
> that in the day skips ditches
>
> and in the evening dinners.
>
> I can scream loud
>
> until I become weak

---

[2] This scene is visible on TheSepulnannitura, n.d.).

we are that race

that fucks so little.

We are that race

that clogs the cinema

to see naked women

and jerk off at home.

Yet, nature teaches us

both on the mountains and downstream

that you can be born caterpillars

to become butterflies.

We are that race

that is among the strangest

that caterpillars we are born

and caterpillars we remain.

We are that race

it is useless to pretend:

it has conquered our misery

and we were pregnant

[*No' semo quella razza che non sta troppo bene che di giorno salta fossi e la sera le cene.*

Lo posso grida' forte fino a diventa' fioco no' semo quella razza che tromba tanto poco.

Noi semo quella razza che al cinema s'intasa pe' vede' donne 'gnude e farsi seghe a casa.

Eppure, la natura ci insegna sia sui monti, sia a valle che si po' nascer bruchi

pe' diventa' farfalle.

Noi semo quella razza che l'è tra le più strane che bruchi semo nati e bruchi si rimane.

Quella razza semo noi l'è inutile far finta: c'ha trombato la miseria e semo rimasti incinta]
(nonsonsolofilm.it, 2013).

The world of Cioni is without redemption or the possibility of change. It is an immutable place that denies any expectation, it is in a risk zone, where the fiercely masculine culture is celebrated in the People's House, through the debate "Can the woman afford to be equal to the man?" Everything, in this world, is altogether surreal and subversive. The story ends with an unexpected development: Bozzone gets to sleep with Mario's mother (played by Alida Valli) in exchange for cancelling a debt. The desperation of Mario contrasts with the felicity of Bozzone and his mother. Bozzone is so happy that he accompanies the woman at Mass and concludes that "God exists;" later, at the table, Bozzone recites the sweet and very bourgeois poem by Jacques Prevert, *Cet amour (This Love)*. These radical changes leave Mario in deep disorientation.

Being in risk zones is a rare skill. Needless to say, there are many examples of true comedy also in the Seventies and in the following decades. One exemplar: the saga of ten films that tell the story of the accountant Ugo Fantozzi, the character conceived and played by Paolo Villaggio. The world of Fantozzi is already fixed in the first two films, *Fantozzi* (1975) and *The Second Tragic Fantozzi* [*Il secondo tragico Fantozzi*], both directed by Luciano Salce. Fantozzi, married to his wife Lina and father of the ugly Mariangela, works in the so-called Mega-firm, led by the powerful Galactic Megadirector Conte Maria Rita Vittorio Balabam, where he has as colleagues the accountant Filini, the surveyor Calboni, and Miss Silvani, of which Fantozzi is madly infatuated. Fantozzi is a loser, a person who has failed and has achieved nothing of what he wanted in life. He is harassed and humiliated by his colleagues and bosses. The social satire of bourgeois conventions and the habits of the rich is presented in some famous scenes, where a populist reinterpretation of reality is provided.

This is the case where Fantozzi and his office colleagues are obliged by their boss, Professor Guidobaldo Maria Riccardelli, to watch for the umpteenth time the Battleship Potëmkin in the company's film club. It is Fantozzi who pronounces the liberating phrase "In my opinion [...] the Battleship Kotiomkin [instead of Potëmkin for legal reasons] is a crazy shit!" [*Per me [...] la corazzata Kotiomkin è una cagata pazzesca!*], rebelling against the dominant, conformist aesthetic. We are in unknown territory, where the politically correct philosophy and respect of the cultural establishment, are definitively reversed.

More directly political is the satire in the films starring the comedian Antonio Albanese, playing his famous character Cetto La Qualunque. In the trilogy, *Whatsoeverly* [*Qualunquemente*] (2011), *Everything Everything Nothing Nothing* [*Tutto tutto niente niente*] (2012), *Cetto Is Back, Doubtlessly* [*Cetto c'è senzadubbiamente*] (2019), directed by Giulio Manfredonia, Cetto is a Calabrian politician, sleazy and devoid of any morality and scruples, in an Italian society oppressed by corrupt politicians and by corrupt customs, and devoid of any ethical ideal. In the third film of the saga, Albanese/Cetto discovers that he descends from the Bourbons, the ancient kings of Naples and Sicily. Cetto's attempt to recreate the kingdom and become king of the Italians gives rise to ridiculous and farcical vicissitudes. During those, Cetto provides a demeaning picture of Italian society: "I love the Italians, they are a flock that follows the dog and I bark very well! They have lost faith in politics, in economics, in democracy, and we offer them monarchy, Italians have been believing all kinds of bullshit for years, and we are the right shit at the right time!".

Cetto's spectacular and intense sexist approach to life, his attraction to escorts, has clear metaphorical force in evoking the politician and former Prime Minister Berlusconi, the powerful media entrepreneur. As can be expected, the figure of Berlusconi is the subject of some satirical or political films focused on his opaque past. Again, satire is not humorous but involves Italian society. In *The Caiman* [*Il caimano*] (2006) Nanni Moretti addresses the relationship between Silvio Berlusconi and the people. In the film, Berlusconi is Prime Minister but under investigation by the judiciary for tax fraud and other charges. Presented as a politician with a dark and disturbing power, Moretti concludes his film with the noir image of Berlusconi leaving the court while the people assault the judges who condemned him.

The cinema of Nanni Moretti, director and actor in his own films, provides an analysis of the changes in Italian society, with dazzling and in-depth insights able to grasp new imaginaries and their significance. In *Ecce bombo* (1978), the delusion of the after-Nineteen-Sixty-Eight youth is represented as an intimate, personal state of uncertainty (Todini, 2004). *Red Wood Pigeon* [*Palombella rossa*] (1989) is a satire of the end of the ideals of left-wing parties and their cultural vision. The fall of the Berlin Wall has definitively revealed the nature of real socialism and demolished the libertarian illusions connected with it. The film is considered the cinematographic manifesto of the crisis of left-wing ideologies (Sesti, 2004) that Moretti expresses through the figure of a Communist Party member, Michele Apicella, who has lost his memory in an accident and who tries to find it during a game of water polo, practiced by him.

A crucial point is that, once again, the political aspects are filtered through the meanings and feelings of the protagonists and interpreted in terms of a more general crisis of values. An eloquent moment is Michele's interview with a young interviewer, in which the latter uses stereotypical terms of a banal and conformist language, such as "Marriage falling apart" [*Matrimonio a pezzi*] *Kitch*, "Even if my environment is very cheap" [*Anche se il mio ambiente è molto cheap*]. Michele reacts violently to this way of speaking about persons and events, shouting several times "But what kind of language is that?" [*Ma come parla?*], "It is not the subject [...] it is the expression!" [*Non è l'argomento [...] è l'espressione!*], and finally concludes "But how you speak! Words are important! How you speak [...] Who speaks badly, thinks badly, and lives badly. You have to find the right words: words are important!" [*Ma come parla! Le parole sono importanti! Come parla!... Chi parla male, pensa male, e vive male. Bisogna trovare le parole giuste: le parole sono importanti!*]. The moralistic approach to language appears to be a crucial way to denounce the docility with which people adapt to the conformity and deceptive, alienating nature of words, unable to express the truth (Sesti, 2004, p. 3). Words, in all Moretti's films, are endowed with a crucial responsibility in connecting speakers and reality, constituting the crucial semantic components of the film: they denounce the effort and difficulty of reciprocal understanding, the distance between individuals in modern society.

Thus, the symbolic force of films such as *Red Wood Pigeon, Ecce Bombo, Berlinguer, I Love You, Totò and the King of Rome*, the characters of Fantozzi and

Cetto La Qualunque, can all be associated with the particular narrative register in which the story, events, and language are far from a realistic narration but enable an independent and surreal level of understanding. Coarse and vulgar expressions, in films such as *Berlinguer, I Love You,* and *Cetto Is Back, Doubtlessly,* are a kind of metaphorical construction and contribute to evoking an alternative world, a social imagery different from the conformist approach to life and current political and social values. Similarly, it is no coincidence that Bozzone, one of the characters of *Berlinguer, I Love You,* usually vulgar and scurrilous, recites love poems and goes to church as a good bourgeois when he finds a woman and feels satisfied.

9.4 Other Media

Satire in newspapers and magazines, typically associated with cartoons and inserts, mostly appears (with some exceptions) less free, deep and corrosive than that of films and other forms of expression. As Lagioia (2015) observes, it is difficult for satirical cartoonists to be truly subversive, as they also unconsciously tend to be adapted to the political and economic interests of the newspaper. The weekly *Candid* [*Candido*], founded in Milan (1945–1957) by the two important writers and journalists Giovanni Mosca and Giovannino Guareschi (cf. Sect. 9.2), represented a satire that was viscerally anti-communist. An interesting aspect of its ideological anti-communist approach is the marked annoyance at any apparent reduced aversion or compromise of the national ruling class, in particular the Christian Democracy and the Western states, towards the Communists, seen as a total and unapproachable enemy. The same approach characterizes the saga of Don Camillo and Peppone, touched on in Sect. 9.2, presented in the pages of *Candid* in the form of tales from 1946.

The satire of *Candide* can be exemplified by reference to some cartoons published around 1950–1951, the period in which the Italian Republic joined the Marshall Plan, the Council of Europe, and the Atlantic Alliance, and finally in 1951, the European Coal and Steel Community. The fierce aversion to communists and the nostalgia for the autarchic politics of Fascism are drawn in eloquent cartoons referring to contemporary events concerning the political struggle between communists and the government, the latter considered too acquiescent. I recall the macabre joke on the massacre that occurred during the strike of January 9, 1950, at the United Foundries [*Fonderie Riunite*] of Modena (a city in Emilia-Romagna region) called by the union in protest against dismissals, entitled "The last gift of the Italian Communist Party has arrived from Modena" (January 22, 1950). There the State police fired on protesters, killing six workers and injuring 200 people: coffins drawn in the cartoon are labeled as a gift of communists. "Celebrations for Verdi" (December 3, 1950) provides an opportunity to compare the acronym VERDI, interpreted as Vittorio Emanuele King of Italy [*Vittorio Emanuele Re d'Italia*], with LEPRI, "hares, the fearful animal par excellence" associated with Luigi Einaudi President of Italian Republic [*Luigi Einaudi Presidente Repubblica Italiana*]. In other words, the current Republic and its representatives are seen as fearful and inept, compared to past regimes. Finally, "Communist apparatus" (July 23, 1950) depicts Italy with a gun pointed at its head, the communist apparatus. Guareschi despises the ruling class of the Republic, seen as submissive towards communism: "A worried gentleman tells Italy: Look lady, there's someone pointing a gun at your head," "Yeah, I know, but he has a firearms license."

The evil [Il Male] was published from 1978 to 1982, a tragic time for Italy, and was a special and not repeated apparition in Italy's journalistic and satirical world. Produced by Pino Zac, Vincenzo Gallo, and other known left journalists and intellectuals, it had immediate success by proposing a cynical and aggressive reading of political facts and figures. Its satire was based on a vulgar and debasing representation, and a derisory and desecrating approach, whereby the sad events of terrorism are the subject of fierce irony and mockery. One of the inventions of *Il Male* was falsifying the front page of newspapers. A famous hoax was the news that the film actor Ugo Tognazzi—who, of course, consented—was the leader of the terrorist group Red Brigades [*Brigate Rosse*], published on three false front pages of Italian newspapers, *Paese Sera, Il Giorno* and *La Stampa*. In *Paese Sera* the news was: "Ugo Tognazzi arrested. He is the leader of the BR […] Also Vianello [another Italian comedian] in the same strategic direction: Five hundred carabinieri hunt him. Faked the breakup of the couple at the time of 'One two three' [a television comic program]. From behind the scenes, they directed the subversive movement. Many arrests of comedians. Congratulations by Pertini (the President of the Republic)." Ranting and demented texts accompanied images and caricatures that were often fierce and blasphemous.

It is no accident that The Evil was often subject to censorship. Some famous covers illustrated the heavy and offensive approach to power. The cover of the February 1978 issue, entitled "This is the last straw (lit. The measure is full)," shows a chamber vase on which are bas-relief faces of Enrico Berlinguer, leader of the Communist Party, Giulio Andreotti, the powerful Christian Democrat politician, several times minister and prime minister, and Ugo La Malfa, leader of the Republican Party. In the February 7, 1979 issue, the title "What face did he show up with?" refers to the image of Andreotti's face shaped in a vulgar and degrading form: if "face is an image of self-delineated in terms of approved social attributes—albeit an image that others may share" (Goffman, 1967, p. 5), then the subversive result relates not only to Andreotti but to the entire institutional establishment. The link is clear between the type of satire and figurative language used in The Evil, and similar contemporary forms of semiotics used, for example, in the film *Berlinguer, I Love You*, discussed in Sect. 9.3.

The front page of the August 29 edition proposes a worldly and allusive image with which The Evil [*Il Male*] represented Pope John Paul II, depicted as a rich tourist, a sort of playboy, who heads for a luxury pool saying: "Fucked if with communism I used to swim!" Profanities, obscenities, and derisory scatological representations bring the reader to a desacralized dimension, where everything and everybody appear without sense, and interpretation is substantially governed by emotions and cultural assonance. It is of note that this kind of political message will become increasingly common in the rhetoric of Italian political struggles in the following decades and typically of populist parties such as the *Lega* [League] of Umberto Bossi and the *Movimento 5 Stelle* [5 Stars Movement] of Beppe Grillo (Baldi, 2023).

As one can expect, television could also provide an arena for satire. However, satire did not find a suitable stage in television. In the decades of the so-called first republic, until the Nineties, satire was close to being domesticated. With the liberalization of the broadcasting sector things changed, but not much, because satire was checked by ownership and large networks linked to political power. In January 2001 the show Satyricon, played by Daniele Luttrazzi, was broadcast on the Second Channel of State TV. The show was understood as a parody similar to Letterman's talk show, of which it took the same structure and headings. The explicit and derisory satire was introduced by an initial slogan: "The program that is going to air contains fellatio, cunnilingus, masturbation, feces, urine, sadomasochism, Bruno Vespa (a famous TV journalist close to power), and anything else the fetid mind of Daniele Luttazzi has fermented in the last period. His explicit language is meant to upset fools. To everyone else, have fun!".

The episodes of Satyricon contained interviews and other interventions by Luttazzi, always very explicit also for allusions to the Mafia origins of Berlusconi's wealth and also always very sarcastic towards the political establishment. Sexist gags and sexual allusions were very explicit, as in the interview with Anna Falchi, a showgirl, who was invited to take off her underwear, causing fierce criticism from right-wing politicians and journalists, with the consequence that the program was temporarily suspended. Berlusconi, who became Prime Minister in 2002, explicitly requested its closure. Over the past decade, another comedian has taken a central role in the left-wing satire of politicians i.e., Maurizio Crozza and his TV show *The Crozza's Brothers* [*I fratelli di Crozza*] on a private channel. The show is based on imitations that provide critical and derisive representations of politicians. The effect, however, is estranging: Berlusconi who falls asleep while talking; Enrico Letta, the secretary of the Democratic Party, who speaks in a professorial and a little confused way; Giorgia Meloni, the current prime minister, apodictic and sure in her Roman speech, with swirling eyes; the president of Campania, De Luca, polemicizing with the northern regions; and folkloric, Zaia, the president of Veneto, inconclusive and confused; and so on…

Lagioia (2015, p. 9) underlines the distance of humorous representations of the idiosyncracies and expressions of politicians, from satire, in the sense that "The problem with Crozza's humor is its being nihilistic. When I watch his sketches on TV, I am convinced that the world was really reduced to those linguistic codes, […]. It is the representation of an eternal world." By contrast, what we have discussed in Sects. 9.1 and 9.3 is something that comes from *outside*. It is a language, a semiotic construct that has "a clandestine and disturbing presence. The comedian does not challenge power with the language of power" (Lagioia, 2015, p. 9). The comic effect begins where there is a gap with the language of power, an irreconcilability. Of course, Crozza's parody reproposes the language of power, and in this sense it moves within its own logic. In any case, the picture that is created is neither benevolent nor conciliatory, but a corrosive and debasing image of the powerful, where politicians appear as puppets, meaningless people, that repeat an empty and ridiculous script.

9.5 Conclusions

This chapter has addressed some aspects of Italian satire, focusing on cinema and, only secondarily on other media. Italian comedy is, especially in films, above all a critique that through social denunciation affects politics and politicians. We have seen that Italian satire has had to deal with a dramatic history and complex social, political, and cultural events and changes. In cinema, satire displays two main directions. On the one hand, condescending and indulgent parody of past political and social events and of the faults of Italians; on the other hand, a lashing and provocative critique of social and political imagery and behaviors is instantiated, starting from Totò to recent filmography. A feature of this satire is the recourse to vulgar language, sexual allusions, and a derisory representation of society, institutions, and politicians. This kind of expression has the result of creating real detachment from conformist thinking, a provocatively different imagery.

References

Anile, A. (2001). Brothers of Italy. In A. Anile (Ed.), *Totò and Peppino, brothers of Italy* (pp. 12–35), Einaudi (in Italian).
Baldi, B. (2023). The strategic use of debasing and vulgar language in Italy's contemporary politics: Beppe Grillo and Matteo Salvini. In O. Feldman (Ed.), *Debasing political rhetoric: Dissing opponents, journalists, and minorities in populist leadership communication* (pp. 165–180). Springer.
Bowdle, B. F., & Gentner, D. (2005). The career of metaphor. *Psychological Review, 112*(1), 193–216. https://doi.org/10.1037/0033-295X.112.1.193
Brunetta, G. P. (2009). *Italian neorealist cinema: From "Roma, open city" to "persons unknown."* Laterza (in Italian).
Butler, J. (1997). *Excitable speech: A politics of the performative.* Routledge.
Del Boca, A. (2005), *Italians, good people?* Neri Pozza (in Italian).
Gentner D., & Bowdle, B. F. (2008). Metaphor as structure-mapping. In R. W. Gibbs Jr. (Ed.), *The Cambridge handbook of metaphor and thought* (pp. 109–128). Cambridge University Press.
Goffman, E. (1967). *Interaction ritual: Essays on face to face behavior.* Pantheon Books.
Gotor, M. (2019). *Italy in nineteenth century: From the defeat of Adua to the victory of Amazon.* Einaudi (in Italian).
Jakobson, R. (1933/2009), *The end of cinema.* Book Time (in Italian).
Lagioia, N. (2015, November 5). *What's left of satire in Italy.* Internazionale. https://www.internazionale.it/reportage/2015/11/05/satira-italia-crozza-male (in Italian).
Lakoff, G., & Johnson, M. (1999). *Philosophy in the flesh: The embodied mind and its challenge to western thought.* Basic Books.
Lotman, J. R. (1973/2019). *Semiotics of cinema and features of cine-aesthetics.* Mimesis (in Italian).
Nonsolofilm.it. (2013, May 21), *Berlinguer I Love You quotations and dialogues* (in Italian). https://www.nonsonsolofilm.it/berlinguer-ti-voglio-bene-citazioni-e-dialoghi/.

Pasolini, P. P. (2008 [1975]), *Corsair writings*. Garzanti (in Italian).
Rossi, F. (2002). *The language in play. At Totò's lecture on rhetoric*. Bulzoni (in Italian).
Sesti, M. (2004). Palombella Rossa. In *Encyclopedia of the cinema* (pp. 1–7). Treccani (in Italian). https://www.treccani.it/enciclopedia/palombella-rossa_%28Enciclopedia-del-Cinema%29/.
Sperber, D., & Wilson, D. (1986/1995). *Relevance, communication and cognition*. Blackwell.
TheSepulnannitura. (n.d.). *Poetry Bozzone—Berlinguer I love* [video]. YouTube. https://www.youtube.com/watch?v=Xs-OrCeueb4.
Tirino, M. (2017). Please! Totò and the subversion of bourgeois hypocrisy: A sociocultural analysis lecture on rhetoric. *H-ermes. Journal of Communication, 9*, 7–36 (in Italian). http://siba-ese.unisalento.it/index.php/h-ermes/article/view/17328.
Todini, S. (2004). Ecce bombo. In *Encyclopedia of the cinema* (pp. 1–7). Treccani (in Italian). https://www.treccani.it/enciclopedia/ecce-bombo_%28Enciclopedia-del-Cinema%29/.

Benedetta Baldi is Full Professor of Communication and Discourse Analysis at the University of Florence, Italy. She is President of the Second Cycle Degree Course in Communication Theories. Her research includes different fields of linguistics and pragmatics, language teaching and communication theory, specifically political discourse and the relationship between media and socio-cultural imaginary. Her latest books in this field are *Opinione immediata* (2018), about public opinion and media, and *Il linguaggio del potere* (2021), addressing the persuasive and manipulative nature of political discourse.

Chapter 10
The Power of Funny: Indigenous High Art as Quiescence and Rebellion

Liz Sills and Pamela G. Monaghan-Geernaert

Abstract In 2006 Apsáalooke artist Wendy Red Star released a print entitled *The Last Thanks*. Reminiscent of da Vinci's *The Last Supper*, the piece features Red Star (in a traditional elk tooth dress) seated amid plastic skeletons wearing stereotypical Native headdresses at a table littered with unhealthy, prepackaged food. The piece calls to mind popular, celebratory images of the first Thanksgiving, confronting its audience with the genocidal legacy of the arrival of non-Native people on the North American continent. *The Last Thanks* uses funny imagery to address this history with a message of looking toward the future with resilience while realistically confronting the horrors of the past. This research analyzes the rhetoric of Red Star's work and explores the precedent for Native artists using humor to cultivate resilience in the face of aggression. We explore the humorous rhetorical tropes within the image and the implications of the choice to express the message in a high art format, lending itself to an extra-cultural audience for a jarring and subversive effect. Ultimately, we address the effect of Native humor on non-Native audiences and the ability of humor to celebrate—and indeed flaunt—strength in the face of oppression.

10.1 Introduction

Why do Native Americans hate April?

Because April showers bring mayflowers and

Mayflower brings white people.

Why do Native Americans hate snow?

L. Sills (✉)
Department of English, Communication, and Global Languages, Northern State University, Aberdeen, SD, USA
e-mail: elizabeth.sills@Northern.edu

P. G. Monaghan-Geernaert
Department of History and Social Sciences, Northern State University, Aberdeen, SD, USA
e-mail: pamela.geernaert@northern.edu

Because it's white and settles on their land.

We expect that our readers are at least tacitly acquainted with the genocidal colonial history of the United States. We hope that myriad wars between the colonizers and the existing American population and the tens of thousands of Indigenous deaths that resulted are embedded in the national public mindset. After all, a great deal of the country's mythos is built on the glorified absence of Indigenous nations. As King (2012, pp. 54–55) eloquently expresses in *The Inconvenient Indian*:

> Dead Indians are the only antiquity that North America has. Europe has Greece and Rome. China has the powerful dynasties. Russia has the Cossacks. South and Central American have the Aztecs, the Incas, and the Maya. North America has Dead Indians.

As the dominant-culture mindset relegates Native culture to representations of warrior-like athletic prowess and in King's words, "New Age spiritual flimflam" (ibid., p. 59), representations of the non-antiquated, modern Native-lived experience are often omitted. Early Hollywood, notoriously cast clay-covered, white actors in one-dimensional Native roles. Native parents are forced to cope with their children living awash in mass-mediated portrayals of Dead Indian stereotypes (Nesterhoff, 2021). This means that the perspectives of the 9.7 million American Indian or Alaskan Native people living in the United States (Jones et al, 2021) are missing from the dominant popular culture mindset.

Speaking of tropes of antiquity, we also expect that our readers are familiar with the iconic 1490s Leonardo da Vinci painting *The Last Supper*. The picture has been considered a masterwork of composition for centuries and continues to find new life through avenues like the recent, wildly popular *Da Vinci Code* franchise. The painting features Jesus Christ surrounded by the twelve apostles seated in a row at a dinner table, celebrating a Passover ritual meal before Jesus is betrayed to the Romans.

We now invite the readers to picture *The Last Supper*, but with a few tweaks. Instead of Christ at the center of the table, [as can be seen] the reimagined image features a Native woman in an elk tooth dress and feathered headband. Instead of apostles, she is surrounded by plastic skeletons. Instead of Passover allusions, the scene includes cartoonish decorations that indicate a Thanksgiving dinner. And instead of Seder foods, the red-checkered tablecloth is scattered with commodity food of bologna, Kraft singles, Wonder Bread, and Oatmeal Crème Pies.

This new vision of a life-punctuating meal is the stuff of a 2006 photograph by Apsáalooke artist Wendy Red Star entitled *The Last Thanks*. This 24 × 36-inch pigment print (see Fig. 10.1) has been displayed in a variety of museums, most notably in a six-month tenure at the Museum of Contemporary Art in Chicago, IL. Red Star's website describes the print as employing "a comic pastiche in service of an urgent commentary about the dispossession and genocide of Native peoples in the United States" (Red Star, 2022).

Red Star's image embodies the dilemma of Indigenous artists in the US. On the one hand, artists are trained in the Western canon and expected to dialogue with it to obtain gallery or museum exposure. On the other hand, artists want to express their

10 The Power of Funny: Indigenous High Art as Quiescence and Rebellion

Fig. 10.1 Wendy Red Star, *The Last Thanks*, 2006

cultural trauma in a way that is necessarily non-Western. *The Last Thanks* appears to bridge that divide by expressing an Indigenous perspective through a Westernized high art medium. But to what effect? The appeal to high art may indicate that Red Star is quiescent and willing for Apsáalooke to kowtow to the sweep of dominant popular culture. Conversely, the image is designed to be discomfiting, thus indicating a spirit of rebellion. Gaventa (1980) might attribute the dichotomy to the "'split' consciousness" of powerless groups who are aware of their grievances but do not feel they have agency to do anything about their situation. Red Star's description of the work as "urgent commentary" implies that she expects some social agitation to emerge from her efforts.

The present analysis will establish that Wendy Red Star's photograph *The Last Thanks* and many of her other works signify both quiescence and rebellion through humor. Referencing the Western visual art canon through parody signifies the undeniable dominance of said canon. At the same time, the funny elements of her work add a tongue-in-cheek twist that enable rebellion, at least at a cognitive level. This pivot enabled by humor gives the artist a unique rhetorical niche in which to express modern Native perspectives that deviate from the popular narrative.

10.2 Grounds for Apsáalooke Protest

The question viewers of Red Star's photograph must ask is "How did we get here?" The history of the Apsáalooke people, as with many other tribes, is situated in dispossession, genocide, and forced migration—otherwise known as "the Indian problem." From the beginning of Europeans' arrival to "America" the goal of settling the land was strong. Escaping persecution themselves, settlers wanted a better life that was free from religious oppression and open to economic prosperity. This mindset underlies the Doctrine of Discovery and the philosophy of Manifest destiny. Both of these concepts led to physical and cultural genocide of people native to the area.

The Doctrine of Discovery dates back to 1492 when then Pope Nicholas V issued a decree to "subjugate the Saracens and pagans and any other unbelievers and enemies of Christ," and "reduce their persons to perpetual servitude," to take their belongings, including land, "to convert them to you, and your use, and your successors the Kings of Portugal" (Slattery, 2005). The right to conquer non-Christian lands based on the Doctrine gained popularity. The conquest of America becomes legally justified in 1792 when Thomas Jefferson claimed the Doctrine of Discovery as international law (Dunbar-Ortiz, 2014).

Corruption harkens back to days of coercive behavior in treaty making and treaty breaking. The general population might believe that the mistreatment of Native Americans existed in the past but Native Americans and Red Star's *The Last Thanks* reminds us that it is still prevalent today. Land confiscation was designed to force the Crow (and all tribes) to conform to European traditional values. Despite the egregious amount of land taken from tribes, Indian reservations did not enable assimilation. Instead, reservations became fraught with poverty, dependence on the federal government, and further resentment of Europeans. Red Star uses humor in her image *The Last Thanks* as a way to perhaps tame the pain of colonization.

Even Native artwork can be a site of modern cultural oppression. The question of Native art is complex—so complex, that it had to be codified by the federal government. In 1990 the Indian Arts and Crafts Act was enacted. The IACA is a

> Truth-in-advertising law that prohibits misrepresentation in the marketing of Indian art and craft products within the United States. It is illegal to offer or display for sale, or sell, any art or craft product in a manner that falsely suggests it is Indian produced, an Indian product, or the product of a particular Indian or Indian tribe or Indian arts and crafts organization, resident within the United States (U.S. Department of the Interior, n.d.).

The codification enacted to protect Indian people and Indian art begs the question "Who is an Indian?" and "What is Indian art?" On the surface this seems to be simple. However, the answer to these two questions is complicated, contested, and reinforces colonization. The explanation will highlight why Red Star's art is important, timely, and humorous.

Blood quantum is the degree of Indian blood a person possesses. Tribes that use blood quantum to determine enrollment set the minimum level of blood quantum a person can have to become tribally enrolled. The Crow tribe requires one quarter blood quantum to become a tribally enrolled member. It is important to note that dogs, racehorses, and Indians are the only three "things" that quantify their belonging by blood quantum. The effect of blood quantum for IACA purposes has been felt by many artists. As Shiff (1992) states: "Imagine you wake up on November 29, 1990, to find yourself a Native American artist but not an Indian, your authentic art transformed into imitation during the night because you don't have federal tribal membership."

The second method to determine who is an Indian is based on lineage. In this method, Indian status is given to individuals who can "prove" that they are descendants from one of the original enrollees of the tribal rolls. This method relies on record keeping of tribes and federal agencies. As much of this early enrollment was at a time of great transition in the government's dealings with the tribes, the ability to capture who was an original descendant and the ability to track the documentation made this method problematic (Shiff, 1992). This method often leads to the long standing joke that "my great-great-grandmother was a Cherokee princess."

Using either method above still does not completely grasp the concept of "Indianness." The cultural, spiritual, and emotional connection to heritage might/should lie at the basis of identity. Nor do these methods fully explain native humor that is entirely culturally based. Many "Indians" grow up in an urban setting, do not practice any "traditional" culture activities, and are unable to speak their tribal language. Their blood quantum or lineage does not guarantee that they identify as Indian. To the contrary, some individuals might not have enough blood quantum to be tribally enrolled but nevertheless follow cultural practices and strongly identify as Indian.

The second question that needs to be addressed in the IACA is "What is Indian Art?" Simply defined, Indian art should be any art produced by an Indian. The IACA act discusses art which could be deemed "traditional" such as pottery, silver & turquoise jewelry, and beadwork. IACA's goal is to protect "knock-off" pieces of traditional art, such as dream catchers made in China. However, Indian artists are as diverse as is the work they produce. Traditional pieces can have high value with tourists and collectors. But Indian art is more than commercial. Wendy Red Star's *The Last Thanks* is an example of such diversity as the photograph is not produced for mass distribution to tourists. In fact, the sarcastic humor in the art is intended to elicit feelings in tourists similar to Red Star's provocative piece.

Jimmie Durham produces art with equal shock factor, here too tapping into sarcasm as a way to elicit a humorous response. Durham, a non-enrolled Indian artist notes that when IACA was implemented he lost the "right" to be an Indian artist (Shiff, 1992). Durham has now focused on highlighting the problems of IACA and the underlying colonization and profiteering of Native peoples. His 1986 installment "On Loan from the Museum of the American Indian" parodies the anthropological collection of Native American artifacts. "Pocahontas' Underwear" is a key piece of this installment and features panties adorned with feathers and beads. Additionally, the exhibit contains the work "Current Trends in Indian Land Ownership"—a series of maps starting with an entirely dark one indicating that Indians "owned" everything. In the last map, the dark spots of Indian possession have become so small one hardly sees them. Durham's graphic, like Red Sky's photograph, is both comic and biting; their target is an entire history.

In some instances, the art itself has been colonized. Apsáalooke ceremonial clothing has been adapted as traditional materials become harder to secure (Molinari, 2013). For example, dresses are now made of wool that once were made of buckskin. Now included in ceremonial attire are symbols of modern, and often pop, culture. Many high school graduates are adding beaded medallions to their robes including Batman, Hello Kitty, and favorite sports teams. The irony and humor of ceremonial medallions in the form of Hello Kitty needs to be noted. Art critic Margaret Dubin suggests that this fusion of social and cultural practices helps Native and non-Native society coexist (Molinari, 2013).

Working within the constricting framework of being a Native artist, Red Star's humor still gets traction with audiences thanks to its use and subversion of the unique visual rhetoric of high art. She capitalizes on the nuances of the relationship of a viewer with an artistic image, turning the trappings of elitist gallery culture to her advantage. She recognizes the mythical sanctity of some dominant-culture visual art tropes (i.e., *The Last Supper*) but then profanes them through irony to grab the audience's attention. Her use of ironic humor allows her audience to more comfortably process ideas that they might turn away from if they were presented in a more factual, literal way.

Of course, audiences are aware that they are co-conspirators in artifice when they observe an image created. Western art is often analyzed in its relative degrees of separation from reality (Freeland, 2001). Baudrillard (2005) famously coined the term "hyperreality" to describe images whose relationship with reality is so cartoonish that their meaning is rooted mainly in other images (p. 120). "For art, reality is nothing," he quips (p. 77). Barthes (1980) analyzes photography with the same spirit, pointing out that this medium, purported to document visual experience in a literal way, can really only relate to reality as a mask, a form of theatre. John Dewey promoted art as a source of knowledge and a way to grapple with reality. When audiences see reality being perceived in a malleable way, they can appreciate that their lived experience is a product of perception. Humor also needs to have someone see/hear the joke to be effective. What is sacred might naturally be profaned, and it is in that sacrilegious freedom that Red Star addresses social issues through captivatingly ironic high art. By turning the (serious) image of *The Last Supper* on its (humorous) head the artist is able to confront and offend, interacting with a "great" image. Audiences are forced to reconsider not only visual tropes but the ideas behind them, and in doing so they embrace the humor of the piece.

Consider the venues in which high art like Red Star's work is displayed: museums, with their elitist veneer. American art museums were explicitly designed with a "civilizing" function in mind so that the poor, huddled masses immigrating to the country might be brought up to cultural speed (Freeland, 2001, p. 98). Despite this mission, less than half the population frequents art museums, and the people who do tend to have considerable income and education. Museums set the standard for an upper-class sense of "taste," for "quality," for the traits that make a piece of art "great" i.e., the sort of meaningful icon discussed above. By using their influences to set such a canon, museums make themselves the holy sites of high art with layers of humor, ranging from slap-stick funny to subtle innuendos.

However, the canon of high art today is forced to face-off with a carnival of criticism. Various movements within the art world call into question the "greatness" of the establishment (Freeland, 2001). This sort of commentary reminds the viewing public that art is artifice and that it is meant to be questioning and questioned. Audiences might find this process offensive, as profaning the canon often involves ridiculing the ideas that are represented by sanctified images as well as attacking what some viewers come to view as a living, breathing being. The public outrage and heartbreak caused by environmental activists who defaced classic works of art such as da Vinci's *Mona Lisa* and Vermeer's *Girl with a Pearl Earring* in 2022 illustrated the implications of agitating the pillars of the high art world (Petras & Borresen, 2022). For Baudrillard (2005, p. 26), though, such subversion is the logical outcome of art's hyperreality:

> But what could art possibly mean in a world that has already become hyperrealist, cool, transparent, marketable? What can porn mean in a world made pornographic beforehand? All it can do is make a final, paradoxical wink—the wink of reality laughing at itself in its most hyperrealist form, of sex laughing at itself in its most exhibitionist form, or art laughing at itself and its own disappearance in its most artificial form, irony. In any case, the dictatorship of images is an ironic dictatorship.

Art wants its audiences to continue to crave perspective-altering artifice. Thus, it doubles down on its own artifice by making itself even more artificial. This results in pictures that convey double meanings i.e., irony.

Pictures can force or finesse. Sometimes they confront their audience into becoming immersed in them; Barthes (1980) opines that photographs are violent in this way, enabling the fascinating "spectacle of degeneration" condemned by Baudrillard (2005, p. 37). On the other hand, pictures can fight natural human aversions to seeing things like death through the complex subversion that is irony. This process is still a species of confrontation, because as "the spiritual form of the disillusionment of the world" (pp. 120–121) it must turn accepted meaning on its head. But the confrontation is contemplative, congenial, and by not evoking harshness or avoidance it invites dialogue with the viewer via a greater variety of emotional experiences. Booth's (1974) *A Rhetoric of Irony* elaborates that double-meaning discourse builds community and inspires audience interest and pleasure, establishing its gravity and relevance by doing so. He describes the appreciation of irony as "that glorious ironic leap upward to the ironic sublime" (p. 114). His invocation of Kant's notion of the sublime implies that irony makes us feel that we are strong in the face of any uncomfortable idea that might be expressed having been cushioned by deep thought and perhaps by humor. Irony's grinning absurdity protects viewers from their natural visual reactions to difficult images.

In short, for Red Star to convey her ideas, she must entrance her audience into engaging in dialogue with her work. She must reiterate reality in a way that allows viewers to step back and critically analyze it. In so doing, she is using the long-canonized visual language of Western art that is reinforced by the venues in which people encounter her pictures. But by twisting those tropes to engage uncomfortable realities in an ironically funny way, she is able to immerse viewers in ideas they would normally avoid. Even notions of death—that hardest thing to see—can become more engaging when genocide is expressed through plastic skulls, and nutritional deficiencies are observed as part of a festive banquet spread.

10.3 The Power of Humor

The "superiority theory" of humor suggests that it can reinforce and reproduce societal hierarchies (Westwood, 2004). Humor can also function as or moving toward resistance, especially in its subversive forms like parody (Gilbert, 2003) and other species of satire that can function as a "discourse of inquiry" (Baym, 2005, p. 268). But its enthymematic nature means that humor does not succeed unless it reiterates common perceptions or power structures. Sometimes this results in a process of rite and anti-rite wherein beliefs are critically examined after they are shared (Mintz, 1985). In other instances, only the function of "rite" remains—where comedy only deals with reiteration. Collinson (1988) illustrates this potential in his observation of British shop-floor workers who maintain their position in the workplace pecking order by using humor to ridicule subordinate colleagues as "miserable or lazy" (p. 194).

Not all funny utterances involve irony, of course. But irony is an incredibly useful tool for political humor such as Red Star's artwork. Jones (2010) notes the effective use of funny ironic incongruity in political entertainment such as The Colbert Report, a popular parody news show that aired in the early 2000s. By spoofing the George W. Bush administration in ironic ways Colbert was able to expose the absurd aspects of the federal bureaucracy by appearing to praise its rationality. In so doing, the show engaged in the kind of "postmodern playfulness" (p. 182) that younger contemporary audiences found refreshing compared to the pseudo-factual, modernist traditional news. Red Star's work operates similarly—by ironically spoofing traditional Western art she is playfully exposing its inconsistencies.

10.3.1 Pacification

Some scholars have even noted the "'pacificatory' qualities of joking" (Collinson, 1988, p. 182) that work as a "safety valve" to prevent progressive or valuable action from taking place where it might have done so if steam had been allowed to build up. This might be among the motivations for trends like managers bringing in corporate comedians to entertain workers by expressing ostensibly dissenting viewpoints in a humorous manner. Exercises of apparent comedic dissent like the Russian Esquire magazine's repeated superficial spoofs of Vladmir Putin (Galperin, 2008) could cause more potent criticisms of him to fizzle out. Humor can serve as a 'discounting cue' that makes criticism seem undesirable in the face of the happy affective payoff of laughing (Young, 2008, p. 123). Thus, by hiring a comedian to spoof them, management might be discouraging workers from taking greater action.

These factors may lead to the status quo from which Westwood (2004, p. 777) deduces that "one would be hard pressed to provide any concrete instances in which humor or comedy actually had a material subversive consequence." However, material consequences might not always be precisely the point. Although the criticisms leveled through comedy might not bring about immediate revolution, they are made more memorable by their humorous presentation (Young, 2004). Humor also proves attractive thanks to the anticipation of a happy affective payoff (Baym, 2005; Young, 2008)—so that arguments presented in a seemingly innocuous, funny way can attract a more attentive audience than those that seem aggressive or depressing. Furthermore, Gossett and Kilker (2006) emphasize that subtle acts of resistance—those that do not achieve sweeping material results—should not be discounted as "mere coping devices or safety valves" (p. 67).

10.4 Native American Humor

Humor is used in a variety of ways among Native Americans. Within Native Communities it is used to tease, taunt, and poke fun at oneself and others. Native Americans tease each other as a way to show affection. It is often said that if a Native American teases a non-Native American, that is a sign that the non-Native is accepted into the community (Johansen, 2005). Humor is also used as a way to poke fun at oneself. Humility is a strong virtue and expressing humility is often accomplished through self-deprecating jokes. The importance of humor can be seen with the First Laugh ceremony. For Navajos the first laugh is an important milestone for a child and is celebrated with a ceremony including a feast provided by the person who provoked the child's first laugh (Hill, 1943).

Outside of Native communities, humor can be used to shed light on the damaging effects of colonization. Native American humor often functions as catharsis in the face of oppression, contemporary and historical (Lincoln, 1993). The sting of highlighting oppression through Native humor has been felt by the federal government and steps were created to control humor. The Bureau of Indian Affairs realized the political strength of Native humor and in the 1920s banned Native clowns (primarily Kachina's in the Southwest) as part of the religious crimes code (Lincoln, 1993).

Wendy Red Star's *The Last Thanks* is only one of several pieces by the artist that highlight Native American humor. Each one of her pieces are equally controversial, shocking, poignant, and satirical. Red Star has been defined by museum curators as an activist (Gobnick, 2015). Her artwork is intentional in calling to light the problems that plague Native Americans. Some of her pieces focus specifically on the past, addressing the historical images that are often stereotypical of Native peoples. She calls to light the absurdity of these stereotypes to make the viewer uncomfortable. However, the absurdity is part of the comedy. Viewers can see that she is poking fun at them for having these stereotypical views. The reason the art 'works' is that the stereotypes are well known.

Wendy Red Star produced two pieces of art that point to the myth that Native Americans are somehow more innately in tune with nature. In "Four Seasons," Red Star is surrounded by items in nature. "Posing amid blow-up deer, cut-out coyotes and wallpaper mountains, Red Star uses her series to go after the standard blather about Native American's inevitable 'oneness' with nature" (Gobnick, 2015). In this piece of art, the absurdity of the relationship with nature is developed by the artist being "natural" and the environmental elements being "unnatural." The ridiculousness is designed to challenge the viewers presumptions about the relationship between Native Americans and the land. In her piece "My Home is Where my Tipi Sits," Red Star photographs the landscape of the reservation. The series of color photographs highlights reservation features including government housing and broken down 'rez' cars. The photos also show the poverty and despair of reservation life—rendered sardonically humorous by showing the irony of what viewers expect to see and what the reality is in fact.

Using humor to offset the trauma of colonization has been a staple of Native people (Deloria, 1969). Humor serves an important function in helping persecuted people process tragedy by giving them a way to poke fun at their oppressors (Amada, 1993). Native nations have survived physical and cultural genocide, loss of land, boarding schools, relocation and now oversight of how they can create and sell Native art. Native humor is part of the resilience of a people; their ability to express it through art is critical (Garrett & Pichette, 2000).

10.5 Analysis

The Last Thanks reflects societal power dynamics vis-a-vis Apsáalooke people, but undermines the dominant colonial culture. We use here a critical/cultural analytical approach to illuminate that interaction. First, we'll overview the nature of the domination Red Star is facing and then we'll examine the funny tropes in the photo in their conversation with that power structure.

A notion of powerlessness marks the Apsáalooke lived experience, as well as that of other Indigenous tribes throughout the United States whose aegis of control has been confined to reservations where treaty rights have been violated. If we understand power as a situation in which someone can get someone else to do something against their will, then we understand that tribal communities tend to be on the receiving end of that spectrum. Gaventa's (1980) *Power and Powerlessness* offers us a useful analogy to dissect the situation. As he reviewed various mechanisms of power, he observed that they operate in three dimensions: (1) decision-making conflicts, (2) mobilization of bias i.e., creating a culture with rules and customs that maintain a particular power structure, and (3) control of the symbolic convergences that create meaning in everyday life. He posited that effective wielding of the second dimension creates an atmosphere governed by the "rule of anticipation" that a subordinate party will not challenge dominating forces out of anticipation that such a challenge would precipitate painful retaliation. Once power is exercised via the three dimensions of mechanisms, that defensive strategy devolves into an ingrained sense of powerlessness within a subordinate population, leading to fatalism, self-harm, and apathy.

Is the kind of control achieved through the three dimensions of mechanisms outlined by Gaventa (1980) permanent? No. There is potential for rebellion if a subordinate group senses shifting power relationships on the part of the hegemon and takes the initiative. But if the third dimension, in particular, was maintained well, rebellion is often quashed before the idea even fully takes shape:

> As long as elements of the sense of powerlessness or the assuming consciousness that grow from non-participation may be maintained, then although there may be a multitude of grievances, the 'unified' or 'critical' consciousness will likely remain precluded (Gaventa, 1980, p. 19).

Gaventa uses these dimensions as a framework to understand the attempted rebellions and more comfortable quiescence of a small Appalachian community dominated by an international company, local elites, and union corruption, concluding that "[...] the quietness of this segment of America's lower and working class perceived at a distance cannot be taken to reflect consensus to their condition or seen to be innate within their socio-economic or cultural circumstances" (Gaventa, 1980, p. 253). That is, silence is not consent in a very political way. Silence is, however, a result of decades of domination and failed rebellion. If standing up to power will harm me or at best not do any good, reason the members of a silent population, then why bother? Thus, rebellion yields to the tranquil appearance of quiescence.

The situation in Gaventa's (1980) Appalachian town is easily analogous to life on the Crow reservation. There, generations-long fights for treaty rights illustrate the strength of the first dimension of power. In the second dimension, the political power structure within the tribe often exhibits cronyism and collusion with government agencies against whom the citizens of the reservation at large would rather rebel. The third dimension of power is expressed, among other ways, in education. The reservation border town of Hardin, Montana's education system is aired in Colton's (2000, p. 97) *Counting Coup*: "[...] in a school with a 49 percent Indian population, the certified staff at Hardin High includes *no* Native Americans, and the curriculum offers *no* classes in Native American Studies—*nothing* in Crow language, culture, or history." If Apsáalooke children aren't taught to make meaning via their own cultural roots, then they have little reason to fight for that culture in their adulthoods. Given all of this oppression, the question becomes whether people are continuing to rebel or simply acquiescing to the dominant culture out of a sense of perpetual powerlessness.

Enter Wendy Red Star and her tongue-in-cheek high artwork. On the one hand, she is expressing discontent in a way that could be seen as an attempt at rebellion, as the broader cultural consciousness shifts towards inclusion. On the other, by using the medium that she does she may be admitting that there will never be a way to impactfully express anything except through the dominant culture's *lingua franca*, thus illustrating the triumph of the third dimension of power. We will now address the sorts of humor used in *The Last Thanks* and attempt to position them within the realms of quiescence and rebellion.

Ostensibly, Red Star is accomplishing two things in her work: (1) Speaking truth to power in a way that only humor can, and (2) Punching up by doing so. She makes use of incongruous humor to accomplish this. The contrast between *The Last Supper* and *The Last Thanks* is incongruous, and so is the contrast between the cartoonish Native stereotypes and the grim Native reality.

Incongruity is the soul of a great deal of humor—perhaps all of it, according to some scholars (Cundall, 2021). Gimbel (2020, p. 28) summarizes the concept in terms of joke-telling: "[…] standard joke architecture thereby revolves around an incongruity between the set-up and the punch line when viewed through the primary interpretation, which is then resolved when both are viewed through the secondary interpretation." That is, the punch line acts as a minor premise that modifies our understanding of the set-up's major premise, leading to a conclusion that is funny because of the absurdity of the contrast. Take, for example, the classic Mitch Hedberg one-liner: "The shirt is dry clean only, which means it's dirty." The listener is expecting to hear something about cleaning the shirt during the set-up, but the punch line reveals that Hedberg finds the process of dry cleaning so onerous he's stepping outside of the societal expectation for cleanliness. The contract between the expectation and the outcome, especially because that contrast involves jarring, clever phrasing, strikes the listener as surprising in an absurd, non-threatening way that elicits laughter.

The same contrast between expectation and outcome can be found in nonverbal humor as well, and in the case *of The Last Thanks* it shows up decisively in the visual tropes of Red Star's photograph. The photo is rife with examples of gently violated expectations. The overall pastiche of imitating *The Last Supper* but using that mainstay of Western spiritual art to express the secular gutting of a non-Western culture. (Of course, the underlying congruity of the images predicts the death of the protagonist at the center of the table.)

All of the painting's elements that mimic and then twist da Vinci's original work create a sense of incongruity. Building on that baseline absurdity, Red Star confronts her audience with the contrast between popular culture notions of traditional Native life and modern Native realities. At the center of the table dressed in her elk tooth dress and surrounded by the sorts of foods eaten by people living in Reservation food deserts, Red Star represents genuine Native traditions as well as the consequences of colonization—another contrast worth nothing, albeit a less whimsical one. All around her, however, are representations of the sorts of images white U.S. schoolchildren are inundated with as the Thanksgiving holiday approaches: stereotypical Native headdresses made of construction paper, an inflatable polyester turkey wearing a pilgrim hat, and childlike images of the vast, open tracts of land that represent the need for white American expansion. Building on the foundation of these incongruities, Red Star drives her message home through an overarching macro-level contrast. The entire image revolves around the collision of the popular notion of happy Indians together with grateful colonists giving thanks for the bounty of the land vs. the grim reality of colonial genocide, represented by the plastic skeletons placed in the positions of da Vinci's *The Last Supper* apostles.

Through these examples we can appreciate Red Star's ability to use humor to encourage her audience to grapple with the unseeable grimness of death. The skeletons, easily the most obvious representations of genocide, appear ludicrous with their construction paper headdresses and their gap-toothed plastic smiles. The inflatable turkey, representing false harmony with the colonists, towers laughably over the rest of the figures with a permanent agog look on its face. The use of primary colors throughout the scene (with the exception of the more subdued tones of Red Star's outfit) suggests a general sense of childishness. All of this combined whimsy pulls in the viewer with the pretext of comfort and fun, and only upon the closer examination after being enthralled with the image does the audience appreciate its message of exposure and condemnation.

Biting humor invites contemplation. Kramer (2021, pp. 79–80) elaborates the connection between the two:

> Happily, a humorous attitude facilitates a philosophical attitude, and vice versa. Consider any number of seminal thought experiments involving evil demons, brains in vats, what it would be like to be bats, teletransporters, and famous violinists surreptitiously attached to our backs. These mental exercised cultivate unconventional ways of thinking about issues we might otherwise complacently ignore. They are also kind of funny; at least, if we are open-minded, they elicit a 'hey that's funny,' as in 'strange,' unexpected,' 'novel,' or an enlightening variation of 'WTF!', but about matters we thought we already knew quite well. Humor, like philosophy, takes nothing for granted; this is good, because I'm pretty confident that we're wrong a lot more than we're right.

Incongruous humor rips us from our assumptions and deposits us, comfortably, into the realm of the unexpected. We are then forced to reconcile the difference between the expectation and outcome through a thought process that might lead us to question the presumptions that prompted the initial expectation. *The Last Thanks* asks dominant-culture observers to mesh: (A) their notions of the myth of the Dead Indians who happily relinquished their territory and cultures to colonists, with (B) violent genocide. The ostensible, intended message at the end of that process is that the happy myth of Thanksgiving is as empty as the inflated pilgrim turkey in the background of the image.

Red Star is punching up by employing incongruity to galvanize audience reconsideration of the American history they were taught in elementary school. That is, she is an underdog ridiculing a dominating culture that wields more power than her own. Funny punching up has the advantages of exposing and leveling social inequalities, addressing the ethics of power imbalances, and engaging in a non-violent form of political rebellion. But our dichotomy of quiescence and rebellion begs the question of whether Red Star is really doing any punching. After all, humor can trivialize very serious situations (Julin, 2021). Plastic skeletons might trigger the idea of genocide, but they do not sincerely convey loss of life. Thus, they can act as a sort of safety valve that enables audiences to congratulate themselves on their open-minded reinterpretation of history without experiencing any impactful emotions.

According to Gaventa's (1980) paradigm, if Red Star's work really punches up then she is engaging in rebellion. If not, then she is acquiescing to the dominant discourse and maintaining powerlessness. So, which is she doing? Thanks to her use of funny, ironic visual tropes she is certainly capitalizing on the ability of images to immerse and encourage contemplation of subjects that viewers might otherwise avoid. On the other hand, the very medium that she's using so well is one created and dominated by an elitist white Western tradition. Because of that, her work is showcased in venues (museums) that are only attended by a fraction of the population; it's accessible online, of course, but only to those who know to go looking for it. This dichotomy can be bridged only by that crucial question of whether the punch is landing.

It's tempting to say that Red Star is engaging in a sort of Trojan Horse acquiescence. She admits fealty to the medium of the dominant culture and speaks its language only to turn that medium against the Western-centric perspectives that it usually champions. Then again, we need to ask what sort of change Red Star is seeking through her attack. If it's consciousness-raising, then the Trojan Horse is effective—she has a public forum full of people who probably don't often think about Native issues and who may or may not have ever encountered a Native person in their everyday life. These people are inclined to be contemplative because they have entered the art museum by choice and are likely to be captured by the visual irony of *The Last Thanks*. Oddly, Red Star is perhaps being rebellious *and* acquiescent. Gaventa (1980) discusses a consciousness-raising effort by the downtrodden citizens of the Appalachian communities he studies to appeal to the British company that controlled their land and their quality of life. Although the activists got great buy-in from the British public who saw news specials covering their suffering, they were unable to move the massive corporate owner—the only entity who could actually improve their situation. Gaventa cites this as an example of something that buttressed their feeling of powerlessness; a factor in the second and ultimately third dimensions of power. Red Star, on the other hand, is part of a community that has been quashed for much longer than the Appalachian miners had been at the time they took their stand. Her culture has rebelled and been denied *ad nauseum*. So instead of attacking the first or second dimensions of power, like the Appalachian miners or like her ancestors, Red Star has chosen instead to interact with the third dimension and the symbols it entails.

Symbolic, rhetorical acquiescence can be a path toward rebellion. Although a print in a museum is unlikely to change legislation, it can knock common historical fallacies off their pedestals. Thus, it can begin the process of changing power structures—rebelling—by reversing the process that created them. Red Star attacks third-dimension mainstay symbols like pilgrims and turkeys and replaces them with horrifying (but still viewable) alternatives. Her approach is cheeky and fun and therefore appealing, so it's able to get the job of subversion done well. And once the symbols of dominance are called into question, so is that dominance itself.

10.6 Conclusion

Humor separates and unites, elevates and lowers, and plays with the boundaries between in-groups and out-groups. Gaventa (1980) paints a dichotomy between quiescence and rebellion, but sometimes a cultural situation calls for both at once. If a group has become entrenched and their powerless status seems irreversible, they must first acknowledge that status quo (quiescence) and then spin it to their advantage (rebellion). In such a situation, a strictly rebellious *eidos* would simply precipitate a clapback of the entrenched power. But reclaiming power *through* the structure created by the hegemon is a form of subversion that can get real traction—and can only be accessed after acquiescence has granted access to that structure. One is reminded of the traditional Malay proverb, "When the great lord passes, the wise peasant bows deeply and silently farts." Obviously, the peasant would prefer not to bow, but they can get a bit of their own back regardless.

Native, funny, high art illustrates the simultaneous nature of quiescence and rebellion. In the case of Wendy Red Star, the use of traditional Western art forms constitutes a bow to the great lord. But the satire creates a stink, and the lord is left with little choice but to accept it and move on if he is to preserve the trappings of his status. Humor is certainly more pleasant than farts; the impression left by Red Star and other Native people working in high art lingers a lot longer as well.

References

Amada, G. (1993). The role of humor in a college mental health program. In W. F. Fry & W. A. Salameh (Eds.), *Advances in humor and psychotherapy* (pp. 157–181). Professional Resources.
Barthes, R. (1980). *Camera Lucida: Reflections on photography*. Hill and Wang.
Baudrillard, J. (2005). *The conspiracy of art*. The MIT Press.
Baym, G. (2005). The daily show: Discursive integration and the reinvention of political journalism. *Political Communication, 22*(3), 259–276.
Booth, W.C. (1974). *A rhetoric of irony*. The University of Chicago Press.
Blue Legs v. United States Bureau of Indian Affairs, 867 F.2d 1094 (8th Cir. 1989).
Colton, L. (2000). *Counting coup: A true story of basketball and honor on the little big horn*. Warner Books.
Collinson, D. L. (1988). 'Engineering Humour': Masculinity, joking and conflict in shop-floor relations. *Organization Studies, 9*(2), 181–199.
Cundall, M. (2021). Got IT?: Introducing incongruity theory. In J. M. Henrigillis & S. Gimbel (Eds.), *It's funny cause it's true: The lighthearted philosophers' society's introduction to philosophy through humor*. The Lighthearted Philosophers' Society.
Deloria, V., Jr. (1969). *Custer died for your sins: An Indian manifesto*. Avon Books.
Dunbar-Ortiz, R. (2014). An indigenous peoples' history of the United States. Beacon Press.
Freeland, C. (2001). *But is it art?* Oxford University Press.
Gobnick, B. (2015, April 7). At the Met, Wendy Red Star pops Indian clichés. *artnet News*. https://news.artnet.com/art-world/metropolitan-museum-wendy-red-star-pokes-indian-clichc3s-285643.
Galperin, A. (2008). Putting on Putin. *Columbia Journalism Review, 46*(6), 10–11.

Garrett, M. T., & Pichette, E. F. (2000). Red as an apple: Native American acculturation and counseling with or without reservation. *Journal of Counseling & Development, 78*, 3–13.

Gaventa, J. (1980) *Power and powerlessness: Quiescence and rebellion in an Appalachian valley.* University of Illinois Press.

Gilbert, L. (2003). Moking george: Political satire as "True Threat" in the age of global terrorism. *University of Miami Law Review, 58*(3), 843–889.

Gimbel, S. (2020). *Isn't that clever: A philosophical account of humor and comedy.* Routledge.

Hill, W. W. (1943). *Navajo humor.* Banta.

Johansen, B. E. (2005). Catharsis vis a vis oppression: Contemporary Native American political humor. *Simile, 5*(2), np.

Jones, J. P. (2010). *Entertaining politics* (2nd ed.). Rowan & Littlefield.

Jones, N., Marks, R., Ramirez R., & Rios-Vargas, M. (2021). *2020 census illuminates racial and ethnic composition of the country.* United States Census Bureau. http://www.census.gov.

Julin, G. (2021). What's the punch line? Punching up and down in the comic Thunderdome. In J. M. Henrigillis & S. Gimbel (Eds.), *It's funny cause it's true: The lighthearted philosophers' society's introduction to philosophy through humor.* The Lighthearted Philosophers' Society.

King, T. (2012). *The inconvenient Indian: A curious account of Native people in North America.* University of Minnesota Press.

Kramer, C. (2021). I laugh because it's absurd: Humor as error-detection. In J. M. Henrigillis & S. Gimbel, (Eds.), *It's funny cause it's true: The lighthearted philosophers' society's introduction to philosophy through humor.* The Lighthearted Philosophers' Society.

Lincoln, K. (1993). *Indian humor: Bicultural play in Native America.* Oxford University Press.

Mintz, L. E. (1985). Standup comedy as social and cultural mediation. *American Quarterly, 37*(1), 71–80.

Molinari, K. E. (2013). Adapt and adopt: Apsaalooke (Crow) beadwork and regalia from the nineteenth century to today. *Journal of Northwest Anthropology, 47*(2), 203–213.

Nesterhoff, K. (2021). *We had a little real estate problem: The unheralded story of Native Americans & comedy.* Simon & Schuster.

Petras, G., & Borreson, J. (2022, November 30). *From Mona Lisa to The Scream: Climate protesters deface art in Europe—and now the US.* USA Today. https://www.usatoday.com/in-depth/graphics/2022/11/30/climate-activists-attack-paintings-mona-lisa-scream/10699588002/#:~:text=In%20more%20than%20two%20dozen,reports%3A%20Global%20temperatures%20are%20rising.

Red Star, W. (2022). The Last Thanks. *Wendy Red Star.* http://www.wendyredstar.com.

Shiff, R. (1992, Autumn). The necessity of Jimmie Durham's jokes. *Art Journal, 51*(3), 74–80.

Slattery, B. (2005). Paper Empires: The legal dimensions of French and English Ventures in North America. In J. McLaren, A. R. Buck, & N. E. Wright (Eds.), *Despotic dominion: Property rights in British settler societies* (pp. 50–78). University of British Columbia Press.

The Crow Tribe of Indians, Plaintiff-appellant, v. Campbell Farming Corporation; Robert Earl Holding; Sinclair Oil Corporation, D/b/a Sunlight Ranch company; Sun Valley Company; and KMH ranch Company, Defendants-appellees, 31 F.3d 768 (9th Cir. 1994).

U.S. Department of the Interior (n.d.). Indian arts and crafts board. *The Indian Arts and Crafts Act of 1990.* https://www.doi.gov/iacb/act.

Westwood, R. (2004). Comic relief: Subversion and catharsis in organizational comedic theatre. *Organization Studies, 25*, 775–795.

Young, D. G. (2004). Late-night comedy in Election 2000: Its influence on candidate trait ratings and the moderating effects of political knowledge and partisanship. *Journal of Broadcasting & Electronic Media, 48*(1), 1–22

Young, D. G. (2008). The privileged role of the late-night joke: Exploring humor's role in disrupting argument scrutiny. *Media Psychology, 11*(1), 119–142.

Liz Sills is an Associate Professor of Communication Studies at Northern State University. Her interests lie in rhetorics, philosophies, and cultural consequences surrounding comedy, humor, and any other catalysts of mirth that constitute The Funny. Her work can be found in *Comedy Studies*, *The Philosophy of Humor Yearbook* and in the 2013 Eisner award-winning volume *Black Comics: Politics of Race and Representation*. Sills is a past president of the Lighthearted Philosophers' Society.

Pamela G. Monaghan-Geerneart is an Assistant Professor in the History and Social Sciences department at Northern State University. Her research includes examining culturally appropriate delivery of health care and education. She focuses on acknowledging historical barriers and generational trauma, and responding by developing ways to Indigenize systems and services. Her work has been published in the *Journal of American Indian Education* and *The Annual Review of the Interdisciplinarity Justice Research*. Additionally, she sits on the American Indian Advisory Council, advises the Native American Student Organization and reviews for the Crazy Horse Memorial Scholarship.

Chapter 11
The Cultural Background of Political Humor "Sung" by the Spanish People

María del Mar Rivas-Carmona and María del Carmen García-Manga

Abstract The purpose of this paper is to analyze the relationship between culture, politics, and humor in one of Spain's most popular celebrations, the Cádiz Carnival. The protagonist, in contrast to the magnificence of other carnivals in the world, is the discourse written by the ordinary people to be sung. Groups such as "*chirigotas*" and "*comparsas*" compose and rehearse humorous, satirical, and even biting or acidic lyrics that portray all the current events, competing for weeks in an official contest broadcast live on television. The Final of the Gran Teatro Falla Contest has become a true political thermometer and a popular indicator with which to detect issues concerning the citizenry. Its shrewd and humorous lyrics go viral through the internet and social networks, criticizing local, regional and national political powers, while addressing topical social issues. All this is accompanied by characterization and scenography in accordance with the lyrics, so that costumes, acting, staging, and voices are of the utmost importance. This study will employ a Relevance Theory pragmatic analysis of the lyrics by groups that competed from January 21, 2023 to the grand finale almost a month later.

Preamble: Spain, Humor, Politics, and Culture

The carnival of Cádiz suffered brutal repression and was banned between 1937 and 1947 during the 40-year fascist dictatorship of General Franco. Many carnival authors and performers were murdered by the rebels after the coup d'état of 1936 (Decarlini, 2023).

The traces of fascism and the dramatic rupture between brothers who were divided between "the two Spains" have never healed, despite the "model" transition to democracy that everyone praises about Spain. We are currently witnessing a resurgence of neo-fascism that for fifty years was muted, silent or camouflaged among the

---

M. M. Rivas-Carmona (✉) · M. C. García-Manga
Faculty of Philosophy and Letters, University of Córdoba, Córdoba, Spain
e-mail: mmrivas@uco.es

M. C. García-Manga
e-mail: fe2gamam@uco.es

© The Author(s), under exclusive license to Springer Nature Singapore Pte Ltd. 2024
O. Feldman (ed.), *Political Humor Worldwide*, The Language of Politics,
https://doi.org/10.1007/978-981-99-8490-9_11

democratic right. All this is reflected in cultural manifestations and humor, because Spain is a nation that even laughs at its own misfortunes. Moreover, through humor (whether white, black, satirical, or sarcastic), messages are conveyed that many would otherwise not dare to communicate.

The generation that survived the civil war kept quiet because it could do nothing else. The heirs of the victors do not even want to hear about historical memory, but many children and grandchildren of the generation of the defeated, murdered, disappeared, and repressed, seek moral reparation. "Fear brings silence, and that silence makes people stop talking about their loved ones and stop them from existing… [But] *music and art are very powerful tools to bring back to consciousness what is forgotten*" (Decarlini, 2023).

Domínguez-Pérez's (2011) *The summer that brought a long winter,* or documentaries such as *They died singing* (2020), speak of these roots and explain why today the people are not afraid to sing the truth in the streets, in the theater, or in front of the cameras. Speaking the truth cost many their lives. If they did not keep quiet before, they will do so even less now.

11.1 Introduction: The Cádiz Carnival as a Poetic-Journalistic-Humorous Phenomenon

There is no doubt that the Carnival of Cádiz is a musical, poetic-theatrical, humorous, and also journalistic phenomenon (Moreno-Rodríguez, 2019). Humor is the common thread, the vehicle that transports and overcomes all filters to make the most daring criticisms and political and social claims, ranging from the local, regional, and national, to international levels (Gigliotti, 2023). In fact, "[c]arnival turns Cádiz into the epicenter of the most rogue, daring, irreverent, ironic and politically incorrect humor" (EFE, 2020).

The Carnival of Cádiz, urban in character and clearly influenced by the Italian and French carnivals, constitutes a festival of wit that is prepared throughout the year, but which culminates every February when the voice of the people, presented through the different groups, offers a repertoire of lyrics in the streets of the city and/or in the official competition of carnival groups (COAC) in the city's Gran Teatro Falla. Carnival represents the breaking of rules, freedom, and lack of inhibition, typical of the Christian festival of debauchery prior to the arrival of Lent.

Carnival suffered relentless censorship and even saw its name banned, changed into "typical Gaditan festivities" (Ramos-Santana, 1985), but the carnival tradition managed to survive as a social phenomenon through the ingenuity of authors, musicians, performers, and artists at the service of freedom of expression. Perhaps as a legacy of the censorship era, one of its most effective and intelligent weapons is that of the "double entendre," which evaded regulatory restrictions without having to stop describing the injustices committed against the people.

11 The Cultural Background of Political Humor "Sung" by the Spanish People

Each year, each group of performers chooses a mask, which they use to portray a real or fictitious character, called a *"tipo"* (a 'type'). In Cádiz the *tipo* is more than a costume because it embodies a personality, a character who takes on an independent life and is felt as "responsible" for what is sung (Barceló-Calatayud, 2014). In the past, the costumes were made by the artists' mothers, wives, and girlfriends. Nowadays, many of them are made by professional dressmakers and are as much a secret as the lyrics of the songs.

The lyrics are interpreted polyphonically, recreating these stereotyped identities in a caricatured or realistic way. The groupings represent a collective voice, though individual at the same time, because they all address the audience directly from the "I" of the first person singular, through the aforementioned character or type; the ultimate sender responsible for the text, obviously, is the lyrics' author(s). This direct and equal, non-hierarchical communication with the audience of the contest in the theatre or the audience listening to them in the street, leads to the use of a very colloquial, almost familiar register, despite the fact that every year the close context of communication is increasingly transcended, given that by being recorded and broadcast on social networks carnival has become a mass phenomenon. However, the ludic intention and the search for a rapprochement with the public lead to a linguistic relaxation in which the communicative intention or purpose prevails (Payán-Sotomayor, 1993), and we find ourselves with the most spontaneous and genuine version of the speech of Cádiz.

Together with this informal language of Cádiz, all the paralinguistic resources that accompany the message are fundamental to complement the communicative stimuli: music, kinesics, disguise, etc. All these codes collaborate in the playful-critical pragmatic intentionality that the listener has to interpret.

Here, in short, is a discourse full of naturalness, spontaneity, closeness, and familiarity that nevertheless has been deeply planned, structured, organized, and designed to achieve communicative complicity and a humorous and/or emotional reaction in the audience (Solís-Llorente, 1966). This ad hoc discourse has, in turn, a receiving audience that also seeks entertainment through laughter; therefore, it is essential to speak of "feedback" between audience and performers. If the intended humorous or emotional effect does not occur, there is a communicative failure that prevents the success of the interaction.

Hilarity and emotion can come from linguistic stimuli such as hyperbole, repetition, ambiguity, wordplay—or from silence, a gesture, or a certain intonation. All this conscious shaping of humorous discourse obviously requires a greater inferential cognitive effort on the part of the recipient (Shilikhina, 2017), but the contextual effects (laughter, tears of emotion, exclamations of approval, etc.), more than compensate for this effort to the satisfaction of artists and audiences.

The main types of musical compositions are *presentation*, *cuplés*, *paso dobles* and *popurrí* (medley of well-known melodies with rewritten lyrics), presented by four main types of groups: *quartets* (3–5 members); *chirigotas* (7–12 members); *comparsas* (10–15 members); and *choirs* (18–35 voices and 5–10 musicians).

The *chirigota* is the funniest carnival form and its main function is to make people laugh, although it is complemented with satire and sarcasm to carry out biting social critique. *Chirigotas* are usually accompanied by guitars, snare drum, bass drum, and, of course, the most typical carnival instrument: the *pito de carnaval*, an elongated whistle with a very characteristic and very humorous sound. The whistle is generally used to introduce each of the *coplas* of the groups.

In this chapter we will analyze the humorous and vindictive discourse of the *chirigotas* that took part in the Cadiz carnival of 2023.

11.2 Relevance Theory and Carnival Humor

As Jiang and colleagues (2019) point out, "[h]umor is a universal phenomenon but is also culturally tinted… Generally, humor is present in all human cultures. However, people from different cultural backgrounds may see humor in different ways."

The phenomenon of humor was not studied in detail until the 1980s with the advent of communication linguistics and the pragmatic-discursive approach. Among the various theories that study humorous discourse, we highlight the General Theory of Verbal Humor (TGHV) (Attardo & Raskin, 1991) and especially the Theory of Relevance and Humor (Torres-Sánchez, 1999; Yus-Ramos, 2003, 2016).

In the case of carnival lyrics, the humorous intention transcends purely verbal resources i.e., the explicit, and is accompanied by non-verbal elements related to the speaker's attitude, kinesics, incongruities, logical-cognitive-sociological aspects, and even contextual assumptions of a cultural, environmental, psychological and social nature, shared by both senders and receivers in the communicative process ("shared knowledge"). The humorous intention can also justify a reorganization of the information that provokes double meanings and ambiguities; in fact, it is common in lyrics to maintain two simultaneous interpretations to finally opt for a rupture of expectations, a final punch line, which provokes surprise and consequent hilarity.

From the beginning of discursive and pragmatic studies, the context became a key element to achieve an adequate interpretation of the message. In order to determine communicative intention, in every interaction there is an inferential process that takes into consideration both the context in which meaning is produced and the context in which it is interpreted. In their Relevance Theory, Sperber and Wilson (2004) maintained that the expression and recognition of intentions is probably the essence of human communication (Sperber & Wilson, 2004). In order to infer meaning, the receiver relies on verbal and non-verbal, explicit and implicit clues, and throughout this inferential process the interpreter chooses the most interesting or "relevant" meaning i.e., the one that provides the greatest cognitive/contextual effects with the least mental effort to process them.

Humorous language serves as a clear example of the strategic use of a wide range of verbal and non-verbal resources that become communicative clues helping to interpret the message. When a communicative situation provokes humor, it is usually accompanied by relevant information that might be intended to provoke different emotions, vindicate ideas, or criticize ideological positions. In the words of Donnelly (2013), the receiver might expect to laugh, and perhaps even does laugh, but s/he may perhaps also stop and think. When senders and receivers share a greater number of "contextual assumptions," that is, when they have a similar worldview and know it because it is "mutually manifest" (Sperber & Wilson, 1986, p. 41), the intention is communicated more effectively. Consider, in the case of the carnival, how the communication of meaning occurs most effectively between those who share the same assumptions and worldview.

When constructing a hypothesis of meaning, as receivers we start from the explicit content or 'explicatures' (in the case of carnival discourse, both verbal and non-verbal) that are completed with the implicit content or 'implicatures' (Sperber & Wilson, 2004, p. 261). We must emphasize that in the "acted" discourse of carnival, in which so many elements interact, the non-verbal communicative clues connect immediately with the cognitive schemas of the receivers (Tanaka, 1992; Yus-Ramos, 1998).

11.3 Spanish Culture, Humor and Politics in the Cádiz Carnival 2023

The Carnival of Cádiz is a carnival of progressive and anti-fascist ideas—by tradition, by history, and because it belongs to the people.

Spain has been and is considered a model of democratic transition because the passage from Franco's dictatorship to democracy was achieved without great social conflict. But when fifty years later fascist voices that for decades remained adapted or "reconverted" to the democratic right resurface, voices are heard that argue against going back to the past. However, as the well-known phrase attributed to the Spanish philosopher Jorge Ruiz-de-Santayana goes: "Those who forget their history are condemned to repeat it."

Carnival, of course, in its profound review of socio-political and cultural reality, does not forget history.

11.3.1 Catholic Religion, Holy Week, the Civil War, Fascism

As we have pointed out, although the communicative intention of carnival discourse is always primarily humorous, its lyrics can deal with themes of profound social and cultural depth. These lyrics take on a humorous sense not only in and of themselves, but also when coupled with their visual and auditory context. Many can be very harsh and vindictive when taken out of the carnival's context, where visually we find *tipos* or characters who take on a life of their own, dressed in comic and sometimes even bizarre costumes, and whose gestures are almost histrionic; acoustically, they are accompanied by melodies, instruments, and forms of singing that contribute to the comicality of the communicative event. The public distinguishes the seriousness of

Fig. 11.1 *"Los alarmistas"* (The Alarmists) singing in the street. *Source* Carlospasky, n.d.

the themes from the humorous treatment they receive, and appreciates and enjoys the wit and good humor of the artists and composers, many of whom become social referents in Cádiz.

This is the case of the street *chirigota* lyrics from Rota's "Los alarmistas" (The "alarmists"/alarm technicians) (see Fig. 11.1), when they sing about the exhumation of Franco's General *Queipo-de-Llano* in a jocular, although critical, tone. *Queipo-de-Llano* had many soldiers and civilians assassinated, including many carnival-members, because humor could become a threat to the regime.[1] For this reason, when he was exhumed this year from the Basílica de la Macarena, he was the subject of the following lyrics of numerous carnival groups.

> From the Macarena he left on a Thursday **nigh**.[2]
>
> Gonzalo Queipo-de-Llano for a little **drive**.
>
> Fed up with driving around with all his bones in the **car**,
>
> He got a flat tire after a roundabout not very **far**.
>
> And instead of in a **niche**, he ended up in a **'ditch.'**[3]
>
> [laughter from the audience in the street]

---

[1] Vidarte (1973) notes how *Queipo*'s propaganda chief spoke of 150,000 executions ordered by *Queipo* in Seville in barely half a year during the conflict. The Hispanophile Ian Gibson (1989) blamed Queipo-de-Llano for ordering the death of the famous poet Federico García Lorca in "The Death of a Poet 1936."

[2] Some words here are bolded/italicized to emphasize the puns and play on words.

[3] Our translation of the lyrics tries to keep a certain syntactic sense in English, while maintaining the content of each poetic verse.

11 The Cultural Background of Political Humor "Sung" by the Spanish People

[*De la Macarena salió un jueves por la **noche***

*Gonzalo queipo-de-llano" 'pa' darse una vueltecita en **coche**.*

*'Jarto' dar vueltas con 'tós' los huesos en la furgo**neta**,*

*pinchó una rueda justo después de una glor**ieta**.*

*Y se quedó 'tirao' en una cun**eta***] (Carlospasky, n.d., 18:00–18:45)

This song deals with the exhumation of the genocidal, Francoist soldier Gonzalo Queipo-de-Llano who, seventy years after his death, was still buried in the Basílica de la Esperanza-Macarena in Seville. In compliance with the Law of Historical Memory the current Spanish socialist government urged the Brotherhood to remove his remains from the floor of the church. The Virgen-de-la-Esperanza-Macarena, moreover, is the best known and most popular Holy Week brotherhood in Spain, and its procession on Good Friday morning attracts devotees from all over the world.

This song criticizes the long presence of the genocidal soldier's remains on sacred ground. The lyrics combine difficult cultural issues such as religion and its typical and worldwide known, popular manifestation through the Holy Week processions, with historical memory and the Civil War, personified in the Francoist military genocide.

As difficult as it might seem to create humor from this thematic combination, that is the effect that the *chirigota* "Los alarmistas" undoubtedly achieves. Humor arises from a combination of both verbal and non-verbal stimuli. On the one hand, even if we find a topic that is not at all humorous in principle, it shouldn't be forgotten that in carnival practically *everything* is humorous; not only artists and composers know it, but also the public. Humor arises from the clash of expectations with respect to what would be acceptable in other contextual circumstances. No matter how serious a subject might be, it will cease to be so if those who transmit it are gentlemen dressed as agents of an alarm company, with a security camera on their shoulders, a big telephone attached to their uniform, and a sign of an "alarmist" technician (a play on words with "alarm technician"), with comic gestures of complicity with the audience and a mischievous smile from ear to ear. In addition, they play a humorous carnival whistle and sing a medley of very funny and well-known melodies whose lyrics have been rewritten in a parodic way.

From a linguistic point of view, it is humorous that the transfer of the soldier's remains becomes "to take a little ride in a car," like someone going for a nice walk. An ingenious parallelism is established, accessible to all those who share the 'background knowledge' regarding the procession that leaves the Macarena every Holy Week, the funeral procession of the general, and this surprisingly romanticized "ride in a car." The use of extremely colloquial language and Andalusian pronunciation ("*pa*" for "*para*" (for), "*tós*" for "*todos*"(all)) and the curious and meaningful rhymes (***noche**-**coche**/**furgoneta**-**glorieta**-**cuneta***) have a fundamentally humorous effect in Spanish.

There is a hilarious, totally unexpected ending, as the story finds poetic justice in the genocide that sent so many thousands of Spaniards to the ditches; now, by a whim of fate, albeit a carnival one, the perpetrator ends up with his bones in a ditch. The

Fig. 11.2 *"Los llorones"* (The Weepers) singing in the street. *Source* Codigo Carnaval, n.d.a.

audience laughs, not because they actually desire something like that but because they are surprised at the final association of the murderer with the "ditch" [*cuneta*] rhyming with the previous "*furgoneta*" (van) and "*glorieta*" (roundabout). Dramatically, the association with ditches is with carried out reprisals, but not with their executioners. Thus, by presenting the story in reverse the previous mental scheme is ingeniously inverted and provokes a humorous contextual effect in the audience.

Another street *chirigota*, *"Los llorones"* (the weepers) (see Fig. 11.2) also included the exhumation of Queipo-de-Llano in their final medley.[4]

Queipo-de-Llano is leaving the Macarena this m*orrow*,

a Sevillian told me with great *sorrow*.

Deep down he was a good person, a good **guy**,

Though on the radio he encouraged many people to be raped and **die**.

But that's minutiae compared to what Jiménez-Losantos does ref*er*,

and he's still on the **air**. (Ahhhh) [laughter and bravos from the audience]

[*Queipo-de-Llano se va de la Macar***ena**,

me dijo un sevillano con mucha ***pena***.

Él en el fondo era una persona íntegra y ***buena***.

Es verdad que en la radio animaba a violar y matar a no sé cuántos,

pero eso son minucias comparado con lo que suelta Jiménez Losantos

---

[4] The winning *comparsa* of the 2023 COAC Carnival, "La ciudad invisible", also dedicated a *pasodoble* to this theme in the Gran Teatro Falla, highly applauded and appreciated by the public.

y sigue en antena. (Ayyyyy)] (Codigo Carnaval, n.d.a., 6:48–7:25)

This *chirigota* gets laughs, applause, and *bravos* from the audience when in their medley they dedicate a song to the departure of General Queipo from the Macarena church, with the music of the well-known song "Macarena" by the Sevillian duo Los-del-Río. The disguise of weeping old women with black sunglasses and a shoulder scapular, mixed with amusing music and gestures, contrasts again with the lyrics that ironically describe Queipo as a good person ["una persona bu*ena*"] simply because it rhymes with "Macar*ena*" and "*pena*" (sorrow). Also, they comment on how the general used Radio Seville as part of his cruel propaganda to "encourage rape and murder" of Republican Democrats, although in another witty loop, they relate what Queipo broadcast on radio with what the ultra-conservative radio announcer Federico Jiménez-Losantos says today, compared to whom Queipo's was "minutiae."

11.3.2 Mass Media, the Spanish Morning Breakfast of Housewives and Pensioners, the Growth of Neo-Fascism

Spain is a country of radio in the morning and TV programs that accompany the work of all those who can combine it with listening to or watching that medium. These media are very powerful and the big media groups have taken over channels with great influence on the public, in which "pseudo-journalistic"[5] talk shows proliferate that scarcely reflect the true ideological plurality of society, especially promoting conservative ideology of which they have become a loudspeaker. As Fallarás (2022) points out: "The vast majority of the media in Spain are right-wing or extreme right-wing."

In contrast to this reality of the mass media, carnival is a "journalism sung" by the people, in which they freely say what they think, without favoring anyone's interests.

The *chirigota* "Frente Talibán" ("Taliban front," short name for "Those of the Taliban front of the irreverent republic of *Kadik*adistan,[6]" semi-finalists of the Cádiz Carnival 2023) (see Fig. 11.3), identified this year with the Cádiz Taliban "type," offered "sharp criticism" of the "pseudo-journalism" or "sell-out journalism" of Spain's radio and television programs (Roldán, 2023). The subject was worthy of attention given that from these supposedly informative programs political opinions are slipped in instead of news (Geneiro, 2023).

Enjoy the breakfast that every morning they offer *you*

the channels and national media, in programs so *crude*.

---

[5] In the sense that those who speak are not always journalists and because they debate on any topic, as if they were experts on everything.

[6] To highlight the pun with Cádiz: Kadikadistan is a made-up name recalling all these republics ending in –**istan**, but with the beginning of Cádiz spelled with 'k' to resemble the Arabic language.

Fig. 11.3 *"Frente Talibán"* (Taliban Front) singing in the theater. *Source* ONDA CADIZ CARNAVAL, n.d.

Table and tablecloth companions of the vote seekers and the businessmen, ***too***;

felicitators of the capital, emissaries of lies, ahh, and manipulators of the ***truth***.

They're still at the top because they tell you what they ***should***.

Distorted press, ahh, press, prosti***tute***.

They cordially chat with Díaz Ayuso and with Abascal, while they ***drool***.

And knowing what the Borbón in his bedroom and in his mattress ***put***,

they kept ***mute***, they kept ***mute***, and they kept ***mute***.

They say that carnival is journalism that in February the people sing,

but comparing my festival with that sell-out ***press***, to Cádiz is an off***ence***,

for in Cádiz things are said just as they are ***thought***,

Without selling ourselves out to anyone, 'cause we are not ***bought***.

[*Disfrute el desayuno que todas las mañ****anas***

*le ofrecen los canales y medios nacionales en sus burdos prog****ramas***. *Compañeros de mesa y mantel del buscador de votos /y del empre****sario****,*

*del capital felad****ores****, de la mentira emis****arios*** *y de las verdades manipulad****ores****. Ahí siguen arriba porque le dicen lo que deben dec****ir****,*

prensa desvirtuada y prostituida, ay, vivivivi.

La que charla cordial con Díaz Ayuso y con Abascal, mientras se le cae la ***baba****. Y la que sabiendo la que el Borbón metía en su alcoba y en su colchón* *call**aba**, call**aba** y call**aba**.*

*Y a veces puede que el carnaval sea periodismo que por febrero el pueblo c**anta**. Comparar la fiesta mía con esa prensa vendida 'pa' Cádiz resulta una ofensa, que en Cádiz se dicen las cosas /tal como se piensa,*

sin venderse a nadie, y con más vergüenza] (ONDA CADIZ CARNAVAL, n.d., 7:40–9:30)

Far from resorting to suggested implicatures or insinuations, in this *pasodoble* the inferential work is already given to the receiver and the information is made explicit. Thus, the author and the performers do not hold back when they sing (as above):

They're still at the top because they tell you what they ***should***.

Distorted press, ahh, press, prosti***tute***.

They cordially chat with Díaz Ayuso and with Abascal, while they ***drool***.

And knowing what the Borbón in his bedroom and in his mattress ***put***,

they kept ***mute***, they kept ***mute***, and they kept ***mute***.

Adding to the impressive text are the expressiveness of their gestures accompanying the lyrics, as well as the underlying music emphasizing the repetition of the main ideas, accusing the press of being servile to the right and the ultra-right, and of keeping quiet in the face of the excesses of the king emeritus.

In the last verse they end by rejecting the comparison of carnival with the press, for carnival is the people's truth, not sold to anyone: "for in Cádiz things are said/ just as they are ***thought***, /without selling ourselves out to anyone,/'cause we are not ***bought***."

Journalists such as Roldán (2023) minimized the critical nature of these *chirigota* lyrics, claiming that "[their] aim is to bring a smile from the very heart of the Gran Teatro Falla of Cádiz to the rest of the world," but the intended cognitive effect on the audience, apart from making them laugh or smile is in our opinion clearly vindictive too. Humor is thus the vehicle for launching the strongest criticisms and exposing the greatest truths.

The audience at the theatre appreciates the relevance of the messages while laughing at the witty and humorous way they are delivered. In this case, the *chirigota*'s costume is as 'irreverent' and surreal as its name, dressed as Cádiz Taliban hybrids with seagulls' nests and fishermen's nets on their turbans, toy weapons, and even a tank with a Cádiz license plate. An amusing melody introduced with the carnival whistle, and exaggerated gestures, accompany the main ideas and words.

Rhymes strategically match the key words such as mañ*ana*-progr*amas* (morning-programs), empres*ario*-emis*arios* (businessmen-emissaries), b*aba*-call*aba* (drool-kept mute), of*ensa*-p*iensa*-verg*üenza* (offence-think-dignity), which accurately summarize the content: the morning programs are emissaries of politicians and businessmen whom the press flatters; as opposed to this, in Cádiz people say with dignity what they really think.

Recognizing the names of the programs and media presenters, and seeing the bravery of the artists who weave the ideas in a poetic and ingenious way, makes the audience burst into laughter as the witty lyrics progress. This, because a Taliban from Cádiz with a seagull's nest in his turban or an imam (homophone of "magnet" in Spanish) with screwdrivers, spanners, and screws attached to his hat can say things that an ordinary citizen would not dare.

11.3.3 Anti-immigration, Racism, Fascism in Political Institutions

Spain has always been a land of welcome, and in the 10th century it was a model of coexistence between Christians, Arabs, and Jews. There is no need to go back to the Middle Ages, as in the post-war period of the last century it was the Spaniards themselves who had to emigrate to other places. However, with the rise of the ultra-right, the 'anti-other' sentiment is growing in a certain sector, as can be seen in the lyrics of the *chirigota* "Fariña de mis ojos" (The "flour" of my eye). Racism and xenophobia are traits that sadly form part of parties such as Vox, led by Santiago Abascal, condemning the arrival of immigrants on open boats from the Mediterranean (see Fig. 11.4).

> I crossed the whole country to get to your beach…
> And when I got to the **Strait**, Santi Abascal was there **straight**:
> "Here no reds (leftists) are allowed, **guys**, no rogues with **lice**."
> And Abascal cut the road… And there it was when I saw [long suspenseful pause]

Fig. 11.4 *"Fariña de mis ojos"* (The Flour of My Eyes) singing in the theater. *Source* Ortega Palomares, n.d.

11 The Cultural Background of Political Humor "Sung" by the Spanish People

the Nazi in the Mediterranean. [great laughter from the audience]
[*Cruce yo todo el país para llegar a tu playa...*
*Y cuando llegué al est**rech**o, Santi Abascal allí de**rech**o:*
*"Aquí no se admiten **roj**os, maleantes con pi**ojos**".*
Y Abascal cortó el camino... y allí fue cuando yo vi ((pausa))
al Nazi en el Mediterráneo] (Ortega Palomares, n.d.).

This *chirigota* from Santoña, Cantabria, was a semi-finalist with a 'type' that is easily recognized by the public, a Galician drug trafficker based on a real character (see Fig. 11.4). To add to the humorous effect, they wore a wig, suit, gold watch, and gold medal (a Galician scallop shell) and, of course, the red clown circles on their cheeks. As a play on words, "Fariña" in Galician means flour and is a colloquial name for cocaine. In turn, "Far**iña** de mis ojos" imitates the expression "la n**iña** de mis ojos" (the apple of my eye).

With music from the well-known song *Nací en el Mediterráneo* (I was born in the Mediterranean) by the Catalan singer-songwriter Joan Manuel Serrat, one of the emblematic songs whose lyrics are known by everyone throughout Spain, the author, José María Barranco, varies the beginning with the word *nací* (I was born) becoming "nazi," personified in Santiago Abascal, leader of the far-right Vox party.

Although out of context the subject matter is far from funny, the humorous treatment aims to provoke hilarity in the audience and succeeds. The costume, the exaggerated gestures, the attitude and, above all, the change of Serrat's well-known lyrics to include Abascal, a politician representing the far-right, turns the idyllic song about how proud we Spaniards are to be Mediterranean into a song against the racist and xenophobic intolerance of the far-right.

In the original lyrics, Serrat sang of his love for the Mediterranean Sea, but they were changed in a parodic way, causing surprise and hilarity. The public has in mind the original verses: A tus atardeceres *rojos* se acostumbraron mis *ojos*/como el recodo al *camino*..." (My eyes got used to your red sunsets,/like the bend does to the road...), but they unexpectedly become "Aquí no se admiten *rojos,* maleantes con pi*ojos*/y Abascal cortó el *camino*..." ("Here no reds [leftists] are allowed, guys,/no rogues with lice."/And then: "Abascal cut the road..."). The unexpected appearance of a character like Abascal in the midst of a beautiful and romantic melody, together with the surprising change of lyrics, provoke laughter from the audience. The key words and rhymes are retained, but the meaning is diametrically opposite, and the presence of the far-right in the Mediterranean is associated, through background knowledge and cognitive assumptions shared by author/performers and audience, with the rejection of immigrants arriving in the Mediterranean fleeing a worse world in Africa, explicitly extended by Abascal to all those who are left-wing ("*rojos*": red). The audience, while disapproving of the intolerance, laughs heartily at the composer' ingenious witticisms.

11.3.4 Aristocracy; Andalusian Latifundia; Spanish Monarchy

There are historical and cultural issues that continue to be part of the Andalusian sentiment. One of these is the historical claim to land. As Aguaza (2017) points out: "Andalusian society has historically been characterized by a very marked social structure, which has had the possession of land as its dividing line."

The relationship between Andalusians and their aristocracy has therefore been historically conflictual, given that most of the land belonged to a very few lords, while the peasantry had no land of their own to cultivate and no stable work on the land of others. Latifundism, which had been established in the Middle Ages, and the absenteeism of rural landowners, left the people destitute (Checa-Godoy, 2013). At the beginning of the 20th century, the Second Republic attempted an agrarian reform that was aborted by Franco's uprising leading to the Civil War, so that many Andalusians had to emigrate in droves, abandoning land that did not provide them with work. With the arrival of democracy, a profound agrarian reform program was introduced, but the vestiges of large estates still remain in large tracts of fenced-off private land (Checa-Godoy, 2013).

La Chirigota del Barranco still sings of this Andalusian historical injustice (see Fig. 11.5).

Fig. 11.5 *"La Chirigota del Barranco"* (Barranco's Ravine Chirigota) singing in the theater. *Source* Codigo Carnaval, n.d.b

This blessed land goes on with the same cross on its **back**,

providing for so many vultures, amongst marquises and other aristo**crats**.

We know well that all that their ancestors inherited was stolen from the **peasants**.

We know well that in the lands they ploughed up the sweat that's spilled was our grand**parents.**'

I wonder if there is any who **would** renounce their title so sudde**nly**.

I don't consider them that **foolish,** although some of them really look like that… appar**ently**. [crazy gestures and laughter from the public]

[*Sigue esta tierra bendita con la misma cruz a cu**estas**,*

*manteniendo a tanto buitre entre marqueses y duqu**esas**.*

Ya sabemos bien que 'tó' lo que han 'heredao' todos sus antepasados

*se lo robaron al p**ueblo**.*

*Y sabemos bien que en las tierras que han 'arao' el sudor que hay 'derramao' era de nuestros ab**uelos**.*

*Y no hay ninguno que así de p**ronto** al título prefiera renunc**iar**;*

*no creo que ninguno sea tan t**onto**, aunque alguno lo llegue a aparenta*] (Codigo Carnaval, n.d.b).

The humorous, verbal, and non-verbal vehicle that surrounds all the lyrics of the "Chirigota del Barranco" makes them capable of transmitting very harsh criticisms and accusations that the audience accepts willingly. They are disguised as 19th century Andalusian bandits (see Fig. 11.5), with blunderbusses and exaggeratedly large sideburns, accompanied by a cannon and a donkey, their gestures and smiles as exaggerated as their sideburns. In the *pasodoble* "This blessed land goes on […]" these "bandits" paradoxically complain about what others stole, but in fact they act as Robin Hoods who turn out to be good against those who for centuries have abused the people. The audience laughs, especially when they wonder if any privileged person will ever give up their perks and they reply that there is no such foolish aristocrat, although many actually look like fools, clearly alluding with their words and gestures to some that audience members immediately have in mind.

Not only the aristocracy; the monarchy is also not spared from acid criticism. Spain has a parliamentary monarchy i.e., the king reigns but does not govern, a task belonging to the parliament. Nevertheless, the monarchical institution, restored after Franco's dictatorship, is a fundamental part of Spain's identity as a nation, as in the United Kingdom.

Carnival in Cádiz could not occur without lyrics dedicated to the Royal House. One of the contest's most acclaimed groups, the *chirigota* del Bizcocho "Los mi alma," disguised as ghosts or spectral figures all dressed in white (see Fig. 11.6), with white chains and white make-up, dedicate the following song to King emeritus Juan Carlos I and his grandson Froilán (also amusingly known by his real/royal long name Philip-John-Froilan-of-all-the-Saints):

Fig. 11.6 *"Los mi alma"* (My Soul) singing in the theater. *Source* Todo Carnaval, n.d.

Felipe-Juan-Froilán-de-tós-los-Santos is making a bigger and bigger mess of **things**.

The only difference between his grandfather and the **kid**

is that, whenever he goes out on the **town**,

he never '*robs*' us of our expectations and lets us **down**. [great laughter]

[*El Felipe Juan Froilán de tós los Santos,*

el mushasho cada vez la lía más parda.

Ya solo se diferencia de su abuelo

en que este siempre que sale nunca defrauda] (Todo Carnaval, n.d.)

The Sevillian *chirigota* "Los mi alma" (My souls),[7] awarded fourth prize in the COAC 2023, cannot help but criticize the wanderings of the current king's nephew and, incidentally, of his grandfather, the emeritus King Juan Carlos I, who is now "exiled" in Abu Dhabi for defrauding the state financially. The boy's wanderings have led to him being sent to Abu Dhabi with his grandfather to avoid further scandals, making two "exiles." Unlike his grandfather, the young man (according to the authors) never "*defrauds*" every time he goes out, this playing on the double meaning of the verb "*defraudar*" in Spanish: legally it means to defraud, to steal; the other meaning is to disappoint, to frustrate a hope. The play of meanings, in which the

---

[7] People from Seville are known as "my souls" because they use the expression "mi alma" to call others all the time.

Fig. 11.7 *"El niño de Isabelita"* (Lizzy's kid) singing in the theater. *Source* El Español, n.d.

grandfather "defrauds" (fiscally) and the grandson never "'*robs*' us our expectations and lets us down" (he does not stop making the news because of his mischief), gets a hearty laugh from the audience.

The brilliant *chirigota* from Rota, "El niño de Isabelita" (Lizzy's kid), also mocks the emeritus King (see Fig. 11.7).

> Juan Carlos de Borbón has many girlfr**iends**.
> Today he has one, tomorrow another, it never **ends**…
> He likes Corinna, Nicole, Sofia, **May**…
> He likes a different one every **day**.
> Juan Carlos's shotgun still works o**kay**.
> …He's going to take them all to Abu Dhabi, to Abu Dhabi, ehhhhh.
> [exaggerated gestures and dancing, and laughs from the public]
> [*Juan Carlos de Borbón tiene muchas novias.*
> *Hoy tiene una, mañana otra…*
> *Le gusta mucho la josefa, la corinna, la nicole, la Sofía…*
> *a él le gusta una diferente cada día.*
> *a Juan Carlos la escopeta le funciona todavía.*
> *…Se las va a llevar a todas a Abu Dabi, a Abu Dabi, eh*]
> (El Español, n.d.)

In this *chirigota*, the combination of gestures, intonation, characterization, and lyrics achieves a very humorous effect on the audience. 'Typecasting' Queen Elizabeth II's son, Britain's Prince Charles, now King Charles III (see Fig. 11.7), and to the rhythm of Bad Bunny's reggaeton, they mock with great humor the life that the Spanish emeritus king is living in Abu Dhabi at the expense of the Spanish people's money.

11.3.5 On Women Politicians

In a chapter dedicated to carnival humor, we cannot fail to mention a song that has gone viral and like other funny and catchy carnival songs has become a recurrent earworm for many people. The street *chirigota* "The alarmists" (see Fig. 11.8) dedicated a section of their medley to the controversial president of the Madrid Community, Isabel Díaz-Ayuso, from the right-wing Popular Party, presenting a version of the well-known *ranchera* folk song "Me gustas m*ucho*" (I like you a lot) by a famous Spanish singer, Rocío Dúrcal, renamed as "Me gusta Ay*uso*" (I like Ayuso).

> When I was studying geography, my teacher used to tell me that in the center is "Madr*izzz*,"
>
> but I have my suspicions that it's further to the right, just like Bert*ín*.
>
> Although their mayor is nice and f*unny*, he's not the one for ***me***.
>
> The president is more witty and z*any*, she's the best of all "Madr*izzz*."
>
> She seems angelic, but she opens her mouth and lets out such outrageous th*ings*.
>
> With what she says I ***laugh*** always so, so very ***much***.
>
> I like Ayuso, I like Ayuso, *indeed*!!
>
> but I can't vote [**votar**] for her, I don't live in "Madr*izzz*".
>
> [...]
>
> From Vox they're mad as *hell* 'cause she's not doing *well* promoting ***equality***,
>
> but they haven't realized that for her equality means: "I don't ***care what it is***."

Fig. 11.8 *"Los alarmistas"* (The Alarmists) singing in the street. *Source* IIB Sweetwater Beachcombing in Rota, n.d.

As I speak Andalusian and I'm from the *South,* let me explain what "**botar**" *means*:

"*Botar*" means "fuck off *now*" if you spell it with a "*b*"!!

I like Ayuso, I like Ayuso, *indeed*!!

but I can't throw her away, I don't live in "Madr**izzz.**"

I like Ayuso, I'd like her *more*, if I could tell her "walk the hell out the *door*."

[*Cuando estudiaba geografía mi maestro me decía que en el centro está "Madrizzz",*

pero tengo mis sospechas que está más a la derecha igualito que Bertín.

Aunque su alcalde es muy gracioso y muy chistoso, no es el que me gusta a mí. La presidenta es más bromista, pedazo de humorista, lo mejor de "to Madrizzz". Parece angelical, pero es que abre la boca y suelta cada gran barbaridad.

Con lo que dice yo me río siempre una "jartá".

Me gusta Ayuso, me gusta Ayuso a mí,

pero no puedo yo votarla, no vivo en "Madrizzz".

[…]

Desde Vox están que trinan porque ella es que adoctrina fomentando la igualdad, pero no se han dado cuenta que para la presidenta igualdad es que "igual le da". Como yo soy del sur y hablo en andaluz, lo de botar no sé qué entenderán.

Botar con "b" "po" significa "pal carajo ya".

Me gusta Ayuso, me gusta Ayuso a mí,

pero no puedo yo botarla, no vivo en "Madrizzz".

Me gusta Ayuso, me gustaría más de que pudiera yo botarla "pal carajo ya"]

(IIB Sweetwater Beachcombing in Rota, n.d.).

This street group, disguised as alarm technicians, reviews with humor and sarcasm some of the most famous controversies of the female Madrid president's mandate, during four and a half minutes that have been reproduced thousands of times on social networks.

The *chirigota* begins by singing:"When I was studying geography, my teacher used to tell me that in the center is 'Madrizz,' but I have my suspicions that it's further to the right just like Bertín," alluding to the geographical situation of Madrid, which now seems to be more "to the right" (in a clear play on meanings between the geographical right and the ideological right there in power), just like the popular conservative singer Bertín Osborne.

Throughout the *copla* there is phonic interplay between Andalusian speech and the speech of "Madrizzz" (an exaggeration of the Madrid pronunciation of the word Madrid, parodically transcribed in correspondence with the phoneme/θ/instead of /d/). However, the performers are very Andalusian and laugh "*una jartá*" (a lot, they crack up) when the apparently "angelic" politician "spouts every hugely outrageous thing." These contrasts cause great hilarity in the audience.

Curiously, in this relaxed Andalusian pronunciation, the singers justify the key to the song, given that throughout the *copla* they express that they like Ayuso, but cannot "vote for her" because they do not live in Madrid [*no puedo yo **votar**la, no vivo en "Madrizz"*]. Finally, they end up explaining that they mean "***botar***," which means "to throw someone out" ("*'Botar'* means "fuck off *now*"/if you spell it with a '*b*'!!"). The homophony of the lexical units "*botar*" and "*votar,*" with clearly differentiated meanings, is thus disambiguated, breaking the ambiguity of the text's orality.

In this way the audience can confirm their cognitive schemas which foresaw that a *chirigota* from Cádiz could not be happily praising a politician representing the most rancid ultra-right. The presuppositions and expectations of those who listen to the *chirigota*, and who intuit and await a satisfactory explanation and resolution, finally find their confirmation, amused by the ingenious phonetic solution, provoking a reaction of laughter and applause.

11.4   Final Considerations

From the remoteness of the province of Cádiz, the critical view of the authors of the lyrics and the masterly interpretation of the groups stand out as "free journalism," critical and without self-interest, using humor as a vehicle to approach facts that affect society and politics, continuously alluding to relevant socio-cultural references recognized by the audience of the Gran Teatro Falla where the official competition takes place, and by the general public who follow them locally in the streets of Cádiz or throughout the country via the media and social networks.

From this brief review of the carnival's thematic and socio-cultural features, we have also seen how the pragmatic framework is the most appropriate one to be able to adequately explain the unquestionable cognitive effects of the humorous discourse. An integral and comprehensive interpretation of the phenomenon of humor cannot be reached if we do not pay attention to the humorous attitude of the sender or to the linguistic and paralinguistic resources that coexist in the generation of humor in carnival *coplas* that find in the (meta)pragmatic approach powerful explanatory tools for such a complex and productive phenomenon.

References

Aguaza, F. (2017, March 13). *The struggle for land in Andalusia*. El Salto. https://www.elsaltodiario.com/campesinado/la-lucha-por-la-tierra-en-andalucia (in Spanish).

Attardo, S., & Raskin, V. (1991). Script theory revis(it)ed: Joke similarity and joke representation model. *Humor: International Journal of Humor Research, 4*, 293–347. https://doi.org/10.1515/humr.1991.4.3-4.293.

Barceló-Calatayud, A. M. (2014). *The "type" in the carnival of Cádiz*. Universidad de Cádiz (in Spanish).

Carlospasky. (n.d.). *Street chirigota "Los alarmistas"* (Video). YouTube. https://www.youtube.com/watch?v=KVT9BESbrhA (in Spanish).

Checa-Godoy, A. (2013). *Landownership.* Andalupedia. http://www.andalupedia.es/p_termino_detalle.php?id_ter=11710 (in Spanish).

Codigo Carnaval. (n.d.a). *Street chirigota "Los llorones"* (Video). YouTube. https://www.youtube.com/watch?v=GHR5bU9zgsk (in Spanish).

Codigo Carnaval. (n.d.b). *Chirigota "La Chirigota del Barranco"* (Video) YouTube. https://www.youtube.com/watch?v=alGxGLBAy5I (in Spanish).

Decarlini, J. (2023, February 12). *The brutal repression of the carnival members in Cádiz after the coup d'état.* Diario Público. https://www.publico.es/sociedad/brutal-represion-carnavaleros-cadiz-golpe.html#analytics-buscador:listado (in Spanish).

Diputación de Cádiz. (2020). *They died singing* [documentary]. Carnaval de Cádiz TV. https://www.youtube.com/watch?v=7PBGG5ZGdoQ (in Spanish).

Domínguez-Pérez, A. (2011). *The summer that brought a long winter.* Quorum. (in Spanish).

Donnelly, L. (2013). *Women deliver, the world receives: Cartoons for and about every woman.* http://www.womendeliver.org/assets/Cartoon_Book.pdf.

El Español. (n.d.). *Chirogota "El niño de Isabelita"* (Video). YouTube. https://www.youtube.com/watch?v=vhx1VZPvBiY (in Spanish).

EFE. (2020, July 20). *The most scoundrel humor takes the streets of Cádiz.* Canarias7. https://www.canarias7.es/hemeroteca/el_humor_mas_canalla_toma_las_calles_de_cadiz-KDCSN455935 (in Spanish).

Fallarás, C. (2022, February 22). *'Ayusers' vs 'losers': In Spain the media are right-wing.* Diario Público. https://blogs.publico.es/cristina-fallaras/2022/02/22/ayusers-vs-loosers-en-espana-los-medios-son-de-derechas/ (in Spanish).

Geneiro, A. (2023, February 2). *Breakfast club.* Voz digital. https://www.lavozdigital.es/carnaval/frente-taliban-republica-irreverente-kadikadistan-vera-iman-20230203231411-ntv.html (in Spanish).

Gibson, I. (1989). *The death of a poet 1936.* Pantheon Books.

Gigliotti, S. (2023, February 12). In defense of Martínez Ares. *Todos los nombres.* https://todoslosnombres.org/cadiz-carnaval-la-letra-de-martinez-ares-contra-queipo-que-senala-a-la-macarena-la-cofradia-llevaba-anos-apurando-la-desgracia/ (in Spanish).

IIB Sweetwater Beachcombing in Rota. (n.d.). *Street chirigota "Los alarmistas"* (Video). YouTube. https://www.youtube.com/watch?v=xZBq6KiGMCc (in Spanish).

Jiang, T., Li, H., & Hou, Y. (2019). Towards a cultural specialty on humor perception and usage. *Frontiers in Psychology, 10.* https://doi.org/10.3389/fpsyg.2019.00123.

Moreno-Rodríguez, J. A. (2019). *Carnival of Cádiz: Critical journalism of a people.* Tal vez (in Spanish).

ONDA CÁDIZ CARNAVAL. (n.d.). *Chirigota "Frente talibán."* (Video). YouTube. https://www.youtube.com/watch?v=rnV2-__Rjec&t=450s (in Spanish).

Ortega Palomares, F. M. (n.d.). *Chirigota Fariña de mis ojos* (Video). YouTube. https://www.youtube.com/watch?v=wIli458EYDw (in Spanish).

Payán-Sotomayor, P. (1993). The carnival language. In A. Ramos Santana (Ed.), *Carnival in Cádiz* (pp. 35–47). Diario de Cádiz (in Spanish).

Ramos-Santana, A. (1985). *History of the Cádiz Carnival.* Caja de Ahorros de Cádiz (in Spanish).

Roldán, A. (2023, February 16). Emissaries of lies. *El Confidencial.* https://www.elconfidencial.com/television/programas-tv/2023-02-16/chirigota-cadiz-coac-frente-taliban-ana-rosa-griso_3576999/ (in Spanish).

Shilikhina, K. (2017). Metapragmatic markers of the bona fide and non-bona fide modes of communication. In W. Chlopicki & D. Brzozowska (Eds.), *Humorous discourse* (pp. 107–130). Mouton de Gruyter.

Solís-Llorente, R. (1966). *Choirs and chirigotas. The lyrics of the Cádiz carnival.* Taurus (in Spanish).

Sperber, D., & Wilson, D. ([1986] 1995). *Relevance: Communication and cognition* (2nd rev. ed.). Blackwell.

Sperber, D., & Wilson, D. (2004). Relevance theory. In L. R. Horn & G. L. Ward (Eds.), *The handbook of pragmatics* (pp. 607–632). Blackwell.

Tanaka, K. (1992). The pun in advertising: A pragmatic approach. *Lingua, 87*(1/2), 91–102. https://www.sciencedirect.com/science/article/abs/pii/002438419290027G?via%3Dihub.

Todo Carnaval. (n.d.). *Chirigota "Los mi alma"* (Video). YouTube. https://www.youtube.com/watch?v=djMnMIr8fMs (in Spanish).

Torres-Sánchez, M. A. (1999). *Pragmatic study of verbal humor.* Universidad de Cádiz (in Spanish).

Yus-Ramos, F. (1998). Relevance theory and media discourse: A verbal-visual model of communication. *Poetics, 25*(5), 293–309. https://www.sciencedirect.com/science/article/abs/pii/S0304422X9700020X?via%3Dihub.

Yus-Ramos, F. (2003). Humor and the search for relevance. *Journal of Pragmatics 35*(9), 1295–1331. https://www.sciencedirect.com/science/article/abs/pii/S0378216602001790.

Yus-Ramos, F. (2016). *Humour and relevance.* John Benjamins.

María del Mar Rivas-Carmona is a Senior Lecturer at the University of Cordoba, Spain. She has previously taught at Harvard University, USA, and the University of Seville, Spain. Her classes focus on Translation, Discourse and Pragmatics, and her research interests include discourse analysis and specialized translation. Standing out among her recent publications are two international co-editions on the discursive aspects of translation, published by Peter Lang (2013) and Narr Verlag (2013).

María del Carmen García-Manga is Associate Professor of Spanish Language at the University of Córdoba. She holds a Ph.D. from the University of Cadiz (2010), a degree in Hispanic Philology (1998) and in Linguistics (2000), and develops her research activity in the areas of Spanish Language and General Linguistics, addressing aspects of semantics, linguistic motivation, morphology, lexicology and lexical creativity, lexicography and teaching–learning of lexical competence in Spanish as a foreign language.

Part III
Framing and Analyzing Political Humor

Chapter 12
Political Humor in American Culture: From Affability to Aggression

Michael Alan Krasner

Abstract This chapter uses Invited Behavior (my original concept) to analyze the power of leaders' humor and to show how changes in American leaders' humor reflect and reinforce recent changes in American political culture, especially the change from legitimacy to illegitimacy and the rise of a fantasy-based, extreme right-wing movement that has captured one of the two major American political parties. During the era of legitimacy, leaders used gentle humor to gain acceptance within that system, inviting the media and the public to follow the cultural norm of deference to the establishment. Now that legitimacy has been substantially eroded, insurgent far-right leaders such as Donald Trump use crude, aggressive humor to debase establishment rivals, inviting their supporters to treat these antagonists as life-and-death enemies. Such humor also reinforces the ultra-nationalist, xenophobic, homophobic, racist, misogynist fantasy world promoted by right-wing talk radio, Fox News, and other media. More traditional leaders such as Joseph Biden continue to employ the gentler humor that was nearly universal when the system was legitimate, inviting their supporters to see themselves as part of a united nation and to defer to established leaders and institutions offering a nearly fact-based view of reality.

12.1 Introduction

Humor is a human universal (Apte, 1985; Brown, 1991). All peoples laugh and most tell jokes, but humor is also culturally specific (Feldman, 2000). What is funny in one culture may be offensive or incomprehensible in another. Even within a particular national culture, conceptions of what is funny may vary sharply across time and across different constituent groups, whether defined by region, religion, race, class, ethnicity, gender, age, or political affiliation.

This chapter uses my original concept of Invited Behavior to analyze the power dynamics of leaders' humor and to show how changes in American leaders' political

M. A. Krasner (✉)
Taft Institute for Government and Civic Education, Queens College, City University of New York, New York City, NY, USA
e-mail: makrasner@gmail.com

© The Author(s), under exclusive license to Springer Nature Singapore Pte Ltd. 2024
O. Feldman (ed.), *Political Humor Worldwide*, The Language of Politics,
https://doi.org/10.1007/978-981-99-8490-9_12

humor reflect and reinforce changes in American political culture, especially the change from legitimacy to illegitimacy and the attendant rise of an extreme right wing, anti-democratic movement that has captured one of the two major American political parties—the Republicans. Part two adumbrates the concept of Invited Behavior, answering the general question: How does humor work to help leaders gain and hold support? Part three analyzes specific examples of successful leaders' humor drawn from the era of legitimacy. As the examples show, in this era leaders from both major parties employed humor to issue inclusive invitations aimed at reinforcing the norm of deference to leaders and support for the system.

Part four analyzes the current era, characterized by a legitimacy crisis and polarization driven by the takeover of one of the two major parties—the Republicans—by far-right forces. In this context, the use of humor by most Republican leaders will depart sharply from the cultural norms of promoting national unity and deference to establishment leaders. Instead, humor will be used by the extremist Republicans to demonize opponents, especially the media and established political leaders, creating what Murray Edelman (1985) calls "political enemies"—those seen as existential threats as opposed to opponents who only differ on policy.

Such humor will be aggressive, crude, and divisive, depending heavily on mockery. As such, it is one example of what a previous volume in this series categorized as "debasing political rhetoric" (Feldman, 2023a, 2023b). This humor also serves to reinforce the fantasy universe promulgated initially in the 1990s and early 2000s by right wing talk radio, Fox News, and Republican leaders such as Newt Gingrich—a universe characterized by ultra-nationalism, patriarchy, white supremacy, anti-Semitism, homo- and transphobia, xenophobia, and misogyny. Recently, the extreme conspiracy beliefs of QAnon, a weird pro-Trump conspiracy theory advanced online by a shadowy network, have been added. They include accusations that the U.S. government is controlled by reptilian aliens and that Democratic leaders run a pedophilia ring and drink a substance derived from those children's blood (Milbank, 2022).

Part five discusses the implications of these patterns for American democracy.

12.2 Invited Behavior and Leaders' Use of Humor

12.2.1 Invited Behavior

As originally conceived, Invited Behavior (Krasner, 2019) focused on how political leaders use social norms that structure situations into invitations and responses to enhance their own power. Examples include signaling for applause in a speech, and (in American politics) telling a joke (inviting laughter).

The broader version of Invited Behavior employed in this chapter and previously (Krasner, 2019, 2021) rests on the idea that considering political interactions generally in terms of invitations and responses illuminates dimensions that would otherwise remain obscure. Doing so reveals the true appeal of the leader and the followers' motivations. The next section uses this approach to analyze humor's power in general terms.

12.2.2 Ten Invitations—Why is Leaders' Humor Powerful?

The following categories overlap in practice but are more clearly discussed separately.

These analytical points apply both to the era of legitimacy and to the era of illegitimacy and polarization, but the means of achieving them—the kinds of humor used—are diametrically opposed, as will be made clear in section four. The crude, aggressive humor of the latter period involves additional invitations that will be discussed in part five.

12.2.2.1 The Attention-Claiming Invitation

Every attempt at humor is an attempt to claim attention, from the direct, explicit method of the person who says to their friends "I have a joke," to the indirect approach of a person who makes a witty remark and waits for the audience to "get it." The leader's invitation is: *Please pay attention to me.*

12.2.2.2 The Invitation to Accept the Leader's Control

Being the center of attention is crucial to leadership, but humor does more than that. A leader who uses humor puts themselves in charge because they are in the superior position of knowing something the rest of us don't know—what we will "get" when the joke or witty remark is understood. Thus, the leader has the opportunity to frame situations and to frame her/himself and the situation as explained in the points that follow.

This relationship is evident in the language of humor. We say someone "***makes*** us laugh." They control us. They produce a physical reaction in us. The power relation is clear.

By making us laugh, by taking control of the immediate social situation, and by reframing the pressing issue to benefit themselves, leaders also take control of the bigger political picture as we shall see in discussing the specific examples below. The invitation is: *Please accept my control.*

12.2.2.3 The Invitation to See the Leader as Superior

The figure in control gains the opportunity to frame themselves as superior, to present themself as above whoever is questioning them, as immune to whatever charge or criticism is being put forward, and as existing on a plane above ordinary reality. By using humor, the leader is putting themself above the situation, framing themself as being above critics and above accountability. Thus, the invitation becomes: *Please see me as too good and powerful to be bothered with the petty concerns raised against me or to do things in an ordinary way.*

12.2.2.4 The Invitation to Pleasure

Successful humor also invites potential followers to the gifts of laughter and (possibly) relief from tension. The invitation is: *Please accept from me the gifts of laughter and relaxation.*

12.2.2.5 The Invitation to See the Leader as Benevolent

If the humor is successful, if the attention to the leader is rewarded by the gifts of laughter and reduced stress, then the leader will be seen as benevolent. The invitation is: *Please see me* [the leader] *as someone who wants to help you* [potential followers]*; please see me as someone who is kind and generous.*

12.2.2.6 The Invitation to See the Leader as Empathetic and Genuine

To make us laugh the leader must understand us—he/she must be enough of a "regular guy" to know what will amuse us, and therefore must be like us in important ways and, like us, a regular person—authentic and trustworthy. The invitation is: *Please see me as a human being who comprehends your situation and genuinely cares about you.*

12.2.2.7 The Invitation to See the Leader as Strong and Likely to Win

As the examples to be discussed will demonstrate, successful political humor instantly reframes the situation (Amir, 2019). When potential supporters and journalists and even rivals laugh at the leader's joke or quip, what was serious becomes funny. What was problematic is solved. The person who can do this, who can instantly transform other people's perception of a given situation, particularly one that was threatening the leader, must be seen as strong and destined for success. The invitations are: *Please see me as someone who doesn't have to take seriously the petty threats that have been raised against me. Please see me as someone who transcends the ordinary and let me bring you along with me as I conquer.*

12.2.2.8 The Invitation to Join the Group Supporting the Leader

By laughing, potential supporters accept the leader's reframing of the situation. By doing it in concert with others, they become for that moment (and perhaps for much longer) part of the group supporting the leader. This experience can reinforce an existing allegiance or lead to a new one. The invitation is: *Please join our group; the group that follows the strong leader; the group that enjoys itself; the group that will win.*

12.2.2.9 The Invitation to Escape Responsibility

This invitation is to escape either the professional responsibility of journalists or the civic responsibility of citizens to investigate and judge the leader's possible corruption, poor judgment or disability. It offers the enticing option of evading potentially burdensome parts of reality—those that create unpleasant tensions—especially those that call the leader's qualifications into question, and instead to join the leader in dismissing these threats as not to be taken seriously. The invitations are: *Please give up your independent critical judgment and instead accept the laughter, strong leadership, and group allegiance that I offer. In particular, please join me in dismissing what threatened me as not worth taking seriously.*

For journalists, accepting this invitation resolves the tension involved in investigating a potential source. If they laugh at the joke and accept the leader's version that the failing isn't serious, they need not fulfil their professional obligation to investigate and risk alienating a powerful figure. (In the terms of Edelman's, 1985 penetrating analysis of symbols and politics, accepting the leader's invitation means giving up referential symbols—those that help make sense of reality by identifying objective elements—for condensation symbols i.e., those that evoke emotions).

This relinquishing of responsibility has a parallel in the physical aspects of laughter. At its extreme, laughter is called helpless laughter, laughter that goes on and on uncontrollably, laughter that we cannot stop. But there is a degree of helplessness at every level as indicated by common expressions such as "She tried unsuccessfully to keep a straight face," or, "I couldn't help laughing." When we laugh, we give up a degree of self-control.

Wallace Chafe (1987) points out that laughing is incapacitating physically and mentally. When you are laughing, you cannot do pushups, light a candle, or work a crossword puzzle. Furthermore, this state of incapacity is enjoyable. As Chafe (1987, p. 21) summarizes the issue: "Humor, in short, has two principal effects: physiologically it incapacitates, and psychologically it diverts attention to itself so that all else is forgotten or ignored. While in the humor state, you can't act effectively, and you like it."

In her brilliant book (2019), Lydia Amir references this point as part of her argument that humor (in the sense of accepting the ridiculousness of the human condition) offers a solution to the tragic dilemmas of human existence. By enabling the simultaneous perception of different points of view, humor reduces the intolerance of ambivalence and helps to moderate extreme emotions, among other beneficial effects. Chafe (1987, p. 18) adds: "[H]umor is an adaptive mechanism whose function is to keep us from taking seriously those things that we ought not to take seriously." Amir (2019, p. 84) summarizes the idea this way: "Thus, the pleasure humor triggers diverts attention away from decisive action on the psychological end, and the physiological incapacitation impedes it."

But for the political realm the point to underscore is that humor's ability to reconcile and transcend contradiction can be manipulated by leaders to bad ends. It can be used to cover up corruption or senility or (simply) bad choices. It can be used to hide what should be exposed and denounced. A political leader may choose to use humor to convince others that they should not take something seriously even when they should.

12.2.2.10 The Invitation to Accept the Leader's General View of Reality

Laughing at the leader's particular reframing humor leads potential supporters into the leader's general conception of the political universe and reinforces supporters' adherence to it. When we "get" a joke, which means when we understand why it is funny and we laugh, we are implicitly and almost instantly agreeing with the joke's point of view (Yovetich et al., 1990). It is only a slight exaggeration to say that humor produces an "Instant Transformation of Perception," because the process of getting a joke and laughing usually occurs without rational consideration. We simply react and, as the previous point indicates, the reaction is primarily visceral, not the product of extended reflection. In laughing we are agreeing with the premise and the conclusion of the joke or witty remark. We are thus accepting the following invitation: *Please accept the world as I define it and accept me as the arbiter of that reality. Follow me; join our movement; trust and believe in me.*

All of these invitations, if accepted, reinforce the cultural norm of deference to leaders, and, more generally, reinforce allegiance to the existing system—that is, they reinforce legitimacy.

12.3 Leaders' Humor in the Era of Legitimacy

12.3.1 The Cultural Context

Rogers Smith (1993) analyzes multiple American cultural traditions: a liberal tradition extolled by Tocqueville (2020) and Hartz (1955) that emphasizes limited government and the rule of law protecting individual rights; a republican tradition that includes civic virtue and popular sovereignty; and an ascriptive tradition that assigns natural superiority to white, straight, Christian men and subjugates women, and minorities—whether of race, religion, ethnicity, or gender-expression. In this Manichean worldview, society divides into the worthy and the unworthy, the righteous and the subversive.

The liberal tradition is encapsulated in the American Dream—the mythic idea that anyone who works hard and plays by the rules can succeed—meaning that they can enjoy at least a comfortable, middle-class existence, or at best become rich. In times of real or perceived economic hardship, when the American Dream is threatened, the classical liberal consensus is likely to be undermined by a surge toward the ascriptive—the sort of racist, nativist, misogynist, anti-Semitic, anti-Muslim, and anti-LGBTQ+ sentiments to which Trump and other Republicans have appealed. This culture elevates "true Americans," deriding others at best as dangerously misguided and at worst as the criminal Mexican immigrants of Donald Trump's announcement speech (Trump, 2015a, 2015b). Recent American history illustrates this shift.

While the strength of the basic cultural components of trust in government and support for major institutions of American society varied during the latter half of the twentieth century, it was very high at the outset—in the 60 and 70% range during the 1950s and 60s (Pew Research Center, 2022) and remained in the 40–54% range at the turn of the century (Gallup, n.d.). This period (1945 to roughly 2000) was also marked by a relatively strong consensus on the nature of reality, with most Americans accepting the version presented by the three main television networks in their nightly newscasts. Groups such as the John Birch society that advanced a conspiratorial view characterizing President Dwight Eisenhower as a "dedicated, conscious agent of the communist conspiracy," were relegated to the political fringes (Mulloy, 2014).

In that era of legitimacy, liberal and republican culture dictated that leaders be accomplished in public service, that is, within the system—either successful generals (Washington, Grant, Eisenhower), or experienced elected officials—and that leaders be dignified, knowledgeable, modest, intelligent, educated, maintaining integrity, mature, restrained, and hard working, as political scientists writing on leadership during this period attested (Edelman, 1985; Neustadt, 1991). But leaders were also supposed to have the common touch, to be able to communicate with everyday folk, to demonstrate their common humanity. They used humor, especially self-deprecating humor to do so (Paletz, 2002). Despite all their prestige and power, they could poke fun at themselves, thus demonstrating that they were not supercilious or egotistical despite their high status and positions. The leaders' self-framing invitation (a variation on invitation number 3 above) was, *Please see me as a likeable human being, not a snob or an elitist.* Leaders in this era also used gentle humor to defuse threats that might have undermined their reputations or threatened their competitive positions.

12.3.2 Defusing Threats—Three Examples

12.3.2.1 Kennedy and Corruption

In the campaign for the 1960 Democratic presidential nomination, then Senator John F. Kennedy faced accusations that his ambitious father, Joseph P. Kennedy, a very wealthy businessman who was also a former ambassador to Great Britain and a former chair of the Securities and Exchange Commission, was using his fortune corruptly on Senator Kennedy's behalf (Kessler, 1996). Had this frame prevailed, Kennedy would have been seen as the undeserving puppet of a scheming fat cat who was intent on buying his son the White House. His campaign would have been doomed.

Kennedy responded with humor. At a speech attended by members of the Washington press corps, Kennedy held up a small yellow piece of paper—the sort used to transmit messages by telegraphy—the email of that era. "I have here a telegram from my father," he said, and pretended to read. "It says, 'Dear Jack, Don't buy a single vote more than necessary—I'll be damned if I am going to pay for a landslide [an overwhelming victory]'" (Kennedy, 1958). The humor proved effective—the audience, including the journalists, laughed—and the issue faded from the media (and public) agenda (Krasner, 2023) despite later revelations that Joseph P. Kennedy had in fact dispersed large sums of money in crucial states such as West Virginia (Kessler, 1996; Loughry, 2006).

Consider Kennedy's joke in more detail; he is saying, "I'm at ease. I'm not on the defensive. I can joke about this. I don't have to account to you, the reporters, and by extension to the people. I can rise above this using humor to do so. I can reaffirm my status as the natural leader, the prince—the one you admire for grace under pressure and to the devil with the issue that created the pressure and tension in the first place." He invites the audience to see him as an undamaged leader, invoking the cultural element of leadership based on ability.

Instead of some labored defense that only serves to call attention to the issue and to offer a further target for attack, the joke invites the audience, including the journalists, to accept the leader's invitation to dismiss the issue, to reject the idea that it is to be taken seriously. The journalists and the audience are thus relieved of the burden of having to investigate, study, weigh evidence, and come to a decision. They can instead relax, enjoy the gift of laughter, and, crucially, defer to the accomplished leader.

In other words, this successful humor has used the cultural element of deference to deserving leaders to defuse the threat to the leader, and (by extension) to reinforce the legitimacy of the existing system.

12.3.2.2 Ronald Reagan and Age

In the presidential campaign of 1984 in the first of three televised presidential debates, Ronald Reagan, anointed as the "Great Communicator," and a heavy favorite against former vice president Walter Mondale, stumbled badly. He appeared generally ill at ease, while Mondale was relaxed and almost jovial, noting that he personally liked the president as anybody would. Reagan seemed at a loss for words when answering questions. Even his presumably well-rehearsed closing statement was halting and barely comprehensible. Media accounts raised the issue of Reagan's age, which he had joked about for years. Mondale seemed to have found the one chink in Reagan's peace-and-prosperity armor that might tighten the race (Pomper, 1985).

Predictably, a journalist raised the issue in the second debate. Reagan responded with, "I have decided not to make age an issue in this campaign. I will not exploit for political purposes my opponent's youth and inexperience." The audience broke into laughter; so did the questioning journalist. Mondale grimaced and then joined in. The danger had been met, the issue blunted, the threat dissolved (PBS Newshour, n.d.).

With this joke, Reagan said: "You've been worrying about my age. You want to know if I've got all my faculties. Well, let me prove it to you, not with a boring recitation of facts and figures, but with a joke. That will show you that my sense of humor is intact. More important, it demonstrates that I'm in command of this situation. After all, I'm relaxed and I just made everybody, including my opponent, laugh, and I sure took the wind out of that solemn reporter's sails." He invites attention; he invites people to enjoy themselves as the recipients of the laughter he gives them; he invites them to join him in dismissing the seriousness of the accusation; and he invites them to accept him as a good and competent leader because he has taken control.

Mondale himself testified to the joke's decisive effect in a documentary with Jim Lehrer (PBS, 2012).

Lehrer [referring to Reagan's joke and the laughter that followed]: Is that when you knew you were in trouble?

Mondale: Yeah. He got the audience with that one. I could tell. That one hurt. I knew he'd gotten me there. *That was really the end of my campaign that night* [emphasis added].

Lehrer: Did you know that night, that it was over?

Mondale: Yeah, I walked off and I was almost certain that it was over, and it was.

Here again, Reagan's humor invokes the cultural element of deference to leaders by inviting the audience to see him as a good leader—alert and capable, generous and human. Thus, he and the system of which he is a part are legitimated.

12.3.2.3 George W. Bush and Impertinence

At the time of the second presidential debate in 1988, the Republican nominee, George W. Bush, the incumbent Republican Vice-President, had through relentless attacks (especially on the issue of crime) taken a ten-point leader in the polls over his Democratic opponent, Governor Michael Dukakis of Massachusetts, and seemed poised for victory. Only a strong performance in the debate would allow Dukakis to regain a competitive position (Farah & Klein, 1989). The moderator, Bernard Shaw, an African-American anchorman from CNN, posed dramatic, personally confrontational first questions to both candidates (PBS, 2012).

Shaw began by asking Dukakis: "Governor, if Kitty Dukakis [the governor's wife] were raped and murdered, would you favor an irrevocable death penalty for the killer?".

Dukakis made no effort to interrupt; no sign of emotion crossed his face when the question was being posed nor when he replied (Author's contemporaneous observation; see also PBS, 1995). His response was the stock answer about opposition to the death penalty that he had been presenting throughout the campaign. One analyst (Hershey, 1989) concluded that "The debate could have ended at that point."

The unintended invitation thus issued was: *Please see me as a weak man, who, when confronted by a shocking, offensive question (and questioner), can defend neither himself nor his wife.*

Compare Bush's response to the next question that also included death and that referenced a widely criticized choice; in this case, Bush's selection of an undistinguished senator from Indiana, Dan Quayle, to be his vice-presidential candidate. Here is the sequence (PBS, 2012):

> Shaw: Now to you, Vice President Bush. I quote to you this from Article III of the 20st Amendment to the Constitution: "If at the time fixed for the beginning of the term of the President the president-elect shall have died, the Vice President-elect shall become president,' meaning, if you are elected and die before inauguration day..."
>
> Bush (interrupting in a mock admonishing tone): Bernie [laughter; Bush smiles as Shaw pauses and then stumbles as he continues]
>
> Shaw: [...] automatically, automatically, Dan Quayle would become the 41stPresident of the United States. What have you to say about that possibility?
>
> Bush: I'd have confidence in him. And I made a good selection. And I've never seen such a pounding, an unfair pounding on a young Senator in my entire life. And I've never seen a presidential campaign where the presidential nominee runs against my vice-presidential nominee; never seen one before [applause].

In contrast to Dukakis's passive, even deferential waiting out of the offensive question and his wooden response, Bush interrupts the impertinent journalist in a spontaneous, genial, humorous way that reasserts his authority much more powerfully than shouted indignation or any other response could have done because the humor instantly brings the audience into Bush's camp and isolates the journalist. Like Kennedy and Reagan, Bush is relying on the cultural element of deference to and respect for leaders.

The clear implication of Bush's single word, his tone, his facial expression, and his body language is this reframing in terms of deference to established leaders: *"You (Shaw) are saying something that goes beyond the bounds of polite behavior (and you are trying to put me on the defensive, as you just did my opponent). I could be hurt or offended, but I'm far too strong for that. I'll put you back into your place by reminding you first of how you are supposed to act, but more importantly the manner of my reminding will reinforce my authority over you and over the audience and, by extension over the voters."*

Bush is saying, I acknowledge that you tried to damage me, but of course you failed and really only damaged yourself by transgressing the norms of polite behavior in general, and in particular of deference to high officials and presidential candidates and of important public ceremonies such as presidential debates.

My tone mocks the idea that you could disconcert me. By the combination of mock hurt and reproach, I convey two messages in simple terms that everyone grasps immediately. First, you should not do this; behave yourself. Second, you can't hurt me.

Bush took command of the situation, repulsed the verbal attack, and isolated the attacker by placing him outside the bounds of polite behavior and making him the object of gentle derision and laughter. He did all of this with extraordinary efficiency and ease—a single word, properly delivered, was all it took. The invitations to the audience, and by extension to voters, were: *Please enjoy seeing me put this ill-mannered fellow in his place; and please see me as a strong, commanding leader who deserves deference (and as a leader in a legitimate system).* But notice that in his case as with Kennedy and Reagan, he did not debase the questioner; he did not make him into an enemy. Thus, he honored the cultural element of a united society, consistent with both the liberal and the republican traditions.

12.3.3 Self-Deprecation in an Era of Legitimacy—From Kennedy to Clinton

As president, Kennedy used self-deprecating humor to endear himself as a modest man who could laugh at himself. In 1961 during a state visit to France, where his French speaking wife captivated Parisians, Kennedy introduced himself at a press conference at the Palais Chaillot by saying (Kennedy, 1961): "I do not think it is altogether inappropriate that I introduce myself to this audience. I am the man who accompanied Jacqueline Kennedy to Paris, and I have enjoyed it."

The specific invitations thus issued include: *Please see me as a modest man who can laugh at himself. Please see me as a loving husband. Please see me as somebody who can appreciate the power of a beautiful, charming woman.* And the general invitation would be: *Please see me as a regular person; please recognize our common humanity.*

But notice the judo effect here. Self-deprecating humor is also self-elevating humor because it coopts potentially damaging issues and in so doing reverses their implications and impacts. By pre-empting this issue, Kennedy protected himself from commentary that said he had been eclipsed in Paris by his wife. Instead, he made the issue his own and used it to enhance his own image and standing, not least because the woman he was ostensibly elevating was his own wife.

Before the 1984 campaign made the age issue an urgent matter, Ronald Reagan had used self-deprecating humor effectively to take control of this issue. Thus, in his first state of the union address (Reagan, 1981), Reagan said: "President Washington began this tradition in 1790. […] For our friends in the press, who place a high premium on accuracy, let me say: I did not actually hear George Washington say that" [laughter]. At the Inaugural Luncheon in 1985, Reagan (1985) said: "There's been quite a few Inaugurations in my lifetime. I missed Abe Lincoln's but – [laughter] – I do remember Calvin Coolidge's" [laughter]. In an address to high school students on Martin Luther King, Jr.'s birthday, Reagan (1987) said: "And just to set the record straight, I may be old, but there's no truth to the story that Abe Lincoln and I walked to school together back in Illinois."

George H. W. Bush (Bush I), Reagan's vice president and successor, was known to mangle the English language on occasion, and he sought to get ahead of this issue by saying this of himself: "Fluency in English is something that I'm often not accused of" (Mears, 2018).

President Bill Clinton, in the early days of his administration, which were characterized by notable failures, offered this tongue-in-cheek defense at the White House Correspondents Association dinner: "I'm not doing so bad; I mean, at this point in his administration, William Henry Harrison had already been dead for sixty-eight days!" (Clinton, 1993).

These examples were intended to demonstrate the speakers' humanity, to underscore that they were authentic human beings, not given to egocentrism and that they would understand and respond to the concerns and needs of everyday Americans. Leaders who had this crucial characteristic in turn legitimated the system. By demonstrating their humanity, they also demonstrated that the system of which they were a part deserved the support and approval of its citizens.

12.4 Leaders' Humor: The Era of Illegitimacy and Polarization

12.4.1 The Political/Cultural Context

By 2015 when Donald Trump began his campaign for president, the culture of unity based on the liberal and republican traditions as well as the consensus on reality that had prevailed before 2000 had largely been eroded. Legitimacy—the main element of political culture—had dropped to record lows. Among the fifteen major institutions of American society included in the Gallup poll's survey, only three—small business, the military, and the police—received endorsements (either "a great deal of confidence" or "quite a lot of confidence") from the public whereas eight of the fifteen had been so evaluated in the 1970s (Gallup, no date). Political institutions ranked especially low, with the Congress at 8%, the presidency at 33%, and the Supreme Court at 32%. The media also fared poorly, with TV news at 21% and newspapers at 24%.

Similarly, the Pew Research Center's survey of trust in government (2022) found only 19% of the American people saying they could trust the government in Washington to do what is right "just about always," or "most of the time." In 2001, the range in various polls had been 49–54%, and in the 1960s it had been over 60%.

The country had also become sharply polarized. A powerful right-wing insurgency, fueled by enormous contributions from the ultra-rich and corporations, has captured one of the two major political parties—the Republicans (Hacker & Pierson, 2021; Mayer, 2016). Debasing rhetoric (Feldman, 2023a, 2023b) had become standard fare for most Republicans as they attempted to demonize their opposition (Milbank, 2022). Instead of drawing on the culture of unity, this insurgency drew on the divisive ascriptive tradition, including longstanding cultural elements as racism, nativism, misogyny, and xenophobia, as well as on newly salient elements such as homophobia and transphobia.

12.4.2 Aggressive, Divisive Humor

In this context, Democratic leaders' use of humor has continued to follow the patterns of the legitimacy era while Republican leaders have used more aggressive alternatives. To this trend Donald Trump added crudeness—coarse language that expressed aggressive sentiments and thus departed further from the norms of the era of legitimacy. As Oliver and Rahn argue (2016, pp. 191–192), this populist style "signals to the people that the [...] [leader] will go to great lengths to protect their interest [...] [T]he psychological distance between populist leaders and their followers is reduced and the bonds among followers solidified." These are the invitations to authenticity, followership, and fellowship I discussed above (in Sect. 12.2.2.9), but also the invitation to accept a fantasy reality.

12.4.2.1 Nicknames—Invitations to Supporters

Trump ridiculed his primary opponents by giving them nicknames reminiscent of a sixth-grader's schoolyard. Jeb Bush, the erstwhile front-runner, known for his low-key, dignified manner, became "Low-energy Jeb" (Trump, 2015a). Marco Rubio, the Senator from Florida, was dubbed "Little Marco" (Trump, 2016b), while Senator Ted Cruz from Texas was "Lying Ted" (Trump, 2016a). In the general election, the Democratic candidate, Hillary Clinton was "Crooked Hillary" (Trump, 2016c). These mocking appellations invited Trump supporters to express aggressively their resentments of establishment politicians, to enjoy emotional satisfaction at the expense of the elite (Denby, 2015). Trump was saying: *Join me in making fun of these stuffed* shirts who look down on people like you and giving vent to feelings of vengeance and violence. He was dividing the country into the worthy and the unworthy.

12.4.2.2 Invitation to the Id

But notice also that the crudeness and childishness of the language called forth raw emotions. If Trump, the supposed titan of business, the very epitome of the American dream, and now a candidate for president, if he could act childish and use schoolyard taunts, then so could anyone else. Trump, by his example, was issuing this invitation: *Join me in crudely expressing aggression against these people who look down on you and me. Join me in using provocative, childish language that in the schoolyard or on the stree, often leads to violence.*

In terms of Freudian psychology, Trump's actions and his language aimed at the most primitive part of people's psychological makeup. This was *the invitation to the id*, the part of the human personality that contains the most primitive and the most powerful impulses—to aggression, to violence, and to killing (Freud, 1905/1960).

12.4.2.3 Trap Invitation to Rivals

In addition, the mockery posed a special kind of invitation to the rivals being mocked. They were both challenges and traps. The challenge was this: *I'm calling you a name! What are you going to do about it?* The rival is being challenged to stand up for themself, to fight back.

But this challenge is also a trap because responding in kind, as Rubio tried to do (Berenson, 2016), means the rival is fighting on Trump's chosen ground—Reality TV—where Trump had starred for fourteen years. Trump could play this game brilliantly, while his opponents struggled. Predictably, this response only reinforced Trump's support (Krasner, 2019). The alternative response—to stick to the issues and ignore the provocation— was likewise a trap because in the rough-and-tumble, melodrama frame that Trump had established, it looked like weakness. In this sense, the mocking humor of name-calling is best understood as a *trap invitation to rivals*. They are trapped between the traditional elements of leadership that say, on the one hand, be strong and defend yourself, and on the other hand, be dignified and restrained.

12.4.2.4 Invitation to the Media

Finally, the name calling was an invitation to the media: *Please cover me because I will be unpredictable—I'll do things no other presidential candidate has ever done. And I'll provide drama—what will my rivals do in response to my taunts and mockery?* The media responded by giving Trump vastly more coverage than any of his rivals, a bonanza of free publicity that contributed powerfully to his success (Confessore & Yourish, 2016; Krasner, 2019).

12.4.2.5 Aggressive Defusing

Trump also used mocking humor to defuse threats from journalists. Here is one prime example, from the first Republican candidates debate of 2015, moderated by Megyn Kelly of Fox News (CBS News, 2015) (presented in script form to make clear the interaction):

> Kelly: Mr. Trump, one of the things people love about you is you speak your mind and you don't use a politician's filter. However, that is not without its downsides, in particular when it comes to women.
>
> You've called women you don't like "fat pigs, dogs, slobs, and disgusting animals" [laughter].
>
> Your Twitter account…
>
> Trump: Only Rosie O'Donnell [laughter].
>
> Kelly: No, it wasn't [applause].
>
> Your Twitter account [applause].
>
> Trump: Thank you.

Note the similarity and the difference between this situation and Kennedy's in 1958. Trump's laughter-producing riposte defuses the accusation in the same way that Kennedy's set piece joke did. As I argued above, (in Sect. 12.2.2.9), in both cases the leader is saying to followers and to the media, *"Maybe this is true, but don't take it seriously. Don't bother inquiring further. I may be doing something wrong, but don't hold me to account because my destiny transcends such petty issues. It's okay for me to do this because what I can do for the country far outweighs such minor concerns."*

But notice also the key difference. Trump's humor is divisive. It targets an enemy, ostensibly Rosie O'Donnell, but really all women, especially the offending journalist. It invites pleasure-taking in debasing someone else; the invitation is: *Please join me in humiliating this woman in particular, and all women in general.* It targets feminists and invites a return to patriarchy.

By contrast, there is no targeted enemy in Kennedy's humor. Everyone is invited to follow the chosen leader, to enjoy the pleasure and relief that comes from dropping the issue. This is one crucial difference between humor in an age of legitimacy and humor in an age of illegitimacy and polarization.

An even more flagrant example of abusive mockery against a journalist involved Trump's unfounded assertion that people in New Jersey, presumably Muslims or Arabs, had celebrated the destruction of the World Trade Center on September 11, 2001: "There were people over in New Jersey that were watching it, a heavy Arab population, that were cheering as the buildings came down" (Trump, 2015b).

Trump claimed his assertion was supported by reporting from *Washington Post* reporters Serge Kovaleski and Fredrick Kunkle, but when they contradicted him, he attacked Kovaleski, who suffered from a disability—arthogryposis—that produced erratic movements of his hands and arms (Haberman, 2015). At a rally in November 2015, Trump, who knew Kovaleski well, pretended to speak as Kovaleski. Changing his voice to a high-pitched, strained, hoarse tone, he widened his eyes as he leaned backwards from the waist, loosened his mouth, rocked back and forth and sideways, and flapped his arms and hands, saying, "Uhh, uhh. Don't know what I said. Uh, I don't know what I wrote…He's going like, 'I don't remember (Trump, 2015c).'" Of course, this episode earned Trump widespread condemnation from the mainstream media (DelReal, 2015), but it also invited supporters to see him as someone who would break norms, and therefore as someone different from ordinary politicians, and as someone who would stop at nothing to serve their interests.

In all these cases, Trump was also drawing on the divisive ascriptive tradition to say that as the representative of the truly good people he could, as a leader, debase those who opposed him because they were the enemies of the good.

12.4.2.6 Trump in the White House

As President, Trump most often expressed aggression directly, but he did resort to mockery during the Covid crisis, saying of a journalist, "He's got a mask that's so large I think it's the largest mask I've ever seen so I don't know if you [referring to Prime Minister Benjamin Netanyahu who was on a conference call] can hear him." (Trump, as quoted by Slisco, 2020).

12.4.2.7 Trump in 2023

As a candidate in 2023, Trump returned to using crude mocking humor against both journalists and opponents. At a nationally televised town hall meeting in May 2023, he repeatedly mocked E. Jean Carroll, who had recently won a judgement against him in a civil case that included her accusing him of rape. He called her a "whack job," and said he felt sorry for her then husband (Trump, 2023a). Trump also referred to Nancy Pelosi, the former Speaker of the House of Representatives, as "crazy Nancy Pelosi, as I affectionately call her […]" (Trump, 2023a). These comments brought laughter from the audience (composed of Republican voters) as did a reference to President Biden's needing a script (Trump, 2023a), and an attack on the moderator, CNN's Kaitlin Collins as a "very stupid person" if she did not know that the 2020 election was stolen (Trump, 2023a).

Trump's camp renewed the use of mockery against rival Republicans as well. In response to former Trump supporter Chris Christie's entering the race against Trump, Donald Trump, Jr. mocked Christie's obesity by posting an altered version of the Krispy Kreme Doughnuts logo as though it were Christie's campaign logo (Trump, 2023c). In the same vein, Trump himself posted a video altered to make it appear that Christie had made his campaign announcement at an all-you-can-eat buffet (Nash, 2023).

In response to his indictment for illegally retaining top secret government documents and obstruction of justice, Trump used humor to denigrate his accusers. Speaking to a crowd at his Bedminster, New Jersey golf course, Trump said (Trump, 2023b), "The prosecutor in this case [...] I will call a thug. I've named him Deranged Jack Smith" [laughter].

By this use of debasing humor, Trump is invoking the ascriptive tradition to make Smith in particular and any critic in general a member of the unworthy challengers to white, male, Christian hegemony. He is dividing the political world into good and evil, making his critics the evil political enemies, existential threats to the righteous order, and setting the stage for violence against them.

12.4.2.8 Humor Condoning and Inciting Violence

Earlier, in the fall of 2022, other Republicans had taken aggressive, debasing humor even further in their response to an attack on Speaker Pelosi's husband, Paul, who was brutally beaten in their San Francisco home by an intruder who had intended to kidnap the Speaker for political reasons (Long et al., 2023). Speaking at an election night rally, Republican Representative Andy Biggs (2022) said: "We're going to show Nancy Pelosi the door very soon. [...] She's losing the gavel but finding the hammer."

A second Republican member of the Congress, Clay Higgins of Louisiana, posted a photograph of Speaker Pelosi with her hands covering her face and captioned it: "That moment you realize the nudist hippie male prostitute LSD guy was the reason your husband didn't make it to your fundraiser" (Capps, 2022).

A third instance (there were others), came from Kari Lake, the Trump-endorsed gubernatorial candidate in Arizona, as reported by *The Guardian* (Pengelly, 2022):

> The Republican candidate for governor of Arizona, Kari Lake, drew laughter at a campaign event in Scottsdale on Monday with a remark about the attack on Paul Pelosi, husband of the Democratic US House speaker, Nancy Pelosi: 'Nancy Pelosi, well, she's got protection when she's in DC,' Lake said. 'Apparently her house doesn't have a lot of protection.'

On June 9, 2023, one day after former President Trump was indicted for mishandling classified documents and obstructing justice, Lake addressed the Georgia State Republican Convention as follows:

> I have a message tonight to Merrick Garland [the U.S. Attorney General] and Jack Smith [the federal prosecutor who indicted Trump] and Joe Biden—and the guys back there in the fake news media, you should listen up, as well, this one's for you: If you want to get to President Trump, you're going to have to go through me, and you're going to have to go through 75 million Americans just like me [applause and cheers]. And I'm gonna tell you, yep, most of us are card-carrying members of the NRA [National Rifle Association, that advocates fewer restrictions on guns] [standing applause and cheers]. That's not a threat; that's a public service announcement [laughter] (Lake, 2023).

The first three examples issue the following invitation: *Please join me in taking pleasure from physical attacks on our political rivals.* Like the humor previously described, these "jokes" condone and encourage violence and the attendant dehumanization of the targets of violence.

The fourth goes a step further. It issues this invitation: *Join me in encouraging violence against officials of the federal government by agreeing that it's okay to laugh about it and that such violence is really a public service.* This is the ultimate expression of the divisive ascriptive tradition because it justifies outright warfare against opponents.

12.4.2.9 Biden's "Old-Fashioned" Humor

By contrast, President Biden's humor echoes the humor of the era of legitimacy. With regard to the issue of age, Biden's line at the White House Correspondents dinner in April 2023 (NBC News, 2023) that "I believe in the first amendment, not just because my good friend Jimmy Madison wrote it," referring to one of America's founding fathers, who died in 1836, parallels almost exactly Ronald Reagan's joke about George Washington. On another occasion, Biden took a page from John F. Kennedy's humor book and introduced himself to a women's group at the White House by saying (Biden, 2023): "My name is Joe Biden [laughter]. I'm Dr. Jill Biden's husband" [laughter]. These self-deprecating jokes extend the same invitations to recognize the leader's humanity and to respect the political establishment as were dominant in the era of legitimacy.

12.5 Conclusion

These diametrically opposed styles of humor reflect and reinforce the intense polarization of current American politics. On one side, supporters of white nationalist, Christian patriarchy, ally themselves with major segments of the corporate elite. They portray the political, media, and cultural establishment as a threat to everything that patriotic Americans should hold dear. Their weaponized, debasing, divisive humor encourages violence in the context of a fantasy world of heroic resistance to demonic opponents. This is humor weaponized in a crude, aggressive manner that is the ultimate expression of the ascriptive tradition.

On the other side, a mixed coalition that operates mostly under the aegis of the Democratic Party includes some corporations, a few anti-Trump Republicans, and the remnants of various movements, including labor, civil rights, environmentalism, women, and LGBTQ+. This often-strained constellation generally supports leaders who continue to use a gentler form of humor that recalls the era of legitimacy and reflects a more nearly fact-based version of reality. They draw on the liberal and republican traditions that promote unity and equality and leadership based on virtue and experience.

As noted above, the far-right insurgents gain strength from tapping powerful, primitive emotions and impulses—fear, resentment, racism, misogyny, aggression—among others. Unfettered by reality or scruples, they can shape their messages, including their humor, to suit their political needs. Whether or not the coalition seeking to sustain America's deeply flawed democracy can employ fact-based communication, including a gentler, inclusive humor, to compete successfully in this struggle is the vital question of our day.

How the question is answered is no joke.

References

Amir, L. (2019). *Philosophy, humor, and the human condition: Taking ridicule seriously.* Palgrave MacMillan.

Apte, M. (1985). *Humor and laughter: An anthropological approach.* Cornell University Press.

Berenson, T. (2016, March 1). *Here are Trump and Rubio's best schoolyard insults.* Time. https://time.com/4242827/donald-trump-marco-rubio-insults/.

Biden, J. (2023, March 27). Remarks by President Biden at the SBA women's summit. https://www.whitehouse.gov/briefing-room/speeches-remarks/2023/03/27/remarks-by-president-biden-at-the-sba-womens-business-summit/.

Biggs, A. (2022, November 8). *Andy Biggs jokes about attack on Paul Pelosi.* YouTube. https://www.youtube.com/watch?v=U666WJS82eo&t=29s.

Brown, D. (1991). *Human universals.* Temple University Press.

CBS News. (2015, August 7). Transcript of the 2015 GOP debate. https://www.cbsnews.com/news/transcript-of-the-2015-gop-debate-9-pm/.

Capps, A. (2022, October 31). *Clay Higgins mocks hospitalized husband of Nancy Pelosi in deleted tweet after attack.* Lafayette Daily Advertiser. https://www.theadvertiser.com/story/news/local/2022/10/31/louisiana-rep-clay-higgins-mocks-nancy-pelosi-husband-paul-pelosi-deleted-tweet-hammer-attack/69605531007/.

Chafe, W. (1987). Humor as a disabling mechanism. *American Behavioral Scientist, 30*(3), 16-26. https://journals-sagepub-com.queens.ezproxy.cuny.edu/doi/abs/10.1177/000276487030003.

Clinton, W. J. (1993, May 1). Speech at the White House Correspondents Association dinner. https://www.c-span.org/video/?40370-1/1993-white-house-correspondents-dinner.

Confessore, N., & Yourish, K. (2016, March 15). *$2 Billion worth of free media for Donald Trump.* New York Times. https://www.nytimes.com/2016/03/16/upshot/measuring-donald-trumps-mammoth-advantage-in-free-media.html.

DelReal, J. (2015, November 26). *Trump draws scornful rebuke for mocking reporter with disability.* Washington Post. https://www.washingtonpost.com/news/post-politics/wp/2015/11/25/trump-blasted-by-new-york-times-after-mocking-reporter-with-disability/

Denby, D. (2015, December 15). *The plot against America.* The New Yorker. https://www.newyorker.com/culture/cultural-comment/plot-america-donald-trumps-rhetoric.

Edelman, M. (1985). *The symbolic uses of politics.* University of Illinois Press.

Farah, B., & Klein, E. (1989). Public opinion trends. In G. Pomper (Ed.), *The election of 1984: Reports and interpretations* (pp. 103–128). Chatham House Publishers.

Feldman, O. (2000). Non-oratorical discourse and political humor in Japan: Editorial cartoons, satire, and attitudes toward authority. In D. De Landsheer and O. Feldman (Eds.), *Beyond public speech and symbols: Explorations in the rhetoric of politicians and the media.* Praeger.

Feldman, O. (Ed.). (2023a). *Political debasement: Incivility, contempt, and humiliation in parliamentary and public discourse.* Springer.

Feldman, O. (Ed.). (2023b). *Debasing political rhetoric: Dissing opponents, journalists, and minorities in populist communication.* Springer.

Freud, S. (1905/1960). *The ego and the id* [Strachey, J. (Trans.)]. Norton.

Gallup. (n.d.). Confidence in institutions. https://news.gallup.com/poll/1597/confidence-institutions.aspx.

Haberman, M. (2015, November 26). *Trump says his mocking of New York Times reporter was misread.* https://www.nytimes.com/2015/11/27/us/politics/donald-trump-says-his-mocking-of-new-york-times-reporter-was-misread.html.

Hacker, J., & Pierson, P. (2021). *Let them eat tweets: How the right rules in an age of extreme inequality.* Liveright.

Hartz, L. (1955). *The liberal tradition in America.* Harcourt Brace.

Hershey, M. (1989). The campaign and the media. In G. Pomper (Ed.), *The election of 1988: Reports and interpretations* (pp. 73–102). Chatham House.

Kennedy, J. F. (1958, March 15). *Remarks of Senator John F. Kennedy at the Gridiron Club,* Washington, D.C. https://www.jfklibrary.org/archives/other-resources/john-f-kennedy-speeches/washington-dc-19580315.

Kennedy, J. F. (1961, June 2). *Press conference.* https://www.jfklibrary.org/archives/other-resources/john-f-kennedy-press-conferences/news-conference-12.

Kessler, R. (1996). *The sins of the father.* Warner Books.

Krasner, M. A. (2019). The new American electoral politics: How invited behavior and reality TV explain Donald Trump's victory. In O. Feldman & S. Zmerli (Eds.), *The psychology of political communicators: How politicians, culture, and the media construct and shape public discourse* (pp. 13–30). Routledge.

Krasner, M. A. (2021). Dividing America through new-culture speech. In O. Feldman (Ed.), *When politicians talk: The cultural dynamics of public speaking* (pp. 257–274). Springer. https://doi.org/10.1007/978-981-16-3579_15.

Krasner, M. A. (2023). *Jokes and politics: The power of leaders' humor.* Taft Institute for Government & Civic Education. https://taftinstitute.org/application/files/4516/8775/5646/TI-Jokes_and_politics-The_Power_of_Leaders_Humor_June_2023.pdf.

Lake, K. (2023, no date). *Kari Lake has a message for Merrick Garland and company.* YouTube. https://www.youtube.com/watch?v=gUVEabpyaAM

Long, C., Rodriguez, O., Mascaro, M., & Balsamo, M. (2023, October 28). *Intruder attacks Pelosi's husband, calling, 'Where is Nancy?'* AP. https://apnews.com/article/paul-pelosiassaulted-156ece77186eb11b97260af3c5122f67.

Loughry, A. (2006). *Don't buy another vote, I won't pay for a landslide.* McLain Printing Com.

Mayer, J. (2016). *Dark money: The hidden history of the billionaires behind the rise of the radical right.* Doubleday.

Mears, W. (2018, December 1) *George H. W. Bush: Great in experience, not as communicator.* APNews. https://apnews.com/article/north-america-financial-markets-usnews-ap-top-news-ronald-reagan-d90885dbd04d41e9b3f7da8f34555291.

Milbank, D. (2022). *The destructionists: The twenty-five year crack-up of the Republican Party.* Doubleday.

Mulloy, D. (2014). *The world of the John Birch Society: Conspiracy, conservatism, and the cold war.* Vanderbilt University Press.

NBC News (2023, May 1). *Biden jokes about age at 2023 White House Correspondents Dinner.* https://www.google.com/search?client=safari&rls=en&q=biden+age+joke+white+house+correspondents+dinner+2023&ie=UTF-8&oe=UTF-8#fpstate=ive&vld=cid:1d5791c4,vid:OpNDWsVBnyQ.

Nash, C. (2023, June 7). *Trump posts edited video of Chris Christie launching campaign at all-you-can-eat buffet.* Mediaite. https://www.mediaite.com/politics/trump-posts-edited-video-of-chris-christie-launching-campaign-at-all-you-can-eat-buffet/.

Neustadt, R. (1991). *Presidential power and the modern presidents: The politics of leadership from Roosevelt to Reagan.* Free Press.

Oliver, J., & Rahn, W. (2016). Rise of the "Trumpenvolk:" Populism in the 2016 election. *The Annals of the American Academy of Political and Social Science, 667*, 189–206. https://doi.org/10.1177/0002716216662639.

Paletz, D. (2002). *The media in American politics* (2nd ed.). Longman.

PBS. (2012). *Debating our destiny* (complete edition). https://www.amazon.com/s?k=debating+our+destiny&crid=27PO27ZBAJ6HE&sprefix=debating+our+destiny%2Caps%2C102&ref=nb_sb_noss_1.

PBS Newshour. (n.d.). *Carter vs. Reagan: The second 1980 presidential debate.* YouTube. https://www.youtube.com/watch?v=3HB2sz4bAbU.

Pengelly, M. (2022, November 1). *Republican candidate draws laughter with mockery of attack on Paul Pelosi.* The Guardian. https://www.theguardian.com/us-news/2022/nov/01/kari-lake-mocks-paul-pelosi-attack.

Pew Research Center. (2022, June 6). *Public trust in government: 1958–2022.* https://www.pewresearch.org/politics/2022/06/06/public-trust-in-government-1958-2022/.

Pomper, G. (1985). The presidential election. In G. Pomper (Ed.), *The election of 1984: Reports and interpretations* (pp. 60–90). Chatham House.

Reagan, R. (1981). *Address before a joint session of the Congress reporting on the State of the Union.* The American Presidency Project. https://www.presidency.ucsb.edu/documents/address-before-joint-session-the-congress-reporting-the-state-the-union-2.

Reagan, R. (1985, January 21). *Remarks at the inaugural luncheon at the capitol.* https://www.reaganlibrary.gov/archives/speech/remarks-inaugural-luncheon-capitol.

Reagan, R. (1987, January 15). *Address to high school students on Martin Luther King, Jr.'s birthday.* https://www.reaganlibrary.gov/archives/speech/address-high-school-students-martin-luther-king-jrs-birthday.

Slisco, A. (2020, October 23). *Trump mocks reporter for wearing "largest" mask as U.S. reports 71,000 daily COVID cases.* Newsweek. https://www.newsweek.com/trump-mocks-reporter-wearing-largest-mask-us-reports-71000-daily-covid-cases-1541827.

Smith, R. (1993). Beyond Tocqueville, Myrdal, and Hartz: The multiple traditions in America. *The American Political Science Review, 87*(3), 549–566. https://www.jstor.org/stable/293875.

de Tocqueville, A. (2020). *Democracy in America* [H. C. Mansfield & D. Winthrop (Eds. & Trans.)]. University of Chicago.

Trump, D. (2015a, August 19). *The Donald Trump conversation: Murdoch, Ailes, NBC, and the rush of being TV's "rating machine."* Hollywood Reporter. https://www.hollywoodreporter.com/news/politics-news/donald-trump-murdoch-ailes-nbc-816131/.

Trump, D. (2015b, November 22). *"This Week" transcript: Donald Trump and Ben Carson.* ABC News. https://abcnews.go.com/Politics/week-transcript-donald-trump-ben-carson/story?id=35336008.

Trump, D. (2016a, February 25). *Transcript of CNN-Telemundo debate.* Washington Post. https://www.washingtonpost.com/news/the-fix/wp/2016/02/25/the-cnntelemundo-republican-debate-transcript-annotated/.

Trump, D. (2016b, March 3). *Transcript of Republican debate.* Washington Post. https://www.washingtonpost.com/news/the-fix/wp/2016/03/03/the-fox-news-gop-debate-transcript-annotated/.

Trump, D. (2016c, April 16). *Speech: Donald Trump—Watertown, NY.* https://www.youtube.com/watch?v=hmQGhyoC5RY.

Trump, D. (2023a, May 13). *Read: Transcript of CNN's town hall with former President Donald Trump.* CNN. https://www.cnn.com/2023/05/11/politics/transcript-cnn-town-hall-trump/index.html.

Trump, D. (2023b, June 13). *Donald Trump speaks to supporters in Bedminster, N.J.* YouTube. https://www.youtube.com/watch?v=T0vivQ3ix8I.

Trump, D., Jr. (2023c, June 7). Tweet. https://twitter.com/donaldjtrumpjr/status/1666410955641683970?s=46&t=VKhHDNfTleIY1cw-jjdztg.

Yovetich, N. A., Dale, J.A., & Hudak, M.A. (1990). Benefits of humor in reduction of threat-induced anxiety. *Psychological Reports, 66*, 51–58. https://doi.org/10.2466/pr0.1990.66.1.51

Michael Alan Krasner is Associate Professor Emeritus of Political Science at Queens College, CUNY, USA, and also co-directs the Taft Institute for Government and Civic Education that promotes political participation. His articles have appeared in the *Journal of Peace Research, New German Critique, Social Policy, New York Affairs, and Urban Education*, and he is the co-editor of and a contributor to *Immigrant Cross-Roads: Globalization, Incorporation, and Placemaking in Queens NY* (2021).

Chapter 13
Political Humor: Theoretical Questions, Methodological Suggestions

Sam Lehman-Wilzig

Abstract The advantage and disadvantage of an anthology like this one is that the reader receives a fascinating picture regarding the variety of political humor around the world—but such variety makes it difficult for any coherent picture to emerge regarding political humor writ large (globally). The present concluding chapter raises several questions regarding the possibilities for such "universal" theorizing and offers some methodological proposals for carrying out such research. Although it is clear that the subject of political humor is at base qualitative, with a high degree of subjectivity, nevertheless it might well be possible to employ more rigorous approaches to the phenomenon that after all has existed for well over two millennia and still found almost everywhere around the world.

13.1 Introduction

The chapters of this book offer a very broad picture of political humor around the world. However, other than Feldman's introductory chapter that presents a systematic categorization of the different types of political humor and its other aspects, each chapter focuses on a specific country or ethnos/nationality. This provides us with an interesting, localized picture; however, such pinpoint studies demand an effort on the part of the reader to try and find commonalities between the various countries and nations covered.

Moreover, even if such an effort were made, at this stage it would not enable any hard and fast conclusions, for two reasons. First, the methodologies of these studies (especially how and what to choose as examples) are quite different, and often not explicitly explained. Second, the types of political humor covered are very varied—from standup sketches to political cartoons and even to carnival presentations—and almost everything else possible in between. Third, the major contribution of this book: the chapters focus on the political culture of the respective countries as explanation for the types (and intensity) of their respective political humor. However,

---

S. Lehman-Wilzig (✉)
Department of Communications, Peres Academic College, Rehovot, Israel
e-mail: wilzis@biu.ac.il

© The Author(s), under exclusive license to Springer Nature Singapore Pte Ltd. 2024
O. Feldman (ed.), *Political Humor Worldwide*, The Language of Politics,
https://doi.org/10.1007/978-981-99-8490-9_13

as political culture around the globe is extremely variegated, there is little possibility for commensurable findings and conclusions.

In this concluding chapter, therefore, I will raise several theoretical issues—and provide a few methodological suggestions for future research. I use the word "attempt" advisedly, fully aware that the entire subject of political humor is highly "amorphous" and subjective i.e., it lies mostly in the eye (and mind) of the beholder. To quote U.S. Supreme Court Justice Potter Stewart's definition of "pornography": "I shall not today attempt further to define ["hard-core pornography"].... But *I know it when I see it*." (Whether that quote in itself can be considered "political humor" is an interesting question, a general point to be pursued later on below.)

13.2 The Qualitative Problematics of Categorizing Political Humor

The first problem when trying to categorize political humor in any systematic fashion is that much of it cuts across several categories. The chapters highlight three main types:

Destructive Humor as practiced by Philippines President Duterte and U.S. President Trump—directed against political opponents e.g., Chap. 2, or against groups e.g., Chaps. 5 and 7.

Educational Humor that indirectly teaches current events to the mostly non-politically involved citizenry, through satirical shows, jokes, and even high art—raising usually avoided issues e.g., Chaps. 3 and 10. *Legitimate (Positive) Criticism Humor* that lays the groundwork for change, whether personnel or policymaking e.g., Chaps. 2 and 4.

Clearly, many times a specific example of political humor can cross boundaries and be categorized in two (and even infrequently, all three) of these categories. Certainly, educational humor can also be designed to create (policy) change; when politicians are highly incompetent or vicious, then using destructive humor to damage their reputation can also be seen as an attempt to bring about electoral change.

The second problem for any researcher using such categories is the reverse challenge: it isn't always altogether clear to which category an example of political humor belongs—or whether it is "political" at all (see further below for examples). What you might consider overly harsh ("destructive"), someone else could view as proper comeuppance ("legitimate") against a politician who uses vicious humor against opponents. Or what one researcher might view as merely "educational" i.e., getting the facts out there to uninvolved citizens, another scholar could categorize as trying to bring about change by undermining a party's fake news.

This brings up a different, problematic research issue. As just noted above and also in several chapters (e.g., Chaps. 3 and 10), political satire can serve to provide ("educational") political information to many citizens who otherwise would not seek it out or even be aware that a problem exists. However, this depends to a large extent on the level of political involvement and savvy of the general population—itself a function (in part) of the country's safe or precarious situation. For instance, given the country's ongoing history of conflict and wars, one would be hard put to find many Israelis who are not aware, or don't have an opinion, regarding Israel's key national security issues. Thus, a political joke in Israel about an army general or the Minister of Defense could hardly be considered "educational" as everyone is acutely aware of who they are, as well as their foibles and idiosyncrasies. This would not be the case with exactly the same joke regarding a similar major political personality in a country such as Switzerland that hasn't fought a war in over a century and a half. Thus, perhaps more than almost any other subject (and definitely not less), researchers of political humor must be highly aware of the historical and cultural nuances of the countries they are studying.

To be sure, deep political knowledge among the citizenry does not negate the widespread use of satire or political humor in general. Indeed, the opposite could be the case: the more politically involved and knowledgeable the citizenry, the greater amount of political humor is disseminated. Here too Israel is a good case in point as it has numerous media venues for political satire and humor in general. Examples abound: (1) newspaper editorial cartoons, with the caricaturists using pseudonyms: Dosh, Ze'ev; (2) televised political satire programs: *Nikui Rosh* (Head Cleaning); *Zehu Zeh* (That's It); *Eretz Nehederet* (A Wonderful Country); *Ha'Yehudim Ba'im* (The Jews are Coming), etc.

Indeed, one could suggest—something worthy of future research in political satire—that the more a specific ethnic (or other type of social) group has been oppressed over its history, the greater its use of political satire or other forms of humor, whether during those periods of persecution and/or even when finally sovereign over its own destiny. In short, if this were found to be true (even as a generalization), that would add an extra element to the interconnection between culture and political humor.

As a matter of fact, some chapters in the present book offer hints of this without explicitly expressing this observation. For instance, as shown in Chap. 3 in some detail, modern Greece has quite an aggressive culture of political humor. Could this be (in part) a function of the dictatorship it suffered through decades ago? Or is it merely a continuation of, and/or further building on, 2500 years of political satire from Aristophanes? One hardly needs to mention that the Jewish people (Chap. 8), one of the most persecuted over the past centuries, has a long history of self-effacing humor (and also jokes that are subtly critical of their oppressors). Although Chap. 10 focuses deeply on only a few examples of Native American satire, it would not be surprising if wider research would also find many examples of such anti-persecutors humor among the various American tribes (North and South).

13.3 Does Female Sexist Political Humor Exist?

Several chapters in this book describe the theme of sexist political humor e.g., in Greece (Chap. 3) and the U.S. (Chap. 12). However, in all cases the brunt of the "joke" is a woman—and the "humorist" jokester is a man. Interestingly, sexist humor is not much found among female politicians—at least not as presented in these chapters. In fact, if one can judge from the female leaders presented in this book, it would seem that they almost don't use humor in public. Two examples, both from Chap. 5 (the Philippines—not known for restrained political humor): Corazon Aquino who "was not known for making jokes or humorous statements during her presidency;" and Gloria Macapagal-Arroyo whose one attempt at humor can hardly be considered "funny."

This too is an interesting subject for future research. If women leaders do tend to use political humor far less frequently, is this a matter of a very different humor "style" between male and female politicians? Or rather merely a result of the fact that at present, there are far fewer women leaders than men so that we don't have enough "representative examples" to make any realistic comparisons?

To be sure, such research might have to deal with a conundrum: if it turns out that female leaders use less political humor (certainly the more aggressive forms), is this because of their gender? Or perhaps those societies that have greater sex equality in their political leadership—e.g., the Scandinavian nations—also have lower levels of aggressive political humor (or humor in general). It cannot be mere coincidence that this book and the following second book (Feldman, 2024) do not have even one chapter from Sweden, Denmark, Norway, Finland, and Iceland—this despite this series' editorial staff putting out a general call to all researchers worldwide to contribute their scholarship on the general subject of political humor. In this age of increasing gender studies, the question of female political humor begs for elucidation

Along this specific line of inquiry, it bears noting that women who are not politicians are involved in political humor as part of their overall humor routines. In Chap. 10, for instance, we see how a woman uses her artistic skills to satirize the political situation of American domestic colonialism. And of course, there are female comedians who occasionally touch on political issues e.g., America's Sarah Silverman and Amy Schumer; Israel's Orna Banai and Tom Yaar.

One way of testing whether the central factor underlying gender disparities in the telling of political humor is the particular sex of the humorizing leader or rather a function of wider, societal humor female/male non/aggressiveness is to compare the (non)aggressive "intensity" of such humor between male and female politicians within those restrained countries (e.g., Scandinavia). Along these lines, Chap. 4 on British "phlegm" offers a mere hint that the issue might indeed be "cultural:" In 2022 Liz Truss had the shortest prime ministerial tenure in British history, and during those 45 days she seems to have told only one political joke—as "phlegmatic" as those of the male prime ministers studied: "We all had teenage misadventures. Some people had sex, drugs, and rock 'n' roll. I had the Liberal Democrats." I suggest that in the future, the authors of that interesting chapter expand their study to one of the

U.K.'s longest running (and controversial) prime ministers: Margaret Thatcher. As she was known for a sharp, biting tongue, her political humor would shed greater light on whether "British phlegm" humor is universal, and if not, does it characterize all female leaders in the U.K.?

The Truss joke above suggests another aspect that bears researching in the future: it was directed not only at a competing party but also at herself. Thus, any gender-oriented research on political humor should also differentiate between externally addressed humorous critiques and self-deprecating ones. Women leaders might employ the latter more than their male counterparts, to neutralize sexist expectations that women should act in more genteel fashion. Or perhaps there is no difference on this element, as one can see from the Philippines case in Chap. 5 (e.g., Benigno Aquino III; Rodrigo Duterte): self-deprecating humor seems to be widespread there, and not connected to the gender of the leader.

In general, if future research finds that within any given national culture neither men nor women indulge more than their gender counterpart in relatively aggressive humorous attacks against opponents or groups, then one can conclude that whether societies tend to be aggressive or "civil," the main factor is societal culture in general and not inherent differences between the sexes. This would have significant import for gender studies, adding to (and moderately undermining) the existing literature on gender communication differences in general (i.e., outside the political realm).

13.4 Future Research Agenda

13.4.1 Cross-National, Interactional Humor

There are at least four additional research topics worth pursuing. The first relates to high-level, cross-national, political humor. In short, what are the problems inherent in political humor when leaders (and senior diplomats) try to be humorous when meeting with heads of other states? Are they more circumspect, knowing that the chances of misinterpretation are greater? Or do they actually indulge in more humor to "break the ice," especially prior (or after) difficult political negotiations? The following is a famous example of such humor in a very serious security situation involving two friendly countries: the U.S. and Israel. During the 1973 October "Yom Kippur War," Israel was on the defensive against Egyptian attacks and desperately needed additional American arms—leading to a meeting between Prime Minister Golda Meir and U.S. Secretary of State Henry Kissinger. Golda tried to play on Kissinger's Jewish lineage:

> Henry Kissinger: Golda, you must remember that first I am an American, second I am Secretary of State, and third I am a Jew.
>
> Golda Meir: Henry, you forget that in Israel we read from right to left.

In this case, Golda turned the tables on Kissinger without embarrassing him—a prime condition in diplomacy. However, as both had the same general (Jewish) cultural background, it was easy for her to make a humorous riposte without fear of "misunderstanding" what would be acceptable in such a situation. Obviously, the same is not usually the case when enemies are conversing in their diplomacy efforts e.g., contemporary China and the U.S., or even when the leaders of friendly countries with widely divergent cultures enter negotiations e.g., the U.S. and Japan.

13.4.2 The Influence of Political Humor: Quantitative, Empirical Research

A second research agenda has already been broached by the authors in Chap. 5: "Future studies therefore must validate and examine people's sentiments *empirically* to fully establish the positive effect of presidential comedic strategies towards public opinion. How, and to what extent, citizens sift through the humor to distinguish what (and who) is funny and trustworthy would bring a much nuanced lens to the whole comedic enterprise of presidents." Here they are suggesting a micro-analysis study, focusing on specific voters in an attempt to ferret out not only their perception of different types of political humor, but to what extent this influences their voting decisions. Eminently sensible and doable.

However, it is not a complete solution. The problem with this approach is that it is country specific and not easily translatable to other nations. Therefore, I suggest a complementary methodology, entailing a global perspective, much like other cross-national studies on a variety of subjects e.g., political violence and wars (Gurr, 1970) and religious discrimination (Fox, 2016). In brief:

(1) Create a universal political humor index with a few scales (e.g., mildly humorous to very funny; civil to highly aggressive; etc.).
(2) Have local political scientists[1] score on the index every candidate for a top, elected position (president, prime minister) over the past several decades. The duration would be a pre-determined, specific period of time e.g., tenure in office.
(3) Categorize these politicians by several independent variables e.g., gender; incumbency; Left/Center/Right; etc.
(4) Categorize several dependent variables regarding type of humor employed: crass/aggressive or civil/mildly critical (these can be through a scale); against other politicians or self-deprecating (e.g., John F. Kennedy to Bill Clinton in Chap. 12).

---

[1] Given that several of the dependent variables are subjective i.e., based on the perspective of national culture, one cannot use the same coders/scorers for different countries because no scorer could be aware of the many differences in the way each national citizenry perceives their own politician's humor.

(5) Categorize several dependent variables regarding the addressee/"victim" of the humor employed: against a specific politician; versus a political party; criticizing policies; versus a foreign country/politician[2]; etc.

(6A) Categorize the different venues or media through which the political humor is transmitted by the politicians e.g., TV, radio, cinema (see Chap. 9), social media, newspaper (print or online), public assembly, direct marketing (email, newsletter etc.), carnival musical compositions and theater (Chap. 11), and even art (Chap. 10).

(6B) Categorize the different venues or media through which the political humor is transmitted by *non*-politicians e.g., standup comedian, TV satire program, political cartoonist, etc.

(7) Categorize the nature of each country's political system: fully democratic (completely fair elections), partly democratic (e.g., mostly non-independent media, but with relatively fair elections), autocratic (elections heavily skewed to the incumbent through control of the media and disqualification of legitimate candidates).[3]

(8) Correlate their humor scores (#2 above) with the degree of their electoral success, taking into account (regression analysis) all the dependent and independent variables all the dependent and independent variables (#3–#7).

With a sample of hundreds of such politicians in dozens of countries over a lengthy time period, all sorts of correlations could be found through regression analysis. This

---

[2] Two such joke examples are worth telling, not coincidentally with the same country as the joke's victim: The first we have already seen in Chap. 7 where Poles ask: "Why do we call the U.S.S.R. 'our brother' and not 'our friend?' Because you can choose a friend."

The second joke involves Russian-Jewish immigrants to Israel before the collapse of the Soviet Union. Such an immigrant is invited by an Israeli neighbor for afternoon tea.

Israeli: I hear that it takes a decade in the Soviet Union to get an apartment.

Immigrant: Really can't complain.

Israeli (taken aback): What about a car? I understand you had to wait five years to buy one.

Immigrant: Well, you can't complain.

Israeli (now really surprised): I've seen photos of huge lines waiting to buy some meat.

Immigrant: "I didn't complain."

Israeli (dumbfounded): Then why did you move to to Israel

Immigrant (quizzically): What do you mean? Here in Israel, I'm allowed to complain!

[3] I do not suggest including completely dictatorial regimes. The assumption here is that although they might hold "elections," such political systems are not going to countenance much political humor addressed at the ruling regime e.g., contemporary Russia or Iran. Therefore, such a category should not be included in any regression analysis. However, political humor in authoritarian regimes is certainly a worthy subject of research on its own.

would not negate the need for future research, given that such a study's findings would probably raise more questions that it could answer. Nevertheless, it holds the promise of finding some "universal" patterns regarding the effectiveness of political humor around the world that a few authors in this book seem to take as an unproven given e.g., Panao and Pernia (Chap. 5); Krasner (Chap. 12).

To be sure, such a large-scale research project would not be definitive for two reasons. First, as is clear from the title of Chap. 12 ("...American Culture: From Affability to Aggression"), over time political humor can change its stripes as a result of developments in the political system. A similar transformation occurred when Spain went from fascism to democracy (Chap. 11). Thus, focusing on the country as the unit of analysis will miss such changes if there is no sensitivity to a possible transformation of the political system.

13.4.3 Nationality Without Sovereignty: Political Humor Without the Homeland

The third research project worth pursuing involves "diaspora nationalities" without political sovereignty in a homeland. Two chapters in this book touch on this. Chapter 8 focuses on Jewish humor, not necessarily in the Jewish state of Israel; Chap. 10 looks at Native American tribal political satire—an agglomeration of "internal diaspora" communities. "Purer" forms of such national cultures exist globally e.g., the Kurds, Roma ("gypsies"), and certainly did in the past e.g., American black slaves, even for a long time after their legal emancipation (as noted in Chap. 8). These communities usually do have the right to participate in elections within the countries they live in, sometimes even with representation within the political system. Nevertheless, one could expect their political humor to be significantly different from that of the specific country in which they find themselves (such as Jewish humor throughout the past two millennia until the State of Israel was established).

13.4.4 Political Humor Frequency

Finally, a fourth research approach that understandably has not been touched upon in this book's chapters, continues the quest for "empirical" findings but from a purely *quantitative* standpoint. By its very nature, political humor is subjective, involving cultural perception among other difficult-to-quantify aspects. Nevertheless, one cannot summarily dismiss the question of *frequency* i.e., how *often* does political humor manifest itself? The politicians' jokes, satirical media sketches, etc., that the authors bring to bear are all interesting and instructive—but cannot give a complete picture of the political humor situation in any given country. Thus, some sort of *quantitative* methodology needs to be developed, offering a general picture of the amount of political humor expressed.

Here, too, this would not be easy—nor definitive. For example, much political humor is oblique—making it hard to decide whether to be included. Here's an example from Israel (or any country where Jews reside):

> Son calls Jewish-Israeli mother: Mom, I have great news: I was just elected President!
>
> Mother: That's nice, dear. In which synagogue?

The difficulty here is in distinguishing between the personal and the political. Indeed, this conflation of the public and the private is standard in Middle Eastern societies, as well as in other traditional-minded areas around the world. Should that joke be considered "political"? Hard to decide: *Yes*—it remarks on the non-importance of political leadership; *No*—it is all about prioritization regarding the centrality of one's local community. Indeed, this latter point is why counter-intuitively (given incessant conflict) Israel consistently ranks near the top of global "happiness" surveys; its politics might be a mess (and very aggressive), but it's the local, familial, that really counts for the populace—and on that familial and local, social level in general, they are highly satisfied.

This is true for almost every Israeli—except for the politicians themselves whose entire life revolves around politics. Indeed, when I asked a few members of Knesset (Israeli Parliament), each a former political science student of mine, what was the toughest part of their job, the answer was invariably: "Having to attend a wedding or bar-mitzvah event every evening from one of my political party's Central Committee (or other important politico) members!" Here again, we see the admixture of the political and the personal, rendering such jokes difficult to categorize, or even to decide whether to be included in a study of *political* humor.

A final Israeli joke that made the rounds back in the 1960s, is especially nonplussing in this regard:

> In the 1960s, Prime Minister Levi Eshkol's third wife was much younger than he was. Night after night, when he arrived home after a long and tiring day, he was too exhausted or distracted for any "romance." His wife asked a woman friend what to do to raise his libido for some intimacy.
>
> The friend suggested: "Buy a black bra and a white bra. Cut the bras in half and stitch together one black cup with a white one. When you're both undressing for bed, make sure he sees this bra on you." "Great idea!" Eshkol's wife replies and carries out the project. The next night as the two are undressing, she removes her blouse and sexily calls out to him across the bedroom. He slowly turns and looks at her, considering the scene for the moment. Then he cries out: "You're right! I knew I forgot to tell Moshe Dayan something important!" [Defense Minister Dayan, a bona fide war hero, was famous for his black eye patch.]

Are jokes about politicians' (lack of) love life to be considered "*political* humor"? Or, for that matter, anything else that deals with their personal lives? I leave you (and future researchers) to ponder the issue. Clearly, measuring political humor frequency is not a hard and fast science; nevertheless, even a general number would provide a useful indication of its centrality within a nation's political arena.

13.5 Conclusion

To conclude, the issue of political humor is no laughing matter! It potentially has huge consequences during election campaigns, in the conduct of domestic politics between elections, and even on the plane of international diplomacy. Moreover, it can have significant spillover effects on society e.g., treatment of women and minorities. This book (and its complement, Feldman, 2024) offer several fascinating observations that form the foundation for more systematic future research that could provide us with a wider, systematic lens on this fascinating, and quite important, topic.

References

Feldman, O. (2024). *Communicating political humor in the media: How culture influences satire and irony*. Springer.

Fox, J. (2016). *The unfree exercise of religion: A world survey of religious discrimination against religious minorities*. Cambridge University Press.

Gurr, T. (1970). *Why men rebel*. Princeton University Press.

Sam Lehman-Wilzig served as Chair of Bar-Ilan University's Department of Political Studies (2004–2007), and also its School of Communication (2014–2016) in Israel. He was also Chairman of the Israeli Political Science Association (1997–1999). He now serves as the Academic Head of the Department of Communications at Peres Academic College (Rehovot, Israel). He has published 44 academic journal articles; 28 chapters in academic books; and authored four scholarly books, the latest: *Virtuality and Humanity: Virtual Practice and Its Evolution from Pre-History to the 21st Century* (Springer Nature, 2021). His areas of expertise are: New Media; Technology & Society; Political Communication; and Extra-Parliamentary Behavior. Further info: www.ProfSLW.com.

Index

A
Abascal, Santiago, 202–205
Absurd humor, 119
African-American humor, 139, 152
Aggression, 6, 13, 51, 52, 56, 60, 61, 68, 175, 230, 232, 235, 246
Aggressive
　discourse, 53
　function of humor, 6
Andalusian Latifundia, 206
Anti-immigration, 204
Anti-LGBTQ, 223
Anti-Muslim, 223
Anti-Semites, 16, 142, 150
Apsáalooke, 25, 175–178, 180, 184, 185
Aquino, Corazon, 88–90, 242
Aquino III, Benigno Simeon, 94, 95, 243
Arabs, 12, 102–106, 108, 112, 204, 231
Aristocracy, 206, 207
Asian cultures, 69
Attention claiming invitation, 219

B
Begin, Menachem, 15, 17
Ben-Gvir, Itamar, 112
Biden, Joseph, 217
Black humor, 8, 103, 146. *See also* gallows humor
Blair, Tony, 68, 72–74
Bonding humor, 141
Book of Esther, The, 104, 144, 145
British
　humor, 67, 70, 71, 79, 80
　phlegm, 24, 67, 70, 71, 75, 79, 243
　political humor, 68, 80

Brown, Gordon, 51, 52, 59, 62, 74, 80
Bush, George W., 22, 73, 182, 225–228

C
Cádiz Carnival (Spain), 19, 25, 193, 194, 197, 201
Cádiz *chirigotas*, 193, 195, 196
Cameron, David, 71, 74–76
Cancel culture, 31, 36, 40–43, 150
Caricatures, 1, 37, 68, 79, 97, 111, 123, 124, 171
Carnival *coplas*, 212
Cartoons, 1, 18, 42, 68, 73, 79, 107, 126, 128, 130, 132, 141, 170, 239, 241
Categorization, 62, 239
Censorship, 41, 119, 131, 160–163, 165, 171, 194
Chamber Quintet, The, 109
Chinese culture, 69
Christian Democrats (Italy), 165, 171
Christianity, 69, 126, 128, 145, 146, 149
Christians, 145, 204
Cinematographic comedy, 159
Clinton, Bill, 22, 228, 244
Colbert Report, The, 18, 182
Collective imagery, 160
Comedy, 1, 2, 17–19, 21, 23, 31–33, 35, 36, 39–43, 52, 77, 79, 86, 131, 148, 150, 151, 153, 159, 165, 168, 182, 183
Communism, 119, 120, 126, 128, 154, 164, 171
Comparing ethnic groups, 12
Comparing national characters, 13
Comparsas, 193, 195
Comprehensive Theories, 6

Confrontational encounters, 49–51, 61, 62
Contesting hierarchy, 62
Contrasts in humor, 11
Control invitation, 219
Court jester, 117
Crow reservation, 185
Cynical and provocative irony, 160
Cynical and tragic view of the world, 162

D
Daily Show, The, 17, 18
Dajare (literally, "wordplay"), 10
Da Vinci, Leonardo, 176
Defensive function, 8
Democratic Party (Italy), 172, 234
Diaspora, 246
Díaz-Ayuso, Isabel, 210
Diplomacy, 72, 77, 244, 248
Discourse Humor Theory, 117, 122
Disparagement humor, 19, 69, 141
Divisive humor, 229, 234
Duterte, Rodrigo, 17, 95, 243
Dziad(y) (an ancestor, grandfather), 126

E
Eastern cultures, 69
Emotional framework, 86, 88
Eretz Nehederet (A Wonderful Country), 7, 241
Eshkol, Levi, 15, 20, 247
Estrada, Joseph E.
  Erap joke, 92, 93
Ethnic humor, 6, 12, 142
Ethnic identity, 12
Ethno-national humor, 1, 3, 4, 10

F
Facebook, 17, 18, 33, 111
Fascism, 160, 162, 170, 193, 201, 204, 246
Face threats, 51, 52, 54, 62
Feminism, 134
Feminist humor, 134, 231
Fictional politics, 31, 36
Freud, Sigmund, 2

G
Gallows humor, 8, 144. *See also* black humor
Gaventa, John, 177, 184, 185, 188, 189
Genocide, 8, 176, 178, 182, 184, 187, 199

Gentle humor, 25, 217, 224
Germany, 18, 107, 109, 112, 148
Graffiti, 1, 2, 14
Great American Joke, The, 31, 33–37, 43
Greece, 49, 54, 55, 62, 72, 164, 241, 242

H
Harel, Asaf, 107
Hatano, Akira, 15
High Art, 25, 175, 177, 180, 181, 189, 240
History of Jewish humor, 19
Hitler rants, 106, 107
Holocaust
  commemoration, 101, 103
  deniers, 105
  humor, 8, 19, 24, 101–105, 107–110, 113, 148
  Remembrance Day, 105, 107
Hostility, 4, 6, 9, 12, 140, 148
Humor as defense mechanism, 6, 8, 9
Humor as strategic rudeness, 56
Humor, categories of, 32, 73, 119
Humor, intellectual function of, 9

I
Im/politeness, 49, 51, 61
Immigration, 204
Impoliteness strategy, 50, 52, 54, 62
Incongruity, 2, 4–6, 31, 33, 34, 38, 50, 68, 120, 140, 186
Incongruity theory, 5
Individualistic society, 69, 159
Inferiority theory of humor, 140, 150
Instagram, 18, 33
Invited behavior, 217, 218
Irony, 2, 23, 52, 57, 58, 73, 74, 79, 80, 86, 117, 126, 135, 160, 162, 163, 171, 180–182, 184, 188
Israel, 7, 15, 19, 20, 22, 101–109, 111, 112, 241, 243, 245–247
Italy, 76, 162, 164–166, 171

J
Japan, 16, 19, 21, 22, 244
Jews, 5, 8, 9, 12, 13, 19, 104–107, 109, 110, 141, 143, 145–147, 150–152, 204, 247
Johnson, Boris, 71, 76, 77, 80
Joke, 1–5, 9–16, 17–24, 32–34, 37–40, 42, 43, 55, 68, 72, 74–76, 80, 85–93, 95–97, 106, 110, 119, 130, 133, 135,

Index

140–143, 146, 147, 150–154, 162, 170, 179, 180, 183, 186, 217–222, 224, 225, 231, 234, 235, 240–243, 246, 247. *See also* "put-down jokes"

K

Kaifu, Toshiki, 22
Kapwa (a connection with the collective), 24, 85, 86
Kapwa-infused leader, 86
Kennedy, John F., 16, 17, 38, 224, 234, 244
Khrushchev, Nikita, 15
Kimmel, Jimmy, 39
Kondabolu, Hari, 42

L

Last Thanks, The, 175–179, 183, 184, 186–188
Lazopoulos, Lakis, 60, 61
Leadership typology, 85
Left-wing, 24, 56, 101–105, 108, 111–113, 159, 164, 169, 172, 205
Levy, David, 20
LGBTQ, 4, 112, 132, 234
Lincoln, Abraham, 9, 17, 38, 228
Los alarmistas, 198, 199

M

Macapagal-Arroyo, Gloria, 93, 242
Machiavelli, Niccolò, 15
Magazines, 18, 33, 164, 170, 182
Mandela, Nelson, 74
Manga, 1, 18, 193
Mass media, 3, 14, 18, 22, 79, 201
McCain, John, 14, 36, 39, 154
Metaphors, 1, 2, 10, 57, 58, 77, 110, 161, 162
Mickiewicz, Adam, 127, 128
Mitsotakis, Kyriakos, 54, 56, 58, 60, 61
Mocking humor, 4, 87, 95, 141, 143, 230–232
Mondale, Walter, 17, 38, 225
Mori, Yoshiro, 22
Movies, 18, 79, 159, 162, 163
Muslims, 103, 139, 231

N

National character, 13, 23, 24, 85, 86
Native American
   history, 37, 159, 176, 178, 179, 185, 241
   traditional artwork, 178, 183, 185
Native people, 37, 175, 176, 179, 183, 184, 189
Nazi propaganda, 146
Nazis, 102, 104, 105, 108, 110, 111, 113, 147, 148, 152, 153
Nefeli Meg, 60
Negative humor, 150
Neo-Fascism, 193
Netanyahu, Benjamin, "Bibi,", 104
New Democracy (ND, Greece), 56, 61
Newspapers, 18, 33, 75, 91, 108, 126, 132, 141, 154

O

Obama, Barack, 17, 35, 75, 104
Obuchi, Keizô, 21

P

Pagan ritual/paganism, 128
Palestinians, 13, 101–105, 111, 112
Parody, 1, 2, 18, 19, 22–24, 32, 39, 43, 68, 72, 73, 79, 101, 103, 104, 106, 110, 113, 117, 126, 135, 159, 162, 172, 173, 177, 182
PASOK (Greece), 55
Philippines, 17, 24, 87, 88, 90–92, 94, 95, 240, 242, 243
Pleasure invitation, 220
Poland, 109, 110, 117–121, 123–125, 128, 131, 132, 134–136, 146
Politeness, 50–52, 62
Political advertising, 67
Political debates, 52, 117
Political humor, 1–4, 6, 10, 14, 15, 18, 19, 21, 23–25, 31–33, 35, 36, 40, 49, 50, 52, 62, 68, 71, 79, 80, 85–87, 97, 117, 119, 122, 126, 135, 143, 154, 182, 217, 218, 220, 239–248
Political polarization, 24, 31, 117
Political satire, 2, 18, 21, 24, 32, 36, 49, 50, 52–54, 58–61, 86, 92, 118, 125, 160, 240, 241, 246
Positive humor, 150
Poster, 19, 37, 119, 120, 128, 141, 150
Prejudice, 1, 11, 13, 40, 139–141
Presidential jokes, 85
Presidential speeches, 88
Presidents as comedians, 88
Protest, 13, 14, 53, 57, 90, 93, 103, 104, 107, 110, 111, 113, 126, 130, 131, 134, 170, 178

Puns, 1, 3, 10, 57, 61, 80, 132, 143, 198, 201
Put-down jokes, 16

Q
Quiescence, 175, 177, 185–187, 189

R
Rabin, Yitzhak, 102, 108, 112
Racism, 6, 106, 107, 140, 204, 229, 235
Ramos, Fidel V., 90, 91
Reagan, Ronald, 17, 38, 74, 225–228, 234
Rebellion, 177, 185–189
Red Star, Wendy, 25, 175–189
Regression analysis, 245
Relevance Theory, 193, 196
Relief/release theory, 6, 140, 150
Religion, 12, 19, 23, 24, 32, 41, 69, 102, 117, 122, 126, 128, 130, 141, 146, 197, 199, 217, 223
Republican Party (U.S.), 171
Ridicule, 2, 6, 16, 40, 53, 58, 68, 80, 86, 96, 97, 104, 105, 109, 152, 182
Right-wing
   government, 102, 108, 112, 124, 134
Rozanov, Mysh, 111
Rubin, Louis D., 31, 33, 34, 42, 43
Russia, 122, 135, 146, 151, 176, 245

S
Sapir, Pinchas, 20, 21
Sarcasm, 23, 74, 76, 79, 80, 86, 144, 145, 165, 179, 195, 211
Satire, 1–3, 7, 8, 17–19, 21–24, 32, 35, 36, 49, 50, 52–54, 58–61, 67–69, 86, 92, 97, 101, 103–107, 110, 112, 113, 118, 125, 159–163, 168–173, 182, 189, 195, 240, 241, 245, 246
Saturday Night Live, 7, 18, 154
Self-deprecating, 9, 38, 67–69, 71, 74, 75, 77, 78, 80, 87, 93–95, 97, 104, 147, 183, 223, 227, 228, 234, 243, 244. *See also* self-disparagement
Self-disparagement, 9, 19. *See also* self-deprecating humor
Semiotic construct, 172
Sexist humor, 54–56, 141, 242
Sexual function of humor, 7
Siege mentality, 101–103, 106, 108, 113
Simpsons, 42, 132
Social function of humor, 7

Social justice, 10, 139, 140, 147, 150, 153, 154
Social networks, 19, 50, 51, 193, 195, 211, 212
Social satire, 117, 159, 160, 168
Socio-cultural characteristics, 12
Spain, 12, 193, 194, 197, 199, 201, 204, 205, 207, 246
Spanish carnival, 197
Spieprzaj dziadu" phrase (Please piss off, old geezer), 130
Stereotypes, 1, 3, 12, 13, 20, 55, 56, 139–141, 153, 154, 160, 164, 176, 183, 186
Sunak, Rishi, 68, 78
Superiority theory, 4, 6, 51, 141, 182
SYRIZA (Greece), 55

T
Talmud, 140, 143, 145
Theater, 8, 19, 21, 72, 79, 131, 132, 194, 245
TikTok, 18, 33
Torah, 12, 143, 146
Trap invitation, 230
Trump, Donald, 10, 24, 31, 33, 38–40, 217, 223, 228–234, 240
Truss, Elizabeth, 78, 243
Tsipras, Alexis, 57–61
Twain, Mark, 35
Twitter (since July 2023 rebranding to "X"), 18, 33, 41, 53, 150, 231

U
Uncertainty avoidance, 68, 70
United Kingdom (U.K.), 24, 67–79, 207, 242, 243
U.S.A., 24
U.S.S.R., 119

V
Violence inciting humor, 233
Visual culture, 180
Visual rhetoric, 180

W
Washington, George, 9, 15, 17, 21, 36, 39, 40, 223, 224, 228, 229, 232, 234
Weil, Uzi, 109, 110
Western cultures, 69, 186

What do you take us for, a couple of goyim?, 149
Women, 4, 5, 16, 33, 34, 56, 85, 95, 120, 134, 139, 141, 142, 152, 166, 167, 201, 210, 223, 231, 234, 242, 243, 248

Y
Yom Kippur War, 102, 243

Yoshida, Shigeru, 21
YouTube, 18, 58, 106

Z
Zaralikos, Christoforos, 58, 59
Ziv, Avner
    model for understanding humor, 6
Zu Arzenu (This is Our Country), 110